ROBERT E. GRINDER

*PHILOSOPHY OF EDUCATION*

*Exploration Series in Education Under the
Advisory Editorship of
John Guy Fowlkes
and
Edward A. Krug*

# PHILOSOPHY OF EDUCATION

## LEARNING AND SCHOOLING

Donald Arnstine
*The University of Wisconsin*

*Harper & Row, Publishers*
*New York, Evanston, and London*

*To*
*BARBARA*

# CONTENTS

# EDITOR'S INTRODUCTION

MANY BOOKS HAVE BEEN WRITTEN ON THE PHILOSOPHY, PSYCHOLOGY, principles, and methods of education, and, as might be expected, there are marked similarities and wide differences among them. A great number of these books deal with theoretical or applied goals, and leave the practice and application of educational ideas to teachers and administrators.

This book is exciting and timely because it intertwines theory and practice, and yet gives more than adequate treatment to educational psychology, philosophy, principles, and methods. As the Table of Contents shows, a myriad of elements which constitute the processes of teaching and learning are presented in the pages to follow.

The reader may be surprised to find relatively few references to philosophy and psychology, in and of themselves. In a note from the author to me, the reason is given:

> Dear John Guy:
>
> You'll note that the reference to "philosophy" and "psychology" are brief; that is because they are not really *topics* of the book; they are its *tools*.

It is my belief that this volume will be revealing, inspiring, and helpful to both the theorists and practitioners in the field of education.

JOHN GUY FOWLKES

# PREFACE

THOUGHT AND ALL ITS PRODUCTS OWE THEIR EXISTENCE TO A COM-
munity, and never has this been more apparent to me than in the
writing of this book. The community from which the book grew is
far too large for me to express by gratitude to each of its members,
but there are some to whom I am especially indebted. To mention
them is not to count them as adherents of the views that are expressed here. It is rather to acknowledge that without their support
and criticism, the ideas advanced here would be far less clear—if
indeed they could have reached expression at all.

An analysis of experience can be no better than the extent to
which one is open to it in the first place. Peter Benjamin Stein
enabled me to see at firsthand how experience can sensitively be
apprehended in all its qualitative richness. Endless arguments with
Peter Franklin Stone helped me to see that opinions do not come
armed with their own reasons; and that if reasons are not offered in
response to challenge, then one opinion is as good—or as bad—as
another.

That I should ever have inquired into matters of schooling at all
is due to the encouragement of Robert E. Mason. His teaching convinced me of the importance of knowing how the young are educated, and of the correlative importance of thinking carefully about
it. It was also my good fortune to have been able to continue my
education under the guidance of Harry S. Broudy, whose own
teaching has served as a standard for thoroughness, care, and professional responsibility.

My gratitude is extended to the Research Committee of the

Graduate School of the University of Wisconsin for research support in the summer of 1964, when this work was begun. And my debt to Thomas J. Johnson is great for many conversations during that time, which helped me to see more clearly the relation between theories in psychology and philosophy.

Theory and speculation are easily entangled in the sticky webbing of their own language and presuppositions. While I am not free from all the baggage of undue complexity (and from the other evils that go along with it), I owe to William H. Hay my good intentions and my efforts to succeed in this regard. At least some of my foggier thinking was penetrated and laid to rest by his questions.

The editorial reading of the manuscript of this work was borne with patience, intelligence, and good will by Edward A. Krug. Whatever blunders remain, they pale in comparison to those that were caught by his good sense and his knowledge of education and educators. I am also indebted to John Guy Fowlkes for providing me with the opportunity to write, and for editorial criticism of a fundamental nature. The vigorous and comprehensive reactions of John L. Childs forced me to reconsider the manuscript in its entirety. He helped me find a multitude of errors, and to see more clearly where this work joins and where it departs from the tradition from which it springs. He also sensitized me to many omissions in this work each of which will serve as a point of departure for fresh inquiry.

I am indebted most of all to my wife Barbara. Writing a book makes strong demands on life at home, and she made a home in which working and living were never in competition. While fulfilling her own academic duties, she unfailingly met my speculations with patience, good will, and good arguments. The book and I are much the better for it.

Parts of Chapter VIII of this book appeared initially in the *Teachers College Record*, 67 (1966).

DONALD ARNSTINE

*"Philosophy of education"* is not an external application of ready-made ideas to a system of practice having a radically different origin and purpose: it is only an explicit formulation of the problems of the formation of right mental and moral habitudes in respect to the difficulties of contemporary social life.

—John Dewey, *Democracy and Education*

# I

# CONSIDERATIONS OF METHOD

THIS IS A BOOK ABOUT THE KINDS OF LEARNING APPROPRIATE FOR schools to promote. All of us learn, and what we learn is decisive in our becoming who we are. But what makes learning worth thinking about is not only its significance in human affairs, or the universality of its occurrence; it also merits attention because of its elusiveness. We learn just by growing up in the midst of others, but what we learn is often a matter of chance. We do not always learn what we want to, and we do not always learn when we want to. Nor do we always learn what others would like us to learn.

Because civilizations are perpetuated through a process of experiencing and learning, adults try deliberately to direct the learning of their young. And because a modern democratic civilization is not likely to be maintained when only a few people are so educated, we establish schools in the hope of promoting learning in the entire younger generation. But the mere existence of schools does not guarantee that the learning we desire will take place. To foster learning in others in a systematic way is sometimes even harder than it is to learn ourselves. And when those others, with all their differences, are put together in the same classroom, the problems of promoting learning are made still more acute.

In the light of the public school's role in maintaining a democratic civilization, and in the light of the problems attendant upon efforts to promote learning, I shall, in this book, examine the kinds of learning we seek to make available to all the members of the younger generation. Questions about learning raise psychological problems about the efficiency of means, but questions about what is appropriate raise problems of values, or the desirability of ends. In this study, attention will be given to problems of both means and ends in education, but since the primary emphasis is on desirable practices for the promotion of learning in schools, the approach will be evaluative, hence philosophic in nature.

The school tries to eliminate the factor of chance in learning as much as it can. It goes about its job deliberately and selectively. Yet the ways that people learn in school have much in common with the ways they learn out of school. The school refines and controls the kinds of events from which people haphazardly learn elsewhere. Thus the relation of deliberately controlled schooling to the accidental pattern of acculturation is much like that of a carefully wrought drama to the vagaries of life itself. And just as drama fails when it loses touch with reality, so schooling can be expected to fall short of its intent if it ignores the kinds of events from which people learn outside of school, and instead presumes to engage in practices somehow unique and peculiar to itself:

> For anything so overdone is from the purpose of playing, whose end, both at the first and now, was and is to hold as 'twere the mirror up to Nature. . . .

The intent of this book in inquiring into learning and schooling is to hold up a mirror to experience. Not experience just as we live it, but experience that has been examined in an effort to find out why it happens the way it does. When we ask about the conditions under which people learn, we must investigate men's actions and men's minds. The investigation itself can be no better than the relevance, the consistency, and the clarity of the procedures with which it is conducted. But the final test of the value of the inquiry will lie in the extent to which what is discovered about learning and schooling accords with what does in fact occur in ordinary human experience. The school teacher practices no mysterious and isolated art, nor yet does he simply seek to reproduce the prosaic events of living and growing up. Rather, he stands to those events as the dramatist does to the enculturating influence of society. He plans, selects, and controls in the hope of producing certain effects on others.

To compare schooling to a drama is to suggest that teaching is an art. Indeed it is, but it is a practical art. To plan, select, and control the conditions brought to bear on schoolchildren in an effort to help them learn, requires the thoughtful direction of means to the achievement of anticipated ends. The practitioner improves the practice of his art not only through increase of experience, but also by acquiring greater understanding (which can be developed through study of the experiments and discoveries of others) and through the elaboration of rules of procedure that follows upon greater understanding.

The intention in this book is to pursue the kind of inquiry that might result in greater understanding and in the elaboration of more effective rules of procedure. While the mode of inquiry falls under the heading of philosophy of education, I have imposed no *a priori* limits on how such an investigation should be conducted. Yet others who have examined teaching and schooling have put limitations on their mode of inquiry. These limitations emerge from their conception of teaching, on the one hand, as a sort of fine art, and, on the other, as a science. These compartmentalized conceptions of teaching put serious obstacles in the way of making it more effective through inquiry and research.

Those who view teaching as an art attach great importance

to the factors of intuition and inspiration in schooling. Learning is often conceived as the spontaneous product of an almost mystical union between teacher and student:

> When a teacher teaches his subject in a living way, these effects [of the "discipline of the subject"] upon *him* can be seen and felt by the pupils, who themselves come to participate in it through contact with him. His love for the subject, his excitement in it, is directly conveyed, and this is not a mere emotional infection but an intellectual passion which is the pupils' very actie education. . . . In this way, it is character, shown by the way of the teacher's whole approach and attitude, which "teaches" more effectively than anything else.[1]

The teacher's character unquestionably affects the quality of his teaching, and there is much of importance that happens in the learning process which eludes clear verbal descriptions. The teacher in the course of his work makes intuitive judgments, too, but this cannot be all that is important in the promotion of learning. For if it were, the improvement of teaching would be essentially a matter of each individual teacher's own subjective judgment. And if this were the case, all inquiries into learning and teaching would either be useless or not held accountable to public canons of inquiry, reasons, or evidence. Introspection and subjective judgment may under certain conditions improve one's character, but they are surely not the most dependable route to the improvement of teaching.

Those who view teaching as a science put great faith in the collection and use of empirical data as a means of improving teaching. The impression is easily given that, once enough reliable data are collected, a fully developed science of teaching will emerge that will provide clear rules for the statistically predictable production of learned students:

> The development of a science of effective teacher behavior is almost certainly the most urgent research problem that faces the profession today. If teaching is not a science, then it must be an art—that is, a skill possessed only by teachers who either

were born that way or have been lucky enough to stumble on its secrets by chance.[2]

But this, too, is a misconception which would seriously thwart inquiry into teaching and learning. Since teaching is an activity with a practical intent, it is much like scientific research (the practical intent of which is to discover and refine knowledge). It would, of course, be a mistake to confuse scientific *research* with science itself, for science not only involves a tested method of conducting inquiry, but it also comprehends organized bodies of theory and knowledge. There are rules for the conduct of scientific research, but simply to follow those rules does not guarantee that that research will be productive, nor should those rules, in and of themselves, be called a science. In like manner, there are rules for effective teaching, but no "science of effective teacher behavior" is any more likely to make a science of those rules or to guarantee the occurrence of desirable learning than can the canons of scientific research guarantee original and theoretically productive results.

The Baconian conception of science as the mere piling up of empirical data is not a fruitful guide to inquiry about the physical universe, nor is this procedure likely to contribute a great deal to the improvement of teaching. Theory and hypothesis, and sometimes intuitive guesses, guide the collection of data when research is conducted in the natural sciences. In like manner, they must also guide inquiry into teaching and learning. But even more prominently in this latter inquiry, theories and hypotheses are suffused with choices based implicitly or explicitly on values. For simply to ask the question, "Under what conditions could learning be most effectively promoted?" assumes that he who asks is able to recognize what would constitute a successful effort at teaching. Success is a concept that means different things to different people, but the choice cannot be an arbitrary one, nor can it be made simply on the basis of an accumulation of data unguided by evaluation and the projection of directing hypotheses. Thus it vitiates research into teaching and learning to limit it to the gathering of empirical data; it is a delusion to assume that the practice of teaching is dependent for its improvement solely on such data. Inquiry so limited by the demands of a pseudoscience is not likely to be very helpful to anyone concerned about schooling.

The chapters that follow will try to shed some light on the improvement of school practices by seeking an understanding of the conditions that make learning possible. Insofar as understanding is sought, considerations of empirical evidence and conceptual clarity become relevant. But at the same time I will try to show where choices must be made and what kinds of values are operative in the making of those choices. Throughout, I will also try to show that, no matter how much prior planning and choosing is done in an effort to promote learning, the need cannot be avoided to act immediately and intuitively in the process of teaching itself. But it will be seen, too, that even these acts can thoughtfully be prepared for in advance.

To be concerned about the improvement of school practice is not to ignore the importance of educational aims. Those aims have always been, among educators and laymen, an arena of serious debate. But one reason (although not the only one) those debates have not been settled is that aims are sometimes cast in terms so general as not clearly to indicate any differences in school practices. But practices widely differ anyway, and the differences are often the result of inability to see their connection to aims and consequences, and of failure to examine critically the beliefs that are presupposed by those practices.[3] A single example may make this more clear. Most educators subscribe to the slogan that the schools should meet individual differences. But how shall this be achieved? Suppose the children in a classroom differ widely in measured I.Q. score, interest in and aptitude for the subject, relevant prior knowledge, and home background. These differences can be taken into account (that is, "met") by grouping the students homogeneously, by varying the content or the mode of its presentation to suit individual students, or by enabling each student to pursue whatever he finds of interest. Individual differences can be met in these (and other) ways, yet they are so divergent that it is to be wondered whether the same ends are being achieved.

In fact, individual differences among students are usually met in one of two general ways. School methods and materials may be varied in an effort to help students advance as far as they can in acquiring a specified body of subject matter knowledge, or, on the other hand, students may be allowed the freedom to explore whatever content or areas seem relevant to their own unique personalities. In the first case, individual differences are conceived only as obstacles to be overcome en route to having all students do different amounts of the same thing. In the second case, individual differences tend to dictate what each student will do. In the first instance, the differences among students are held to be reducible and of less importance than the similarities to be acquired. In the second instance, these same differences are taken as given and irreducible, and are held to be of greater importance than anything that could be acquired.

It might be supposed that very different consequences would result from conducting such widely varied practices. Indeed, one might wish to question the wisdom of either practice, or to criticize both, but no such inquiries are likely to proceed so long as attention remains focused on simply "meeting individual differences." School practices are means, but to consider means apart from the ends they are likely to serve and apart from the beliefs that are presupposed by them is neither rational nor very practical. Suppose, then, that we shift our concern to educational ends, to which those means are so intimately bound. Here we encounter another kind of problem.

When deliberations about educational ends are put in clear and precise terms, debate itself may become endless. Thus people concerned about education have argued long over such matters as the nature of man, a proper hierarchy of values, and the purpose of life. In these arguments, the practices of schooling become incidental. They are treated as *mere* means to certain exalted ends, and the consequences that they may in fact have, are seldom thoroughly explored. While school keeps, ends are debated; but concrete school practices remain as unenlightened as ever.

Another approach to the statement of educational ends is to put them in terms to which no right-minded person would object.

It can then be hoped that the business of fitting educational practices to those ends will proceed. That this procedure promises little for the improvement of schooling can be seen by considering one such worthy statement of educational ends. Several centuries ago, John Milton announced:

> I call, therefore, a complete and generous education, that which fits a man to perform justly, skillfully, and magnanimously all the offices, both private and public, of peace and war.

It is probably just because no one would strongly object to Milton's statement that it is so useless. If school practices differ widely, and yet the practitioners all agree as to the worthiness of a stated end, then something must be wrong with the statement of that end. And indeed, all that mars it is the fact that it gives little if any indication of the practices that would make it operational in schools and in the lives of children and youth. A great many statements of educational ends suffer from such shortcomings, and the result is that those who subscribe to them are free to engage in whatever practices suit them. Thus the actual, if unintended, function of such statements of educational ends is to distract attention from what might operate to achieve them. And again school keeps, as unenlightened as ever, while in this case ends are agreed upon.

School practices cannot be made rational without due consideration of the ends they are likely to serve, and those ends themselves remain vacuous without consideration of the particular practices that would either help or hinder their achievement. In this book, I shall directly inquire into school practices for two reasons. First, those who are concerned about schooling are interested in what happens in the schools. Whatever aims for schooling people hold, and whether they are justified in holding them, there is no doubt that teachers and administrators are engaging in certain very particular activities. There is also no doubt that they and others have some interest in how those activities are conducted. To present a lesson may or may not fulfill some aim, and it even may achieve an end contrary to the one intended. But it is at least to *do* something, and what people do is what they are concerned about, and often hope to do better.

The second reason for being primarily concerned with school methods and practices is that I believe it holds more promise of achieving concrete and practical results than does concern with statements about school aims. Of course, neither ends nor means can be made rational in isolation from each other. But while there may be doubt about what methods to select in order to reach a given end—because the end is so often put in such a general way —we are on much firmer ground when we infer the ends which particular methods are likely to serve. For these reasons, then, and without ignoring the aims and intentions that guide educational practice, the emphasis in the chapters to follow will be on the methods, practices, and organization of schools.

When the practices of schooling are inconsistent, and when they bend readily to the dictates of fashion, the thinking that guides them is usually unclear or has not been carried far enough. The varied methods of meeting individual differences that were discussed earlier illustrate these shortcomings in thought. Practice can be illuminated and made more effective by clarifying the thinking that guides it, and this end can, in turn, be served by clarifying the language which constitutes that thinking. The analysis of concepts that guide educational practice will, then, be one of the ways in which this book will address the problems of learning and schooling.

But people concerned about schooling are interested in what is done. *Their* dominant interest is not in language and concepts, and they do not normally seek analyses of their discourse. Their concern is, quite properly, with practice. However much the clarification gained by conceptual analysis might in theory rationalize school practices, as a matter of fact, such analysis seems far removed from what goes on in the classroom and often has little influence on the conduct of schooling. There is little point in offering another book about schooling without the hope of its contributing to the improvement of practice. Thus the argument in this book will be carried beyond mere clarification and, once clarification is gained about the consequences of adopting particular school methods, good reasons will be sought for selecting some methods rather than others. To do this, knowledge will be utilized that is relevant to learning and schooling, and that knowledge will be sought wherever it can be found. In some instances, scientific research into learning will be consulted; at other times, the careful examination of experience common to everyone will serve as a source of what we need to know.

In order to judge that some practices may, and others may not, be appropriate for schooling, more than reliable knowledge and conceptual clarity is required. The making of choices always presupposes commitment to certain ends or values. When it is relevant, I will try to make as clear as possible what kinds of value choices are operating in the selection of any particular school methods. This inquiry into learning and schooling, then, will undertake to utilize, with as much conceptual clarity as can be attained, whatever knowledge and explicitly examined values may be relevant.

## NOTES

1. Louis Arnaud Reid, *Philosophy and Education* (New York: Random House, 1965), pp. 152, 153, 155.

2. Donald M. Medley and Harold E. Mitzel, "The Scientific Study of Teacher Behavior," in Arno A. Bellack (ed.), *Theory and Research in Teaching* (New York: Bureau of Publications, Teachers College, Columbia University, 1963), p. 81. It might be noted in passing that poets, painters, and pianists, who work very hard at developing their craft, might take exception to the notion that either they were "born artists" or they stumbled on their skills by chance.

3. In noting the extent to which all of our acts are based on presuppositions that in many cases remain unexamined, John L. Childs has written, in personal correspondence, "We never deal with any situation with a naked mind."

# II

# LEARNING
# AND DISPOSITIONS

MUCH ATTENTION HAS BEEN GIVEN RECENTLY TO THE CONCEPT OF teaching, both in in the form of linguistic analysis[1] and of carefully designed empirical observations of the "teaching act."[2] Much has been learned from these studies, but it is not to the purpose here to review them. This is chiefly because, whatever we wish to call teaching, our schools exist wholly for the purpose of fostering learning. If teaching procedures are at all rationally governed, they will, sooner or later, bend in whatever directions are found to be compatible with what is known about learning. Since the results of teaching are not always related to what teachers had anticipated, studies of what teachers actually do must perforce include much that bears very little relation to the sorts of learnings that would be accounted desirable. Thus it is proposed that the more economical course is to examine what happens when people learn, and hope that implications can be found for deliberately instituting some of those situations. To understand learning, in short, is to be able to judge what is and is not appropriate teaching.

It is a commonplace that schools are places where pupils learn, or where they are supposed to learn. But no matter how universal agreement may be to this innocent-appearing statement, there is very little precision about what it means. That people disagree about *what* pupils ought to learn would be cause enough for concern, but the problem lies deeper than that. For our ordinary use of the term "to learn" does not clearly indicate the sort of process to which a person has been subjected when it is appropriate to say of him, "He learned."

Since the conditions under which people learn are focal to this study, it is important to be as clear as possible about what will be meant by the term "learning." In ordinary discourse, learning refers to a broad range of events. Thus when a person has acquired some information, it is normal to say that he learned. Or, we say that the acquisition of a habit, or an attitude, or a skill is an instance of learning. For most practical purposes, these varied uses of the term learning are clear enough. In each case, some change resulting from experience is indicated, and the type of change is roughly suggested by noting what was learned. But language that serves well enough for ordinary discourse may not be suitable for the purposes of specialized inquiry into learning. No specialized inquiry can proceed very far without some precision in the key terms that are used, and learning is at the very center of the present inquiry.

We say that a person learns to catch a ball, to come home on time, to like strawberries, or to be kind, and that he learns the principal crops of Argentina. To say that a person has learned these things is to suggest fairly clearly what he can do. But it is equally clear that in each of these cases, a person has been subject to different sorts of events and different things have happened to him. When learning is spoken of as a process, the different *kinds* of processes that might be meant are clearly enough indicated when we specify the *outcome* of the process (e.g., learning a fact, or learning an attitude). But when we simply ask, "How shall learning be facilitated?" no indication is given of the sort of process that is under investigation. The only sensible response to the question so put is to ask, "Learning what? The learning of facts? or of habits? or of what?" The task at hand then, is simply to specify the kind of learning on which this study will focus.

Changes in overt behavior, knowledge acquired, new skills, habits, and attitudes, are all legitimate aims or outcomes of schooling, and all of them in ordinary discourse are properly called "learning." But when the role of schooling in general education is considered, I shall try to show that the particular *processes* to which these learning outcomes refer are each, for one reason or another, narrowly restricted. For this reason, the discussion of learning in subsequent chapters will emphasize the kind of learning that occurs when a disposition is acquired.

This choice of a referent for the term learning is made not only for the sake of clarity, but also for convenience. For, as I will later try to point out, the process of acquiring dispositions is one that cannot be said to have occurred *unless* other processes (which are also typically called learning: e.g., acquiring information, skills, etc.) have also occurred. Thus, it will be convenient to speak of a process of learning broad enough in scope to include other kinds of learning processes of which it is composed. In the sections of this chapter that immediately follow, I will try to better clarify this by exploring the concept of learning as it is used in connection with acquiring new behaviors, knowledge, skills, habits, and attitudes. I will then set forth what is meant by the phrase, "to acquire a disposition," and show how it is related to the aforementioned kinds of learning.

## LEARNING AND CHANGES IN OVERT BEHAVIOR

We may begin our examination of the concept of learning by noting some of the ways in which people have tried to define it. Perhaps as broad a definition of learning as one is likely to find is this one:

Learning is a process whereby a change in behavior results from some form of experience—activity, training, observation, and the like. Changes in behavior which result from such forces as bodily injury, fatigue, or use of drugs is not considered learning. . . . [and] some behavior changes result primarily from maturation.[3]

This definition is probably too broad to be very serviceable for our purposes. There are innumerable processes by which one's behavior may be changed, but not all of those processes can properly be called learning. When the bus driver refused my dollar bill on the grounds that he was out of change, I fished in my pocket for a couple of dimes. My behavior clearly changed, but no one would be likely to call the process from which that change resulted a case of learning. Nor would it be likely for anyone to say that I learned that the driver was out of change, or that I learned to produce my own dimes. Rather, I *understood* the driver was out of change (because he told me), and I already knew how to get dimes out of my pocket.

If the process from which a change in overt behavior results does not necessarily separate learning from other events, neither is the notion of overt behavior crucial to a definition of learning. It is quite an ordinary use of the term to say of a person that he learned something, even though his behavior, either at the moment or immediately thereafter, did not change. Of course, it is reasonable to say that we have *no warrant* for claiming that someone else has learned unless there is an observable change in his behavior *sometime,* but the *warrant* (observed behavior) *for an event* (learning) *should not be mistaken for the event itself.* To put this another way, that which constitutes public evidence for the occurrence of an event need not be included in the definition of the event itself. There are cases in which a person might learn without performing any overt act *at that time.* There would be no use denying that a genuine case of learning had occurred, although only some change in behavior at some later time would constitute public evidence that this was so. We can make this point clearer by examining an instance of learning which is contrary to a definition of it that includes the notion of a change in overt behavior.

Suppose that you are exchanging recipes over the bridge table with your friends. "You know," somebody says, "I understand that people in Malaya eat grasshoppers." You make a face and voice your distaste. The first speaker then points out that Malayans are as used to eating grasshoppers as you are to eating beef, and when you object that it's "more natural" to eat beef, your friend counters by noting that Indians would become ill if forced to eat it. You become hesitant at this juncture, and the conversation moves from a defense of the eating habits of others to proposals to adopt those habits for oneself. Your tentative objections are overridden when others point out that, had we not adopted the menus of others, we might be without such staples as corn and potatoes or such delicacies as frogs' legs.

By the time the conversation has returned to grasshoppers, you have succumbed both to the reasoning of your friends and the pressure of the social climate. To yourself, you admit having looked at matters rather narrowly, that tastes may indeed be a matter of habituation, that even you have come to enjoy eating some things you found repugnant at first, and that you, too, might be willing to give grasshoppers a fair trial. To conclude our rather lengthy example, we add that you live to a ripe old age and are never once served grasshoppers, nor do you ever have the opportunity to dine in a restaurant that serves them.

Although the evidence afforded in the example is not conclusive, surely it is reasonable to conjecture that you have acquired a new disposition or changed an old one. And while it may be a disposition toward getting along with friends (especially when they disagree with you), it may also be a new disposition toward eating strange and exotic foods. In either case, it would undeniably be appropriate for you to say that you learned something. But as in the case of many of the things we learn, the occasion was not such that you could immediately manifest your learning in overt behavior. Yet at some future time, you might very likely make a deliberate effort (if your disposition really had changed) to vary your menu. Thus the absence of an immediate change in overt behavior does not vitiate your claim (had you been asked) that learning had occurred.

In the same sense, most people who travel by commercial airlines learn what to do in case of emergency (stay calm, fasten the seat belt, operate the oxygen mask as the stewardess demonstrates, follow her instructions, etc.), without, fortunately, ever having to display overtly what they learned. It is possible that overt behavior in a situation later on will verify to others the occurrence (or nonoccurrence) of prior learning. The airplane may, in fact, become involved in an emergency situation and you may, in fact, be served snails the day after the conversation about grasshoppers. In these situations, one's overt behavior will serve as public evidence as to whether or not you have learned.

For the above reasons, I shall exclude from the meaning that will be adopted for the term learning the stipulation that it be manifested—either immediately or at any specifiable future date—in overt observable behavior. Much learning is, of course, manifested overtly and at once, but some learning does not show up until much later and, when it does, its behavioral manifestation may take a variety of forms (you might at a later time eat whatever is served to you, you might deliberately order squid or calves' brains, you might encourage your children to broaden their tastes, etc.). Ordinary uses for the term learning acknowledge this to be the case. For this reason alone, the claim made by some educators, that unless some overt change in behavior is *observed* learning has not *occurred,* is a mistaken claim. And it would follow that the correlative pedagogical proposal—to formulate *all* educational goals in terms of directly observable changes in behavior—is too restrictive. It is true that aimlessness in teaching can be avoided by seeking overt changes in behavior as *evidence* of the occurrence of learning, but it is dangerous to confuse evidence of the occurrence of an event for the event itself. The evidence (overt behavior) that some learning has occurred may not be manifest until long after the occurrence of learning itself. And when the evidence for learning becomes manifest, it may not come in the form that was anticipated.

## LEARNING AND KNOWING

While the notion of learning which involves some overt change in behavior has attracted some educators, the concept has caused enough discomfort to have encouraged efforts to temper it. The most usual of these attempts has been to point out that verbal behavior, the use of language, is, after all, a form of overt behavior. It is then said that while a person's bodily movements may not be observed to change, we can induce changes in a person's verbal responses, and that these changes also constitute learning. Thus, if we wish to know whether a person has learned something, we can simply ask him an appropriate question.

What sort of a response does such an appropriate question elicit? If I wish to know whether Johnny is learning history, I might ask him, "Do you know who is called the father of your country?" Johnny may answer, "Yes," but if I am still left wondering whether Johnny has learned any history, it is because I asked the wrong question. The kind of question I must ask, in order to find out if Johnny has learned any history (assuming learning to mean change in verbal behavior), is a question that elicits information from Johnny. So if I ask, "Who is called the father of your country?" and Johnny answers, "George Washington," I can then assume that Johnny has learned at least some history. To put this another way, a year ago Johnny would have answered, "I don't know." Since his verbal behavior in response to my question has changed, I infer that Johnny has learned.

Another way of formulating this conception of learning, and indeed, a more familiar way to those who have no particular stake in strict behaviorism as a comprehensive account of psychological phenomena, is to say that learning is the acquisition of knowledge. To learn is to come to know, and he who has learned now knows something he did not know before. Acquiring knowledge may be an important school aim, but I shall try to show in what follows that to call the process of acquiring knowledge learning leads to confusion. Knowledge is always acquired when learning in the broader sense of acquiring dispositions occurs, but it is not the same thing as acquiring dispositions. In the same sense, we always acquire something when we make a trade, but acquiring something is not the same thing as trading. The matter may be put more precisely: given all the sorts of events to which the term learning is *normally* applied, the use of it to indicate *only* the acquisition of knowledge is unnecessarily restrictive and may be misleading. This can be made clearer by again looking at an example.

No difficulty in communication would be encountered if one were told, "After attending the medical school and spending a year as an intern, Watson learned to be a good doctor." Similarly, it is quite clear what is meant when one hears, "In medical school, Watson learned the structure of the heart." While the meaning of both these sentences is quite clear, the use of the term learn is altogether different in each. Because these different usages (as well as others to be taken up later) persist in ordinary discourse, confusion and sometimes controversy arise over what is meant by learning when people claim that schools are (or ought to be) places where pupils learn English, or learn manners, or learn chemistry, or learn citizenship, etc.

It is not my intention here to legislate for ordinary language. What makes terms like learning ambiguous also affords them the richness that sometimes makes art of much educational discourse. But at the risk of sounding dry, and in the hope of being able to communicate clear and possibly even useful meanings, the remainder of this discussion will proceed on the assumption that such clarity and meaningfulness can be achieved only when so crucial a term as learning is used unambiguously. Hence we must continue with the task of sorting out the various usages of the term.

If learning is taken to mean the process of coming to know, in the sense of acquiring knowledge, then "learning to become a good doctor" and "learning the structure of the heart" must be phrases intended to indicate that the same sort of process is occurring. Yet it is obvious that these two phrases refer to quite different sorts of processes. Learning to be a good doctor involves the acquisition and development of a great number of abilities and attitudes, most of them founded on knowledge. Acquiring and developing these abilities is a case of learning *how* (e.g., how to conduct a diagnosis, make an incision, etc.); acquiring and developing these attitudes is a case of learning *to* (e.g., to remain calm during an operation, to keep free of personal prejudices when diagnosing and treating patients, etc.). Learning the structure of the heart, however, involves the acquisition of specific information, and would normally be called a case of learning *that* (e.g., that the heart is a certain kind of muscle, that it has four chambers, etc.).[4]

Attempts have been made to reduce the concept of knowing *that* to knowing *how*.[5] Thus it might be said that one who possesses a given piece of information—who, in other words, knows *that*— is one who, in fact, knows *how* to make certain verbal responses in appropriate situations. (And similarly, one who has *learned that* really has *learned how*.) This claim may be true but it is equally true that the distinction between knowing *how* and knowing *that* is still a serviceable one. As long as human behavior is such that a reasonably clear empirical distinction can be made between expository verbal utterances and other behaviors, the concept of knowing *that* and knowing *how* will have distinguishable referents.

The acquiring and developing of abilities and attitudes—learning *how* and learning *to*—are not processes like acquiring knowledge, or learning *that*, as Professor Gilbert Ryle has forcibly pointed out.[6] It is always possible to find out precisely when someone learned *that* something was the case: Watson learned the structure of the heart last Thursday afternoon. But precisely when does one learn *how* to exercise an ability or an attitude effectively? It does not make a great deal of sense, usually, to try to specify the hour, the day, or the week that Watson learned to be a good doctor. Learning to be a good doctor is a lengthy process that proceeds through imperceptible stages, but it is not so with learning the structure of the heart. It is true that knowledge of the heart's structure may consist of many separate items of knowledge, but it can be said that the acquiring of each item is a discrete event.

If these two kinds of acquisition are, in fact, such different sorts of processes, why indiscriminately apply the same term (learning) to both? If we asked how we should promote learning, we would, of necessity, have to provide at least two wholly different answers, depending on which sense of learning was meant. Despite all this, many theoreticians and practitioners speak as if there were but *one* efficient and workable way to promote learning.[7] This error, as might be expected, is based on the mistake of failing to recognize the wide variety of situations to which the term learning is normally applied, only two of which have been mentioned thus far.

Let us look more closely at the contexts in which "learning" and "coming to know" are used. The participle "learning" generally indicates a single, extended process, a continuing state of affairs that covers a more or less indefinite period of time. If we ask, "Has he been learning for a long time?" our question implies that the learner was in a different condition with respect to what he was learning at the beginning of that time than he was at a later period. We may also ask if one is learning slowly or quickly.

But the participial forms "knowing" and "coming to know" behave differently. If we should ask, "Has he been knowing for a long time?" the question, odd as it may sound, does *not* imply that the knower was in a different condition with respect to what he knows at different periods of time. What he might have known at one point in time, during the period he was knowing, was just what he knew at a later point in time. On the other hand, if we should ask, "Has he been coming to know for a long time?" our question would imply not the existence of a single, extended process over time, but rather a discrete series of events over a period of time. We should be asking, "Over a period of time, did he come to know X, and to know Y, and to know Z?"

We cannot tell *when* a person "learned history," because no one has ever finished, nor can we ever tell exactly *when* a person learned historical-mindedness. But we *can* tell precisely when a person came to know that George Washington is called the "father of his country." The reason for this, to use Professor Ryle's terms,[8] is that "coming to know" announces an achievement, a completed event, while learning, in the sense in which it has just been used, indicates a task—a continuing process. Thus it makes no more sense to say "he came to know slowly" than it would to say "he won the race slowly." Winning a race is not a gradual or time-consuming affair, although running a race is. To win is an achievement (and to run, a task); it is either done or not done, and to say "he is winning the race" is only a loose way of indicating that someone is running a race and is at the moment ahead of his rivals, or seems to have more energy left than they do, etc. To come to know is also an achievement. One may be in the dark for a long while, but when one comes to know something, he does so at once. Before that precise moment, he simply did not know, and afterward he did. It makes no sense at all, then, to say, "He is coming to know that George Washington is called the father of his country." Nor does it make any sense to say, "he slowly came to know" a particular item of knowledge. If the student understood the language, he knew the fact in question as soon as he was told.

If the distinction made here between learning and coming to know has been a fair one, it would then be a mistake to claim that learning *means* coming to know. It would not, of course, be a mistake to say that when one is learning (in the sense of acquiring dispositions), he comes to know a great many things. Coming to know, or knowing, then, is one of the things that happens during the process of learning. A question of the form, "What are the conditions under which a person comes to know?" may be intended to find out how people learn in such a way that they come to know. Or, it may have nothing at all to do with how people learn.

The upshot of all this is that, on the basis of how language is normally used, the term learning often indicates a broader range of events than the phrase "coming to know" indicates. Acquiring knowledge may occur during the course of learning, but usually that is not all that occurs. Thus in our subsequent discussion, learning will not be used to mean *simply* coming to know, although its referent may *include* coming to know.

The reader should be warned, however, that the usage of learning adopted here does not accord with some usages typical in educational discourse. Learning is, for example, sometimes equated with "discovery," and the latter term is usually intended to mean the pupil's own successful effort at making valid inferences about something previously unknown, on the basis of having been provided with some relevant information. There is unquestionably great value in schools' promoting such events, but on the basis of the usage indicated in the foregoing discussion, neither discovery nor the making of inferences is to be identified with learning. For to discover and to make an inference are but ways of coming to know, and they share the same linguistic features as coming to know.

A very different usage of learning, but one still contrary to the usage presented here, is offered by advocates of programmed instruction. These educators claim that their devices promote the acquisition of knowledge.[9] This may indeed be true. They also claim that their devices promote learning; what they generally mean is that the acquisition of knowledge *is* what people mean by the term learning. On the basis of the foregoing discussion, this is false. Some people may, for their own reasons, wish to equate learning and the acquisition of knowledge, but it has been argued here that this is a confusing way of using these terms. To simplify the matter, we might say that *knowledge is not "learned" at all; it is acquired.* This usage might avoid confusion when we consider the role of knowledge in the process of acquiring dispositions and in the achievement of educational aims.

## LEARNING AND SKILLS

Just as it has been indicated that, for our purposes at least, learning is to be understood as a process broader than the mere acquisition of knowledge, so also is it broader than the mere acquisition of a skill. Having a skill normally means being able (or knowing how) to perform, according to prescribed rules or models, some activity that is at least so complex or difficult that it cannot typically be performed on the first or the first several attempts. A skill, then, requires practice. Swimming is a skill. So is the making of an incision, or the playing of a violin, and so is reading. Now the peculiarity of a skill, and what so often confounds the meaning of the phrase, "to learn a skill," is the fact that it is seldom exercised by itself. The exercise of a skill is usually involved in some broader and more inclusive activity, although the skill itself may be acquired apart from those broader activities. We may illustrate this point by looking at the four examples of skills just noted, seeing how they are normally exercised, and how that exercise is related to the ways in which they are acquired.

The skill of swimming is one that is often exercised for its own sake, apart from any other activity or purpose. On hot summer days, people often plunge into a pool or lake and swim. Not *to* any place in particular or for any purpose, but simply for the pleasure of swimming. The skill of reading is quite different. No adult reads for the sake of the pleasure of reading itself. We read *something*—this book, that article, this poem, that essay. If the swimmer is asked, "Why are you swimming?" he might reply, "To get to the boat," but it is just as likely that his response will be strictly in terms of the exercise of the skill: "I like to swim." Not so with the reader. If he is asked why he is reading, his answer will normally include some reference to what he is reading (e.g., "I am reading a detective story because . . ." or "I like to read poems").[10]

We also speak of skilled surgeons and skilled violinists, but the exercise of these skills is more like that of reading than swimming. If the surgeon skillfully making an incision is not calling into play *more* than his skill, we would be likely to say, with no fear of being self-contradictory, that he is a skilled surgeon but a doctor of doubtful repute. Likewise, if the violinist playing a cadenza is not exhibiting *more* than his skill, we are likely to call him a skillful violinist but a poor musician. For such a performer we reserve the epithet, "mere virtuoso."

How are skills like these acquired? In all cases, they involve practice in following a prescribed set of rules or an exemplar. But there are crucial differences in the acquisition of different sorts of skills. After appropriate practice, if the swimmer is able to swim rhythmically and with a variety of strokes for reasonably long distances, we say he is a skillful swimmer. And by skillful swimmer we mean *good* swimmer. But when, after appropriate practice, the violinist is able, rhythmically and with no mistakes, to play scales, arpeggios, and exercises, we *may* say he has become skillful but we are not ordinarily prepared to say he is a *good* violinist. The same holds for doctors and readers. Since there is much more to being a doctor than skillfully making incisions, and much more to reading than skillfully deciphering written marks on a page, we do not, with respect to people who exercise these sorts of skills, equate "skillful" with "good."

Skills may be *acquired*, then, in isolation from other activities, but some skills are never exercised that way and, in the case of the exercise of these latter skills, "skillful" and "good" are not normally equated (one who swims the sidestroke skillfully is a good swimmer; but one who practices pizzicato skillfully is not necessarily a good violinist). In the case of activities where skillful does not mean good, then, something *in addition to* the skill itself is acquired by the practitioner. For this reason, "Smith learned to be a swimmer" and "Smith learned to be a violinist (or reader, or doctor)" are sentences in which the term learn *means different things.* Likewise, "to learn to swim" is a usage of "learn" different from that in the phrase "to learn to play the violin (or to learn to read, or to learn medicine)." That is, some skill-learning involves, either sooner or later, the acquisition of more than the skill itself.

Since our discussion later on will focus on learning, it is necessary to distinguish between these two particular senses of "learn." If this is done, we can avoid the confusion normally engendered by the claim that Jack has learned to read. What would such a claim mean? It probably means more than "Jack has learned how to decipher marks on a page." But does it mean that Jack can profitably read poetry as well as prose, philosophical or speculative writing as well as expository, scientific explanations as well as a narrative of Dick and Jane? Does he skim or read intensively at appropriate times? Does he know when to read for detailed content and when to search for an author's arguments? All of the foregoing activities are called reading, and properly so, but none of them in particular is indicated by the phrase, "Jack has learned to read." (That reading may include any or all of these activities also points up the folly of those who debate over the alleged one best way of teaching reading.)

All that is intended here is that our stipulated usage for learning *exclude* the sense of "learning how to decipher marks on a page" as a full meaning for "learning to read." Earlier, I rejected as a definition of learning the mere acquisition of knowledge because, among other reasons, it was too restrictive; that is, other learnings were occurring, too, that were not covered by the phrase, "acquiring knowledge." For the same reason, I shall reject as a definition of learning the mere acquisition of a skill, in the sense of its being separate from its connections to other activities and purposes with which and according to which it is normally exercised. Learning to be a violinist involves a set of processes and events qualitatively quite different from those involved in learning to be a swimmer; it would only confuse further inquiry to label both sets of events as learning.

In ordinary language, "He is learning to swim" is quite intelligible. Unfortunately in some respects, we shall have to dispense with this usage in the hope that the gain will be greater than the loss. Instead, we shall say, "He is acquiring the skill of swimming." This is admittedly awkward, but it will pay off when we talk about schooling. For we can now distinguish "Jack is learning mathematics" from "Jack is acquiring the skill of mathematical computation." What the latter sentence means is quite clear. Jack is learning to add a column of numbers, or divide one number into another, or perhaps factor an equation algebraically. What the former sentence means should also be clearer by now. If "Jack is learning mathematics," he is doing *more* than acquiring and practicing a skill; he *may* also be learning *why* computations work as they do or what situations (e.g., a problem in physics or economics) are appropriate for the exercise of such skills. These distinctions are frequently recognized by those concerned with schooling, even though the blanket use of the term learn tends to obscure them.

The confusion of skill acquisition with other and more broadly conceived kinds of learning has probably led to an inadvertent narrowing of educational aims and teaching methods.[11] For example, it is thought that people learn to be logical or to think critically by taking a course in logic. Yet in such a course, people may acquire logical skills without ever learning to use them in practical or theoretical situations where they might be appropriate. Drawing inferences is a skill, and like any other skill it improves with practice. But exercises in logic are not necessarily conducive to the drawing of inferences about current personal, social, and economic problems. Yet if a person does not accurately and fruitfully draw inferences in the latter areas of concern, it will not likely be said of him that he learned to be logical (or to think critically)—no matter how skillfully he can infer the mortality of Socrates from given premises. When we say that someone has learned to be logical, we mean that more than the acquisition of certain skills has occurred. It is this latter sense of the term learning that will be adopted in subsequent discussion. Learning will indicate a broader range of events than the phrase "acquiring a skill" indicates. Skills may be acquired during the course of learning, but according to the usage adopted here, that will not be *all* that is acquired.

## LEARNING AND HABITS

People often say that their children are in school to learn good habits. There is no doubt about what this means, since it is normally taken to mean "to learn good ways of behaving." But many ways of behaving are not habits. It would be reasonable to suppose, then, that the process of learning a habit is not the same as the process of learning something which is not a habit. In this section I will point out that confusion is engendered by using the term learning to connote the acquisition of habits. Most of this confusion results from the fact that "habit" is used to indicate so many different and often conflicting sorts of things.

Whatever else it may imply, the concept of "habit" makes reference to the frequency of some act. One who has a habit of $x$ may be expected to perform $x$ under the same set of conditions under which one without the habit would not. In this minimal sense, "habit" means just what "disposition" means. But "habit" is seldom used synonymously with "disposition." We might say, "Smith has the habit of drinking," but if Smith is an habitual drinker, we would not be likely to say, "Smith has a disposition to drink." If Smith has not got a habit of drinking, we might say, "Smith is disposed to drink when . . ." and then mention specific conditions under which Smith drinks—thus implying a variety of situations in which Smith does not drink. This is to say that, at least in some usages, the owner of a habit is less discriminating about when he will practice that habit than is the owner of a disposition. To put this another way, the owner of a habit can be expected to practice his habit *whenever* an occasion makes such practice possible, whether or not it is appropriate to that occasion. Thus if one has the habit of dressing neatly, he can be expected to dress neatly whenever he dresses; if he has the habit of being punctual, he can be expected to be on time whenever he has an appointment. The occasion, of course, may not be consciously recognized. Such would be the case with the habit of smoking, although it can be expected to be practiced at almost any time there is something available to smoke. Likewise, the habit of pulling at one's ear during conversation can be expected to occur in any social situation.

Common to all the examples of acts mentioned above are (1) their probability of occurrence, given the conditions that allow them to occur, and (2) their relative automaticity; that is, the agent performed the acts on a situational cue, rather than first deliberating about whether he should or should not perform the acts. This latter aspect of habits is worth examining more closely. Whether habits are relatively automatic depends, of course, on what behaviors we wish to include as habits. To take an extreme case of an exception we might note what is sometimes called the "habit of intelligence." Now, being intelligent requires all sorts of behaviors, none of which could normally be classified as routine or automatic. Minimally, intelligent behavior is behavior deliberately governed by awareness of conditions and consequences of events. Such behavior is not what we would call habitual. Hence "the habit of intelligence" is, apparently, the "habit of being nonhabitual." Yet it is self-contradictory to say that one can have a habit of not acting according to habit. "The habit of intelligence," then, is an imprecise use of ordinary language and does not constitute an exception to the claim that habits are marked by automaticity.[12]

Are there other legitimate exceptions to this claim? It is common to speak, for example, of the habit of honesty. Yet to behave in an honest way is not to behave automatically and under the control of external cues. What is involved in such a "habit"? We can neither be so blunt as to say knowing right from wrong nor so verbose as to resurrect a Platonic dialogue. We might say that an habitually honest person not only must have a fairly clear set of values that afford him guidance in a wide variety of complex situations, but he must also be sensitive enough to complex situations to know when honesty might become an issue. However, behaving according to this kind of sensitivity and according to a set of situationally operative values is not normally called a habit. Among other things, intelligence is involved, and intelligence is not a habit. Thus to speak of a habit of honesty is to call to mind the relatively automatic behavior evidenced by the unthinking person who replies with an affirmative answer to the question, "Have you planned a surprise party for me?"

Some people are acutely aware of situations in which the honesty of a particular course of action is problematical, and they attempt to find reasons for their decisions consonant with deliberately chosen values. Such a person is the man who asks himself whether he *ought* to deduct a certain item on his income tax return, or whether he *ought* to sell yesterday's bread to someone who is willing to pay the price of fresh bread. But rather than call this sort of behavior a habit of honesty, it might be clearer to call it a disposition to be honest, since the behavior, far from being automatic, is thoughtful and highly discriminative of situations.

As I have already indicated, the distinction made here between a habit and a disposition may be a rather fine one, and it is undoubtedly contrary to some ordinary usages. But it is a necessary distinction to make, because we want to see whether the acquisition of habits can conveniently be called learning. As has already been pointed out, a habit refers to behavior that is recurrent. Brushing one's teeth in the morning may be a habit, but being intelligent and being honest cannot be. The reason is that the act of brushing one's teeth is discrete, overt, observable, repeatable, and nondiscriminative—i.e., we do it every morning. But behaving intelligently and honestly has none of these characteristics. What enables us to say that a person is intelligent or honest is the fact that his behavior varies to suit different circumstances; the *quality* of his acts may be repeatable, but the acts *themselves* are not.

Repeatable acts performed more or less automatically, the sort of behavior that is indicated by the term habit, are acquired by the process of conditioning. Conditioning, whether it be explained by contiguity, drive-reduction, reinforcement, or whatever else, is a process that occurs in both men and animals whereby the probability of the occurrence of a response is increased. Through conditioning, a pigeon may acquire a specific sequence of movements, a child may acquire tastes for certain foods, and an adult may learn not to bid no-trump on an unbalanced bridge hand. All these behaviors are properly described as habits, and because of instances like these, some theorists have gone so far as to equate conditioning with learning. But this judgment (and it is a judgment, not a fact) is over-hasty, for it reduces all human learning to the behavior of animals without language and all human behavior to complex habits. Whether these sorts of reductions will withstand close scrutiny will be examined more closely in the next two chapters but they appear prima facie to be questionable. Intelligent and honest behavior as they were described earlier in this section would seem to involve more than just complex habits. The relations between learning and conditioning are doubtless subtle and complex: Conditioning may occur during the course of learning, and learning may occur when one is being conditioned. Another way of putting this would be to say that habits may be acquired when one is learning, and one may learn while he is acquiring habits. But this is not to say that learning and the acquisition of habits (or conditioning) are one and the same thing. For this reason, in the subsequent discussion the acquisition of habits will be related to the concept of learning in a way similar to the acquisition of knowledge and skills: Habits may be acquired when one learns but that is not all that is happening. In order for one to say that learning has occurred, more than habits must be acquired.

## LEARNING AND ATTITUDES

It is often said that, when a person's attitudes change or when he acquires new ones, he has learned. Again, we have a case of a very loose sense of the term learn and an inadequate one for any effort to discuss without ambiguity the conditions that facilitate learning. In the present discussion, we will use the term attitude as a way of indicating preferential behavior toward some object. Thus, if a person readily eats bananas when offered them and occasionally buys them himself, we may say that he has a positive attitude toward bananas.

What has happened to a person who has undergone a change of attitude? Has he learned? More precisely, we are here asking about the conditions under which a person's preferences, as manifested in the choices he actually makes, underwent change. We find a wide variety of answers. We may change attitudes by means of direct exhortation, relying on persuasive rhetoric, or by the subtler means commonly found in advertising. We may appeal to a person's reason, pointing out how certain of his present attitudes may conflict with his other attitudes or values. We may gradually shape an attitude through conditioning or reinforcement, providing immediate rewards each time an attitude is displayed that approaches the one we wish to be adopted. Or we may more quickly alter an attitude by administering punishment following its display. We may change a person's attitudes by carefully attending to the kinds of groups and the attitudinal climates of those groups of which he is a member. Or we may change an attitude by involving a person in a particular sort of activity, the conduct of which requires attitudes contrary to those he already holds. We may change an attitude by involving a person in a particular sort of dramatically presented vicarious experience.

There are, doubtless, other ways of changing attitudes and

some of those already mentioned have, from time to time, been explained as variants of the same process, but the point should be clear: When a person's attitudes are undergoing change, he may be experiencing any one of a number of quite different processes. And if this is the case, to call *all* of these processes "learning" would be to use that term in a loose and ambiguous manner. Attitudes may be acquired by a variety of means; some of these means operate within a context of learning and some do not. Hence it would be confusing to define the term learning as the acquisition of attitudes.

## LEARNING AS THE ACQUISITION OF DISPOSITIONS

We have now examined a variety of processes and a variety of possible outcomes of schooling. All of these outcomes normally serve, at one time or another, as specific educational aims. These outcomes may or may not occur during the course of learning but, since they may be secured in a wide variety of ways, and since these ways are made up of quite dissimilar sets of events, it has been held inappropriate for the purposes of this inquiry to apply to them all the single term, learning. In the present section, reasons will be given for using the term learning to indicate the process by which dispositions are acquired. For the moment we shall only point out that clarity, consistency, and convenience will result from using learning in this way, and that this usage of the term, far from being contrary to ordinary usage, is at least what people often have in mind when they talk about the kind of learning they expect and hope the schools to foster.

### THE ASCRIPTION OF DISPOSITIONS

When we ascribe a disposition to something or to someone, we are not describing his present condition so much as we are predicting how he will probably behave under a certain range of conditions at some future time. To say that Harry is cruel (i.e., is disposed to cruelty, or has a disposition to behave cruelly) is to make a claim similar to that made when one says that the wood splits in dry climates. Of course, we can always be more certain about the properties of wood than we can about the characteristics of people. Thus our prediction about when the wood will split can be made with greater accuracy than our prediction about Harry's cruel behavior. Yet neither must Harry be presently behaving cruelly nor must the wood be presently splitting in order that the dispositional or predictive statement be true. What does validate the statement is the occurrence of repeated occasions on which Harry acts cruelly when the opportunity arises, or on which the wood (or other wood of the same type) actually splits after exposure to a dry climate. A disposition, then, is not some sort of a thing or mysterious unobservable property of a thing; rather, it is a concept that has its use in predictive statements. To ascribe a disposition to something or to someone is to say he has a tendency to behave in certain ways when certain conditions are realized. Ascribing a disposition, then, allows for the making of a prediction (although it may also be *used* as a sort of explanation—e.g., "Why did Harry kick the dog?" "Because he is cruel."). In the case of Harry, our observation of his past social behavior allowed us to predict how he would behave toward others under certain conditions. In the case of the wood, our previous experience with it in dry climates allowed us to predict how it would act on future occasions.

Of course, it would be inappropriate for us to ascribe to Harry a particular disposition toward others if we had observed him interacting with others on only one or a very few previous occasions. Likewise, had we seen the wood splitting only once before or under a limited set of conditions, we could not be very certain that it was a dry climate rather than something else (e.g., improper aging that might result in the wood's splitting no matter what the climate) that was responsible for the splitting. Thus the basis for our making dispositional statements about people or things is our relevant experience of those people or things on a variety of occasions. Just how many and how varied those occasions must be will vary with the type of disposition being ascribed (e.g., the ascription of Harry's cruelty will require fewer observations than the ascription of his intelligence, since the latter disposition has a wider range of expression than the former).

In a like manner, the verification of a dispositional statement is generally made only after the occurrence of several relevant tests or observations. If Harry has been described as being cruel, and we observe his cruelty on a single future occasion, we may defeat the dispositional claim by saying, for example, that anyone would have behaved as Harry did under those circumstances. If the wood has been described as having a tendency to split in a dry climate, we may defeat the claim by saying, for example, that any wood would have split under *those* weather conditions. The precise determination of what constitutes adequate verification of dispositional statements may be a matter of scientific determination. Yet in our daily affairs, the willingness with which we assent to the ascription of a disposition varies directly as our testing of the ascription accords with scientific procedures. That is, the more and the more varied are the situations during which we observe an ascribed disposition being exercised, the more likely we are to assign credibility to the ascription. A cruel disposition may have been ascribed to Harry but we should be doing him an injustice (i.e., "jumping to a conclusion") if we agreed with the ascription only on the basis of having seen him kick a dog after he tripped over the animal. But if we are able to observe Harry behaving cruelly to dogs, children, and adults, and on occasions of not only great provocation, but of slight, and of no provocation as well, we should be justified in agreeing that Harry has a cruel disposition.

We may summarize the foregoing by again calling attention to the differences between the ascription of a disposition, the grounds for making it, and the means of verifying it. When we ascribe a disposition to Harry, our statement is meaningless unless it has reference to Harry's behavior, but it need not refer to his present behavior, nor does it ever refer to any one particular act in the past, to any one particular act in the future, or to any particular past or future date. Since dispositional statements about people refer to *ranges* of behavioral acts, they cannot be wholly based upon nor reliably verified by a single act—although the consideration of increasing numbers of single acts constitutes increasingly more adequate grounds and verification for dispositional statements. It is perfectly reasonable to say that Harry *has* the disposition—that it is "in" him; this way of speaking gains additional support from the fact that Harry *feels* disposed to do this or that. But if we are challenged to justify to others our ascription of a disposition to Harry, we cannot usually say, "Look at Harry." We can say, "Ask Harry." But it is usually wiser to point out a range of things Harry has done in the past. Even so, ascribing a disposition does not *mean* these past behaviors, else it would be no more than a historical generalization. In a sense, a dispositional statement is a *use* of history for predicting the future. For this reason, it cannot be justified simply by recounting the past, but must also achieve a measure of verification on the basis of what Harry does in the future. And just as historical generalizations are not disconfirmed by future events, the *past reference* of a dispositional statement is not necessarily falsified if Harry's future behavior is no longer compatible with it. We are then free to say, "Harry's disposition has changed." But we have given sufficient justification for ascribing a disposition to Harry if we can point to a number of relevant cases of his behavior in the past.

It is important to keep the prior grounds and the future verification distinct from the ascription of a disposition itself. To be disposed to do certain sorts of things is not to do them. Thus one may correctly be said to have a certain disposition—on the basis of previously observed behavior—even though the kinds of behavior to which the disposition refers may not be immediately forthcoming. Therefore, to confuse the test (i.e., observing the behavior) of a disposition with the disposition itself is to mistake a tendency to behave for a behavioral act. The fruits of this confusion are readily apparent when some educators rigidly insist that all school outcomes be understood as specific behavioral acts. To do so would be foolish, although it is not foolish to recommend that all school outcomes be *tested* by reference to the behavioral acts of students.

## THE OPENNESS OF DISPOSITIONAL CONCEPTS

The grounds on which dispositional statements are made and the ways they are verified point up another property of such statements which is of special importance when we consider the dispositions of people (whose behavior is less precisely determinable than that of inanimate objects). It is just because the exercise of a human disposition may take so many different forms that singular events are inadequate either as bases or as verifications of dispositional statements. Cruelty, for example, is a dispositional concept, but it has no single or uniform set of exercises. It may be manifested by some persons only in verbal behavior, in others, only physically. It may be directed only toward insects or animals, children or the infirm, men or women. It may be exercised by some people on almost any occasion, by others only in certain kinds of situations. The multiform exercise of dispositions is even more pronounced in cases of such wide-range ones as intelligence or stupidity, which may (or may not) be actualized on almost any conceivable occasion.

It is for these reasons that, in ascribing dispositions, we often aim at greater precision of communication by specifying the object of the disposition, the manner of its exercise, and the conditions under which it is most likely to be exercised. Still, it is never possible fully to specify all the conditions for the exercise of any disposition, since this would call for a crystal ball that afforded exact knowledge of the future.[13]

It might be noted in passing that this openness of dispositional concepts brings into sharper focus the absurdity of talking only about "behavioral goals" for schooling, if by "behavior" specific acts are meant.[14] It makes perfectly good sense to say that schools aim to develop intelligence, open-mindedness, honesty, kindness, and a host of other virtues, and that these virtues are all dispositions. Each of these dispositions, of course, connotes a *range* of behaviors, examples of which can easily be given, but the limits of which cannot be set with certainty. Yet those who make a show of being "scientific" sometimes express impatience with this sort of nonspecificity. Feeling more comfortable about what they have already observed and what they can precisely predict, they have even gone so far as to suggest the elimination of dispositions as school concerns, on the grounds that dispositional statements are vague, and that vagueness (any vagueness, apparently, about anything) is wicked.[15] The alternative to this "vagueness" would be to insure that students will make only specific responses to specific stimuli. (That this is a bizarre notion of schooling will be discussed in detail in Chapters III and IV.)

## CONDITIONS FOR THE EXERCISE OF A DISPOSITION

When a disposition is ascribed to someone, we are given some notion of how he will behave when certain conditions are realized. What sorts of conditions, then, must be realized—both within and without an individual—for any sort of disposition to operate?

It will be convenient to approach the question by looking at an example. Suppose we describe Mr. Crag as a hard and callous person, insensitive to the needs and desires of others. On the basis of this ascribed disposition, we should expect Mr. Crag to say and do things of a particular sort when the opportunity is present. What constitutes an "opportunity," so that Mr. Crag will be able to exercise this callous disposition?

In the first place, Mr. Crag must be in an appropriate situation. If he is at home working on a crossword puzzle, he cannot exercise his callous disposition toward others. Let us then imagine that he is conversing with friends on the topic of public health insurance for the aged. Now if we know about Crag's disposition, we can expect him to make certain sorts of statements about health insurance or about the people who might benefit from it. (It is important to remember, of course, that Crag or anyone else *might* make the same statements from motives wholly apart from a callous disposition.)

Suppose that Crag is extremely shy, or that he stutters badly, or that he is otherwise socially unskilled. If so, he may say nothing at all. This serves to remind us that one must have acquired some *skills* relevant to a particular situation in order to exercise a disposition. A boy with very poor aim either improves his marksmanship or fails to exercise his aggressive disposition by engaging in snowball fights. Returning to our example, unless Mr. Crag has some minimum conversational and social skills, he will not be able to exercise his callous disposition in the situation into which we have put him.

Suppose now that Mr. Crag has never before heard of public health insurance for the aged. In such a case, he could have no beliefs about it, and the mere mention of such insurance could not afford an occasion for the exercise of his callous disposition. The exercise of a disposition is an action and if we are to act at all (even if only verbally) with respect to some object, we must have some *beliefs* about it. It does not matter whether the beliefs are correct or incorrect, substantiated, or only assumed; what is important is that the having of some belief is also necessary for the exercise of a disposition.

Finally, just as the having of relevant skills, knowledge, or beliefs is necessary for the exercise of a disposition, so is it necessary to have some relevant *attitude*. If Mr. Crag is to exercise his callous disposition in the social situation we have constructed, he must not only be equipped with certain social skills and knowledge relevant to the topic at hand, but he must also have an attitude or set of preferences toward public health insurance, toward those who might benefit from it, or toward those who will pay for it. It is not easy, of course, to distinguish the relevant attitude from the callous disposition; given Crag's disposition, we should not expect him, for example, to favor giving aid to the elderly. And in this particular instance, Crag's attitude might be one of not caring one way or the other. But this would be a function of his callous disposition, and it would probably eventuate in his having an attitude of opposing public health insurance (i.e., "I don't care whether you want to help older people or not, but don't ask *me* to pay for it."). Thus as we observe Mr. Crag talking with his friends, we see him exercising his callous disposition as he brings certain (social) skills to bear on his attitudes about what he knows or thinks he knows.

We can now summarize what has been said. To ascribe a disposition is to make possible a prediction about how a person might act under certain conditions. To have a particular disposition, then, is to have a tendency to act in certain ways in certain circumstances. For the action to be actually performed, the circumstances must, of course, be realized. These circumstances include, minimally, the occurrence of a situation to which the exercise of the disposition would be relevant, some manner of skill by which the exercise of the disposition may be carried out, and some belief about and some attitude toward the object of the exercise of the disposition. The distinction that is being made here is between the ascription of a disposition and its exercise. *Ascribing* a disposition is the same as describing a trait of character. In neither case is a speaker obligated to specify precisely how and on what basis a person will act on a particular occasion. But the *exercise* of a disposition always involves particular skills, knowledge, and attitudes. By analogy, we can point out that an airplane flies without having to commit ourselves about its altitude, speed, and course. But when the airplane is flying, it must be flying at a particular altitude and speed, and on a particular course.

A dispositional statement is not about an event, but the exercise of a disposition *is* an event and that exercise can be specified respecting its components. This is also true respecting the acquisition of a disposition. This, too, is an event (although it would be more accurate to say that it is an extended series of events) and it, too, can be specified respecting its components. This is only to say that no disposition can be acquired unless relevant skills, attitudes, and knowledge are also acquired. And it is these skills, attitudes, and knowledge which are employed, in some form at least, in the later exercise of the disposition. But because the skills, attitudes, and knowledge relevant to the exercise of a disposition are hardly ever acquired all at the same time, the acquisition of a disposition is understandably a time-consuming affair— more similar in this respect to the acquiring of a skill than it is to the acquiring of certain items of knowledge. At this point we are ready to consider why it would be helpful to use the term learning to indicate the acquisition of a disposition.

## Learning As Acquiring Dispositions

Most people who are concerned with schooling (or, at least, most of those who pay for it) are hopeful that those who attend schools will behave differently than they would have had they not gone to school. If school makes any difference at all in one's life, it must make a difference in how he acts; otherwise, we have no way of telling *what* difference it made. To this extent, at least, the ultimate test of the efficacy of schooling is behavioral, although we need not embrace the tenets of a crude form of behaviorism which insists that all school aims be cast in terms of specific behavioral acts. But however much people may agree that it is the students' behavior that is the ultimate measure of schooling, they disagree strongly about the sorts of things that, once acquired, lead to particular kinds of behavior. These disagreements, in turn, lead to disagreements about what the schools ought to teach. Thus one school of educational thought holds that the acquisition of certain kinds of knowledge is instrumental in leading to actions that are desirable.[16] Another school of thought holds that the acquisition of certain attitudes and emotional states will lead to certain desired actions.[17] And still another school of thought holds that only the acquisition of particular desired acts themselves will lead to the exercise of those acts later on.[18] Each of these schools of thought is likely to use the term learning to describe the process (as well as the outcome) by which its recommended offerings are acquired.

Despite their differences about *how* students should behave as a result of having attended school, those who hold these varying points of view would probably agree that changed patterns of action ought to be the eventual outcome of schooling. And most of them would also agree that no one is in a position precisely to specify *just* what actions ought to be the outcome of schooling.[19] For such specificity would not only require omniscience on the part of educational planners, but would also imply that the graduates of schools be denied the freedom to choose their actions.

In the light of these agreements and disagreements on the part of those concerned with schooling, it would appear that most of them are agreed that the outcome of schooling is to be a set of dispositions, however much proposals about methods of schooling may conflict. If, by dispositions, we mean tendencies to act, and if the range of actions connoted is never precisely specifiable, and if the acquisition and exercise of dispositions always involves particular knowledge, skills, and attitudes, then it would appear that those who are concerned with schooling have as their aim the acquisition of dispositions. They may, of course, disagree about *how* dispositions are acquired, or about *which* dispositions ought to be acquired. What actually goes on in this process is a matter of some dispute, and will occupy most of the remainder of this book. But despite disagreements about the process of learning, we can profitably conceive it as eventuating in the acquisition of dispositions. If we do so, then we shall not disregard the various concerns of those who wish students to acquire knowledge, or to develop attitudes and emotional states, or to acquire skills. For we have seen that a disposition cannot be exercised—and, for the same reasons, cannot be acquired—without one's also acquiring relevant knowledge, skills, attitudes, and overt acts. Thus the particular aims of various schools of educational thought can never be excluded from any consideration of learning defined as the acquisition of dispositions.

## Learning to Learn as a School Aim

Cruelty, narrow-mindedness, stupidity are all dispositions. On the definition stipulated here, the acquisition of any of these deplorable traits would count as learning. But no one would wish to foster such learning in schools. Thus when we speak of the sorts of learning that are *appropriate* for schools to foster, we must narrow our conception of learning still further so that those which are undesirable will be excluded.

If cruelty, narrow-mindedness, and stupidity are undesirable learnings for schools to promote, then their contraries—kindness, broad-mindedness, and intelligence—surely are desirable. Yet a list of learnings that would be desirable might well be endless. It is necessary, then, to seek what might be common to any sorts of learnings—i.e., to the acquisition of any sorts of dispositions—that would be accounted desirable.

Dispositions that are held to be undesirable are dispositions that make it difficult for one to acquire new skills or refine old ones, difficult to acquire new and reject old beliefs, and difficult to change attitudes. But new or more refined skills, new knowledge, and new attitudes are just what is required to deal effectively with the changing conditions of living. Undesirable or bad dispositions, then, render people incapable of dealing effectively and successfully with novel situations. For while people can deal successfully with the familiar largely on the basis of habit, life is nothing if not a continual encounter with the unfamiliar, and success in such encounters depends on flexibility, breadth, insight, increase of knowledge, and willingness to risk. It would follow, then, that the kinds of dispositions that are desirable for schools to foster are those dispositions that make possible the acquisition and refinement of new skills, new knowledge, new attitudes. This is simply to say that desirable dispositions are those that allow for the possibility of acquiring new dispositions. Or, to put it another way, the learning that is (or, I am proposing, ought to be) the special concern of schools is learning that leads to more learning.

Although educational thinkers may be opposed on many particular issues, and may suggest other school aims as well, few of them would deny the value of learning to learn as an educational aim.[20] Of course, it may be claimed that learning to learn is far too vague an aim for schooling, especially if it is elevated to the position of the school's chief aim. If learning to learn is so important, then *what* are students supposed to be learning to learn? Surely, no suggestions for a curriculum can be found in an aim stated so broadly as this. This is indeed true, and the curriculum will become a subject of discussion later on (in Chapter X). But for the moment we can at least see that, while learning to learn as an aim does not specify any *specific* skills or information for students to acquire, it does serve as a *criterion* by which school practices can be evaluated. The point can be illustrated with an example although a more careful defense of the point will have to wait until later.

Let us suppose we visit a high school history class. The first half of the period is spent in recitation. The teacher's questions about points of historical fact are answered by different students on the basis of their familiarity with the text. In the other half of the period, each of three students writes on the blackboard a list of antecedents to a certain historical event. One list is composed of economic events, another is of political, and a third is of military events. Suggestions from the rest of the class add to the lists, and the extended lists are copied down by each student at his seat. When the class is over, we ask the teacher what the purpose of the previous hour was; he tells us that he wanted to make sure that his students learned what he felt to be important facts about the period in history under investigation. When we ask him why he thinks the students ought to be acquainted with these facts, he answers—after a little prodding—that without facts there can be no understanding of history, and without history one cannot be a well-informed (which is to say, a good) citizen. Now we can examine the teacher's remarks and the events of the classroom in the light of our foregoing analysis.

Whatever the teacher's purposes might have been he was probably not content to state them solely in terms of the acquisition of historical facts. For to most people—including most teachers —to stuff the head with information that has no apparent utility seems a rather vain and laborious, if not impossible, task.[21] For this or some other reason, then, the teacher has implied that he aims to promote the acquisition of a disposition: citizenship.

But did the events we observed in the classroom meet our criterion of learning to learn? The teacher implied that they did not, for he said his aim *then* was to promote only the learning (we should have said "acquisition") of certain facts. But if the classroom is used for the acquisition of facts, when is the aimed-for disposition learned? The teacher might be quick to point out that children do not neatly acquire facts one day and dispositions the next, but that the learning of dispositions is a natural concomitant of acquiring facts. If he focuses on facts, the dispositions will naturally follow. He is correct in this, of course, but the dispositions that do get learned as a result of his teaching practices are probably not the ones he had in mind.[22]

In the first place, the teacher was mistaken in thinking that facts were acquired in his classroom. The only students who *might* have acquired any facts (for how long they retained them is another question) were those who had not read the textbook. Those who did read carefully (the conscientious students, we must suppose) acquired no facts but instead spent the class period giving evidence that they had acquired them. It is not easy to see how this sort of behavior is related to learning to be a good citizen.

The teacher in this case required his students to read a specified number of pages in a particular text. Some students did, and tried to retain—at least for a day—the information they acquired, while other students did not. During the class period, students individually offered evidence of their retention of information (or at least of that information the teacher thought important enough to be worth asking about); the majority of the students, most of the time, simply heard spoken aloud what they had already read or should have read. Under these conditions, of course, it is difficult to remain awake and even more difficult to attend to what is being said. The more enterprising students can be depended upon to have invented their own devices for passing the time while the recitations and blackboard work was going on. In this sort of setting, dispositions are being learned, to be sure, but it is not comforting to speculate about what sort of dispositions they might be. Aside from considerations of citizenship, what the students in this situation are *not* doing is learning to learn. And this should be reason enough for calling into question the classroom practice that has been described.

## SUMMARY

The term learning is normally used to indicate both a process (i.e., what is going on) and a product (i.e., what happened as a result), and the particular process that is indicated usually turns out to be whatever events resulted in a given product. Thus, for example, if knowledge is taken to be a learning outcome, the process of learning will be taken to be the process by which knowledge is acquired. Since different people choose to call different products (e.g., skills, knowledge, etc.) by the name of learnings, they also assign the term learning to a number of very different kinds of processes. Since this book is concerned with the ways in which learning, considered as a process, might be promoted, the fact that the term learning is used to refer to so many different kinds of processes has been held to be obstructive to careful inquiry.

In order, then, to pursue inquiry into learning without ambiguity, it has been suggested that the major emphasis of the term be put on those processes by which dispositions are acquired. The task of describing the events relevant to and involved in those processes has been reserved for later chapters, but it has been indicated here that the acquisition of knowledge, skills, attitudes, and overt acts are all involved when dispositions are acquired. To this extent, then, this usage of learning embraces most of the learning outcomes (as well as some of the processes by which those outcomes are achieved) which others sometimes hold to be the exclusive ones. For this reason, it has also been claimed that the way in which learning has been used here, far from being contrary to ordinary usage of the term, is consistent with a great many uses of it. The usage adopted here departs from ordinary usage only when the latter becomes ambiguous in indicating things so very different that inquiry into learning would become fragmented into a set of distinct and unrelated inquiries.

Finally, because the school is neither obligated nor expected to concern itself with *all* conceivable learnings, and especially with those that most people would hold to be undesirable, a range of learning has been selected as being especially appropriate for schooling. This latter is whatever learning that could be expected to lead to further learning. Put another way, it has been suggested here that schools are especially suited (if not obligated, in a democracy and in a rapidly changing world) to enable students to learn to learn.

# NOTES

1. See, for example, B. Othanel Smith, "A Concept of Teaching," in Smith and Robert H. Ennis (eds.), *Language and Concepts in Education* (Chicago: Rand McNally, 1961).

2. See, for example, the discussions in Arno A. Bellack (ed.), *Theory and Research in Teaching* (New York: Bureau of Publications, Teachers College, Columbia University, 1963).

3. Herbert J. Klausmeier, *Learning and Human Abilities* (New York: Harper, 1961), p. 10 f.

4. For further discussion of the distinctions among learning (and knowing and teaching) *how,* learning *to,* and learning *that,* see Gilbert Ryle, *A Concept of Mind* (New York: Barnes and Noble, 1949), chap. 2, and Israel Scheffler, *The Language of Education* (Springfield, Ill.: Charles Thomas, 1960), chap. 5.

5. See Ryle, *op. cit.,* p. 54.

6. *Ibid.,* p. 59. Of course, cases can be adduced which do not neatly fit these categories. "Learning *that*" may not always indicate the acquisition of knowledge, as in the case of someone's learning that honesty is the best policy. And "learning *how*" may not always indicate the acquisition and improvement of an ability, as in the case of learning how the economic system works. [See Scheffler, *op. cit.,* and Jane Roland, "On the Reduction of 'Knowing That' to 'Knowing How,' " in B. O. Smith and R. H. Ennis (eds.), *Language and Concepts in Education* (Chicago: Rand McNally, 1961).] It would interfere with the purpose of the present discussion of learning to compound complexities of these usages although the way in which one might deal with them may be indicated by the following treatment. When one learns how the economic system works, he has learned *that* a great many things are the case (and he has not necessarily acquired or improved the sort of ability normally indicated by "learning *how*"). If one has learned *that* honesty is the best policy, he may have acquired some knowledge of a norm. He may, on the other hand, have acquired a disposition (to be honest, which would be a case

of learning *to*), or he may have acquired both. In short, when we are told that someone has learned *that* honesty is the best policy, we cannot be at all sure *what* was learned unless the speaker expands on his statement.

7. This point will be elaborated at greater length in the subsequent discussion of behaviorism (Chap. III) although this school of thought is not alone in reducing learning to a single process.

8. See Ryle, *op. cit.*, pp. 149–153.

9. See, for example, Eugene Galanter, "The Ideal Teacher," in Galanter (ed.), *Automatic Teaching: The State of the Art* (New York: Wiley, 1959).

10. A possible exception might be the man in a waiting room who read a tract on Lawsonomy (in which he had no interest) because that was all there was to read, and there was nothing else to do. But even this is not so much a case of reading for the pleasure taken in it as it is a case of an activity instituted to avoid boredom. In Chap. XIII, we will explore further the important implications of boredom for schooling.

11. See the illuminating discussion of this point in Scheffler, *op. cit.*, p. 98 f.

12. John Dewey, among others, speaks of a "habit of intelligence," although he attempts to avoid the confusion noted here by distinguishing between routine habits and active habits. But one might still ask, "Are they *both* habits? That is, is the *form* of behavior the same in both cases?" See Dewey, *Democracy and Education* (New York: Macmillan, 1916), pp. 57, 58, 62.

13. Cf. J. O. Wisdom, "Some Main Mind-Body Problems," *Aristotelian Society Proceedings*, LX (1959–1960), p. 204.

14. That behavioral change as the aim of schooling is not only mistaken but also has serious moral consequences is discussed by Thomas F. Green, "Teaching, Acting, and Behaving," *Harvard Education Review*, 34 (1964), 517.

15. John D. McNeil, "The Influence of Programmed Learning upon Curriculum Research," *Phi Delta Kappan*, 44 (March, 1963), 262.

16. For a lucid exposition of this point of view, see Harry S. Broudy, *Building a Philosophy of Education* (2nd ed.; Englewood Cliffs, N.J.: Prentice-Hall, 1961).

17. See, for example, Arthur Jersild, *In Search of Self* (New York:

Bureau of Publications, Teachers College, Columbia University, 1952).

18. See, for example, Will French and Associates, *Behavioral Goals of General Education in High School* (New York: Russell Sage Foundation, 1957). For an extended discussion of these three points of view in respect of their treatment of the development of attitudes, see Barbara D. Chambers, *The Role of Attitudes in Schooling*, unpublished Ph.D. dissertation, The University of Wisconsin, 1964.

19. It may be that some of those who urge the use of programmed instruction in schools would not concur in this statement. See, for example, French, *op. cit.*

20. Although the worth of learning to learn is not to be measured by the number of people who endorse it, it may be worth noting its appearance in the thinking of writers who otherwise sharply disagree about educational values. Thus it is implied in John Dewey's notion of growth in *Democracy and Education,* pp. 59–60; in Harry S. Broudy's notion of the forms of intelligent behavior both in *Building a Philosophy of Education,* pp. 293–310 and in *Paradox and Promise* (Englewood Cliffs, N.J.: Prentice-Hall, 1961), pp. 39–40; in the discussion of generalization by Florence B. Stratemeyer *et al.,* in *Developing a Curriculum for Modern Living,* 2nd ed. (New York: Bureau of Publications, Teachers College, Columbia University, 1957), pp. 75–76; in Jerome Bruner's discussion of attitudes and values toward intellectual activity, in *The Process of Education* (Cambridge, Mass.: Harvard University Press, 1960), p. 73; and in Solon T. Kimball's and James E. McClellan's discussion of the "main business" of schooling, in *Education and the New America* (New York: Random House, 1962), pp. 289–294. A more explicit statement of the operation and of the value of learning to learn is to be found in Harry F. Harlow, "The Formation of Learning Sets," *Psychological Review,* 56 (January, 1949), 51–65; Dewey treats the subject more explicitly under the heading of "plasticity" (in *Democracy and Education,* pp. 52–54). And yet another exemplification of what is meant here is found in Joseph J. Schwab's discussion, "The Teaching of Science as Enquiry" in *The Teaching of Science* (Cambridge, Mass.: Harvard University Press, 1962). The science classroom, in Schwab's view, "would engage in an *enquiry into*

*enquiry"* (p. 65), and the teachers' role would be "to teach the student how to learn" (p. 67).

21. But not all educational thinkers disapprove of acquiring knowledge for its own sake. One group of writers, discussing the social studies curriculum, deplores the employment of such studies for the achievement of citizenship, critical thinking, problem-solving, family living, and democratic practice. The writers do not hold these goals to be without value, but they do believe that they cannot be achieved through deliberate teaching. Such goals can best be achieved, if at all, if schools focus on a single goal: "the task of imparting complex and difficult bodies of knowledge." See Albert R. Kitzhaber, Robert M. Gorrell, and Paul Roberts, *Education For College: Improving the High School Curriculum* (New York: Ronald Press, 1961), pp. 110–111.

22. See David R. Krathwohl *et al. Taxonomy of Education Objectives, Handbook II: Affective Domain* (New York: David McKay, 1964), p. 20.

# III

## *THEORIES OF LEARNING AND SCHOOLING*

SCHOOLS ARE INDISPUTABLY USEFUL IN PERFORMING A CUSTODIAL function. Classrooms are handy places to send youngsters when their parents and guardians are too busy to take care of them. The objection of many parents to some recent teachers' strikes only underscores the schools' custodial function. If the teachers aren't in the classroom, parents complained, where shall we send our children?[1] Under the industrial and economic conditions that obtain in America at mid-century, children are practically useless in an economic sense (except as consumers). Thus, to have some place to put children while adults work acquires an urgency not found when the young are gradually inducted into adult roles by helping adults at their occupations.

But few people, indeed, view the school *only* in its custodial role—as a place to keep young children off the streets and older ones off the increasingly competitive labor market. For it is also expected that what is done in schools will have an impact, sooner or later, on the behavior of the children who attend them. In the last chapter, these anticipated changes in behavior were discussed in terms of acquiring dispositions. In the next chapter we shall consider the conditions that make it possible for this sort of learning to occur, but first we must attend to some current theories about how people behave and learn. We shall see that some of these theories, while founded on centuries of tradition, only confound our understanding of learning, and thereby continue to confuse our practices in the schools.

We could not attempt to examine here all the theories of learning that are current, but we can discuss some important features that are common to many of them and thus discover major families of theories. The family resemblances between two groups of learning theories are of special interest to us because of their present impact on schooling. Following much current usage, we shall call these two families of theories about human behavior ego-psychology and behaviorism. In the following discussion we do not imply that there actually exists any single learning theorist who endorses all the features attributed to either of these families of theories. Instead, the analysis will focus on those key structural features common to all theories in the family. Thus when we consider ego-psychology, the analysis applies equally to related theories that are variously called self-psychology, personality theory, holistic-dynamic pschology, etc. And when we speak of behaviorism, our discussion is equally relevant to theories of drive-reduction, contiguity, reinforcement, etc. Because we are seeking generality, we shall refer to specific theorists who have discussed both learning and schooling only in order to clarify some specific points.

## EVALUATING ANY THEORY OF LEARNING

If we are interested in finding out how to conduct school practices, it is helpful to know how people learn. To arrive at the latter, we must examine theories of learning. We soon find, however, that the theories conflict: they explain learning in different ways and call attention to different events when the promotion of learning is under consideration. It does no good simply to "pick the best" from each of the theories as a guide to teaching, for we cannot do any intelligent picking until we have a way of judging what might be best. Since the proponents of each of the theories are about equally convinced of the adequacy of their own views of human behavior and learning, sober educational thinkers are often likely to adopt an attitude of waiting until more evidence (i.e., data) is gathered before they settle on any theoretical guides to teaching.

For at least two reasons this attempt to keep an open mind only courts empty-mindedness. First, we must operate our schools *now* and with as much forethought as possible; neither the children nor their parents will wait for school to open at some indefinite time in the future "when all the evidence is gathered." Second, it is not likely that all the evidence ever will be gathered. If it continues to be collected as it is at present, evidence will continue to support all the disputes about learning that are current now. For we shall see that when investigators go after "facts," what they are willing to *call* a "fact" is necessarily dependent on the theory or conception of human behavior or human nature that they hold. Imagine that you are asked to judge between conflicting theories about the properties of water. One theorist says it is tasteless and another insists it is salty. You ask for evidence and the first theorist offers you a drink of lake water, the second offers sea water. Assuming you are only a layman on matters of liquids, you ask for further evidence before you decide. It should be clear that, as long as the first theorist keeps bringing you samples of lake water, and the second keeps bringing samples of sea water, you will *never* be able to decide whether water is "really" tasteless or salty, other than by a purely arbitrary choice. Among conflicting theories of learning, matters are much the same: the "facts" of human behavior are drawn from different wells and are quite reasonably fitting for the different theoretical buckets which contain them.

How, then, are we to discover whether any given theory of

learning is adequate? The man who thinks water is salty does not accept lake water as contrary evidence because, for him, it is simply not water. To evaluate his conception of water we cannot question his facts—that is, his samples of sea water. Instead, we ask what his reason is for choosing to call water only clear liquids that are salty. In other words, we examine the assumptions he holds about water. These assumptions may not be very factual at all. We may accept them, of course, but we may also reject them, and if we do, we may be in a position to look elsewhere (e.g., in lakes and rivers) for samples of water to be counted as further evidence. Although the analogy is rather crude, we must treat theories of learning in the same way. We must examine the assumptions on which they are based as well as the evidence that is brought forward in their support, for that evidence is found only in places where the theorist's assumptions tell him to look. So we examine the assumptions to see if it is worth looking elsewhere for evidence.

We can put this in a different way by saying that empirical investigations alone (the seeking of factual data) will never adequately reveal the relative adequacies and inadequacies of theories of learning even though they all purport to be empirically grounded. If "empirical study" means simply staring at the world and recording what is seen, no theory will ever be supported or refuted. Every theory of learning depends for its existence on the making of inferences about what *cannot* be seen, heard, felt, or smelled, but which are taken as explanations of what *is* recorded by the senses. The families of learning theories that we are calling ego-psychology and behaviorism do not disagree so much on their reports of what any careful observer could see, so much as they disagree about what is *not* seen but which is taken to account for what *is*. However occult it may sound at the moment, it is our task to seek for that which is not seen.

If we may trust that all empirical investigators are confronted with the same range (i.e., visible, audible, etc.) of events in a world common to them all, then we may suppose that the differences in the events they select for study and the differences in the inferences they make on the basis of often quite similar sets of events, are differences in the assumptions they have made (consciously or not) about the nature of the reality with which they are dealing. In the present instance, the reality in question is that of the nature of man, or of mind. These assumptions, in turn, can be traced back to philosophic world views that have for several millennia dominated Western culture. The chief task of the following discussion will be to show that ego-psychology and behaviorism are inadequate as theories of learning—and hence inadequate as guides to teaching—principally because the philosophic world views on which they are based and according to which they make sense do not themselves adequately square with experience. We do not, of course, find correct and incorrect philosophies the way we find mistakes in mathematical proofs. Yet we can try to show that some philosophies, at least, no longer work when they are carried from the rarified air of theory to the humid turbulence of practical affairs. For these kinds of affairs are now more carefully conceptualized and better understood than they were when the philosophic world views underlying ego-psychology and behaviorism were developed.

In the last analysis, then, our test of the adequacy of a learning theory must be one of compatibility.[2] When we move from the theory to its underlying assumptions and the philosophic world view on which it is based, we must ask whether that way of looking at the world squares with our own experience of it—with our expectations, our judgments, and our actions. How this sort of test would be conducted will only become clear (if at all) in the course of the specific analyses that follow, but it will proceed in much the same way that empirical investigators find mathematical systems useful. We may recall that mathematicians are able to devise a limitless number of mathematical systems, and that each one is as "correct" (i.e., valid) as any other. The reason for this is that the only criterion of "correctness" for such a system is that all of its axioms and theorems remain consistent with the postulates from which it starts. Thus it makes no sense to ask *which* mathematical system is the "right" one or the "correct" one; they are *all* right (valid) as long as they are self-consistent. And truth or falsity—as long as such terms connote some reference to the empirical world—are irrelevant considerations.

Theories of learning and the philosophies on which they are based might, of course, be viewed in the same fashion, and thus judged only on the basis of their internal consistency. If we found that several such systems were equally consistent (that is, valid) and were asked to choose between them, we should have no basis for making a choice other than the elegance of one system or another. Our criterion, then, would be primarily an aesthetic one, and we should find ourselves choosing between equally valid philosophies and learning theories on the same grounds that mathematicians might choose (if they felt any necessity for it) between equally valid mathematical systems.

But if a mathematician were asked to choose among such equally valid systems, he would doubtless ask what his choice was supposed to be *for*. If a system best suited to surveying were requested, the mathematician would choose a Euclidean system. If a geographer interested in measuring large areas of the earth's surface made the request, the mathematician might choose a non-Euclidean system. If an astronomer asked for a system to suit his purposes, still another non-Euclidean system would be chosen. The application of mathematical systems to the empirical world should thus be clear. Although there may be an infinite number of systems that are *valid*, only certain systems have any *utility* when we want to deal quantitatively with particular portions of the universe. Interstellar space is curved and Euclidean geometry is limited to the measurement of plane surfaces; hence, while Euclidean geometry is neither true nor false in itself, it is a poor choice as a means of making measurements in interstellar space. When it was used for such measurements in the past, astronomers eventually found themselves burdened with a mass of incompatible and confusing data.

Most educators would say that the purpose of trying to choose among alternative theories of learning is to guide the learning of people. Yet it is interesting to note that some theorists have made their choice of a theory of learning on the basis of its demonstrated utility in changing the behavior of rats and pigeons. This is a perfectly reasonable basis for choosing a theory, but it is not reasonable to make the additional claim, as some theorists have, that such a theory is equally useful when it is applied to the behavior of people. Such a claim makes about as much sense as claiming that a geometry useful for measuring distances between city blocks is equally useful for measuring distances between galactic systems. Of course, there is no reason to deny the physical continuity that exists between space in cities and interstellar space or between pigeons, rats, and men. But to note the similarities among all conceptions of space and among all kinds of living organisms makes it in no way sensible to use the same measuring instruments for both rats and men or for both earthly and interstellar space.

If a learning theory along with its philosophic underpinnings is to be chosen for its utility in dealing with human learners in an empirical world, then it must be chosen for the same reasons that a physicist or an astronomer chooses one rather than another mathematical system. Such a choice cannot be made simply on the grounds of internal consistency, simplicity, elegance, and, perhaps, a respectable and ancient tradition. While these grounds cannot be wholly ignored, the final test of a choice must be its utility in explaining and predicting a wide range of events that fall within our experience of human action.

In the remainder of this chapter we shall ask if the families of learning theories in question provide an internally consistent set of answers to questions about human behavior—and especially learning—that are compatible with our own carefully examined experience of those events. And we shall ask if the theories and the philosophies on which they are based prove genuinely useful in devising school practices that would result in what we have called learning.

## THE CONCEPTION OF LEARNING IN EGO-PSYCHOLOGY

Curiosity and practical necessity have made man himself the subject of his oldest and most unremitting studies. The imposing question "What is man?" is a perennial one, although it is currently put in a less pretentious way: "What makes men behave the way they do?" One significant issue runs through the long history of study and experiment and speculation about man, dividing the questions and answers of the investigators into two camps. The issue is that of the principle by which man and his behavior are to be explained. One camp has maintained that man is but a natural creature made up of the same elements found anywhere else in nature and subject to the same laws that govern the rest of nature. To this group of thinkers it is clear that answers to the question "What is man?" will be found with the same instruments, the same techniques, and the same research designs that are employed in finding out what any other thing in the natural universe is like. By the same token, they answer questions about why men behave the way they do by investigating the natural laws to which all living organisms are subject.

Contemporary empirical investigators within this camp often refer to themselves as "behaviorists," although, with their philosophical allies, they are often described as "naturalists." This latter term would be a useful shorthand were it not for the fact that it has the unfortunate feature of implying that all thinkers who fall outside the group are somehow unnatural. For this reason, when the occasion arises, we shall refer to them as "mechanists," using the term only with descriptive intent.

The members of the other camp are more diverse in their views, but they all agree that what distinguishes men from all other natural creatures is something more than simply greater complexity. And they all agree that men are not subject to the same laws that govern all other natural creatures—at least not subject to those laws the way other organisms are. Because this sort of agreement is negative in nature—that is, they agree about what is *not* the case— thinkers in this camp have plenty of room for a wide variety of opinions about what man is like and why he behaves the way he does.

Traditionally, explanations that have emerged from this camp have been cast in supernatural terms, but it would be inaccurate to maintain that all those who oppose the views of the mechanists described above are, therefore, upholders of supernatural (or, as indicated above, unnatural) beliefs. Those contemporary empirical investigators whose views I am bringing together under the heading of "ego-psychology" are all members of this camp, but not one of them explains man or his behavior by appealing to anything recognizably supernatural, either within man or outside of him. But in seeking to avoid the mechanistic explanations of the other camp, they most usually appeal to determining principles of action found *inside* men. Whether these inner principles are subject to outside (i.e., environmental) influences or not, they are said to be, at least in part, subject to men's conscious control (a feature which distinguishes this group from Freudians, who find man's interior dark and difficult of access, and normally beyond his power of conscious control). This determining interior or core within man is somehow different from his exterior—the physical, three-dimensional man with whom laymen are familiar. To distinguish it from the concrete, behaving man we all see, this inner core is often referred to as a "self" or "ego." The self or ego, expanded into a theoretical structure, becomes the principle by which man and his behavior are explained. For this reason the term ego-psychology is often used to refer to empirical investigators of this persuasion. We shall adopt the older but still useful term "vitalism" to designate thought, whether empirical or philosophical, that is compatible with this point of view and unsympathetic toward mechanism. As we explore the problems raised by vitalism and mechanism, we shall gradually come to see the need for finding still another approach to explaining man's behavior.

In an age of science, the sort of extreme view which is most likely to attract the attention of educated men is extreme scientism. Some of the upholders of mechanism are extremists in this sense, in that they have reduced all human action to the physically determined and determinable bumping around of measurable bits of matter. But an environment of cities and industries, atomic power, and wristwatches that wind themselves is rich soil for the growth of extreme varieties of mechanism. Such views of man's behavior have not been without effect on school practices. Of course, the schools are still strongly influenced by extreme views that are contrary to the pronouncements of science as is readily seen in religious teaching and in much of what passes for moral education. But with the exception of some religious leaders themselves (many of whom have already given up theism), no one in an age of science dares to champion an extreme form of vitalism that *wholly* rejects all aspects of mechanism. Thus we will find no ego-psychologist who vigorously maintains that *all* of a man's acts are determined or determinable from within himself, and independent of environmental influence.

The absence of a thoroughgoing vitalism complicates the views of ego-psychology, but it is easy to see why extremism in these theories has been abandoned. After all, if two men were dropped from the Tower of Pisa, we should only replicate Galileo's findings. Falling men, like all other bodies, fall at the same rate. We must conclude, then, that men are governed, at least in some respects, by the same physical laws that hold for the rest of nature, and ego-psychology is bound to grant this point.

But ego-psychologists, like most other psychologists, are not particularly interested in the rates at which men fall through space. What they are interested in is why some men should *want* to fall through space. This is a psychological problem, not one of physics or physiology. But even here, the ego-psychologist dares not take an extreme vitalist point of view. Some of man's hopes and fears and joys and anxieties may indeed be unique, but some of them appear to be so obviously explainable in mechanistic terms that ego-psychology has had to make its peace with mechanism. Perhaps an illustration will make this clearer.

The psychologist Rollo May has defined very succinctly the point that is fundamental to all ego-psychology. In seeking to explain the behavior of higher organisms (such as man), he points out that we sometimes err in assuming that it can be understood wholly in terms of elements that are found lower on the evolutionary scale. This mistake

> has led us to overlook the self-evident truth that what makes a horse a horse are not the elements it shares with the dog but what constitutes distinctively, "horse."[3]

Now, on these same grounds, what makes a man a man (and behave like a man) are not the elements he shares with the rat or pigeon. If this statement is to be at all meaningful, it must make a difference for the way we talk about the behavior of men. Explanations and predictions of human actions should be unique to humans, and different from the sorts of explanations and predictions made for rats and pigeons. But ego-psychologists do not apply this principle to *all* of human behavior. For example, Schachtel notes that an infant may repeatedly be thrown into the air by a loving parent who exhibits both pleasure and warmth and who affords the infant protection and security. Under these reinforcing conditions, the infant comes to enjoy and look forward to being thrown into the air. If related and unpleasant experiences do not intervene, the child in later life might even consider it quite exhilarating to fall through space.[4]

There is nothing so particularly striking about this explanation and prediction of the child's behavior except that ego-psychology admits it, despite its close similarity to mechanistic explanations. That is, a behaviorist would claim that in this case the child (like any other organism) acquired a new set of behaviors subsequent to reinforcing stimuli (the pleasure-behaviors of the parent). The difference is that while the behavorist explains *all* human behavior in this way, the ego-psychologist does not. Some behavior, he claims, cannot be explained simply on the basis of some concatenation of environmental stimuli impinging on the human subject. It is explanations of this kind of behavior and this kind of learning that we are interested in examining.

Because people, like animals, have a tendency to seek food when they are hungry, and because people, like animals, have a tendency to seek to repeat the kinds of experiences they found rewarding in the past, the ego-psychologist admits these mechanistically explained behaviors into the repertoire of human actions. This sort of behavior has been referred to as "opportunistic becoming"[5] or as "deficiency motivation."[6] Action released by such motivation tends to fulfill what are claimed to be "basic needs" (or deficiencies) common to all individuals—e.g., the needs for safety, belongingness, love, respect from others, and self-esteem.[7] If these needs are not fulfilled, psychological illness is the result. Hence action motivated by these needs conforms to the familiar behavioristic model of tension reduction (the need produces tension in the organism, which is reduced by action that is successful in satisfying the need). Learning, on this model, is explained wholly in terms of stimuli and responses. But what happens to the man whose basic needs are satisfied?

The behaviorist answers that if the need-satisfied man does anything at all besides going to sleep, he can be expected to continue the behaviors previously found to be reinforcing or to work toward satisfying other needs. Not so for the ego-psychologist. It is his claim that few men, indeed, ever reach the stage of need-satisfaction, even relatively speaking. But until a stage is reached where one is no longer feeling the pressure of a great many needs, he will not even have an opportunity to be fully human. For the man who has reached his full potential as a human is *not* driven by his needs (as lower organisms always appear to be), and does not feel the burdensome pressure of a threatening environment. He does not act merely to reduce tensions, nor are his acts to be explained simply as responses to stimuli over whose appearance he has no control. What initiates and guides his acts under these conditions, then? *He* does. Or rather, his self does. That which has been formulated to explain the nature of this kind of behavior-directed-from-within has been called "propriate striving"[8] or "growth motivation."[9]

Growth-motivated people no longer behave in the simple stimulus-response patterns common to lower organisms because they are no longer dependent on their environment for stimulation and direction in their acts. They are behaving in ways fully human because they have become, for the moment at least, self-sufficient.

> The determinants which govern them are now primarily inner ones, rather than social or environmental. They are the laws of their own inner nature, their potentialities and capacities, their talents, their latent resources, their creative impulses. . . .[10]

Herein lies a paradox, for when the ego or self is most fully functioning, it is least aware of itself. On these matters, ego-psychologists become lyrical as they describe what amounts to a nearly beatific state: self and environment are transcended, and inhibition disappears as the self is lost in its activity. The self-actualizing person is able

> To "be himself," to emit behavior—"radioactively," as it were—rather than to repeat it, to allow his inner nature to express itself. . . .[11]

The fully functioning man is able

> in his inner life to transcend the material universe . . . , able to live dimensions of his life which are not fully or adequately contained in a description of his conditionings, or of his unconscious.[12]

Learning, in the course of deficiency-motivated behavior, has been characterized as an affair of tension reduction; it does not occupy the focus of attention for ego-psychology. How is learning characterized during growth-motivated behavior? What is it like, and how it is initiated?

To begin with, growth-motivated behavior *is* learning for the ego-psychologist. When the person is functioning fully, or self-actualizing, he is gaining increase of insight, knowledge of self, and increased integration and inner consistency.[13] These are, of course, dispositional changes. The conditions under which this learning can occur are met when the learner's needs are satiated; further tension-reduction would be to no purpose and simply boring. The learner is then at the stage where, if he is neither threatened nor subject to external pressure, he will of his own accord eagerly seek the "higher, more complex delights"[14] that are the fruits of growing, learning, and growth-motivation. Teachers do not set the time for learning, then; the learner does, for only he knows when he is ready for it.[15] Furthermore, teachers do not dictate *what* the child shall learn nor do they pass judgment on the child's learning. Again, only the learner himself can determine these things, since his learning issues forth from an inner region which is not accessible to scrutiny from without:

> . . . growth takes place when the next step forward is sub-
> jectively more delightful, more joyous, more intrinsically satisfy-
> ing than the last; . . . the only way we can ever know what is
> right for us is that it feels better subjectively than any alterna-
> tive. The new experience validates *itself* rather than by any
> outside criterion. . . . In this way, we learn what we are good
> at, what we really like or dislike, what our tastes and judg-
> ments and capacities are. In a word, this is the way in which
> we discover the Self and answer the ultimate questions Who
> am I? What am I?[16]

What prevents this sort of learning are threats to one's basic
needs—that is, any increase in environmentally sponsored tension.
What facilitates this learning, then, is the reduction of such threats.
This is to say that, for the ego-psychologist, an educative situation
is a permissive situation. The learner is accepted and made to feel
safe; he is gratified, praised, and reassured; he is neither evaluated
obtrusively nor invidiously compared with others. The learner will
be free to explore available materials according to his own interests and potentials.[17]

The resemblance of these descriptions of a learning situation is
strikingly similar to the way some people (probably erroneously) interpret Rousseau's *Emile;* even more similar are they to some of the
proposals of the "extreme" wing of the progressive educators who
attracted some attention in the United States in the decade of the
1920s.[18] In these respects, the ego-psychologists' conception of learning, and the educational proposals that emerge from it, have their
roots in a philosophy of subjective idealism[19] and in its close relative, existentialism.

The ego-psychologist is ready to grant that a permissive atmosphere
may not in itself be enough to foster learning for everyone. Some
people are so mired in their deficit-needs and so subject to the
pressures of their environment that special techniques are needed
to bring them to the point of functioning fully. What is needed
in these cases is therapy—administered, ideally, by a professional
psychotherapist, but still possible in many other kinds of interpersonal relations, including those of teacher and student.

The kind of therapy that is appropriate, however, involves no

Freudian analysis of the client's ills, and no issuing of directives to guide the client's rehabilitation. Rather, it is a client-centered therapy, in which the therapist creates the conditions that will enable the client to do his own learning. The therapist, then, tries only to be himself, to achieve empathy for the client's inner world of private, personal meanings, and to assume toward the client a posture of unconditional, warm, positive acceptance.[20] It will be seen, then, that therapy for the ego-psychologist is only an emphatic form of permissive atmosphere. As in the teaching-learning situation, the therapy situation must free the individual to do his own learning. If the learner is simply told what is good for him, he will not learn it; he must find it out for himself through his own searching experience. Carl Rogers has likened this sort of learning to Kierkegaard's "true subjectivity," about which there can be no direct communication.

> The most that one person can do to further it in another, is
> to create certain conditions which make this type of learning
> *possible*. It cannot be compelled.[21]

Learning for the ego-psychologist is, then, a profoundly moving, personal experience in which the whole self is involved. In the last analysis it is a coming-to-know-one's self (which may fairly be interpreted as a dispositional change) by one's own efforts, through a sort of personal knowing[22] or subjective appropriation[23] which existentialists have called the only route to any knowledge at all.[24] And just as the existentialist insists that the only choice worthy of the name is the one made by the chooser himself, so the ego-psychologist insists that the only learning worthy of the name is that which has been initiated, directed, and appropriated by the learner himself. The teacher is responsible chiefly for insuring an environment of freedom for the learner. In any other sort of environment, the learner becomes merely an organism responding to stimuli— like the rats in the behaviorist's menagerie.

In order to test the adequacy of this account of learning, we might begin by examining what the ego-psychologist means by an environment that will promote learning. It is, above all, one of freedom. No pressures are exerted on the learner, no things or events are present to which he must respond, or with which he must deal in some way. Indeed, materials (e.g., books, paints, etc.) *may* be available, but they do not demand some use; they are not means for dealing with any sort of problem. Now, this is a very peculiar sort of environment, for it makes no demands on the person who is in it. But consider how we normally use the phrase, "a person's environment"; we mean whatever is in a person's surroundings of which he is aware, to which he responds, or which affects him in some way. The "environment of freedom," then, is really no environment at all. And it is in this *lack* of environment that one is expected to learn.[25]

Normally, a person's environment is that with which he deals, consciously or not, whether it be present and immediately at hand or distant in time or space. What is the relation of *this* environment to learning for the ego-psychologist? It is but an obstacle —an impediment to learning. Learning, growth, self-actualization, and even psychological health does not consist of adjusting to the environment, or even in mastering it. Rather, it consists of *transcending* the environment.[26] The learning, growing person is independent of his environment. This account of the relation between an individual and environment is, of course, diametrically opposite to the views of mechanists who claim that all behavior, learning included, is but a response *to* the environment. What sort of a self (or mind) must the ego-psychologists assume, then, in order to bring what is normally spoken of as the environment into such disuse, if not disrepute?

The individual's self is able to learn when it is free from having to deal with an environment. If an environmental situation does not initiate the changes that result in learning, then what does? The self itself, obviously. Thus the self—or mind, to use a more traditional term—turns out to be *an immaterial entity* (because it is not the self that we *see* interacting with things in the world) *endowed with creative powers of its own*. And it must have such powers, for if it did not, it would simply remain inert when it was free from the influence of its environment.

Now, the conception of mind as an immaterial, active substance is a hard one to picture. What are the logical implications of such a postulated entity? And what would be the results of school practices that were based upon the assumption that such an entity existed?

Indians who saw a locomotive for the first time probably thought there *must* be a horse inside to make it go.[27] Likewise, vitalists (whether ego-psychologists, subjective idealists, or existentialists) who observe people behaving have assumed that there *must* be something inside of them to make them go. It cannot be a horse, of course. Instead, we call it a "self" (although it could as easily be called a mind, or a soul). The self is immaterial, but the body is quite solid and three-dimensional, and moves about quite readily. That which makes the body move is the self. But how is this possible? How can a nonspatial self exert influence on a spatial body? Whatever ghostly set of gears[28] could effect a casual connection between the immaterial and the material is beyond conceiving. If it were even possible, then, for a self or mind to learn all of its own accord and independent of an environment, it is not conceivable how such learning could be translated into behavior which would constitute public evidence that learning had occurred. The logical implications of the assumed existence of an immaterial, active self, then, are these. Either it is inconceivable that a three-dimensional, material human being could learn, if his learning is a function of such an entity; or, if it were granted that learning could occur, its presence could not conceivably be detected. The self and its environment have been sharply separated and then deposited in two entirely different realms. And neither all the king's horses nor all the king's men can ever bring together what the vitalist has rent asunder.

Whatever the difficulties may be into which the logic of an immaterial mind may lead us, we may still ask about its practical implications. What might happen, then, were we to base school practices on a vitalistic conception of self?

The sort of school atmosphere that is predicated on the theory of learning advanced by ego-psychology is one of permissiveness. In the present century, this notion of schooling has been associated with what has been called "progressive" education. We shall see later that this conception of progressive education, favored by certain social reformers, curriculum makers, and psychologists differed by a great deal from what pragmatic philosophers and other social reformers thought about it. But progressive education had its prophets of permissiveness, and it is these thinkers who based their educational proposals on a conception of child nature quite similar to the "self" of the ego-psychologists'—even though the earlier progressives may have (mistakenly) traced their roots back to Rousseau or, paradoxically, Freud.[29]

It should be clear why permissiveness is called for by most vitalists. If learning proceeds spontaneously from a self when it is made independent of environmental influence, then, there is nothing that a teacher could do to initiate learning. All that could be done would be to make available a variety of materials which might be useful in learning, and to then institute conditions allowing freedom for pupils. The teacher might provide sympathy, understanding, and encouragement, and then wait hopefully for pupils to do their own learning.[30] We might imagine what would happen in a classroom were this to be done. Some children would deal with the available materials as they had in the past, thus repeating past behavior but learning little, if anything, that was new. Others might become frustrated at the lack of direction, and begin to express aggression toward their classmates. Still others might simply be bored, and utilize the time for woolgathering or conversation. And some pupils, of course, might, out of curiosity, explore the available materials and seek to deal with them in new ways. In this latter group, one might expect some learning to occur.[31]

The reason we are justified in expecting results like those mentioned above is not far to seek. If neither school nor teacher provide any particular direction for learning, what does happen in the classroom will be a matter of accident. But this sort of accident is far from being unpredictable. A child may be freed from the pressures of his environment in the classroom, but he cannot be freed from his past, and it is *that* which will operate most strongly in the permissive classroom. If a child is accustomed to looking at pictures in books at home, he might be expected to do the same in a permissive classroom. If a child is used to firm guidance and discipline at home, he might be expected to become frustrated when he is freed from such direction at school. And if a child has been encouraged to explore his environment freely at home, he will bring this disposition with him to school and act upon it in a permissive classroom. Thus a permissive classroom in no way frees every child from his environment so that learning occurs spontaneously. Instead, it merely provides the conditions for the sort of behavior that is the result of children's past environmental interactions.

Under what conditions, then, *could* one expect a child to learn, if only an atmosphere of permissiveness were provided for him? The child will learn in such an atmosphere if he has been accustomed to learning *out* of school. If he has been encouraged to explore his environment at home, if he has been given responsibility and has been encouraged to deal with his own problems, then, he will bring dispositions formed by such experiences with him to school, and he will probably put a permissive atmosphere to good use (providing, of course, that there is enough similarity between his home and neighborhood, and his school environment).

But neither the facts nor the logic of the matter afford us much reason for hope in this respect. In the first place, the sort of home environment that has been described here is an uncommon one. If it were common, there would be little occasion to discuss the problems of schooling since there would be hardly *be* any problems. What makes the job of the schools so difficult is the fact that those who attend usually do not acquire dispositions to learn at home. Neither the strict discipline nor the lack of discipline characteristic of so many urban homes nor the relatively problem-free atmosphere of many surburban homes is conducive to the development of the sort of dispositions to learn that are relevant to the aims of schools and teachers.

But an even more imposing obstacle faces the alleged utility of the permissive classroom that is favored by ego-psychologists. Learning, it is claimed, will occur if freedom, sympathy, and encouragement are provided. But we have seen that this claim will hold only in those cases where children have already acquired dispositions to learn out of school. But how were *those* dispositions acquired? According to the ego-psychologist, they were acquired at home just as they were to be acquired at school. That is, children must have learned at home because their families provided them with freedom, sympathy, and encouragement. But how, under *these* conditions, could children have come to learn? According to what has been said above, they must have been accustomed to learning *already* if the freedom provided by the family were to be of any help. It will be seen that this theory of learning involves us in an infinite regress that takes our study of the child all the way back to the womb. Is it *here* that the child first began the sort of learning which his family's subsequent pemissiveness allowed to flower forth? If this appears bizarre, all one can suppose is that the learning power of the child's self is innate, and requires no experience in dealing with an environment in order to exist. And as has already been indicated, this is just what the ego-psychologist must assume. In the last analysis, what allows a permissive atmosphere to be effective in the fostering of learning is the existence of an immaterial mind or self that is innately endowed with the power of learning. But we have already seen the difficulties that beset this view of mind and human nature.

Assumptions about human nature lie behind our explanations and predictions about the way people behave. Assumptions about the nature of mind are useful insofar as they explain, among other things, what we know about learning. But the assumptions that vitalists make about the nature of the mind or self are inexplicable and, ultimately, a mystery. It is not very helpful to try to explain what we *do* know something (learning) by reference to what we cannot even understand: an immaterial, creatively acting self.

## THE CONCEPTION OF LEARNING OF BEHAVIORISM

Behaviorism is the contemporary heir to a long tradition of mechanistic accounts of human behavior, one of whose earliest and clearest spokesmen in modern history was Thomas Hobbes.[32] Like

Hobbes, who attempted to explain human behavior in terms of mechanically conceived connections that began with the act of sensation, the contemporary behaviorist is unimpressed with postulated entities that cannot be observed, or whose existence cannot be clearly inferred from observations. For most behaviorists, a statement about human nature or human action is meaningless unless all of its referential elements can, at least after analysis, be referred to immediately observable properties or relations. An immediately observable property (like the color green) or relation (like that of heavier than) is called an "undefined concept" because it must be learned through experience and it cannot be described to another person purely linguistically. That is, one cannot *tell* someone else what green looks like, or what it means for a thing to be heavier than something else, unless that other person has consciously seen colored things and has had some conscious experience of the weight of things. As behaviorists judge them, concepts like "ego" and "self," no matter how they are analyzed or understood, still contain important elements that refer to that which is not and cannot ever be immediately observable. Thus such concepts are said to be quite literally meaningless.[33]

So far is the behaviorist from taking seriously the existence of unseen egos, selves, and minds, that he has focused his interest solely on physiological actions that are open to public view. Instead of speaking, then, of the *cause* of human actions (e.g., learning), the behaviorist prefers to speak of the antecedent and subsequent conditions that appear to be *associated*—in a statistical sense—with human actions. The program of the behaviorist is thus quite relevant to a theory of learning.[34] If one could clearly identify the conditions under which people learn, it might be quite unnecessary to speak of causes at all. For a teacher would need only to institute those conditions in his classroom in order to insure the occurrence of what he is aiming at: learning on the part of his pupils.

Once mind or the self has been eliminated from consideration, all the behaviorist has to deal with is observable behavior.[35] This can be described in three ways. A respondent is behavior that is elicited by external stimuli, and is always an involuntary reflex action. Thus the jerking of one's knee at the tap of a hammer is respondent behavior, as is the occurrence of salivation at the presentation of food.

A second category of behavior is the instrumental act, or "operant." Operant behavior is voluntary, in that it functions to produce changes in the organism's environment (i.e., it "operates" on it). Rather than occurring as an involuntary response to external stimuli, an operant occurs when some prior behavior has been rewarded.[36] Because an operant is not closely tied in an involuntary way to an eliciting stimulus, it is said to be "emitted" by an organism, rather than elicited by an external stimulus. Most of human behavior is thus operant behavior. One orders a particular dish at a restaurant because in the past, he has found it rewarding to do so. One chooses a particular vocation because the activities and rewards associated with it have been found in the past to be rewarding.

The third rather broad category of behavior is called "random" behavior. Whenever an eliciting stimulus for a particular act cannot be found, and when that act cannot clearly be labelled an operant, it is called a "random act." Of course, some acts that are not random at all may appear to be so to an observer. In fact, the definitions just discussed exclude *any* act that can be *explained* from the category of random acts. It would appear, then, that if all behavior—whether animal or human—can sooner or later be explained (that is, if enough relevant data is available), there would be no random acts, and the class of random acts would be empty. Meanwhile, lacking full observation and complete explanation, the category of random acts has been proposed to include all behavior that is neither respondent nor operant. Thus a random act would be one that did not serve any deliberate purpose.

When behaviorists talk about learning they refer, of course, to behavior, and in the case of learning they would mean the acquisition of some new behavior. If we should speak of learning as the acquisition of dispositions, then these dispositions, for the behaviorist, would have to be definable ultimately in terms of observable behaviors (i.e., immediately observed properties and relations which could properly be characterized as "undefined concepts"). Under what conditions, then, does a behaviorist allow that learning has occurred? Obviously, random behavior does not itself constitute learning, although given appropriate conditions of reward, it may eventuate in learning. But the acquisition of new behaviors will always be a function of the reinforcing conditions under which respondent and operant behavior occurs. As will be set forth below, learning is always a case of conditioning; and the conditioning will be either respondent or operant conditioning.

Respondent conditioning occurs when an organism makes a response to a stimulus to which it had not responded in the past. This conditioning can be facilitated by pairing the new stimulus with some other stimulus to which the organism does respond. In the classical Pavlovian experiments, dogs were noted to salivate at the presentation of food (i.e., salivation was an involuntary or respondent act). They did not, of course, salivate when a bell was rung. But if a bell was rung each time that food was presented, the dog eventually salivated at the sound of the bell even though food was not presented. Thus the dog's respondent, salivation, occured as a response to a stimulus (the bell) which had not previously elicited that response. On the model of respondent conditioning, then, learning is a matter of acquiring a response to a stimulus that had not previously elicited that particular response. For an example of respondent conditioning in humans, we might note that some children wince when verbally rebuked. Now, a verbal rebuke does not normally elicit wincing, but a slap directed toward a person will. If a child has in the past been frequently slapped *and* rebuked at the same time, he will quite likely wince at the rebuke even though he is not slapped. The wince is a new response to a stimulus (verbal rebuke) that had not previously elicited the response of wincing.

The learning that results from respondent conditioning is involuntary. Since most human behavior is not of the reflex type but is instead, voluntary, we find that for behaviorists, human learning is typically of the sort called operant conditioning, to which we now turn. Fundamentally, learning according to the model of operant conditioning consists in the increased strength of an operant. By "increased strength" is meant the likelihood that the operant will recur. Thus if conditions are such that an operant becomes more likely to occur than it had in the past (i.e., is stronger), it can be said that the organism has learned. We must now examine the conditions that are said to be likely to increase the strength of an operant.

In the classical Skinnerian demonstration of operant conditioning, a food-deprived pigeon is put in a box that has a key in it; pressing the key will introduce food into the box. The pigeon is observed to make a number of "random" movements, but whenever one of these movements depresses the key, a little bit of lunch is served. With the passage of time, the pigeon presses the key more frequently. Thus it is said that the strength of the key-pressing response has been increased. The pigeon has learned.

Now, the lay observer of this phenomenon might offer the following explanation: the pigeon presses the key so that he can satisfy his hunger by eating the food. But for the behaviorist,[37] this is misleading because of at least two untestable assumptions. In the first place, he claims, we have no right to call the pigeon hungry. Hunger, as we normally use the term, is an internal state, and we have no way of finding out about this from the pigeon. But we *can* say that the pigeon has been deprived of food (and specify for how long). Secondly and more important, the claim that the pigeon presses the key *so that* he can get the food is unjustifiable, for it implies a causal relation. Causal relations, as David Hume pointed out long ago, cannot be directly observed; all that we *do* observe are certain events, related to one another in a certain order of time. The assertion of a cause is an inference made from those observations, and the careless drawing of inferences has plagued the study of human behavior since its beginnings.

What the observer *has* seen in the pigeon experiment is this: as long as the pressing of the key produced food that was eaten by the pigeon, the pigeon continued pressing the key at a rapid rate. Presentation of food is then seen to be associated with increased strength (or greater likelihood) of key-pressing behavior. That which follows a particular operant and is empirically associated with an increase in strength of that operant is called a reinforcer or a reinforcing stimulus (note that *this* stimulus is one that *follows* an operant response, not one that precedes and elicits a respondent).

Reinforcement, then, is whatever affects the probability of occurrence of an operant. If the strength of an operant is increased after the presentation of a particular stimulus, that stimulus is called a positive reinforcer; if the operant's strength is reduced, it is said to have been negatively reinforced. To be effective, it is held that the reinforcer must immediately follow the operant behavior.[38] The withdrawal of a reinforcer is normally followed by the extinction (i.e., disappearance) of the response that it had formerly followed.

We are now able to understand the behaviorist's explanation of the pigeon experiment: food is a reinforcer because the pigeon's key-pressing behavior is more likely to be repeated if it is followed by the presentation and eating of food; furthermore, this phenomenon is more likely to occur when the pigeon has been deprived of food. The term "because" in the above statement does not denote a causal relationship; rather, it indicates that a particular series of events conforms to the definition of reinforcement.

One further point must be made with respect to the nature of reinforcement, and that has to do with the distinction between primary and secondary reinforcers. A primary reinforcer is one that alters the probability of a response without the organism's having engaged in any learning; it is, in a sense, "natural." For example, a food-deprived pigeon appears likely to repeat whatever responses were followed by the presentation of food. It does not have to *learn* that food is reinforcing; hence, food is a primary reinforcer.[39] A secondary reinforcer achieves its effect after having been associated with a primary reinforcer. Food is a primary reinforcer for any food-deprived organism, but money, for example, is not. But if an organism is able to use the money for food, then, the presentation of money can reinforce a response and has acquired the status of a secondary reinforcer. The distinction is an important one, since there is little opportunity to utilize primary reinforcement in cases of human learning. Schools can hardly afford to reinforce certain responses of students with food. They cannot afford to reinforce responses with money, either. Hence other secondary reinforcers must be found if learning in schools is to follow the model of operant conditioning.

We have spoken about the ways in which response strength

is altered, but in many learning situations, not the strength of an old response, but rather the appearance of a new response is desired. New responses can result from operant conditioning in three basic ways: through generalization, discrimination, and differentiation (or shaping).[40] "Generalization" is the term used to describe what happens when a response that had been reinforced in one situation is repeated in another, similar situation. Thus a small child may receive secondary reinforcements (e.g., adult approval) after uttering the word "doggie" when he sees a dog (which in this case functions as a discriminating, or cue stimulus). If this situation is repeated often enough, we may expect the probability of the child's saying "doggie" on the appearance of dogs to increase. But the child may also say "doggie" on the appearance of a horse. Thus his response has generalized, in that it was applied to any four-footed animal. Generalization, then, may or may not produce behaviors deemed appropriate by teachers or other adults. If a child identifies all animals as "doggie," generalization has led to inappropriate behavior. But if the child's response, "animal," to the appearance of dogs has been reinforced, subsequent generalization to horses, cows, etc. would be more appropriate.

In the process of discrimination, generalized operants become tied to a narrower and more particular range of cue stimuli through extinction. If, for example, we continue to reinforce the child's response of "doggie" to dogs, but we do *not* reinforce that response when he makes it to other kinds of animals, then, we can expect the child's response of "doggie" to horses, cows, etc. to extinguish. Eventually, the child will utter "doggie" only with reference to dogs. Thus the process of response discrimination produces the sort of results that would normally entitle us to say, "The child can discriminate dogs from other animals."

Response differentiation occurs when the direction of a continuous series of responses (that is, a complete movement) is altered by means of selectively reinforcing some of those responses and not reinforcing others. Thus we can train a dog to touch a doorknob with its nose by reinforcing (e.g., with food) those movements which bring the dog closer to the doorknob and not reinforcing all other movements. Thus movements away from the doorknob are extinguished and movements toward it become more probable. This process of response differentiation is also known as "shaping" behavior, and the series of steps through which the process moves is called "successive approximations." Each movement that is reinforced is a movement that more approximately corresponds to the "criterion" behavior (i.e., the behavior desired by the experimenter) than the previous movement.

For the behaviorist, all learning is a case of one or more of the processes described above, appearing either alone or in some combination. Complex learning occurs by means of an accretion of responses, a process called "chaining." In such cases, the discriminating stimulus for one response becomes a secondary reinforcer for another response. Suppose that a child is given one black and one white coin, and that he can get a candy bar by putting the black coin in a slot. In this case, the child becomes likely (i.e., learns) to select the black coin—which has then become a discriminating stimulus—and drop it in the slot after the primary reinforcement of the candy. Now suppose that the child is presented with a red and a blue lever. If he pulls the blue lever, he gets the black coin, which he then puts into the slot to get the candy. Now the black coin which remains a discriminating stimulus for slot-dropping behavior, has *also* become a secondary reinforcer for pulling the blue lever. The coin has, in a manner of speaking, acquired its reinforcing properties because of its association with getting the candy. Through processes of chaining even more complex than this one, the behaviorist claims to explain all cases of human learning.

Behaviorists have advanced our understanding of the way men behave by casting out of the explanations all references to immaterial minds and selves. But what behaviorists have chosen to retain in their explanations raises some serious questions about their adequacy. We need not comment further on respondent conditioning, since we may grant that while some human behavior is acquired this way, most of it is not. Instead, we shall focus on operant conditioning and pay especially close attention to its key concept, that of reinforcement.

It is said to be a law of operant conditioning that if the occurrence of an operant is followed by a reinforcing stimulus, the strength of that operant is increased. But this law has a peculiar shortcoming, for a reinforcer has already been *defined* as that which increases the strength of the operant that it follows. Thus the alleged law tells us nothing that is not already contained in the definition of a reinforcer. Consequently, armed only with a definition, we have no way of identifying a situation in which reinforcement could be expected to occur. To put this in another way, the reluctance of the reinforcement theorist to tell us *why* a reinforcer reinforces leaves us with no way of identifying what would constitute a reinforcer and what would not. All that can be done, then, is to observe the behavior of an organism. If an operant is seen to increase in strength, we are entitled to say that it is being reinforced. But the explanation breaks down on at least two counts.

First, we cannot be sure *what part* of the organism's environment is doing the reinforcing. It is easy enough to say that the sunflower seed is reinforcing the pigeon's key-pressing responses, but what part of a mountain climber's complex environment is reinforcing his repeated attempts to climb mountains? The concept of reinforcement, in looking only to the behavior of the organism (and thus in ignoring the complexity of natural environments, which differ by a great deal from controlled laboratory situations), is of no help in answering this question.

But the second shortcoming in the concept of reinforcement is even more crucial for one who would attempt to employ learning theory in the practice of schooling. If a teacher wishes to change the strength or direction of a student's behavior, he has only to reinforce certain of the student's responses. But what shall constitute an adequate reinforcer? The theory tells us only that behavior has been reinforced *after* the behavior has occurred—not before. Thus the theory offers no help to a teacher who wants to know how, or with what, to reinforce the behavior of his students.

Some behaviorists, squarely facing the problem of causality, have tried to explain reinforcement by saying that what reinforces behavior is that which reduces a drive. Thus primary reinforcement is adduced to explain increases in operant strength, and given a reason why reinforcers work, we should be able to identify the sorts of things and events which could be useful in teaching and learning situations. But this only raises new problems. Presumably, people have hunger drives and sex drives, but it would be exceedingly impracticable for schools, or even parents, to use rewards of food and women (or men, if the learner is female) as ways of reinforcing certain desired behaviors. Indeed, people may have other drives the reduction of which will constitute reinforcement, but the identification of reinforcers will then depend on what we are willing to call a "drive." But lists of drives (which are not as popular as they were a generation or two ago) are as long and as curious as the ingenuity of theorists permits.

The other way in which the theory of drive-reduction attempts to explain how reinforcers work is to say that what reinforces behavior is that which has been associated through prior learning with drive-reducers. This is to adduce the concept of what has been called (above) secondary reinforcement. The trouble with trying to use this explanation in a theory of learning that might be applicable to human teaching and learning situations is fairly obvious. For while it is claimed that primary reinforcers, in being unlearned, are common to all organisms (at least of a given species), what constitutes a secondary reinforcer for one individual may have no effect at all on the operant strength of another individual. Secondary reinforcers acquire their effect through learning, and the learning experiences of organisms—and especially people—differ markedly. Once more, the concept of reinforcement offers no particular help to a teacher who asks the reasonable question, "How can I tell what sorts of things will reinforce the behavior of my students?"

Attempts have been made to apply the concept of reinforcement to schooling through the technique known as "programmed instruction." Programmers claim that reinforcement for students consists of presenting immediate knowledge of results of their efforts to acquire the information in a teaching program. Although it is said that pigeons will not work for such meager gains, "simply being correct is sufficient reinforcement" for humans.[41] Not only is there nothing in the reinforcement theory that would support such a claim, but it is even contrary to everyday experience. An enormous number of students in schools have considerably less than a passionate interest in the results of their academic efforts. Some students will be reinforced by knowledge of results and some will not; neither can behaviorism tell us who will and who will not, nor does it offer any practicable way of making the "immediate knowledge of results" become a reinforcer.

If the concept of reinforcement has any value at all, it should be useful in facilitating learning. We might test the theory by applying it to a relatively simple example. Suppose we want to train a child to ride a bicycle. Extrapolating from the data gathered on laboratory animals, we need only reinforce bicycle riding behavior. What facilitated the reinforcing of key-pressing on the part of pigeons was the fact that some of the pigeon's random movements *included* key-pressing; the experimenter had only to connect the key to a food-dispensing apparatus in order to insure that key-pressing would be reinforced. We cannot begin in this fashion with the child because he may never emit random bicycle riding behaviors. It may be theoretically possible to shape the child's current activity (which may be climbing trees) into bicycle riding behavior by successive approximations, but practically it would be rather absurd. So we begin teaching the child by presenting him with the bike (which *may* be a discriminating stimulus, depending on the child's response), and perhaps asking, "How would you like to learn to ride a bike?" It would appear, thus far, that common sense has little to gain from reinforcement theory.

If the child balks at our offer, we must either give up the lesson or find some inducement that will encourage him to try. We might suggest that it is fun to ride bikes, or that all the other children in the neighborhood are riding bikes, or that he will be able to go to the swimming pool by himself if he is able to ride a bike. Now these inducements cannot, even if successful, be called secondary reinforcers, because they are presented *before,* and not after the child's response. Yet they are not eliciting stimuli either, since they do not call forth a reflex action in the child. As a matter of fact, inducements appeal to the child's interests and purposes, and they are often successful in their appeal. Yet interests and purposes are not open to direct observation and have, therefore, been legislated out of existence by most behaviorists and by all reinforcement theorists. Three things are clear at this point. First, reinforcement theory is no help to us in finding inducements to get the child to try to ride the bike. Second, unless the inducements are effective, the child will not want to ride the bike, and we will thus be quite unable to teach him—short of threatening him with dire consequences if he does not learn. And third, all that reinforcement theory could possibly suggest would be random presentations of a variety of things, such as food, money, approval, etc.—*after* the child had already *tried* riding the bike—in the hope that one of them would turn out to be a reinforcer.

If our inducements are successful, and the child gives bicycle riding a try, then all that is necessary according to reinforcement theory is to shape his early, awkward efforts into smoother and more graceful ones by reinforcing the desirable responses and withholding reinforcement after unwanted responses. Again the theory is of no help, since what will be a reinforcer can be identified as such only *after* it has operated in reinforcing behavior. Common sense, on the other hand, indicates that we reward the child's attempts on the basis of whatever induced him to try in the first place. If he was convinced that riding is fun, we cheer him as he wobbles unsteadily before he falls. If he was convinced that all the other children could ride, we might reward his first successful efforts by making favorable comparisons between him and other bicycle riders in the neighborhood. These kinds of encouraging remarks on the part of the teacher may indeed be labelled "secondary reinforcement," but in so labelling them, we have added nothing to the description of these events, and we certainly have not explained them. As in other cases where reinforcement is used to cover cases of increased response strength contingent on wanting something, liking something, wishing that something were the case, etc., the term has little more than a ritual function and no explanatory force. Professor Chomsky concludes his own criticism of the concept of reinforcement by noting that

> any idea that this paraphrase introduces any new clarity or objectivity into the description of wishing, liking, etc., is a serious delusion.[42]

The contention of behaviorism, that all learning is ultimately a matter of conditioning, has been readily adopted by some thinkers whose aim for schooling has been the acquisition of knowledge (although by no means do all such educationists believe that learning is nothing but a matter of conditioning). The reason this is so may be that acquisition of knowledge can easily be interpreted to mean acquisition of *verbal* behavior. And it has been empirically demonstrated that certain verbal behaviors can be acquired by a procedure that purports, at least, to apply the principles of reinforcement and response differentiation. This procedure has been packaged and sold under the title of programmed instruction.[43]

Now it can be shown that programmed instruction does not, in fact, exemplify reinforcement theory.[44] What it calls "reinforcement" is immediate presentation to the student of knowledge of the results of his efforts in responding to the items in the program. As we have seen, the theory of reinforcement offers no reason why such knowledge of results should be termed a reinforcer until the student's subsequent behavior has been observed. And we might expect that after being presented with knowledge of results, some students might be observed to continue responding and others might not. Yet even in the case of those students who tend to continue responding, we might find *just as much* association between the increased response strength and (for example) threat of failing school marks or teacher disapproval, as there is between it and knowledge of results. Reinforcement theory does not tell us *which* was the reinforcer although programmers easily assume it was knowledge of results.

Furthermore, the "small steps" presented by the instructional program—that is, the sequence of items to which the student must respond that covers successive and closely related bits of a subject matter area—has been claimed to conform to the principle of successive approximation, or what has been called here response differentiation. This, too, is an error. Response differentiation, as we have seen, applies to behavior that consists of a *continuous* series of movements which may be shaped to head in one direction rather than another. The number of *possible* directions toward which the movements *might* have been directed is, of course, infinite. In any case, only those movements that more closely approximate the desired direction are reinforced, while the other movements are not re-inforced and hence extinguished. This system works remarkably well in shaping quite complex bodily movements of animals.

The so-called "successive approximations" of a teaching program, however, have little in common with response differentiation. In the first place, the student is not faced with an infinite number of possible responses. Either he is faced with choosing among four quite discrete alternatives, or he is asked to write a response under conditions where he would be aware that only a small and discrete number of possible responses could possibly make any sense. Thus the class of behaviors to which the teaching program is relevant—discrete and finite responses—is quite different from the class of responses (continuous and infinite) to which the process of response differentiation is relevant.

In the second place, the success of response differentiation depends on the extinguishing of inappropriate responses. In the teaching program, each succeeding item is graded for difficulty in such a manner that it will be answered correctly 90 to 95 percent of the time. There are, then, hardly any responses that will be extinguished. Thus, if nearly every item in the program is to be responded to correctly, there is nothing that is being approximated. Each separate response is altogether correct, not approximately so.

Finally, the result of response differentiation is one long, continuous motion that conforms to the criterion of the experimenter. But the result (ideally) of the use of a teaching program is a discrete number of verbal responses. The *last* attempt of the organism, in response differentiation, *combines* all of its previous successful attempts into one smooth, continuous motion. But the last attempt of the pupil working on an instructional program is only a correct response to the last item in the program. When the organism that underwent response differentiation makes its final response, it incorporates *all* of its past successful responses. This is not the case for the final response to the instructional program. To make *that* response correctly provides no evidence that all—or indeed any—of the student's previous responses again could be made correctly.

There is, then, only a rather tenuous relationship between pro-grammed instruction and the theories of learning contained in the varieties of behaviorist psychology. Of course, conditioning can produce measurable results in pupils—whether it is exemplified in aspects of programmed instruction or in any other teaching practice (as, for example, traditional drill routines). But these results are probably not the ones that schools intend to produce. The reasons this is so are important both for an understanding of learning and for a conception of educational goals.

However broad the claims may be of those who advocate the use of conditioning as the dominant or sole method of schooling, they all agree that conditioning is an effective way to foster the acquisition of knowledge (or verbal behavior).[45] But acquiring knowledge in this manner raises two serious problems in connection with the ultimate utility of that knowledge. First, knowledge that has been conditioned is more similar to the results of indoctrination than of education. And second, it is very questionable whether knowledge that has been conditioned will have any utility for the student after the period of conditioning is over. Let us examine the first of these two problems.

To indoctrinate is to communicate certain beliefs in such a manner that he who receives them does not question those beliefs, does not become aware of the techniques of criticizing what purports to be knowledge, and does not even become aware that there are situations in which it might be appropriate to question or criticize what has been communicated. Teaching techniques that are based on conditioning—whether they take the form of drill, programmed instruction, or whatever—allow no room for the possibility of alternatives to the beliefs that are presented. For the student, there is but one correct answer and all other responses are simply wrong. Students who master a program quickly are expected simply to move on to another program; they do not question the veracity of the one just completed. Students who take longer to work their way through a program do not spend additional time in questioning its contents, but rather simply take longer to master all the correct responses. Thus a student who has successfully completed an instructional program (or a lesson based on drill work) has had no opportunity to question what he has acquired, has learned no techniques of criticism, and has been given no indication that the beliefs even could have been questioned. Conditioning, then, is the method of indoctrination *par excellence*, whatever particular form it may take in school practice.

Indoctrination, as we have seen, is not a matter of the truth or falsity of the beliefs communicated, but of the *manner* in which the beliefs are communicated. Yet this manner of communication affects enormously what we can do with what we believe. One who has been indoctrinated through conditioning can do very little with the beliefs that he has. Since he understands it to be absolutely true, it never occurs to him either to question it with a view toward modifying it, or to extend it. And because it exists for him in one form only (the form in which it was presented in an instructional program or as a part of drill), its range of application is narrow. Finally, if the conditioning has been quite successful, he who has been conditioned will most likely be confused, threatened, mistrustful, and antagonistic toward any source that casts doubt upon what he has acquired. In such situations, the victim of conditioning (which is a far more apt term than "learner") can be expected to look for support for his views in some authority at least as omniscient and omnipotent as the original source of conditioning.[46] It goes without saying, of course, that whoever presumes to practice the techniques of conditioning on other people must be very confident, indeed, that *what* he is conditioning is so valuable and so true as to be worth it.

We have just spoken of certain habits that are the ultimate products of conditioning. We might wonder about the utility of having students acquire such habits if the school hopes to turn out scientists and engineers, poets and city planners, statesmen and good citizens. We shall return to these habits a little later, and see how they are related to what has been called learning in Chapter II. For the moment, however, we might see what happens to the beliefs that are supposed to have been acquired as a result of conditioning techniques.

In most ordinary life situations, knowledge and beliefs are acquired for a particular purpose; they are acquired so they can be used in some way. After they have been put to use, they are usually forgotten unless the individual sees some likelihood of using them again. The phenomenon of forgetting is deplored by some people as a failure of memory, but this is probably short-sighted. Most people usually do remember what they need to know in order to do what they have to do. It would seem, on the other hand, that to remember *everything* that one has learned would be a cluttered and inefficient way of putting thinking to use.

Apparently, many people who are concerned about schooling think otherwise on these matters. They are of the opinion that it is reasonable for students to acquire knowledge apart from any use to which it might be put. Furthermore, they believe that it is both efficient and good if as much of this knowledge as possible is retained in memory by students. If the techniques of conditioning appear to be useful in furthering these aims, then it is thought the part of wisdom to adopt these techniques. However, despite their particular stage of immaturity, students are on the whole much like other people. Hence they are almost overwhelmingly confused at being subject to an institution that expects them to acquire vast bodies of information for no reason that is apparent to *them* and that expects them to remember so large a proportion of this information.

But like any average intelligent human being, most students have learned to deal successfully with school aims such as those mentioned above. The aim of the school administration, and possibly of the teacher, may be for the student to acquire and remember knowledge. But that is not the students' aim. *Their* aim is to pass the course, be promoted into the next grade, get out of school without undue embarrassment or humiliation and, someday, get a job. Thus the students, in view of their own purposes, are usually willing to submit to conditioning or any other means by which they can acquire knowledge. And they usually try to remember this knowledge, at least until they have passed an examination. But once the examination is passed, and once the student has been promoted, the knowledge has no more utility; it can safely be forgotten, for it has served its purpose. Measures of how much knowledge acquired in a given school year was retained the next year, or several years later, give some evidence (although it is not clear-cut) that the above discussion is not merely speculative.[47] The conclusion that must inescapably be drawn from this is that much of the knowledge communicated in schools by techniques of conditioning is destined for a short life, prolonged only for a little while by the existence of tests and examinations.

But if the knowledge acquired through conditioning is quickly lost, what remains? If conditioning is undergone long enough, it surely must have some relatively long-term effect. As indicated earlier, this effect is the acquisition of a set of habits that is not so much a function of the *content* of the conditioning as it is of the *process* of conditioning itself. And these kinds of habits are not characteristic of what most people think of as an educated person. We might examine these habits in the light of how they are acquired.

Whether schooling involves drill work, or the traditional recitation, or the systematic development of those methods that appear in the instructional program, it is attempting to condition students. The kind of "problem" that the student continually meets under these conditions is that of having to supply information on demand. His problem is to complete the unfinished declarative sentence,[48] to select the right alternative, to offer the right facts when asked. If it is granted that students will hardly ever confront such problems outside of school, for what will the confrontation of such problems prepare students? The answer is not clear. Life and work present their own problems, all of them more complex than these, and most of them additionally involve conflicts of values and purposes. We might speculate that if the school effectively habituates students to think of problems as demands for correct information, that they will continue to perceive the complex problems of living and working in the same way. Not the least of the unfortunate results of such a habit might be that students, once out of school, would be unconscious of the genuine problems presented by social institutions and group ways of life and thought, just because those problems do not appear as simple demands for information. Such lack of awareness of problems amounts to what is recognized as personal and social insensitivity.

But a narrowing of the sorts of situations one is prepared to deal with as problems is not the only unfortunate habit that might result from effective conditioning. As much cause for concern is the *way* one deals with problems. As noted earlier, the person whose verbal behavior has undergone long conditioning is indoctrinated. He sees the answers to questions as absolute and originating in an unquestioned external source of authority; there are no alternatives. Every question has an answer and there is always a right answer. It would be otiose to observe that scientists and artists cannot work on the basis of such habits of dealing with problems, and that a school that produces people with such habits will not produce scientists and artists. It is equally clear that the everyday problems of living and working can be but inadequately met on the basis of the habits of narrowness and dependence on authority that result from conditioning. When what he thinks he knows is challenged, when his authority is not available, the victim of conditioning is personally threatened; he is likely to become antagonistic, confused, irresponsible. When he is confronted with novelty and seeks in vain for an authoritative solution, his confusion leads to impulsive action or action based on habit that is no longer appropriate. When told what to do he responds promptly; given freedom, he searches for the authority to which his conditioning has accustomed him.[49]

These, then, are the results that could fairly be expected from the schools' adopting the conditioning procedures recommended by the theories of behaviorism. They are not theories of learning so much as they are theories of the acquisition of specific and predictable habits. But human behavior based only on such habits cannot be expected to maintain free individuals or a free and open society. As Professor Skinner (not to mention Plato) so clearly implied,[50] people who act on habit alone are prepared to live only in a society that does not change and in which there are some people around who will direct those habits to purposes that *they* choose.

This chapter has attempted to show that ego-psychology and behaviorism, the contemporary forms of vitalism and mechanism respectively, have failed in their attempts to explain how people acquire the sorts of learnings that schools are established to foster in a free society. Ego-psychology fails because it offers no rational explanation of how it can deliver what it promises. Its goals are noble, but it offers no process by which its goals can be reached. Behaviorism, on the other hand, promotes goals that can be reached. But it, too, is inadequate as a guide to schooling, since its goal is a type of habitual behavior that no free society would ever endorse were it fully aware of what was being offered.

In the next chapter, we shall look critically at a conception of learning that has been proposed as an alternative to ego-psychology and behaviorism. Whatever the merits of this theory, the course of the subsequent discussion will show that the shortcomings of the theories of learning examined in this chapter have a common source. This is the sharp separation, made by both behaviorism and ego-psychology, between the human being and his environment—or, as the behaviorist puts it, between the stimulus and the response.

## NOTES

1. Said one parent, in responding to a threatened strike of New York teachers in 1960, "I go to work and what would I do with the kids? They eat at school, and they are taken care of." This type of response by parents occurred nearly twice as often as the next most frequent type of response. See Charles Winick, "When Teachers Strike," *Teachers College Record*, 64 (April, 1963), 594–595.

2. A learning theory and its related educational values and aims, philosophic assumptions, and proposals for teaching, are all so interwoven that it is not unfair (at least in a pedagogical context) to treat them all together as one vast slogan system. In this view, and without intending a pejorative sense of "slogan," the criteria of judgment that will be employed are not unlike those discussed under the headings of "comprehensiveness" and "compatability" in B. Paul Komisar and James E. McClellan, "The Logic of Slogans," in B. O. Smith and R. H. Ennis (eds.), *Language and Concepts in Education* (Chicago: Rand McNally, 1961), p. 210.

3. R. May, "Existential Bases of Psychotherapy," in May (ed.), *Existential Psychology* (New York: Random House, 1961). p. 81.

4. E. Schachtel, "The Development of Focal Attention and the Emergence of Reality," *Psychiatry, 17* (1954), 309–24.

5. See Gordon Allport, *Becoming* (New Haven: Yale University Press, 1955), p. 62 ff.

6. See A. H. Maslow, *Toward a Psychology of Being* (Princeton, N.J.: D. Van Nostrand, 1962), p. 20 ff.

7. *Ibid.*, p. 19.

8. See Allport, *op. cit.*, p. 65 ff.

9. See Maslow, *op. cit.*, p. 23 ff. and Maslow, *Motivation and Personality* (New York: Harper & Row, 1954), chaps. 5, 6, and 12.

10. Maslow, *Toward a Psychology of Being, op. cit.*, p. 32.

11. *Ibid.*, p. 37.

12. Carl Rogers, "Toward a Science of the Person," unpublished paper presented at a symposium at Rice University, Houston, Texas, in March, 1963.

13. See Maslow, *Toward a Psychology of Being*, p. 36.

14. *Ibid.*, p. 53.

15. *Ibid.*, p. 47.

16. *Ibid.*, p. 43.

17. *Ibid.*, p. 50 f. Also see Clark E. Moustakas, "True Experience and the Self," in Moustakas (ed.), *The Self* (New York: Harper, 1956), p. 10 f.

18. See Lawrence A. Cremin, *The Transformation of the School* (New York: Knopf, 1961), chap. 6.

19. See Richard W. Dettering, "Philosophic Idealism in Rogerian Psychology," *Educational Theory, V* (1953), 206–214.

20. See Rogers, "The Interpersonal Relationship: The Core of Guidance," *Harvard Educational Review, 32* (1962), 416–429.

21. Rogers, "Persons or Science," *American Psychologist, 10* (1955), 267–78.

22. See Michael Polanyi, "Knowing and Being," *Mind, 70* (1961), 458–70.

23. See Ralph Harper, "Significance of Existence and Recognition for Education," in N. B. Henry (ed.), *Modern Philosophies and*

*Education* (Chicago: National Society for the Study of Education, 1955).

24. See Van Cleve Morris, *Philosophy and the American School* (Boston: Houghton Mifflin, 1961), pp. 165–173, 204–207, 210–212.

25. The sympathetic attitude of another person—teacher or therapist— may indeed be counted as part of the learner's environment that is recommended by the ego-psychologist. But the learner need not *deal with* the holder of such an attitude. Rather, the attitude of sympathy is meant only to enhance the environment of freedom— to encourage the spontaneity and freedom of the learner.

26. See Maslow, *Toward a Psychology of Being, op. cit.,* p. 168 f.

27. I am indebted for this example to Boyd H. Bode, *How We Learn* (Boston: D. C. Heath, 1940) chap. 3.

28. See the discussion of what Gilbert Ryle calls "the dogma of the Ghost in the Machine," in G. Ryle, *The Concept of Mind* (New York: Barnes and Noble, 1949), p. 15 ff.

29. Despite many permissive elements in his educational scheme, Rousseau allowed for plenty of directive guidance of his pupil, by means of both the deliberate creation of learning situations and the relationship deliberately cultivated between tutor and pupil. As a result of that relationship, the pupil comes to perceive the tutor as a model for emulation. One could, of course, infer that the "freedom" allowed his client by the ego-psychologist results in just such unconscious emulation. See Jean–Jacques Rousseau, *Emile,* Barbara Foxley, *trans.* (London: J. M. Dent, 1911), *passim.*

    It could also be argued that Freud might have been aghast at permissive school practices, given his notion of the chaotic and destructive contents of the subconscious mind. Freud's distrust of what the mind contained is quite contrary to the trust placed in it by ego-psychologists. See, for example, *Civilization and its Discontents,* Joan Riviere, trans. (Chicago: University of Chicago Press, no date), Sec. V and VI.

30. In fairness it should be noted that many existentialists, and indeed some ego-psychologists who are willing to tolerate inconsistency between their conception of a self and their educational proposals, would deliberately face pupils with significant problems of living.

31. But see Chapter VIII for a discussion of the conditions that must be present before children could be expected to be curious.

32. See Thomas Hobbes, *Leviathan,* in E. A. Burtt (ed.), *The English Philosophers from Bacon to Mill* (New York: Random House, 1939), chaps. I–VI.

33. See Gustav Bergmann, "The Logic of Psychological Concepts," *Philosophy of Science, 18* (1951), 93–110.

34. On the other hand, since behaviorism proposes to speak only about empirically observed correlations and contingencies, some of its proponents have claimed to dispense with the need of having any *theory* of learning (or behavior) at all. See B. F. Skinner, "Are Theories of Learning Necessary?" *Psychological Review, 57* (1950), 193–216.

35. The following discussion of learning is taken largely from Fred S. Keller, *Learning: Reinforcement Theory* (New York: Random House, 1954). Keller's views follow closely those of B. F. Skinner, and differ from the views of Clark Hull largely in what they discard. Most conspicuously absent in reinforcement theory is the concept of drive-reduction (and other concepts functionally related to it, like that of the anticipatory goal response) which was considered of great explanatory significance by Hull and his followers. It is still proper, however, to class both reinforcement theorists and drive-reductionists as behaviorists (just as contemporary behaviorists and their philosophical forebears, Hobbes and John Locke, could all be classed as mechanists with respect to their views about human action).

36. The technical term that would be more appropriate here is "reinforced." But for the moment, the concept of reward is more explanatory. The concept of reinforcement will be introduced and explained below.

37. We are using the generic term, "behaviorist," here although it would be more accurate to say reinforcement theorist.

38. Critical students may note that this observation implies a *causal* relation between an operant and what reinforces it. It would thus be more consistent with the logic of reinforcement theory to say that change of operant strength is associated with degree of immediacy of reinforcement.

39. It would appear that the concept of a primary reinforcer (and logically, of a secondary reinforcer, too) necessarily introduces a concept of *causal* relation—and not mere association—into reinforcement theory. For the only way to explain food as an instance

of primary reinforcement is to say that it reduces a drive (i.e., satisfies hunger). If a causal relation is not implied, there could be no distinction between primary and secondary reinforcement.

40. New responses may also appear as a result of avoidance conditioning, which is a function of the presentation of negative reinforcers.

41. See, for example, James G. Holland, "Teaching Machines: An Application of Principles from the Laboratory," in A. A. Lumsdaine and Robert Glaser (eds.), *Teaching Machines and Programmed Learning: A Source Book* (Washington, D.C.: Department of Audiovisual Instruction of the National Education Association, 1960), p. 218 f.

42. Noam Chomsky, review of B. F. Skinner's *"Verbal Behavior,"* in *Language, 35* (1954), 38.

43. "Linear" programming, developed on the basis of reinforcement theory, will be the topic of the following discussion, since the "branching" types of programs (most influentially sponsored by Norman Crowder) do not claim to conform to any particular theory of learning.

44. See Donald Arnstine, "The Language and Values of Programmed Instruction, Part One," *Educational Forum, 28* (1964), 219–226.

45. See, for example, Eugene Galanter, "The Ideal Teacher," in Galanter (ed.), *Automatic Teaching: The State of the Art* (New York: Wiley, 1959), p. 1.

46. See Milton Rokeach, *The Open and Closed Mind* (New York: Basic Books, 1960), especially chaps. 3, 13, and 22.

47. The evidence, such as it is, shows a broad range in degree of forgetting. Studies of secondary school students show losses in mathematics from a tenth (over a summer) to a third (over a year), and in chemistry, losses of 42 percent (over 3 months), to 81 percent (over 5 years). The amount of loss in college science varied from 50 percent (over 4 months) to 94 percent (after a year). Students of college history were found to have lost 40 percent of their initial acquisition after a year. Studies of retention among elementary school pupils appear to be highly inconclusive. For a summary of research in this area, see M. E. Sterrett and R. A. Davis, "The Permanence of School Learning: A Review of Studies," *Educational Administration and Supervision, 40* (Dec., 1954), 449–460.

48. In the instructional program, this may involve, besides memory, the making of a very elementary inference.
49. See Erich Fromm, *Escape from Freedom* (New York: Rinehart, 1941).
50. See B. F. Skinner, *Walden Two* (New York: Macmillan, 1948).

# I V

# THE
# CONDITIONS
# OF LEARNING

## MIND AS ENVIRONMENTAL INTERACTION

THE BETTER WE UNDERSTAND THE CONDITIONS UNDER WHICH
people learn, the more effectively could we institute those conditions in schools. But in order to understand those conditions,
we must understand the relations that hold between people and
their surroundings, so that any intelligent behavior is possible. We
are now assuming, of course, that the use of intelligence is involved in human learning, and that it is not simply a matter of
conditioning as is the case in the learning of lower animals.

It would appear at first that an understanding of the conditions
of intelligent behavior necessitates having some conception of the

nature of mind. You will recall that in Chapter II we saw that some learning can occur without ever showing up in overt behavior. To take another example, suppose that in the past you had noted the connection between the efficiency of drills and saws and the quality of the steel of which they were made. Let us further suppose, then, that you are now disposed, when selecting among tools, to examine the materials of which they are made. But another occasion for the use of such tools has not yet arisen. If you have truly learned, and yet have exhibited no change in overt behavior, it is reasonable to ask, what *did* change? To answer that your disposition changed only begs the question, for we should still want to know what changes occurred in you that resulted in the change of disposition. In ordinary language, we would at this point be likely to answer that you underwent a mental change. Although we observed nothing new in your overt behavior (you never even said, "If I want to make a clean cut in this wood, then. . . ."), your *mind* changed.

No one has even seen, heard, or felt a mind, and it therefore may be quite unscientific to talk about minds at all. Yet most people do frequently make references to minds and, in light of the relation that is said to exist betwen mind and intelligent behavior (and learning), it will be worthwhile to give careful attention to what might be meant when it is said that someone has used, or changed, or improved his mind. If learning is an event that involves mind, it is only after reaching some conception of the nature of mind that we can intelligibly inquire about the conditions under which people learn.

The theories of learning stated or implied in the vitalist and mechanist schools of psychology discussed in Chapter III were found to be inadequate. These inadequacies, in the final analysis, may be attributed to the inadequate theory of mind that lies behind each psychological point of view. Neither does it appear sensible to suppose that human behavior is under the control of a mind that is an immaterial substance, nor does it appear any more credible to suppose that human behavior is merely a mechanical or electrochemical response to environmental stimuli. Thus before we can discuss conditions that facilitate learning in any detail, we must directly consider mind and see why it is something considerably less than supernatural but more than mechanical. We shall begin by noting how our ordinary experience fails to support the implications about mind of ego-psychology and strict behaviorism.

Some shortcomings of reinforcement theory have already been noted, but lying behind this particular variant of behaviorism is a claim about mind shared by all behaviorists. Since, it is said, mind cannot be directly observed, all that can be observed or referred to is behavior. If it is possible to describe, explain, and predict observable behavior, then, nothing is gained by talking about minds at all. Since all mental states have physical correlatives, and overt behavior is both the subject of all inquiry as well as the testing ground of all hypotheses, statements about minds are otiose and scientifically useless.[1]

Because of the importance of this point for behaviorism, we will try to clarify it by putting it another way. For the behaviorist, either there is no difference between a mental event and an overt act (or set of acts), or the statement of the mental event is simply nonsense. To say that someone has an idea or a certain feeling is to mean that he can be observed to behave in a particular way. There is no difference, for example, between being angry and behaving angrily (or exhibiting "anger behavior" which could include, among other things, the statement that one is angry).[2] In what follows immediately below, it will be shown that this point of view is erroneous and that, consequently, any attempt to explain human learning purely in terms of overt behavior, and omitting all reference to events that are not publicly observable—such as thoughts, ideas, feelings, perceptions, and meanings—is bound to fail.

All that is necessary to show that the thesis of behaviorism stated above is false is to show that a statement about unobservable mental events can be at one and the same time (a) free of any necessary reference to overt behavior, (b) intelligible, and (c) verifiable or confirmable as, at least, probably true or false. Here is an example of such a statement: "All men feel pain when they strike their thumbs with hammers." Let us see if the statement satisfies the criteria.

To say that men feel pain is not to say that men exhibit pain behavior. When they strike their thumbs with hammers, men *may* utter exclamations of pain, they *may* gnash their teeth, and they *may* become flushed. But the statement makes no claim about how men might behave upon striking their thumbs. It only makes a claim about how they feel. It is quite possible to feel pain without saying or doing anything in connection with it. Thus the statement makes a generalization about men's private experiences, not about their publicly observable behavior. But apart from any reference to overt behavior, is the statement intelligible? Does it mean anything at all, if not overt acts? A behaviorist speaking *ex cathedra* is likely to answer in the negative. How, he will ask, could we know what "pain" even meant if it referred to the private experiences of others that are not accessible to anyone else? This question can be answered and the original exemplar statement shown to be intelligible by noting the manner in which we learn to use words that refer to private experiences.

Suppose that Mr. Tinker is learning to use language in the presence of Mr. Evers and Mr. Chance, both experienced users of the language. Over a considerable period of time, Mr. Evers and Mr. Chance occasionally say to one another, and to Mr. Tinker, "You are in pain" (or things like it, e.g., "You must be in pain," or "Are you hurt?"). The criteria that Mr. Evers and Mr. Chance use for applying the term pain are, of course, behavioral. That is, it would not occur to them to use the term had they not observed certain overt behaviors that they took to be the accompaniments of pain. After a time, Mr. Tinker will have noted that when Mr. Evers says, "Mr. Chance is in pain," Mr. Chance is behaving in certain ways (e.g., wincing, gnashing his teeth, etc.). Mr. Tinker will also have noted that whenever Mr. Evers (or Mr. Chance) says to him, "You must be in pain," that he (Mr. Tinker) has certain characteristic feelings. Mr. Tinker eventually understands that there is a connection between the feeling of pain (his own) and pain behavior (of, for example, Mr. Chance), after he has noted that Mr. Evers has used the *same term* in reference to *both* events. Some time later, Mr. Evers may say to Mr. Tinker, "I am in pain," and yet exhibit no other relevant behavior (i.e., pain behavior). This is a statement that is now perfectly intelligible to Mr. Tinker. He knows that it refers not to Mr. Evers' overt behavior (of which there was none other than the utterance itself, which obviously did not refer to itself), but to Mr. Evers' feelings, of which Evers was, of course, directly aware although Mr. Tinker was not.

Given this way of understanding the term "pain" when it refers to the experience of other people, the statement beginning "All men feel pain when. . . ." becomes quite intelligible. It might reasonably be assumed that in such a manner we learn to understand a vast number of terms that refer to the private experiences of others. Now it still must be asked, is it possible to confirm the claim that "all men feel pain when they strike their thumbs with hammers?" For if the truth of the statement were not testable, we should still be a bit uncomfortable about its meaningfulness.

The problem that appears to arise when we try to confirm such a statement lies in the fact that pain is supposed to be a private experience. How, asks the behaviorist, can we make a generalization about a range of events, not one of which is accessible to observation? But the question is gratuitous because it assumes that the world consists of such things as public events (like explosions, that are visible to everyone) and private events, like pains, tickles, aspirations, and itches, that no one else can see, hear, or feel. But as will be pointed out in greater detail later, events do not occur already stamped "public" or "private." Whatever we become aware of, whether it be an explosion or a pain is simply an event when it first appears. We have to *discover* which events have a public character, and which are private, and we do so by finding out what other people are aware of on particular occasions, and by comparing their reports of what they see, feel, and hear.

We may, for example, feel hot, and take this to be a sign of a (publicly observable) rise in the room temperature. But we might, instead, be suffering from a (private) feverish condition. The most direct way of telling whether we have become aware of a public or a private event, in this case, would be to ask others in the room how *they* feel, and compare their reports.[3] The only way, then, of establishing a distinction between public and private is to get reliable information about the experiences of other people. The very notion of a science—as some behaviorists suppose psychology to be—which "rests only on information about the public is therefore radically incoherent."[4]

In the light of how we come to understand concepts that refer to private experiences, and how we come to distinguish between experiences that have a public and a private character, it should be clear how we could confirm the statement, "All men feel pain when they strike their thumbs with hammers." We should simply ask a reasonably large sampling of men who have hammered their thumbs whether they felt pain. If someone should answer in the negative, we could assume either that he was lying or that our statement is false; and if all the men in the sample answered affirmatively, we could assume that, if they answered truthfully, the statement is true to the extent that any inductive generalization can be true. Of course, taking a poll of men who have hammered their thumbs is not a very sophisticated method of confirmation. It is no more than common sense. Yet a behaviorist would deny the utility of the whole procedure on the ground that it is not even intelligible to talk about what all men feel.

It has been the intent of the present discussion only to show that the basic assumptions of behaviorism about mind are contrary to ordinary experience. Statements about what people feel, perceive, think, etc. are not reducible to statements about their overt behavior. Just what these mental concepts do signify will be discussed after we have examined the introspective evidence for the existence of mind that is brought forward by ego-psychologists.

The difficulties of following out the logical implications of the concept of mind as an immaterial substance have been elaborated in Chapter III. Yet the ego-psychologist still has what he considers a conclusive argument for the existence of such a mind. For he claims that each of us has firsthand knowledge of his own self. This is not knowledge derived from the observation of behavior, but direct knowledge of our own selves (or minds) as wishing, thinking, feeling, and ultimately, of being conscious.[5] Because of its striking immediacy, this personal sort of knowledge takes precedence over and is ultimately more convincing than any knowledge that is derived from observation of behavior. Looking within ourselves, then—introspection—reveals a conscious, active mind or self that in no way can be identified with any material object. Mind is immaterial, but it exists because we personally and directly know that it exists.

If the mind is truly to be known in this way, it is the only thing which requires such a mode of knowing; all other things are known (in the sense that what is known can be verified by others) by means of particular operations—comparison, discrimination, generalization, etc. But those who hold this conception of mind usually claim that the unique nature of mind calls for this unique mode of knowing. Yet it would appear that this is a circular argument: the mind is declared to be a unique, immaterial substance *after* having been known by the unique mode of introspection—*after* which it is claimed that the mind's uniqueness *called for* a unique mode of knowing.

> Since, however, the doctrine of the completely unique nature of the mental rests upon an assumption of the way in which it is known, the argument is not exactly convincing.[6]

Normally, the term "knowledge" is reserved for those statements which truly purport to describe some aspect of the world and which are open to verification by other persons. If I claim to know something that no one else could ever conceivably confirm or disconfirm, it may be granted that I have had some sort of a perception, but not that I am in possession of any knowledge. What aspires to the status of knowledge must occupy that status for people other than he who asserts it. And in order to achieve this public character, evidence must be available to others. What is gleaned from introspection is available only to one person; thus, however he chooses to take it, it cannot be called knowledge.

To suggest that one finds out about the workings of his own mind by introspection is to suggest that he must take

> a peep into a windowless chamber, illuminated by a very peculiar sort of light, and one to which only he has access.[7]

Through the use of this method, of course, we could never know anything about the workings of anybody else's mind. But we do find out about other minds; the procedure we normally use is to watch other people do and say things, and to compare these performances with one another, and with the doings and sayings of other people. We find out about other minds, in fact, the same way we find out about any other thing or event. And we find out about our own minds in the same way—by noting what we have done and said (either aloud or to ourselves) in a variety of situations. What makes things a little harder in the case of self-knowledge is the fact that our unavoidable prejudices about ourselves may get in the way of our observations (and this would be reason enough for the existence of therapists who might help us see through our own prejudices). On the other hand, we have additional data about ourselves that we don't have for others: we are aware of how we have felt in a variety of situations. This is not to say that we conduct some process of examination into what our feelings are, for the two cannot be present (the inquiry *and* the feeling) in one person at the same time. We are aware of how we feel simply because we *have* the feeling, and not as a result of any investigation. We might, of course, investigate the relation between the feeling and the conditions that might have produced it, since this would yield more information about ourselves.

In short, one gains knowledge of his own or anybody else's mind just as he gains knowledge of any other thing in the universe: not by staring at it until its secret interior is privately revealed, but by examining its manifestations (which, in the case of mind, is behavior) and its connections with and modifications produced by surrounding conditions and events.

> . . . to know mind, in distinction from just *having* qualities that are "mental" [e.g., feelings], one has to go to things that are *not* mind nor mental and to translate qualities that immediately occur into a set of connections between events.[8]

This mode of investigation assumes, of course, that mind and environment *are* interconnected in some way. The method called

introspection is bound to discover a mind that is not only immaterial but is also located in a very special realm of its own, isolated
from the rest of a universe to which the mind's connections must
forever remain mysterious.

Far from being isolated from its environment, mind is intimately
bound up with it. But we have already seen that the sort of relationship that exists is not one of mere reaction to external stimuli.
What are the conditions that hold, then, when an interaction
occurs that is marked by intellectual qualities that we call mind?

The question is not so easy to answer. It is not like asking, "What
are the conditions that hold when two billiard balls interact?" It is
easy to distinguish between two billiard balls, and relatively easy to
establish their weight and density, the friction with the surface
on which they roll, and the direction and velocity of one, so that
the resultant motion of the other when struck by the first can be
established. But it is not so easy to distinguish mind from environment. So long as mind is conceived as somehow "in" an individual,
as an immaterial substance, it is simple enough to say that everything we see is *not* mind. So long as mind is taken merely as a
shorthand term for responses, it is easy enough to tell a person's
response from all other environmental conditions. But the concept
of mind becomes either mysterious or otiose when it is taken in
either of these ways. Where *is* mind, then?

We have a clue to an answer when we hear a phrase like, "He
minded what he was doing." *That* is where mind is: it is the doing
of something in a particular way. To say, "He used his mind"
is but another way of saying: "He minded what he did;" "He acted
in a minded way;" "He did it intelligently." Mind is not a thing
that we call upon for use in this or that situation; if it were, we
should have to ask by what means we call upon it, and find ourselves calling upon mind in order to get mind to operate for us.
This would lead us to an infinite series of acts of calling upon mind
to call upon mind to operate for us, and we should in such a case
never get around to using it. Mind is, then, no ghostly instrument
that guides behavior; it *is* behavior. But it is not just any behavior,
else we should have to assign minds to rats, pigeons, and planaria.

Just what sort of behavior is implied in the term "mind" will be discussed presently. For the moment, it is enough to note that mind is a term applied to certain ways of doing things. To do something is to deal with the environment—to alter it or one's relation to it in some way. Thus it is quite impossible to identify mind at all *apart from* an environment. Behavior that merits the epithet, "He minded what he did," is so bound up with the environment that it would be quite literally nonsense to talk about the nature of mind as a thing or as a way of behaving apart from environmental interaction. This point has been put so succinctly by the anthropologist Clifford Geertz that it is worth quoting at length:

> . . . the accepted view that mental functioning is essentially an intracerebral process, which can only be secondarily assisted or amplified by the various artificial devices which that process has enabled man to invent, appears to be quite wrong. On the contrary . . . the human brain is thoroughly dependent upon cultural [and, more broadly speaking, environmental] resources for its very operation; and those resources are, consequently, *not adjuncts to but constituents of* mental activity. In fact, thinking as an overt, public act, involving the purposeful manipulation of objective materials, is probably fundamental to human beings; and thinking as a covert, private act, and without resource to such materials, a derived, though not unuseful, capability.[9]

Now, if a particular sort of environmental interaction is what is meant by mind; if mind cannot be defined independently of reference to environment; if, indeed, environment is always, in one form or another, a constituent of mind—if all this is the case, then, one cannot find any genuine distinction between mind and environment. And indeed, the distinction we do make when we talk about mind is an artificial although sometimes practical one. It is made (not found) for convenience of communication and action, but it refers to no real distinction between supposedly independent entities.

One may object that this way of talking about mind violates common sense. After all, do we not normally talk about certain empirically observable properties such as weight, hardness, and length as belonging to the environment (and therefore quite independent of mind)? And do we not speak of other kinds of properties, not available to empirical observation, such as feelings, sensations, and thoughts as belonging to mind—and, hence, quite distinct from the environment? We do of course talk this way, contrary to the conception of mind discussed above. But if mind is a term indicating a particular way that a person and his environment are related, it would make no sense to say that certain properties "belong" to the environment, and certain others to mind. It would make no sense because any property that belonged to the one would, in the nature of things, belong equally to the other at the same time. But it would sound odd, indeed, to say that the environment has feelings and the mind has weight, and the peculiarity of putting things this way is directly the result of considering mind and environment as though they were two separate entities. Properties belong neither to one nor the other, but to both. Yet the term "both" does not refer, here, to two things. Rather, it refers to but one thing: an interacting field in which theoretical distinctions ("mind" and "environment") are made in order to facilitate communication and action. We might examine the relations between the properties of objects and mental events a bit more closely, since what is at issue here will make a great difference for what we take to be the conditions that facilitate learning.

It would appear that the properties of objects are revealed to us initially through the organs of sense. Consider a block of lead. We say it has weight or is heavy because we directly feel it to be such. We say that it has color because we see it. We say that it has extension (i.e., occupies space) because we feel and see that it does. Our assignment of properties to the block of lead is in each case the direct result of a sensation, sense impression, or perception that we directly have. *We* have the sensation, but we assign the properties to the *object*. But on what grounds can we claim that the properties "belong" to the object?

Suppose, as Boyd Bode has suggested, we cut off the block of lead from the rest of the universe with a "metaphysical knife."[10] What happens to "its" properties? Without a gravitational field, it has no weight; without a source of illumination, it has no color. Indeed, without a gravitational field, it has no mass at all. Our block of lead has disappeared altogether. If this is the case, then, the "properties of objects" are not integral parts of the objects themselves; the objects extend as far as their gravitational field.

The properties do not "belong" to the object; to what, then, do they belong? *We* perceived the object and, presumably, its properties. Could the properties (i.e., weight, color, etc.) be in *us*—that is, in our minds or in our perceptions? This will hardly do, for if the weight, for example, of the lead were located in perception itself, we would neither have grounds for believing there was any block of lead in the first place nor would we have any use for the block of lead. If properties were but perceptions, we would have no need for a world or environment at all, and varied perceptions would supplant one another in our minds not in relation to changes in an external world, but according only to some inner law of our minds.

The ascription of a property is a direct function of perception. The property belongs not to an object, but is a function of a field. The perception would appear to be in us. But the world is not made up of perceptions *and* properties which can be assigned each to their proper location. Perceptions are always *of* properties (or of relations, such as our seeing that George is taller than Harold). Hence the perception which appeared to be in us is not in us at all but—since it is itself indissolubly bound to the entire field— is itself an event within a field of events. The occurrence of this event—e.g., the perception of weight—is a function of a field of which the practically distinguishable elements, block of lead and sensory organs, are practically defined (and not "empirically found") constituents.

Thus it does not make sense—except for the furtherance of certain practical purposes—to ask, "To what does the weight belong?" and "To what (or whom) does the perception belong?" What is under consideration here is neither the weight nor a perception, but simply the perception of weight. And the perception of weight belongs neither to an external environment nor to an internal mind. It is an event, like an explosion or a headache or a rainbow. We may, of course, have practical ends in view. If we wish to find out whether lead or iron is heavier, we speak and act as if weight were a property of the objects, and we weigh the objects. Similarly, if we wish to call another's attention to a rainbow, we speak as if it were located in the sky, and point in a particular direction. If, on the other hand, we wish to assess people's judgments about weight, we speak and act as if perceptions of weight were in people, and we record their perceptions. And similarly, if we wish to predict the disappearance of a rainbow, we speak as if it were a function of people's perceptions of light striking water molecules, and we speculate about when the rain will stop, or when the light will be blocked, or become too weak for us to see the rainbow. Thus properties and perceptions get assigned to particular locations, depending on the particular purposes of the speaker. But as events, and apart from our practical concerns, perceptions of properties simply *are*. They do not "belong" to something else, nor could they be held to belong to something else, unless mind and environment were taken to be separate and distinct entities.

Because any event allegedly internal to an individual—that is, a property or function of his mind—is, in fact, a function of an entire field with which an individual interacts, it is proper to say that all mental events, or properties, or functions of mind—are simply natural events, the conditions and consequences of which are open to investigation. What we perceive as the heaviness of lead or the green of grass, our feelings of pain or of joy, our thoughts of binomial equations or of God, are all natural events. They are occurrences just as real as the turning of the pages of this book, and they are no more the properties of mind, as distinct from an environment, than the turning of pages is a property of the environment, as distinct from mind.

Knowing something is, of course, different from perceiving, feeling, or merely thinking something. Because knowledge appears to make some claim to being objective, it is often assumed that perceptions, feelings, and thoughts are merely subjective, and hence but events that happen in particular people's minds. Indeed, knowledge has a public status not so easily achieved by other kinds of so-called mental events. But the implication that, because of this, knowledge is somehow a part of the environment while perceptions and feelings are only a part of mind, is falsely drawn. Why this is the case may throw light on the nature of perceptions, feelings, and mind from still another quarter.

Since not so much can be felt or said about a block of lead, let us this time consider a chair. And let us suppose that we perceive it not only as heavy, brown, and made of wood, but also as well-designed, comfortable, and reminiscent of grandfather. What is being claimed here is that each of these perceptions is an event, equally natural, equally real, equally trustworthy. But an objection might be put as follows: we directly *know* that it is heavy, brown, and made of wood, but others may not agree that it is well-designed, they might not find it comfortable, and surely no one else would find the chair reminiscent of grandfather—at least not your grandfather. Hence heaviness, brown color, and woodenness belong to the chair, available to the perception of anyone, while the qualities of design, comfort, and nostalgia are idiosyncratic and thus belong to the mind of the perceiver and not to the chair. Now this objection is misplaced, and the error is in large part due to a frequently held misconception about knowledge.

Since a perception is always *of* a property, and a feeling is always *about* something,[11] they incorporate aspects of both environment and this or that particular person. Because of this, there is no avoiding the conclusion that every perception is relative to him who has it. Each one of my perceptions—which is to say, the pervasive quality of every moment of my entire life—is unique to me and is, therefore, probably different in quality from each one of your perceptions. Not totally different, of course, since much of our environment is presumably shared in common, and our physiological structures are quite similar. Just *how* different our perceptions are is a matter of knowledge. For there is no way of telling whether my perceptions and yours are very similar or totally different if we simply *have* the perceptions. But when by some overt act we *compare* our perceptions, we have made the first move in the direction of having knowledge.

Perceptions may be compared through the use of language or by particular nonlinguistic acts. If I say, "The chair looks brown to me," and you say, "It does to me, too," then we have compared perceptions, found them similar, and are both more confident in thinking that we *know* the chair is brown. Similarly, if I choose to sit in this chair even though others are equally available, and I note that you behave in the same way, I can infer that another similarity in perception has been discovered; and I become a bit more confident in thinking that I *know* this is a comfortable chair. What we know, then—or what we think we know—consists of those of our perceptions that have undergone some test, and that, consequently have been found to be similar to the perceptions of others. This is to say that we do not directly know anything at all. What we do directly is to perceive, and knowledge is always a matter of having performed some operation vis–à–vis our perception.

The difficulties that arise when knowing is confused with perceiving are probably a result of the fact that some kinds of perceptions are both easy to compare, and often found to be similar while others are difficult to compare, and when compared, often found to be quite different. Thus the former perceptions (in that we get in the habit of trusting their similarity to those of others) come to be called acts of knowing (which they are not) while the latter ones are relegated to the untrustworthy realm of mere subjective, mental phenomena. Why this is so can be made clearer by returning to our example.

We perceive the chair as heavy, and easily find out that everyone whom we ask perceives it similarly. No one would question the perception; we are entitled to say we know it is heavy. We can refine our perception by putting the chair on a scale and perceiving the scale to read, say, 20 pounds. Again, anyone else who is invited to perceive the scale will agree with our reading of it. Hence we are entitled to say that we know that the chair weighs 20 pounds. We perceive the chair as brown, but find that our friend perceives it as gray. For the moment, we are hesitant to say we know it is brown. If we find that large numbers of other people perceive the chair to be brown, we are reassured that our perception of brown has a claim to the status of knowledge and that our friend is probably color blind. But there is no question that he has perceived the chair as being gray. His perception of gray is as natural and real an event as our perception of brown. He, too, may ask others and be willing to say, "I know the chair is brown although I perceive it to be gray."

It is just as easy to find out whether the chair is comfortable, but on this point, more disagreement can be expected. We may find it comfortable, others may find it stiff and tiring to sit in. Further, these may be reports of how the chair *looks*. In such a case, it would be improper to say that we know the chair is comfortable. It would be equally improper to say, "I know the chair is comfortable for me." For this statement is misleading. We may see the chair as comfortable or feel it to be comfortable, but these are perceptions, not matters of knowledge. There has been no successful test of our perceptions against those of others. Hence the statement, "I know this chair is comfortable for me," is only a pretentious and unnecessary way of saying, "This chair feels comfortable." Yet the latter statement as the report of a particular event is as meaningful as the statement, "This chair is comfortable (i.e., I know this chair is comfortable.)," or "This chair weighs 20 pounds."

But of what is the chair reminiscent? Here, the comparison becomes difficult. In reminiscence, sensory perceptions, memories, feelings, and thoughts are all mixed, and it is difficult to describe accurately just what the nature of a particular reminiscence is. What can neither be directly observed nor described accurately is, of course, difficult to compare. Yet we do try to compare reminiscences and associations, and sometimes even find similarities. Anyone who listens attentively to the remarks of museum visitors is bound to hear, sooner or later, a comment like, "Yes, that painting does remind one of the countryside near home, doesn't it?" But if our chair happens to remind us of grandfather (because we remember seeing him so often seated in a brown wooden chair, or because the shape of the chair is so much like the shape of grandfather, or for any other reason), we are not likely to find anyone else being so reminded. Hence we should never be tempted to say in the same breath, "It is the case that that chair weighs 20 pounds, and is reminiscent of grandfather." We might say that that brown chair reminds us of grandfather, intending the reference to brown to indicate a property of the chair, and the reference to grandfather to indicate a private event in our mind. This, of course, would be an error. A more appropriate interpretation (if rather awkward for practical purposes) of the latter statement would be: "My perception of what I take to be a chair includes brownness of color and memories, thoughts, and feelings about grandfather. Since nothing in my past experience has led me to think I am color blind, I trust my perception of brown enough to be willing to say that I know the chair is brown. But since my grandfather is not your grandfather, I take it that the feelings and thoughts I have of grandfather when I perceive the chair are peculiar to me, and that you will not share them."

Thus brown is not a property somewhere out in an environment, nor is a reminiscence an event inside of a mind. Brownness and the reminiscence are both simply events that have occurred as a result of the interaction of a field that includes a particular chair and a particular person. The events in question are perceptions, feelings, and thoughts. All the perceptions, feelings, and thoughts a person has are relative to him, but some of them (e.g., "The Columbia river usually looks blue"; "it hurts when one strikes his thumb with a hammer"; "Lake Mendota looks green when it becomes clogged with grasses and seaweed") achieve the status of knowledge when they are noted to be similar to the perceptions, feelings, and thoughts of a more or less extensive group of other people. Thus even knowledge—whether or not special instruments were involved in achieving it—is always relative to some group. How many people must make up this group, and who they are, depends on the particular cultural tradition which supports what people are willing to call knowledge. In some cultures, only a specially privileged group has the authority to judge whether any given perception is to be called knowledge. In our own culture, the group to which perceptions, feelings, and ideas are referred in order to assess their status as knowledge is usually made up of the greatest available number of those who are competent to investigate the matter under consideration. Some perceptions are, of course, so easy for others to verify (e.g., pointer readings, the room temperature) that it would be pointless to compare them with more than a few others. Needless to say, the ease of verifying certain perceptions sometimes hinders instead of helps the gaining of knowledge. For example, all of us nearly all of the time perceive the earth to be flat.

The purpose of the foregoing discussion has been primarily to show that what we call mind and environment are not separate entities, but rather are only the names we give to practical distinctions we make within a total field. Perceptions, feelings, and thoughts are called mental events only for similar, practical reasons, but in fact "belong" no more to mind than they do to the environment. They are simply events, and mind, far from being a ghostly container of these events, is simply the term we use to refer to particular kinds of ways in which people interact with their environment.

## MEANINGS AND COVERT TRIALS

Since learning, for people, involves changes in the environmental interaction that is called mind, it is now necessary to examine more closely the nature of this kind of interaction. Animals lower than humans on the phylogenetic scale appear to be capable of learning, too, and they certainly interact with their environment. Yet we do not ordinarily say that such animals "have" minds, or behave in a minded way. If we examine the simple kinds of environmental interactions characteristic of lower animals, we may see why mind is not normally attributed to them and why they do not learn in the same sense that humans learn. Finally, we may be able to see more clearly what is unique to human behavior so that the term mind can appropriately be applied.

We have already seen that through the process of conditioning, organisms are enabled to make better adaptations to their environment. In conditioning, stimuli may appear together in such a way that the response to one of them later becomes elicited by the other, and operants ("emitted" or instrumental responses) are strengthened or altered when followed by reinforcing stimuli. Since by these means behavior is changed, it seems proper to call them cases of learning, insofar as lower animals are concerned. In any case, it is not clear that lower animals learn in any other way.[12] Both the respondent and the operant forms of conditioning are cases of what might be called trial-and-error learning, and in neither case would it be appropriate to say that the mind of the organism is involved in the process.

The behavior of men changes through trial-and-error, too, but with one important difference from animal behavior. While animals, so far as we can tell, must make all their trials overtly, men need not do so. In the course of dealing with their environment, men are able to make *covert* trials. Hence they need not always take overt action. Instead, some of their trials are made imaginatively and symbolically (although not necessarily through the use of verbal symbols). By conducting trials in imagination, men can foresee the consequences of their acts before overtly engaging in them, and they can thus delay or eliminate trials that might have had undesirable consequences. Thus men's ability to make covert trials before acting allows for greater economy and efficiency in action, allows for more successes and fewer mistakes, and enables men to deal with problems of greater complexity and with an environment of greater breadth than those dealt with by animals. Covert trials are, by definition, unobservable by anyone else. This is not to say they are secret or permanently inaccessible to others, for they are public whenever they are tested or acted upon. Therefore, we can infer that a covert trial has been made anytime we feel it appropriate to say that someone acted intelligently or mindfully. As the course of this discussion proceeds, we shall see that the term mind refers to any behavior in which we have reason to believe that a covert trial has been made, or in which an overt trial was made (for example, discourse) but could have been made covertly.

If the making of a covert trial is the characteristic way of functioning to which the term mind is applied, we will have a clearer idea of what is meant by mind if we examine the relations that hold among the events that constitute such a trial. And again, we can begin such an examination by first noting the relations that hold among the events that constitute the behavior of animals. Consider a pigeon that has been conditioned in a Skinner box to press a bar, after which the behavior is reinforced by the presentation and eating of food. If the pigeon is put back into the box not too long afterward, it can be expected to head for the bar and begin pressing it. However we may wish to avoid using anthropomorphic language, it is obvious that there is some sense in which the bar means something to the pigeon that the walls and floor of the box and the apparatus in it do not. The pigeon perceives the bar and he commences to manipulate it. In some sort of pigeon-like fashion, the perception of the bar "makes sense"; it means, "if pressed, food will be presented." Of course, the meaning of the bar for the pigeon is not like some of the meanings that people have; the pigeon cannot put it into language nor can it, presumably, think about it. Yet even this primitive meaning that is immediately sensed shares some features in common with meanings had by humans.

In the first place, any meaning for a pigeon is direct and immediate. That is, meaning is a part of perception; as far as we can tell, the pigeon is unable to entertain the meaning of the bar *apart from the act of perceiving the bar*. Some human meanings are of this sort, although other ones—the more interesting ones for us—are not.

Secondly, the meaning of the bar, like any meaning the pigeon can have, is anticipatory. For involved in its very perception of the bar is the expectation of pressing it and receiving food. Again, as with the case of the pigeon's meanings, it is not necessary to assume any conscious awareness of anticipation or expectancy. But insofar as the pigeon is equipped with a nervous system which undergoes tensions and relaxations in the course of goal-seeking (for example, when it is hungry) and goal-achieving (for example, when it is eating), it is reasonable to assume that the meaningful perception of the bar is suffused with a gross feeling of tension that normally accompanies any anticipatory perception, in men or animals. And indeed, as we shall see shortly, all human meanings involve expectations although the latter may not be deliberately attended to.

The occurrence of perceptions that make sense—i.e., have meaning, and that are suffused with an anticipatory tension—is characteristic of the interactions that involve animals equipped with distance receptors and organs of locomotion. The behavior of a lion stalking its prey can be described in the same terms. For the lion, the scent of its prey is directly meaningful; that is, the scent *means* that if it is hungry, the lion will stalk the source of the scent, and possibly kill and eat it. And the meaning is anticipatory in tone: the reference of the meaning is to immediately subsequent behavior, and this future reference combines with the tensions produced by hunger. The anticipatory feeling tone may also be tinged with a consummatory feeling tone that appears as a result of past successful stalking and subsequent eating behaviors.

It is worth re-emphasizing the fact that any animal whose behavior is purposeful or goal-seeking can be expected to make a series of overt trials, and that the perceptions occurring in this activity make sense to the animal. That is, the perceptions are both directly meaningful and at the same time are suffused with a feeling tone that is anticipatory in nature. And it is worth repeating that the meaning in such perceptions is anoetic; truth or falsity is irrelevant to such meanings. The lion may find later on that he has been stalking a hunter's device, but the discovery will in no way render meaningless or incorrect the lion's earlier perception of the scent. For animals, a perception is simply a meaningful event; it is not a claim to knowledge or truth.

What marks all animal behavior, and at the same time marks it off from at least some human behavior, is the fact that the direct meanings apprehended by animals are in a sense tied irrevocably to immediate situations or stimulus compounds. And the apprehension of such meanings calls for an overt trial or behavioral response. To put this another way, the appearance of meaning, for animals, is *limited to the appearance of the particular stimulus compounds that elicit those meanings.* They cannot be entertained apart from the immediate situations in which they occur. This is one reason we hesitate to use the term mind in connection with animals. It is also the reason animals are, in a sense, at the mercy of immediate events. Those who marvel at the physical grace and efficiency exhibited by most animals might bear in mind the fact that, since all their trials during goal-directed behavior must be overt, awkwardness and mistakes would lead to an early death.

The difference between animal behavior and the distinctiveness of men's behavior is, as noted earlier, that the trials animals make overtly can be made covertly by men. And what makes possible the covert trials of men is the peculiar role that meanings have for them. For animals, the particular sort of interaction called a "perception" has a quality of feeling and meaning that is direct: meanings and feelings signify acts and events in process of performance, about to be performed, or directly consequent upon what is being performed. For men, meanings serve a broader function and are not tied to immediate events. The felt or qualitative aspects of the environmental interactions to which men are parties serve to indicate things not necessarily relevant to immediate behavior or to the immediate stimulus situation which is being perceived. When events function in this way—as indicators of other events that are not immediately present as a part of the perceptual field—we refer to them by using the term mind. And it is this functioning of events that is characteristic of human behavior.

The foregoing can be summarized by setting forth a definition of mind which accords reasonably with any instance of its use in practical contexts. Mind is the term used to apply to any case in which *one set of events functions in such a way as to indicate, stand for, or point to some other set of events that is neither immediately present nor immediately forthcoming.*

When events function in this way, covert trials are possible. Men are able to deal with meanings that do not involve immediate behavioral responses. In the course of dealing with meanings, men are able to propose, consider, connect, evaluate, and accept or reject possible behaviors and goals without overtly instituting all those behaviors or pursuing all those goals. As in animal behavior, this process remains anoetic—that is, irrelevant to knowledge, truth, or falsity—until some means is employed to test meanings, so that some of them can be elevated to the status of knowledge.

The kind of meanings that allow such manipulation makes possible the performance of covert trials in the course of purposeful behavior, and it is the inference that such trials have been made that entitles us to speak of intelligent, or "minded" behavior. In men, verbal language plays an important role in the making of such trials, but such language is not always necessary for their occurrence.

Artists and musicians, for example, as well as the audiences of their works, employ and try out meanings covertly without the use of verbal language. A baseball player who makes a "fielder's choice," in which he must quickly decide whether to make a play for a runner who is about to score or to throw the ball to first base is using meanings (e.g., the score of the game, the particular inning, which team bats last, and the probabilities of success of each alternative play based on the speed of the runners, the distance of the throw, etc.) without the aid of verbal language.

And the same sense of intelligence, or using one's mind, occurs when, for example, a mother deals with her young son who runs into the house on the point of tears because older children have been bullying him. As she speaks to the child, she must, on the basis of his visual and gestural cues, decide whether to jolly him out of his mood or sympathize with him, whether to be firm with him or protective and, in either case, not to call into question his maleness. She must also take into account a great many related factors, such as the number and size of the older boys, her son's own physical abilities, the conditions which initiated the bullying, how often similar situations have occurred in the past, and so forth. Yet while the mother must act on the basis of considerations like these, she must, at the same time, both say altogether different things to the boy, and listen to what he is saying. It would appear, then, that this is both a common and a clear-cut case of intelligent, mindful behavior that proceeds in important ways without the benefit of discursive language.

The above illustrations serve to point out that a great deal of human behavior in which it is appropriate to say "mind" is involved, is performed without verbal symbols. Each of the above cases offers many instances of covert trials, many of which are never translated into overt behavior. One might even speculate that Kohler's prize ape, Sultan, who without any overt trials used a box as a platform from which to jump for a banana, had conducted covert trials.[13] If so, then, it would be appropriate to say that the ape had in a sense "used its mind." The possible objection that such an interpretation must be false because apes, being apes, couldn't possibly have minds, is a weak objection. The only evidence we ever get for the existence of mind is the way in which individuals deal with their environment. If apes behave in some situations as intelligently as men, there seems to be no good reason for not saying that they acted in a minded way. It must be remembered, of course, that to go further and then claim that, on the basis of such behavioral evidence, apes *have* minds is but to use a metaphor, and a rather misleading one at that. For the claim that apes *have* minds bears the implication that, because men also have minds, apes and men are, to this extent, alike. This claim is, of course, quite false; for the claim that men have minds is as careless a use of language as the claim that apes have minds. In each case, the ascription of mind is but a way of talking about certain types of behavior. Apes may be able to act like men in a few simple situations, but this provides little warrant for saying that they can act like men in any and all situations. We seem to be on safe ground, then, in saying that in a few cases apes have been observed to behave in a minded way. But careless use of language only leads us into unnecessary and essentially silly problems when we say that apes have minds.

The use of language is an enormous aid to minded behavior, although, as we have tried to show, not indispensable to it. What is called language is simply the organized use of minute, economical behaviors (verbal utterances) which serve to stand for meanings that refer to events and possible events, whether those events be the happenings of the commonly shared world or one's own perceptions, feelings, or thoughts. Language carries meanings that are not limited to the appearance of the situations that call forth those meanings—the kind of meanings, that is, distinctive of human behavior. And because men can, in a sense, preserve those meanings in words that can be shared with others, stored, recalled, and combined in various ways, they are able to deal with a range of situations and problems even more complex and extensive in time

than the kinds of situations dealt with through the direct meanings that are a part of perception and feeling. It is this ability
conferred by language that has led men occasionally to identify
it—mistakenly—with mind and with thinking.[14] Thought may
encompass more and reach greater precision and accuracy, when
it is carried in verbal symbols— and especially, when those symbols
are committed to writing. But enough has been said to indicate that
language is but a refinement of thought and a product of minded
behavior. Yet while language may not be the origin of minded
behavior, it is an indispensable instrument for making behavior
increasingly minded.

## TRIALS AND PURPOSES, MEANINGS AND EXPECTATIONS

Mind has been defined as the functioning of events in such a
manner that they serve to indicate other events that are neither
present nor immediately forthcoming. To ask the question "What
purposes does such a functioning of events serve?" easily turns
inquiry toward the origins and emergence of minded behavior out
of simpler forms of behavior. Rather than pursue this much-disputed
topic, it will be enough simply to indicate here the use of minded
behavior. It will be seen that to follow the course of mind as it
interacts with the environment is to lead us directly to the conditions that make it possible for men to learn.

Whenever we speak of mind in connection with behavior, we
have reference to the use of meanings. We also have reference to
the employment of those meanings in covert trials, or in trials
that serve as an economical substitute (e.g., language) for other
trials. But trials of what, and for what? The answer to this should
be plain. Nothing is tried for no purpose at all. A trial is a try
—an effort to achieve some purpose; any trial, whether overt or
covert, is a step along the way to achieving some end. Purposes
and ends are, of course, unattainable without the coming to grips
with an environment. Were this not so (as some actually claim),
we should not have to try anything at all. Goals would be achieved

merely by wishing for them or thinking about them. But since ends are achieved only by dealing in some way with an environment, all trials of any kind serve this purpose. A covert trial, like an overt one, is an attempt to deal with or control some aspect of the environment. Hence the use of meanings, which are the media through which covert trials operate, is in the leverage they afford men in dealing with and controlling events within their environment.

When it is said that meanings have their use in the control of events, it should not be taken simply to mean that by this process men are always found subduing an unruly environment that is external to them. On the contrary, often the best and sometimes the only way of dealing with the environment is willingly to submit to it. The fact that man's increasing control of the external environment has coincided with increasingly greater numbers of people living longer and probably better does not mean (as existentialists are quick to point out) that there are no longer any situations which must simply be accepted and suffered. Yet, through the use of meanings, men are able to control *themselves* in such situations, and by so doing, are in fact indirectly controlling their environment. Typical examples of such control are found in the appreciation of art, in religion, and in various forms of therapy and psychoanalysis. At their best, meanings that are used in these ways enhance living by providing a deeper understanding and sympathy and a fuller enjoyment of the concrete events of experience. At their worst, meanings used in these ways act as an opiate, affording spurious emotional support that fails in crises, while at the same time diverting attention from the pursuit of methods that might beneficially transform the very situations out of which the need for such meanings grew. In any case, meanings arise where purposes are present, and the use of meanings is found in the control they afford, whether direct or indirect, of that part of the environment that is perceived as being germane to one's purposes.

Learning involves some sort of change in mind; mind always involves the use of meanings; and the appearance of any sort of meaning at all is a function of the presence of purposes. To understand better what occurs when people learn, and what the conditions are that facilitate learning, we need to examine what else is implied in the concept of meaning.

We have already noted that the meanings apprehended by lower animals appear always to be a function of, and have reference to an immediate perceptual field. For such animals, meanings are always direct, and are always anticipatory in a relatively immediate sense. In men, meanings function similarly, but they are not necessarily tied to the immediate perceptual field. And the anticipatory feeling tone of the meanings of men may also lack immediate reference, and indeed, often be quite unnoticed. Yet for men as in lower animals, every meaning is anticipatory; every meaning involves an expectation, whether or not one chooses deliberately to attend to it. Thus the apprehension of a meaning may not indicate that a person expects some particular event to occur, either at once or at a later time. But it does indicate that one is at least aware that *if* something happened, then some other particular event would follow.

It will be possible to illustrate the intimate connection between meaning and expectation by citing a few examples. The perception of the gathering of dark clouds, for instance, is at once meaningful. And the expectation that one has, and which is a *part of* the meaning—that is, that it may rain—is obvious and fully attended to by anyone who apprehends such a meaning in dark clouds. In much the same sense, a traffic signal is meaningful and similarly involves clear expectations (of the conditions under which traffic may and may not move). A tree is meaningful, too, although its lack of instrumentality for the achievement of most people's purposes allows for a much wider and less clear range of meanings. But again, whatever meaning a tree may have for a particular person at a particular time, an expectation of some sort is involved. The expectation may be obvious in the case of a paper mill executive who attends to the tree, but it is no less present in the case of the traveller to whom the tree means a shady place to rest. And for the botanist, the meaning of tree involves a host of expectations of a theoretical and taxonomic sort.

As one last example of the intimate connection between meaning and expectations, consider the Wars of the Roses. The historian finds a variety of meanings in this concept and each of these meanings incorporates its own integral expectations, depending on the context in which the concept is employed. If, for example, the Wars of the Roses is mentioned in conversation with another historian, he may expect to discuss a particular set of political and economic conditions in England in the fifteenth century; or he may expect to discuss the troubles of Henry VI, or the relations between the houses of Lancaster and York—and so on. Many laymen who have survived a course in history may also claim to apprehend meaning when the Wars of the Roses is mentioned. But the mention of these wars will give rise to no particular expectations. From this we may conclude not that some meanings are free of expectations, but rather that some concepts with which people claim familiarity are, in fact, virtually meaningless for them. I take it that I understand what someone means when he mentions alpha particles, but I have no particular expectations about them other than that if an alpha particle has been identified, there is probably a physicist in the vicinity. This is, of course, about as little meaning as one can apprehend in a concept or event without its being mere gibberish or a blooming buzzing confusion.

As some expectation is a part of every meaning, so is a disposition. Dispositions are even further removed from overt behavior than are expectations, but nonetheless dispositions are present, if sometimes in a rudimentary or truncated form, whenever meanings are present. The reason for this is not far to seek. We have already noted that there is no meaning to be apprehended in or from a perception if an organism is without purpose. It is because of this that we so seldom run into situations that are genuinely meaningless: we are very seldom purposeless. It is, in fact, *because* we are nearly always in pursuit of *some* purpose (no matter how trivial or evanescent) that we are not always aware of the intimate connection between meaning and purpose. A person devoid of any purpose would be equally devoid of any meanings, although we are not ever actually to find such a person.[15]

Since meanings appear only when purposes are present, those meanings—insofar as they are relatively free of vagueness and ambiguity—are seen in relation to those purposes; that is, meanings are perceived as relevant to what we wish to achieve. Insofar as they are so perceived, meanings serve as potential cues to action in accord with those purposes. This is to say that the apprehension of a meaning disposes us to act. And this is but another way of saying that meaning comes in the form of a trial—an effort to achieve some end. And since what is distinctive of human behavior, or mind, is the fact that the trial is covert rather than overt, overt action may not necessarily be forthcoming. Thus it is accurate to say that meaning *disposes* us to act, but it does not necessarily trigger action.

A meaning, then, just as it necessarily involves particular expectations, also necessarily involves a disposition to act in accordance with the purpose to which the meaning is related. Whether we *do* act is related to the confidence we have in the meaning (that is, whether we have reason to believe the meaning is a matter of knowledge), the importance we attach to the purpose, the nature of the expectation that the meaning involves, and the other meanings of which we are aware that are relevant to the particular situation of which we are a part. On the basis of considerations like these, it would of course be otiose to point out that human action is far more than merely a matter of responding automatically to environmental (or internal) stimuli.

As has been pointed out previously, some dispositions are never acted upon because conditions never arise which would permit such action. Thus a confirmed liberal may be disposed to participate in massive group demonstrations calling for civil rights, such as marching before the Capitol in Washington, but the circumstances of his job, his health, or his family obligations may never permit such action. On the other hand, one who is disposed to eating strongly flavored foods is easily in a position to put salt on meat, potatoes, and vegetables, and can be expected to do so. For such a person, a gustatory perception has a direct meaning involving both expectations—the consequences of which he has evaluated in terms of his purposes—and dispositions which, for lack of other inhibitory factors, trigger immediate action.

It will be seen, then, that when the term mind is applied to human behavior, the following factors will be found operating: the individual is pursuing a purpose; he is dealing with his environment by means of covert trials mediated by meanings; his trials, anticipatory in feeling tone, involve both expectations of consequences, either immediate or distant, and dispositions to act; and the concrete situation in which the individual was involved is finally altered when a covert trial is translated into action, either in the form of controlling some aspect of the environment or of the individual himself. Of all these events that actually occur, however, all that appears to be perceived by *others* is the overt action that institutes control of a situation. It is only when such action *follows* what appears to be a situation of relatively *less* control and is without an intervening period of successive and unsuccessful overt trials, that others are entitled to infer, or normally are even willing to infer that mind was operating, or intelligence was used. In most cases, however, a sequence of events like the one just described is seen as a whole—that is, in such a manner that we do not deliberately *make* an inference that mind was present. Rather we *perceive* mind to be present as a *part* of our perception of the events.

## LEARNING AND CHANGE IN DISPOSITION

Since the kind of learning that involves a change in dispositions is an event in which some change in mind occurs, the foregoing discussion of mind enables us to see more distinctly what these changes are. Mind is present when purposes, meanings, expectations, and dispositions combine to control some aspect of the environment. A change in disposition occurs when all these elements undergo change. One's long-range purposes may remain essentially unchanged, one may retain his expectations of particular consequences following on particular events, and one's overt behavior *may* not even be affected. But in the immediate environmental situation with which one is dealing, his immediate purposes, meanings, expectations, and dispositions do change when learning of the sort that is under investigation occurs. An example may make this point clearer.

Suppose one's purpose is to build a picnic table, although he is an inexperienced carpenter. If he is to build successfully (which in this case is what would be meant by instituting greater control of the environment) he must acquire information about appropriate tools, appropriate wood, ways of putting things together, etc. He must also acquire some minimal skills in handling tools. Finally, he must *learn* to be a minimally competent carpenter. What is implied is, of course, that being a competent carpenter involves more than being in the possession of information about woodworking, more than being in possession of certain tool-using skills, and more than both together. For being a competent carpenter involves, most importantly, certain dispositions about building. It is not necessary to enumerate all the dispositions involved, but the learning of one of them will serve to illustrate the point made above about change in mind.

As the course of building proceeds, our carpenter's more immediate purpose at a particular time may be to cut a piece of lumber in such a way that it will serve as a brace, connecting a bench to the table. Our carpenter *knows* that if his measuring is faulty, the brace will not fit, and his sawing—no matter how skillful—will be in vain. But his disposition is typical of inexperienced carpenters: he enjoys working directly with the wood, and he is anxious to get on with the sawing. So he quickly takes his measurements and cuts his lumber. And he finds that when the braces are fitted between bench and table, no one sitting on the bench could possibly reach the table to eat from it. This immediate perception of the carpenter's is both angry and rueful in its emotional tone. But it may also have a particular meaning for him. He may decide that it is wiser to put off sawing for a while and measure more carefully. If he does, he returns to his work with an altered disposition: he spends proportionately more time and care in making measurements. And in the long run he can be expected to make fewer mistakes and build things of better quality.

Our carpenter has learned in the above example, and the most obvious element in his learning was a change in disposition. But let us examine the learning experience a bit more closely, and see what other changes were involved. In the first place, the *meaning* of measuring as it relates to cutting has changed. It would be difficult to put this change into very precise words, but it might be hazarded that measuring no longer meant "that operation necessary to the cutting of lumber," but instead came to mean, "that operation necessary to cutting lumber in such a way that it properly relates to other pieces of lumber." Secondly, the carpenter's *expectation* respecting measuring as it relates to cutting has changed. Again, words rather poorly describe an event which is nonverbal in nature, but our carpenter now expects the wood that he has measured to fit together properly after it is cut. He does not merely hope that it will, nor does he expect *only* to get some cutting done after the measurements have been taken. We have already discussed the nature of the dispositional change that occurred, but one more change can be discerned: that in the carpenter's *purpose*. Of course, his long-range purpose—to build a picnic table (or, more distant, to get more enjoyment from his back yard in the summer)—has not changed. But a shorter range purpose—that involved in measuring—*has* changed. He no longer measures simply in order to get on with the sawing; if learning took place, he now measures so that the wood he saws will fit together properly.

Earlier, in Chapter II, I indicated that changes in disposition would be focal to the kind of learning examined in this book. Here it has been seen that other changes are involved in this process as well. Yet changes in disposition remain focal to considerations of learning, and for the following reasons. In the above example, it could be charged that the carpenter knew *from the start* that measuring was an operation performed to enable the cutting of wood so that it would fit together properly. And it could be charged that he expected, *all along,* that the wood would fit together after it was cut to measurements. And it could be charged that it was *always* our carpenter's purpose in measuring to enable sawn wood to fit together. Thus, the charge might continue, *none* of these elements changed in the so-called learning experience. For the carpenter, the meaning of measuring, what he expected from it, and his purpose in doing it all remained the same.

Now, these charges might all be true. After all, no one can *see*, in an empirical sense, what something means to someone else, or what another's expectations and purposes are. All of this is but inference based on another's behavior. And when we claim that someone's disposition has changed, this, too, is an inference based on behavior. But *this* inference is more direct and more reliable. And here is why. Suppose that we watch our carpenter measure, saw, and make the discovery of his mistake. Suppose we continue to observe him, and note the time and care he takes in making measurements subsequent to this experience. It would seem fairly evident that we could *not avoid* the conclusion that our carpenter has taken a new attitude toward measuring, if not, indeed, to carpentry itself.

What is being claimed here is that our inference about the carpenter's change in disposition is a direct function of our observation of his behavior. In observing the carpenter, we do not simply note and record—like a machine—items of behavior, and then later put them all together in order to make an inference about dispositional change. *We directly perceive a change in disposition, because that is the meaning of the behavioral changes we observe.* This can be put still another way. After all, it could be claimed we do not *perceive* behavioral change, but rather, we perceive simply this behavior, and this behavior, and this behavior, and so on. To say that this behavior is a *change* from that behavior is to make an inference. Now, change is not a thing or an object, like a stone or a pelican, that we can see. But nonetheless we do not in our ordinary transactions *make* inferences about the existence of change. Thought would be far too clumsy and slow for successful action if such were the case. Our "inference" of the existence of change is a *part of our perception of events*. Most events are such that we "see them change before our very eyes"; it is only events that are very complex or change quite slowly that necessitate deliberately made inferences about whether, and to what extent, they changed. We "see" the traffic light change (do we merely see a red disc, and then see a green one after the red one disappears, and *then* infer a change?) but we do not directly see a society become more conservative.

Thus when we are speaking of organisms who behave in a "minded" way, the *meaning* of successive events that are different yet maintain some similarity is change. If we apply these distinctions to our observation of the carpenter, the *meaning* of his measuring behaviors over the period of time indicated is change. But change of what? To say *merely* that the carpenter's behavior changed would be as silly as it is obvious. For it gives no information to anyone. Of course his behavior changed. How could it *not* change, so long as he was alive? What is being claimed here, then, is this: if our perception of the changes in the carpenter's behavior was meaningful (in terms of what *we* could then expect from *him*), it was not simply a perception of change, but a perception of a particular sort of change: a change in disposition.

Now, what becomes of the charge that for the carpenter, neither purpose, meaning, nor expectation about measuring changed? That we are entitled to say his disposition changed seems clear. But can a disposition change independently of changes in the other elements? It hardly seems likely. If one's disposition toward some process—for example, measuring—changes, then it must *mean* something different to him. Likewise, his *intentions* respecting it must change, as will his *expectation* about what will happen when he acts with respect to it. In other words, whenever we become aware of a change in someone's disposition, it is reasonable to infer that his purpose, meaning, and expectation has also changed with regard to that toward which his disposition changed.

But from this, it must not be concluded that inferences can be made in the other direction. We cannot infer from a change in purpose, meaning, or expectation that a disposition has changed. Suppose our carpenter's purpose was to build the picnic table, but his disposition toward carpentry was one of impatience and mild distaste. And suppose that after working for a while he quits, deciding that the table is not worth the trouble. Here is a case of change in purpose, without any change in disposition. Or suppose that, when turning his bolts clockwise, the nuts fall off the other end. He put the nuts back on, and tightens them by turning the bolts counterclockwise. This is a case of change in meaning and expectation regarding the bolts, but again, there is no change in disposition. And the carpenter's skill in using a saw might improve, without any change in disposition.

Because of all the changes that can be inferred from a change in disposition, because a dispositional change involves so many fundamental changes in mind, the kind of learning that will remain focal in this study will be that in which a change in disposition occurs.

## THE CONDITIONS OF LEARNING

Having discussed the nature of learning (i.e., dispositional change) in terms of the sorts of events that occur when it happens, we are now ready to see what conditions must exist for it to take place. It may be easier, however, first to see why the theories of learning proposed by ego-psychology and behaviorism cannot bear fruit. For the conditions which they claim will foster learning do not make any connection with—and therefore, cannot facilitate any changes within—the events that make up mind. It will not take long to see why this is so.

To foster learning, the ego-psychologist would create a permissive atmosphere. The learner would be presented with no environmental obstacles. He would, presumably, be free to learn. But under such conditions, what *could* he learn? There is nothing in the pupil's environment about which a disposition could change, because no circumstances are present that necessitate the pupil's dealing with anything. Neither meanings nor expectations will change if the circumstances of the environment provide no occasion for thinking, or minded behavior. Purpose cannot change if no purpose is present to begin with. If the teacher is warm, sympathetic, and understanding toward the pupil, will dispositions change? At best, the only disposition that might change is that of the pupil toward the teacher—a rather trivial change, if that is *all* that happens. But, since the teacher is to be permissive, the pupil need not deal with him, either. Hence there appears to be little reason to expect even a change in disposition toward the teacher. The conditions that the ego-psychologist claims will facilitate learning illustrate a truism: give a person nothing to do, and nothing will happen.

The behaviorist, on the other hand, proposes deliberate alterations of the pupil's environment. In order to promote learning, he would introduce cue stimuli or reinforcing stimuli: the former to elicit new behavior, the latter to strengthen or gradually change existing operant behavior. But, as the behaviorist rightly claims, the changes produced by these stimuli are changes in overt behavior. In the course of such conditioning, changes in covert behavior—which is to say changes of meaning, or mind—are of no concern. But a change in overt behavior is not necessarily a change in meaning. The classic example of this is the child who memorizes the pledge of allegiance: ". . . and to the Republicans of which it stands, one nation invisible . . ." One might also speculate about what the closing of the pledge of allegiance, "with liberty and justice for all," *means* to the child who singsongs it in a segregated school. The overt behavior in these cases is acceptable. That there is no change in meaning, no change in disposition, is apparently not important. But a mere change in overt behavior should not be confused with learning. If it is reasonable to call such changes learning in the case of animals, in light of the fact that the meanings they apprehend are always *tied* to overt behavior, it would be a mistake to deal with human learners as if *their* meanings were similarly related to overt behavior.[16] Since human learners are capable of behaving in minded ways, it would appear to be a moral error to treat them as if they could not.

One further point might be noted in connection with the utility of the reinforcing stimulus. It is, as we have seen, a device that alters behavior while at the same time leaving dispositions intact. It acts, for the learner, as a reward that is not intrinsically related to the meaning of his behavior. Adults often behave under the same conditions. They perform personally unsatisfying tasks because they receive a reward that is in no way related to the meaning of what they have done. The reward is usually in the form of wages, sometimes in prestige. Adults habituated to behave in such ways are easily led to perform acts not only intrinsically unsatisfying, but morally reprehensible. The reinforcing conditions that strengthen such behavior are called by a less technical, but more meaningful term. They are called bribes. The school pupil who acquires criterion behaviors through the institution of so-called positive reinforcers, like marks on a report card or the "knowledge of results" afforded by teaching machines, has in effect, been bribed. Evidence that he has not acquired dispositions congruent with what teachers might hope for is easily afforded by what he forgets and what he does out of school. But there is one sense in which learning may have been actually promoted: his disposition toward taking bribes may be changed. If the student spends enough time gaining the acceptance of adults by performing as they wish in return for the rewards they give him, he may very likely learn to be disposed to behave that way all of the time. Thus one possible ultimate learning result—and the only one possible—of applying in schools the proposals of behaviorism is the disposition to do things not for the direct personal or social value of the thing done, but for a reward.

The discussion of mind on which this chapter has focused affords us some clear implications about the conditions that can be expected to facilitate learning. It is only necessary now to spell out what has been implied throughout. One caution must be noted, however. Conditions that enable learning to occur are *not* conditions that *cause* learning to occur. Cases of change in disposition ordinarily involve an active participation of mind, and there are no conditions *exclusive of* or apart from mind that *necessitate* such participation. Thus the most that any teacher or school can do is create the conditions that make learning possible. They cannot force learning to occur. Matters are different, of course, with respect to conditioning; people can be conditioned whether they choose it or not.[17]

It has already been seen that every case of the occurrence of mind is a case of interaction between an individual and his environment. If learning describes a change in mind, then every case of learning necessarily involves some interaction between an individual and his environment. Mind has been seen to occur when events indicate other events that are not present; that is, mind occurs when meanings are present. The key event that marks learning, then, is a change in meaning, and the conditions that facilitate learning are conditions of interaction between individual and environment that facilitate change in meaning.

Under what conditions might meanings change? We have already seen that when the environment offers no impediment to action—when it provides nothing to deal with—that there is no occasion for thought, hence no occasion for minded behavior. Of course, there would be no occasion for change in meaning. What is necessary for meanings to change is some obstacle in the environment that gets in the way of action: something that "makes one think" (of course, nothing *makes* one think; one can always ignore difficulties and behave mindlessly). Now what sort of an obstacle is meant? Some confusion has come to be associated with this feature of thinking and learning, in that the obstacle has come to be identified by some as a feature of the environment external to the individual. Thus it has been thought that overt action is necessary for learning, and it has been forgotten that people can make their own obstacles quite apart from any overt activity.[18] Neither thinking nor learning require doing anything overtly. Why this is so can easily be seen when we understand what constitutes an obstacle to action.

Activity, whether overt or covert, can be balked by an infinite variety of things, many of which are not empirically observable by anyone else. Children who are playing ball meet an obvious obstacle to action when they are told to get off the street, but a headache constitutes just as serious an obstacle to a mathematician who had hoped to finish some computations in a certain period of time. The carpenter whose saw is badly in need of sharpening has a genuine obstacle to action confronting him, but when a Marxist considers the gradual course of economic change in the United States in the twentieth century, this is no less genuine an obstacle to him if he is trying to argue that capitalism must always meet its downfall in class warfare.

The above examples illustrate that, just as activity may be overt or covert, so may obstacles be overt or covert. An intellectual problem is just as real a problem as a crossing railroad train is to a motorist who is late in getting to the airport. What constitutes an obstacle to action may not be observed by anyone other than him who has the obstacle, but the obstacle is no less real, and no less obstructive, for all its privacy. It should be apparent, then, that *an obstacle to activity is whatever is perceived to be an obstacle by whoever is engaging in the activity*. Nor should it be thought that to perceive in this case means to know. Knowing, as was noted earlier, is the result of having performed some operation respecting a perception. But an obstacle in this sense *is* what it is *perceived* to be. It is not simply revealed through the senses, as if it were always there waiting to be discovered. The problem or obstacle, as a blockage arising within activity, is first and most importantly simply felt. Being in a state of doubt, indeterminacy, unsettlement, is not so much a matter of knowing as it is a matter of feeling. We feel blocked, we feel unsettled, we feel some resistance to activity; above all, we feel a tension within activity that was not present before.

That the above definition should make what constitutes an obstacle a subjective affair should offer no difficulty. For an obstacle as a perceived event is neither more nor less subjective than any perception, any feeling, any meaning, or than mind itself. Like the other things mentioned, an obstacle is simply an event, and to *provide evidence* for the occurrence of an event is a wholly different affair from being aware of its existence. What is called subjectivity in this case presents a problem only when it is erroneously assumed that, unless empirical and intersubjective evidence can be offered to substantiate the occurrence of an event, the event did not occur. A perception is an event that occurs whether or not anyone else is able to validate it. If I am seeing green, that is an event, an occurrence, whether or not there is any way for others to verify the event. If, in the course of checking with others, it turns out that they see red when they look at the same thing I look at, this in no way alters the fact that I see green. Whether or not I am color blind has nothing to do with the objective events that are my perceptions. They are what they are, and if they do not correspond to the perceptions of others, something may be wrong with me (or, possibly, with them); but, my perceptions still are what they are.

Now, an obstacle is whatever is perceived to be such by him who has it. An obstacle is thus a particular perception. Whoever *has* (or feels) the obstacle may, of course, deal with it in covert trials, through use of meanings, and find that it no longer remains an obstacle. Or another person may be perfectly justified in saying that the conditions relating to action do not warrant the agent's perceiving an obstacle. Yet these considerations, taken either by the agent in examining the conditions of his perception of an obstacle, or taken by another person in examining those conditions and making a judgment about whether they warrant the agent's having an obstacle, in no way alter the fact that the agent *had* an obstacle.

Thus if an overt or covert obstacle to activity—which itself may be either overt or covert—is necessary for the occurrence of change in meaning or learning, it should be clear that it must be perceived *by the learner* as an obstacle. To put this another way, students are sometimes *given* problems (i.e. obstacles) which, it is hoped, will facilitate learning. But if measures are not taken to insure that these problems are perceived by the students themselves as obstacles to their meaningful or purposeful activity, then there is no reason for thinking that learning will occur. For if the student does not himself perceive an obstacle to activity, he has no occasion to think, no occasion for change in meaning, no occasion for use of mind, and, consequently, no occasion to learn.

Obstacles, disturbances, resistances, or what are most often called problems, are often utilized in school settings as means of instituting learning experiences. But two cautions must be made regarding their use. First, what constitutes purposeful activity for the student may be altogether different from what the teacher thinks it is. Hence what constitutes a problem or obstacle to that activity may not be the same thing that the teacher thinks is a problem. The result is that what the student may learn as a result of dealing with the problem *he* perceives, may be quite different from what the teacher thinks the student is learning. An example may make this point more clear.

Suppose Johnny, who cares little for school studies, is taking the required tenth grade English course. His purposes are to maintain prestige among his peers, keep from becoming bored in class, finish school so that he can get a good job (or get into college), and avoid trouble with the teacher that might endanger his chances of promotion. An obstacle for Johnny will be whatever he perceives as interfering with these purposes. The teacher's purpose, on the other hand, is somehow to get Johnny to learn, among other things, the parts of speech and their function in sentences. The teacher has been told of the virtues of "problem-solving," and consequently he gives Johnny a problem. Johnny is asked to parse a complex sentence on the blackboard. The teacher believes that if Johnny solves the problem, he will learn something about the structure of sentences and the intricacies of grammar. But the teacher has made a mistake, for he has wrongly assumed that the purpose he has *for* Johnny is in fact Johnny's purpose—which it is not. Thus Johnny's problem is not the same problem the teacher presented him.

In the light of Johnny's own purposes, the problem presented to him is not so much one of parsing a sentence as it is to maintain status with his peers while at the same time maintaining his chances of passing the course. If he takes a posture of unconcern toward the teacher's problem, he may advance the former purpose but endanger the latter. If he correctly parses the sentence on the blackboard, he will maintain his chances of promotion, but he may lose status with his peers (who may accuse him of the sin of having done his homework). The upshot of situations like this is that students like Johnny may learn the sorts of attitudes and dispositions that are effective, for them, in satisfying the expectations of widely divergent groups. But it is not very likely that they will permanently acquire much knowledge about grammar, and it is even less likely that they will learn new dispositions respecting the use of language. The moral of the story is this: if teachers are to utilize problems in facilitating learning, the problems so utilized must be the problems that the students themselves perceive. Otherwise, teachers and students are literally working at cross purposes.

The second cautionary note regarding the use of problems in schools has to do with the kind of relation that holds between a problem and a change in meaning. As noted earlier, it is not a necessary one. Even if the problem is perceived by the student as his own, he may not deal with it. He may simply ignore it or avoid it, so that no meanings change and no learning occurs. Whether the student will, in fact, try to deal with his problem is a function of a variety of things: the seriousness of his purpose, the availability of alternative activities and purposes, the availability of means of dealing with the problem (that is, the extent of the student's information and skill, and the availability of relevant instruments and help from others), etc. Thus a teacher who hopes to institute learning by utilizing problems that are perceived by students must have some knowledge about and some control over all these related factors. Otherwise, what starts as problem-solving may end merely in confusion. We will return to these problems of problem-solving in the next chapter, when we ask whether such a teaching method can appropriately serve as the focus of all school learning experiences.

We have seen that when a person is involved in some interaction with his environment—that is, when he is engaged in some purposeful activity—that dispositions may be changed if an obstacle or problem arises within that activity, and if the individual chooses to deal with that problem. It remains only to show how dealing with such a problem may be related to the acquisition of dispositions. If the problem is solved—the obstacle successfully overcome—so that activity is reinstated, the elements constituting the problem will have undergone a change in meaning, and the individual's expectations respecting his own behavior in connection with such a situation will also undergo change. At the same time, the individual's purpose respecting the sort of situation that constituted the problem will also change. When the meaning of a set of events and the related expectations regarding those events change so that one's purpose is also altered, we shall find that one's disposition regarding those events has also changed. The example discussed earlier of the carpenter's acquisition of a new disposition toward measuring and toward carpentry, illustrates the conjunction of all these elements. When these sorts of changes occur together, we are justified in saying that mind has been at work, and learning has occurred.

Human behavior is more flexible, more adaptable, than that of animals. This is so because, among other things, the way that people behave is a function of their dispositions and attitudes, and these are, in turn, connected to meanings that are far wider in scope and complexity, and far more capable of retention, than the direct and situationally anchored meanings apprehended by animals. Yet despite the flexibility, there is a stability to dispositions that far outstrips the capacity to retain knowledge. A disposition, unlike a whim or caprice, is formed around meanings, and meanings, unlike knowledge, are always related to purpose. The virtue of knowledge lies in the fact that it can be shared, and thus can be used to alter and expand meanings. But meanings are more personal; their presence is what we call consciousness; their use is what we call mind. Dispositions, then, are the more or less stable tendencies of mind. More precisely, dispositions *are* mind when the latter is considered in its motive aspect—when mind is considered as the instrumentality by which we tend to act. And it might be added that, whatever particular dispositions are formed as a result of dealing with environmental obstacles, the very fact of having dealt with such obstacles itself helps to form a disposition and make it increasingly stable. Many people, when they encounter difficulties, are disposed to avoid them, or ignore them, or turn to others for help. But repeated instances of dealing in a minded way with obstacles to one's purposes helps form a disposition to deal with problems—perhaps the most valuable dispositions anyone could have.

This chapter has attempted to explain the learning of dispositions as a function of environmental interactions in which obstacles to purposeful activity arise and are successfully dealt with by means of covert trials. Such a series of events is often referred to as "problem-solving." Many writers have claimed that *only* through problem-solving can people learn. Hence they have recommended that all school activities be organized around problem-solving techniques. But probably just as many thinkers, if not more, have opposed this view. They claim that people can learn simply by being told something, whether the telling appears in a book, a lecture, or simply in conversation. They may also point out that people can learn by themselves, simply as a function of their own curiosity.

In the next chapter we shall examine the claims of the champions of problem-solving more carefully. For however reasonable their advice may be, there appears also to be some truth in the claims of their opponents. We shall exhibit in some detail the specific events that occur when problems are solved, and we shall then see when it is appropriate and when inappropriate to institute problem-solving in schools.

# NOTES

1. See Gustav Bergmann, "The Logic of Psychological Concepts," *Philosophy of Science, 18* (1951), 105.

2. See Paul Ziff, "About Behaviorism," *Analysis, 18* (1957–58), 132–136; also reprinted in V. C. Chappell (ed.), *The Philosophy of Mind* (Englewood Cliffs, N.J.: Prentice-Hall, Inc., 1962), 147–150.

3. This example is borrowed from C. H. Whiteley in "Behaviorism," *Mind, LXX: 278* (April, 1961), 164–174. The present discussion owes much to the content of Whiteley's excellent essay.

4. *Ibid.,* p. 171.

5. Hume observed that whenever he essayed to examine himself as wishing, thinking, feeling, etc., all he found was himself *examining* mental states that were no longer present (see *A Treatise of Human Nature,* Part 4, sec. 6). Since Hume, the notion of introspective knowledge has been increasingly less popular among philosophers. Yet one form of support for the validity of the knowledge gained from introspection can be found in R. W. Sellars' "double-knowledge" theory. See, for example, "An Analytic Approach to the Mind-Body Problem," *Philosophical Review, 42* (September, 1938), 461–487. A recent defense of introspective knowledge of one's own self, or mind, can be found in L. A. Reid, *Philosophy and Education* (New York: Random House, 1965), chap. 7.

6. John Dewey, "How is Mind to Be Known?" *Journal of Philosophy, 39* (January 15, 1942), 33.

7. Gilbert Ryle, *The Concept of Mind* (New York: Barnes & Noble, 1949), p. 168 f.

8. Dewey, *op. cit.*, p. 34.

9. Clifford Geertz, "The Growth of Culture and the Evolution of Mind," in Jordan M. Scher (ed.), *Theories of the Mind* (New York: The Free Press of Glencoe, 1962), pp. 730–731. (The italics are mine.)

10. This metaphor is borrowed from Boyd Bode, *How We Learn* (Boston: D. C. Heath, 1940), chap. 13.

11. It may be objected that some feelings are not about anything at all, but are simply "free-floating"; see, for example, C. J. Ducasse, *The Philosophy of Art* (New York: The Dial Press, 1929), pp. 92–93. This, I believe, is a misunderstanding about human experience. It is possible, of course, to have "free-floating fears," but someone who has them does not simply sit around being fearful of nothing in particular. He may *do things*—e.g., work or engage in conversation—fear*fully*, but the fear is not, then, a disembodied emotion; rather, it is a way of doing or saying things. If the emotion becomes overpoweringly strong, he may stop what he is doing and give in to the emotion. But then, either the emotion will be about something or else we will have a case of psychosis: a mindless, unreasoning cowering that could hardly be taken as an illustration of the occurrence of feelings about nothing in particular as found in normal human beings.

12. There is evidence that lower animals do learn in ways other than conditioning, although it is not altogether clear what is happening to the animal. For example, animals that have had an opportunity to explore mazes can be conditioned to learn the maze in a shorter time than animals that have not had such exploratory opportunities. This is taken to be evidence of "latent learning" (i.e., what the animal apparently learned during the course of his explorations). See E. C. Tolman, "The Law of Effect," *Psychological Review,* 45 (1948), 200–203.

13. See W. Kohler, *The Mentality of Apes,* E. Winter, trans. (New York: Harcourt, Brace, 1925).

14. An antidote to the view that mind and thinking are a function of verbal symbols is to be found in Ernst Cassirer, *An Essay on Man* (New Haven: Yale University Press, 1944).

15. It follows from this that the more clear-cut and personally important one's purpose is, the more clear-cut and pointed will the meanings be that he employs in seeking to fulfill his purpose.

Likewise, the less clear-cut and the more superficial or externally imposed are one's purposes, the more vague, superficial and short-lived are the meanings likely to be that one uses in seeking to fulfill his purposes. The implications for schooling that are held by these relations between meaning and purpose will be discussed in the next chapter.

16. Thus the claim of certain behaviorist psychologists—that they have enabled pigeons to learn to play ping-pong—is misleading. In order to play ping-pong, the player must have some conception of what it means to win or lose. The pigeons, of course, have no such conception. Thus they are not "playing ping-pong" at all; they have only "learned" (in this case, acquired new behavior) to strike ping-pong balls. When a behaviorist says that pigeons are playing ping-pong, he is only using a misleading metaphor—an especially dangerous practice in those who claim to use only precise, scientific language.

17. In cases of conditioning in which the total environment of the victim is under deliberate and complete control (as in brainwashing), changes in behavior may result which are subsequently perceived by others as changes of disposition. This may illustrate the fact that one need not necessarily be aware of the dispositional changes he is undergoing. But on the other hand, the result of extreme conditioning could also be taken as a case of a change in habit's having become so pervasive as to resemble or even become a change in disposition. In *Democracy and Education* (New York; Macmillan, 1916), p. 15, Dewey points out that the distinction between a change in habit ("outer action") and a change in "mental and emotional dispositions" is not a sharp one: ". . . in some cases, altering the external habit of action by changing the environment to affect the stimuli to action [i.e., conditioning] will also alter the mental disposition concerned in the action."

18. See Israel Scheffler, "Educational Liberalism and Dewey's Philosophy," *Harvard Educational Review*, 26 (Spring, 1956), 197.

# V

## SCHOOL METHODS:
## ASSETS
## AND LIABILITIES

In the discussion of mind in the preceding chapter, emphasis was placed on the kind of learning that involves a change in disposition. Yet while learning was focal, it might also be said that thinking, too, was equally under consideration. For the environmental interactions in which obstacles to purposeful activity appear, and are dealt with by means of covert trials and overt tests, are the very kinds of events to which we apply the term, "thinking." Thus it has been held by educators in the pragmatic tradition that the way in which we learn *is* just the way in which we think; that, insofar as one is genuinely thinking, he is learning. To this effect, John Dewey wrote,

> While we may speak, without error, of the method of
> thought, the important thing is that thinking is the method of
> an educative experience. The essentials of method are therefore
> identical with the essentials of reflection.[1]

The essentials of reflection, or thinking, are often referred to as problem-solving. In this usage, it should be clear that problem-solving is not intended to suggest a particular *way* of thinking, but rather it *means* thinking. If the method of education (i.e., of fostering learning) is held to be identical with the method of thinking, then problem-solving would become central to all aspects of the school program.

Such a view of schooling has far-reaching consequences. It finds support, however, in the central role of thought in life out of school as well as in learning in school. It was Dewey's claim that the school practices which effectively foster learning are just those that parallel the kinds of out-of-school situations that demand thought. To be sure, when activity is merely habitual or routine, or when it is capricious, thought is seldom undertaken. Such activities are, in fact, defined as being thoughtless. But the opportunity for thinking does appear when, in the course of pursuing some purpose, one encounters an obstacle that makes the outcome of that activity doubtful or uncertain. When any life situation thus presents a problem to us, we are, of course, free to ignore it, or to retreat from it, and engage in some other activity. But again, such behavior is the outcome of a failure to think, and is not characteristic of life situations that are accounted either successful, or intelligent. Problematic situations do not, then, literally force one to engage in problem-solving. But problem-solving could not be expected to occur unless one was in an active situation in which he perceived that he had a problem.

When this conception of learning and thinking as solving problems is translated into a school setting, it results in a program of giving pupils "something to do, not something to learn." If the doing is so undertaken that it eventuates in the appearance of genuine problems, and if pupils are given appropriate help in dealing with those problems, then thinking and learning could be expected to occur. This conception of doing gave rise to the activity curriculum, the purpose of which was to provide within the normal program of the school the conditions essential for that mode of experiencing—of doing and undergoing—which constitutes the matrix within which genuine intellectual or cognitive experiences develop.[2]

The process of thinking is only begun when a problem has appeared in the course of purposeful activity. What is required for a "complete act of thought" is the subsequent acquisition of relevant data, the formulation and refinement of hypotheses, and the eventual public clarification and test of one or more of those hypotheses. For Dewey, these phases of problem-solving constituted the total process of thinking, and were essential components of any experience that was educative.[3] Yet merely to mention the phases of problem-solving is to oversimplify the matter. It is sometimes a problem to be sure just what the problem is,[4] and, once we get into it, we are not always aware of identifiable phases through which our thinking moves.

Problem-solving has sometimes been discussed as if it were a discrete sequence of well-ordered steps or phases. There is, indeed, a beginning and an end to the process, although neither may be very distinctly perceived except in retrospect. For we become only gradually aware of some problems; they seem to "creep up" on us and we sometimes wonder how long we have had them. On the other hand, the solution of a problem is not necessarily a conclusion to action, a resting point. It may itself be the beginning of a new sequence of events or a new problem, and thus not clearly be perceived as a solution. Finally, what happens between the appearance of a problem and its solution follows no necessary order at all. Thus the discussion of problem-solving that follows is intended only to exhibit the elements of the process, apart from the order in which they might occur, and independent of the form in which they may occur (i.e., sometimes language is employed, sometimes not; sometimes elements appear in combination, sometimes alone; etc.).[5]

## THE PROCESS OF SOLVING PROBLEMS

To begin with, a problem is inconceivable without a purpose, for it is just what is conceived to stand in the way of achieving that purpose. Now, it is not at all easy to imagine what a purposeless activity would be like, since we hardly ever encounter it. It sometimes seems as if the activities of children and foolish people are purposeless, but on closer inspection we may find that by the term "purposeless" we only mean a trivial or silly purpose. Or by assigning the term purposeless to someone's activity, we may simply mean that we do not know what the purpose is. And we occasionally call purposeless an activity the purpose of which may simply be weak; that is, whoever is engaging in the activity may be ready to give it up on the slightest provocation.

When it is said that a purposeful activity is the necessary condition for the appearance of a problem, it is probably fair to interpret this as meaning that *genuine* problems do not arise in the course of activities the purposes of which are trivial, or weak. Watching a television variety show, for example, is a purposeful activity, but the purpose is trivial: it counts for little in the lives of most viewers. Hence when through some sort of interference the screen goes blank, it is not seen as much of a problem; one simply does something else. The purposes children have are often weak, and their activities may often be discontinued at the first appearance of the slightest difficulty or when some other activity is suggested. The significance of this for the occurrence of learning is this: if a problem is not dealt with, there can be no problem-solving. Hence, on some accounts, there can be no learning. And a problem will not be dealt with unless whoever has the problem perceives it to be worth dealing with. Yet this cannot happen unless one is engaged in an activity the purpose of which is, to him, relatively important and relatively strong. Important enough and strong enough, at least, to make it worth one's while to expend time and effort in overcoming obstacles in its way. There does not seem to be anything particularly unique or profound in these observations, yet teachers have, from time to time, attempted to institute problem-solving experiences by utilizing the most trivial of children's purposes. The not surprising result of such efforts has been confusion and desultory action—not learning.

The first requisite, then, for the occurrence of problem-solving is that the learner be engaged in an activity (which is sometimes called an "ongoing activity") in which a reasonably strong purpose of his own is being pursued. Given this context, a problem or obstacle to that activity must appear. As we discussed in some detail in the previous chapter, all that is necessary here is that an obstacle, a block, an indeterminacy, an unsettlement of some sort be perceived by the learner. Whether the obstacle that is perceived will turn out to be a genuine problem is a matter for later determination. If the purpose of the activity is seen by the learner to be worth the effort, he will, of course, wish to continue or reinstate the activity. Hence he will be concerned to overcome the obstacle, or resolve the indeterminacy. Or, in more subjective terms, he will be concerned to perform whatever may be necessary to allay the feeling of doubt or unsettlement that is the first manifestation of a problem.

It will be noticed that what has been mentioned thus far have been only necessary conditions for problem-solving; only necessary conditions for the apprehension of new meanings, expectations, dispositions. What follows on these conditions—that is to say, whether learning will result—depends on the particular nature of these conditions as they interact with the temperament (i.e., the dispositions already formed) of the learner. Given awareness of some indeterminacy in action, an individual may simply ignore the feeling and continue his activity. The results of this behavior may be either fortunate or disastrous. He may simply discontinue his activity, especially if his purpose is not strong. He may allay the feeling of doubt with self-assurance or by seeking the reassurance of others. Again, if activity is pursued in the same manner as it had been prior to the appearance of the obstacle, its success may be a matter of chance. But if the individual's purpose is strong enough and he is not disposed to avoid experiment, he may try something out. He may alter his activity.

When one alters activity in response to an awareness of some blockage, he is making a trial. The trial may be overt or covert. When it is overt, different behaviors are simply tried out at once, and abandoned if unsuccessful. To this way of dealing with obstacles we apply the phrase "trial-and-error behavior," and we see it most commonly in the behavior of animals, infants, people who are mentally retarded, and normal people under extreme conditions such as fear, frustration, etc. But by having and using meanings, people are capable of responding covertly to obstacles that arise in the course of carrying out their purposes. It is in the course of making such covert trials that problem-solving, and learning occur.

If it is successful, the covert trial results in overt behavior based upon a new meaning. All that is intended here will be to suggest some of the ways by which new meanings come into being. Probably one of the first things that happens in a covert trial that begins with a felt obstacle to activity, is the making of a guess or a supposition. This guess is not the sort one makes about the outcome of a coin flip where each alternative has an equal probability of occurrence, and one guess is as good as another. Rather, it is more like a crude hypothesis; it is a proposal for action that will reinstate the activity, and it is based on all of the factors relevant to the original activity, and to what is obstructing it, of which the individual is aware. But if this guess or proposal were acted upon at once, behavior issuing from it would be indistinguishable from trial-and-error behavior. Hence what is here being called a covert trial demands that some operation be performed on the guess before overt action is undertaken.

A first guess or crude hypothesis, then, is tested imaginatively for its consequences. This would appear to be the least one could do to avoid mere trial-and-error behavior. To test a guess imaginatively is to examine the meaning of the guess in terms of the expectations it engenders. If these expectations indicate consequences that would be desirable—that is, that would reinstate the original activity, the guess may be acted upon overtly. But as likely as not, imaginative testing of the guess will find it lacking in some respect. If this is the case, other expedients must be tried.

All of the expedients that are tried as a part of the covert effort to reinstate activity fall into two classes: either they are efforts to adduce information that might be relevant to solving the problem, or they are efforts to improve the hypothesis—either by refining it or by generating a new and better one. The first of these classes of activity may be referred to as "data-gathering"; the second as "hypothesis formation." In the data-gathering phase, the original obstacle, as merely felt, undergoes clarification and specification. In the phase of hypothesis formation, information acquired from the data-gathering phase is brought to bear on the formation of increasingly adequate ideas or proposals for action. Again, these proposals are normally put to an imaginative test before they are overtly tried.

There are no special rules for the gathering of data in ordinary situations of learning and thinking (although the gathering of data within the boundaries of scientific disciplines may be subject to very precise limits). The readiest source of data is another person, whether friend, parent, or teacher. The source is simply asked. If such sources are not available or are inadequate, there are plenty of other sources. Data may be found through careful observation, or in a variety of respositories of knowledge—books, museums, films, etc. The use of data, or knowledge, lies in its capacity to clarify the problem, to rule out some hypotheses (as being contrary to what the information has uncovered), and to act as a basis for the formation of more adequate hypotheses—that is, hypotheses with a good chance of guiding successful action.

Two things should be noticed about what data-gathering is *not*. First, it is not an activity carried on for its own sake, and apart from the effort to reinstate or carry forward some purposeful activity. For if it were, the process would have a random aspect to it. If no particular purpose is to be forwarded by the gathering of data, then no clue is provided to indicate *which* data is worth gathering. Granted that some "research" is little more than elaborate data-gathering, the question must be answered, sooner or later, what shall be done with the data? And as often as not, answers to this question show that, despite its volume, the wrong data was gathered. Those who favor problem-solving as a method of schooling deplore the attempt to have pupils acquire knowledge apart from the pupils' having a purpose to which that knowledge is intrinsically related. For it would seem as if the schools were merely subjecting the pupils to random data-gathering—a procedure as senseless for a student as it would be for a physicist or historian.

Secondly, data-gathering is to be distinguished from finding a solution to the original problem. A student confronted with a difficult problem in algebra who looks up the answer in the back of the book is not gathering data. He is not finding information relevant to the problem: he is finding its solution. This may seem obvious, but the distinction between relevant information and a solution to a problem is less apparent in other situations. A child who has been offered one free ticket to a movie may be torn between using the ticket and going swimming with a friend with whom he had made a previous engagement. The moment he recalls the swimming engagement he perceives a problem (depending, of course, on his prior dispositions respecting the treatment of others, the keeping of promises, etc.). The child may be stumped for a solution and apply to a parent for help. Now, the parent may simply say, "You ought to keep your promises and give the ticket away," or "Take the ticket, explain to your friend that you might otherwise miss the chance to see the movie, and tell him you'll go swimming with him tomorrow." In either case, the parent has simply provided a solution for the child, and not data or information that might serve as a means for the child's solving his problem. In such a case, the parent may have helped the child out of a jam, but he has also robbed the child of an opportunity to think. And it is doubtful that a child can learn by any means other than trying to. Teachers, needless to say, often behave in the same manner as the parent in this example. This is especially ironic in the light of that for which teachers are employed.

An hypothesis that is formed is but a refined and informed elaboration of what was earlier called a guess. As a proposal for action, it is a foray into the unknown made on the basis of what is known and what is desired. As such, it might be called an idea, but no matter what it is called, it is valueless until it is tested in some way, either imaginatively or overtly. A tentative solution will remain tentative until it is tried out. What is of especial pedagogical importance with respect to the formation of hypotheses is that no one but the learner himself can do it. Someone else cannot get ideas for him. All that others can supply is information, directions, or solutions. The attempt to supply another with an hypothesis is in fact only to give him information or to tell him what to do. And like the supplying of ready-made solutions, this, too, only cuts short the thinking process for the learner.

Depending on the kind of problem that is being dealt with, the phases of data-gathering and hypothesis formation may be orderly and sharply separated, or they may merge insensibly into one another. A theoretical physicist may spend years in attempting to formulate an hypothesis; the man in the laboratory may spend as much time gathering data. But someone in the act of deciding which of two suits of clothes to purchase, attempting to account for differences in price, durability, color, style, and use, all at once, is hardly aware of when he is considering information and when he is formulating hypotheses.

Those who favor problem-solving as the method of schooling generally insist on performing overt tests of refined hypotheses. Indeed, without some sort of test, there is little reason to have confidence in the hypothesis. And there would be little likelihood of any stable change in meanings or, as a consequence, of any change in disposition. Yet it seems apparent that hypothetical solutions to some kinds of problems cannot be very easily tested overtly. It is, for example, to be wondered just what *would* constitute an overt test of a historian's hypothesis about what particular events were especially causal in some past or present political or economic change. In this case, as in many other cases, whatever test there may be of the hypothesis remains covert or imaginative, and often consists only in the adducing of additional information with which to compare the hypothesis. Any hypothesis, however, must indicate some act, either overt or covert, that will constitute a test of it. Otherwise it could be called an hypothesis by courtesy only, and would in fact be only an unsupported notion. That witches may have been responsible for the evils in Salem, for example, is not a testable statement. Hence it is not an hypothesis.

The pedagogical importance of an overt test of an hypothesis is that in acting, one becomes directly aware of the value of the hypothesis in reinstating the original activity. In most cases, either it works or it does not. Hence, in the event of success, the possible new meanings that attached to the factors in the original blocked situation become more clearly stabilized than they might have become had the test been only a covert one. And if the hypothesis turns out to be a failure when it is overtly tested, the need for further thinking is apparent. Yet even such a failure can stabilize some new meanings, expectations, and dispositions. Learning is not the result only of successful testing of an hypothesis. We learn from our failures as well.

## THE ADVANTAGES OF
## PROBLEM-SOLVING IN SCHOOLS

Problem-solving has been accorded by some the central place in school practice. It is said that the knowledge and skills adults hold to be important will be acquired by students in the course of dealing with problems. But even more important, it is held that the process of problem-solving will afford young people the practice that is necessary if they are to acquire the disposition to solve problems. By solving problems, that is, youngsters learn to be dispositional problem-solvers: a trait of enormous personal and social worth. Whether these claims are justified will be examined more closely in the latter part of this chapter. For the moment, however, we might review the advantages that problem-solving offers for school practice.

In the first place, it seems unquestionable that the process of problem-solving does promote learning[6]; even the most vigorous of its opponents do not deny this, but rather oppose its use on other grounds. At the same time, an understanding of what happens to a learner in the process of problem-solving sheds light on why it is that certain other school practices often fail to foster learning. An understanding of how information is used in the course of solving problems provides insight into the frequent failure of practices designed simply for the presentation and acquisition of information, apart from any particular use of it. An understanding of the importance of purposeful activity to the process of solving problems affords a clue about why substitutes for purposeful activity so often fail. Exhortation, rewards such as school marks and promotion, and punishments, such as school marks, failure, or extra homework, all appear to be substitutes for purposeful activity.

When we tell a student that he *ought* to learn something because it is good for him, or because he will need it to get a job, or to enter college, or because he will be glad someday that he learned it, we are employing exhortation just because purpose is lacking. And when there is no connection that the student can see between his own purposes and what is to be learned, we must implore him to learn despite what to him is seemingly purposeless. Yet evidence is abundant that the only students who will even try to attend to such exhortations are students who have been trained at home to be docile and eager to satisfy the wishes of adults. But because such a disposition is the moving force behind their school behavior, even these students are not likely to acquire new dispositions. They pass the courses and go on to college and to respectable jobs, but their success remains largely a function of docility and eagerness to please—not a function of thinking and learning.

The rewards and punishments of institutionalized schooling are also substitutes for purpose. Their meaning for the student is clear: even if you don't see the point in what is happening, you'd better go along with it anyway; if you do, you'll be rewarded (with high marks, teacher warmth, candy, etc.); if you don't you'll be punished (low marks, teacher antagonism, parental wrath, etc.). As we have already seen, behavior directed toward getting rewards and avoiding punishment cultivates dispositions tending to stabilize *that* behavior, but has little to do with the kind of learning that schools are maintained to promote. A major virtue of problem-solving, then, is its incorporation of the students' purposes in such a way that unwholesome substitutes can be dispensed with.

Another advantage claimed for problem-solving is its tendency to involve students actively in concrete situations. The energy of young people is apparent to anyone who has been around them. Problem-solving is proposed as a way of utilizing that energy rather than suppressing it and risking problems of discipline, as it is claimed "bookish" school studies so often do. And just as overt activity is utilized, sooner or later, in dealing with concrete situations, the solutions to problems are equally a function of observable, concrete situations. Thus the results of problem-solving procedures are plainly visible to learners, and they affect dispositions more directly than do the more abstract situations and results of traditional school studies, which typically begin and end in overt or covert verbalization. Thus new meanings that result from problem-solving methods are directly perceived, while the meanings of less concrete, verbal methods—in remaining covert—are often simply learned by rote or taken on faith.

School practices that depend principally on verbalization also frequently limit communication among pupils and, consequently, limit socialization. Verbalization that remains covert, of course, makes communication impossible. Yet the overt verbalization that goes on in schoolrooms falls into one of two classes. Either it serves as evidence of a student's having acquired information (e.g., the recitation), or it is taken as a sign of cheating. For to give aid in class to another student is taken to be immoral. The proponents of problem-solving, on the other hand, point out that the socializing of students is one of the legitimate aims of schooling. They further claim that the process of solving problems is well suited to achieve this end. For if students have some purposes in common (and there is no reason to assume that they do not), they can share activities that are purposeful. Thus the conditions are present for the occurrence of obstacles in the way of shared purposes and activities, and the possibility is present for shared inquiry, shared problem-solving. In such a manner, learners can acquire dispositions to co-operate actively with others, utilizing the strengths of each and sharing skills and information in the solution of common problems. Adult life is nothing if not social, claim the proponents of problem-solving, and these kinds of shared activities are best suited to promote the kinds of attitudes, skills, and dispositions that eventuate in desirable patterns of social life.

Those who favor problem-solving as the focus around which to orient all school practices may, finally, point to the disciplinary value of using such a method. It might be noted at the outset that a classroom of pupils each of whom is intensely absorbed in dealing with problems that relate to his own purposes is not likely to be a classroom in which the traditional "discipline problems" will very often arise. But it is also claimed that repeated experiences of solving one's own problems result in the acquisition of desirable dispositions toward the way one approaches all of the affairs of his life. This is to say that, whatever *else* is acquired in the way of knowledge, skills, and attitudes as students continually engage in problem-solving, students will, at the same time, acquire the dispositions that are relevant to their being sensitive to the existence of problems, and to their being unafraid of dealing with them. The disciplinary value of problem-solving, then, lies in its imputed capacity to foster problem-solving dispositions. We might examine more closely the more salient and particular of these dispositions.

In the first place, the learner should be expected to become problem-centered. If school experiences are focused on dealing with problems that arise within purposeful activity, it might be expected that learners would become less conscious of themselves and more concerned with dealing with situations. Secondly, open-mindedness and a disposition to innovate should be fostered. Problems are unique, and old solutions to other people's problems cannot be simply borrowed and used. When purposes are strong and the resolution of difficulties is not easy, one must perforce be prepared to consider a wide range of alternatives, be ready to give up old habits, and be willing to experiment. Finally, experiences in problem-solving provide for the cultivation of the disposition of responsibility. One learns to deal with his own problems instead of avoiding them, passing them on to someone else, or simply abandoning his purpose and seeking simpler and less demanding forms of activity. One learns to try out his ideas covertly before hurling himself into fruitless and wasteful action. One learns to take responsibility for his own failures as well as credit for his successes. And, providing that the problems to be solved are genuinely related to the learner's own purposes, he acquires the disposition of seeing things through—of staying with a problem until he has solved it or until it is clear that he cannot solve it.

## THE LIMITATIONS OF
## PROBLEM-SOLVING

Given so imposing a list of merits, it is difficult to see why the method of problem-solving has not fared better in the schools. If it really can produce the educational results discussed above, it stands to reason that competing educational methods should have been swept aside long ago. Yet far from becoming the only, or even the dominant method of schooling, problem-solving—as outlined in the preceding pages—occupies a relatively minor place in public schools. It is only occasionally employed in elementary schools (where it sometimes appears in what is called unit teaching), and even less frequently in secondary schools. Of course, discussions of and proposals for problem-solving still appear frequently in educational literature, but closer examination reveals that most of this does not refer to what has been described here as problem-solving. These current discussions do refer to a sort of problem-solving, but the problems usually turn out to be ones invented by teachers and textbook writers that are simply presented to students. The students are then told to solve them.

It is tempting to ask why problem-solving should be so unpopular, but the inquiry would lead us to historical events which are only tangential to the present discussion.[7] Instead, we shall consider three kinds of considerations that limit the application of problem-solving in contemporary schools. First, some prevalent teacher attitudes incompatible with problem-solving and some currently fashionable educational aims have pre-empted school time and have crowded problem-solving out of the curriculum. It is questionable, of course, whether these are legitimate reasons for abandoning problem-solving. Second, there are difficulties inherent in the method of problem-solving itself that stand in the way of its use in schools. And third, it is by no means clear that problem-solving, as it has been described thus far, is the only way by which people can learn. If these last two considerations could withstand criticism, they would constitute good reasons for seeking means in addition to problem-solving (or perhaps ways of modifying the process) for promoting learning in schools. We might examine more carefully each of these three sorts of considerations in turn.

To begin with, it might be conjectured that most teachers prefer docile pupils.[8] Youngsters who occupy their time in studiously receiving what the teacher or text offers, and in dutifully recalling and repeating it later on, raise no special problems for the teacher. But children accustomed to problem-solving do not behave this way. In class they expect to pursue purposes of their own and they expect to see the point of any activity. Hence, when they are presented with problems that meet only the teacher's purposes, their attitude is one of asking quite seriously, "so what?" If he is like most other people, a teacher may not care for this sort of question, and he may care less for the student who asks it. This is especially true of teachers who are not sure they can give reasons for activities that will make sense to students, who are not secure in their authority, and who have something less than a full command of the material they are teaching. For such teachers, problem-solving is a threatening activity. It uncovers gaps in their knowledge; it leads in directions that are not always predictable. And as it focuses on inquiry rather than transmission, it makes of the teacher another inquirer rather than a transmitter of information. For some teachers, this situation means loss of status, loss of prestige, and perhaps, even loss of control of the class. Whether teachers *ought* to feel insecure when engaging a class or a student in problem-solving is for the moment beside the point. The fact is that many teachers do feel this way, and as long as they do, they will avoid problem-solving, rationalizing their behavior by saying that the method of problem-solving only leads to much chaos and little learning.

Just as great a deterrent to the use of problem-solving in schools is the fact that it is not logically consistent with the aim of transmitting organized knowledge in a systematic way. The rapid expansion of knowledge in the twentieth century, coupled with radically altering vocational patterns and the maintenance of strained and competitive international relations, have all conspired to call the attention of those concerned with schools to the great necessity for more effective and efficient ways of transmitting more knowledge. But the method of problem-solving is concerned with the acquisition of knowledge only insofar as it is germane to the solving of particular problems. Hence to adopt such a method would be to abandon the goal of systematically transmitting logically organized knowledge. Whether this is a good reason for limiting or eliminating the use of problem-solving in schools depends, of course, on the validity of the acquisition of knowledge as the primary aim of education. In any case, the trend in schooling in the United States since the middle of the present century has been increasingly in this direction, and the logical result has been a decreasing employment of problem-solving.

The foregoing considerations may, in part, answer the question why problem-solving is so little utilized as a method of teaching and learning in schools, but they do not necessarily constitute good reasons for abandoning the method. It is time, then, to look into its inherent limitations.[9] For these do constitute genuine obstacles to attempts at utilizing problem-solving exclusively or perhaps, even dominantly, in schools. And they will raise the question of whether there might be other ways of effectively facilitating the process of learning.

It has been noted that since problem-solving is so closely linked with the active, manipulative occupations of students, the method is, consequently, limited by the kinds of concrete subject matters that can be imported into schoolrooms. Insofar as it possibly requires more ingenuity to bring such things and activities into a class than it does simply to present verbal materials, the charge is fair that this constitutes a limitation inherent within the method itself.

Proponents of problem-solving have dealt with this criticism in two ways. In the first place, the criticism presupposes that the learning of students that is guided by adults will occur only in schoolrooms—away from the life of society. But, contrary to this presupposition, many educational thinkers who have favored problem-solving have insisted that the young be enabled genuinely to participate in the life of society outside of school. Schooling thus may be conceived not simply as what goes on in a certain building, but as an active process which includes guided experience in the occupations, citizenship activities, and recreations of adult society. On such a broadened conception of schooling, there would be no need to "import" concrete subject matters into schoolrooms. Instead, the very concrete subject matters and activities in which the community engages would themselves become an important locus of schooling.

In the second place, the criticism has been met by pointing out that as far as work in school classrooms is concerned, concrete materials and physical activities (and shared experiences, as well) are of special importance in the introductory phases of subjects of study.[10] Such phases may occur in the primary grades, in the secondary school, or in college. Their chief object is to create dispositions toward those subject areas based on the interest, appreciation, and "feeling" for the subject that such active occupations promote. Thus such activities are not necessarily required of the more mature student who has begun to study a subject field in depth, and who has by then learned to identify such study with his own purposes. For this latter student, school experiences would be expected to be more abstract, and to involve the acquisition of systematic knowledge within a particular discipline. Yet such behavior might still fall consistently within the boundaries of problem-solving, as long as the abstract activities engaged in remain purposeful for the student. In any case, then, it may be a matter for debate as to how problem-solving's dependence on concrete materials and active occupations is to be regarded. It may be seen as one kind of limitation inherent within a particular way of promoting learning, or as simply a necessity for learning that may be dispensed with at a later stage of development.

What constitutes a more clear-cut class of limitations in the method of problem-solving as a school technique is its inherent dependency on the peculiarities of individual students. In any classroom they exhibit an enormous range of backgrounds and interests, abilities and capacities, attitudes and purposes. Were we assured that they all came to school well-stocked with knowledge, possessed of strong purposes, and disposed to learn, problem-solving would doubtless proceed effectively and without delay. But since only rarely is such a school pupil found, the process of problem-solving is beset with hindrances. A few of the most obvious of these might briefly be noted.

Since problem-solving emerges from the purposeful activities of students, what a teacher can do in a classroom is limited by the sorts of activities that students have found to be purposeful. Even should a teacher seek to initiate an activity, it would have to be perceived by the students as connecting palpably to their own purposes. This raises several problems for the teacher. First, children's interests differ, and an activity seen to be purposeful by some will not appear to be so to others. This calls for considerable ingenuity on the teacher's part; either he must find some activity that appeals to everyone's purposes, or he must direct several different activities simultaneously.

Second, many pupils come to school full of interests that do not easily lend themselves to educational development. This may be because their interests are trivial, or because their interests are personally or socially destructive. While it may be true that any interest—even in stealing hubcaps from automobiles—can probably be developed in socially advantageous directions, it may take more patience and ingenuity to manage it than most teachers possess. This problem is compounded by the fact that in many cases it is exceedingly difficult even to find out what a child's interests are. This situation is aggravated when classes are large and teaching assignments are overloaded.

To the charge that it is wasteful to spend school time in solving problems that emerge in the course of activities the purposes of which are trivial and insignificant, the defenders of problem-solving may have an answer. Even if a pursuit is trivial, to find out that it is so in the course of solving a problem connected with it is itself *not* a trivial event. In other words, it could reasonably be claimed that most adults do, in fact, consider most all the things that they do to be quite important, and that there is great value in acquiring a disposition to weigh the importance of one's activities, in order to see whether it is worth the effort to deal with problems that arise within them. Of course, there is no guarantee that problem-solving in schools will lead to the acquisition of such a disposition. It takes a teacher of no little sensitivity to help students to see that whether one should deal with a problem is itself a problem.

The interests and purposes of some students may not be trivial or socially suspect, but they may be rapidly fluctuating and weak. When this is the case, students may be disposed to abandon the purpose altogether rather than grapple with a problem that arises in connection with it. Again, this puts in an awkward position a teacher who had hoped that the appearance of an obstacle to purposeful activity would as a matter of course be the cue for problem-solving behavior.

One further difficulty that is a function of the learners themselves might be mentioned, since it calls into question the role of acquiring knowledge in schools. When the formally organized knowledge that is possessed by learners is quite limited—as it, in fact, often is—the process of problem-solving may bog down. For what begins as an attempt to formulate a workable hypothesis may turn into an extensive quest for relevant information. For example, a youth may have a problem of whether to try repairing his car or to find a way of earning enough money to buy another old one. Yet he may have to acquire a fairly systematic understanding of several areas of physics and economics before he can arrive at even a tentative solution. The attempt to acquire all this knowledge would require some systematic study of particular content areas, and would doubtless take the student far from his original problem. Such an extensive process of data-gathering might well vitiate the student's original interest in the problem. The method would appear to be severely limited, then, by what students already know, and would appear even to break down altogether when students try to attack problems which call for the utilization of extensive and logically ordered knowledge with which the students are unfamiliar.

The foregoing difficulty serves to point up the fact that the method of problem-solving, insofar as it is effective, deals rather capriciously with formally organized knowledge. In the course of dealing with problems, students in effect "raid" subject matters the way we sometimes "raid" the refrigerator when we are hungry. In any case, formally organized knowledge gets short shrift. In that problem-solving interferes with its systematic acquisition, any attempt to articulate different grade levels of schooling on the basis of the kind and extent of knowledge that has been acquired, would be doomed to frustration.

Not only is the acquisition of knowledge of secondary importance when problem-solving is emphasized, but there is also a danger that students may acquire undesirable dispositions toward knowledge. The successful attempt at an hypothesized solution to a problem only validates the knowledge that may have been incorporated in the hypothesis. Yet people tend to put more confidence in their successes than is warranted by the evidence. Thus students run the

risk of acquiring the disposition to overgeneralize from their problem-solving experiences, erroneously assuming that they constitute
some sort of test of the knowledge that was employed. If students
become sensitized to this danger, the pendulum may swing the other
way, and they may become sceptical of all knowledge and fearful
of making any sorts of generalizations from their experience.

Thus problem-solving, taken as the model of learning in schools,
puts in jeopardy the acquisition, status, and use of knowledge.
Now it may be claimed that knowledge ought to remain a secondary
concern of schools, and that attention ought to be focused primarily
on the kind of learning that occurs when dispositions are acquired.
Yet at least two questions about knowledge will still remain. First,
are there not some things that students ought to know and that
schools ought to teach in light of both their importance and the
improbability of students' acquiring them out of school? And
second, is there not some knowledge about which students ought
to acquire particular dispositions, even if that knowledge is not
directly related to their present purposes? It would seem, *prima
facie*, that both these questions call for affirmative answers. Yet if
the method of problem-solving only interferes with the achievement
of these ends, how are such learnings to be facilitated? We will
deal with this question later in this and the next chapter. Before
considering it, however, we will return to one final cluster of
difficulties that allegedly besets the use of problem-solving in
schools.

It has already been seen that teaching by the method of problem-
solving becomes an enormously complicated affair when particular
children's purposes do not readily lend themselves to educational
development. But the use of problem-solving in schools is always
highly demanding, apart from special problems posed by particular
students. For the method presupposes that the teacher be acquainted with each student well enough to know what his interests
and purposes are. It presupposes that the teacher respect and be
sympathetic toward each student, for without such attitudes the
teacher would not be likely to foster activities based on students'
interests. And it presupposes that the teacher have great familiarity
with a wide variety of subject matter fields, for once a problem

comes under attack, inquiry into several related areas of knowledge may be necessary before a solution can be attempted.

The demands that problem-solving makes on teachers—intimate knowledge of students and genuine respect for them, and unusual command of broad areas of knowledge—are admittedly great. Yet the charge that this constitutes reason enough for abandoning the method of problem-solving is unwarranted. No matter what method a teacher adopts to foster learning, the chances of his success will increase in direct proportion to the extent that he possesses such attitudes and knowledge. A public school teacher without respect for his students, and some acquaintance with the kinds of people they are, and without some understanding of other areas of knowledge, especially as they relate to his own area of specialization, will be an ineffective teacher no matter what teaching method he employs. On the other hand, the charge is fair that problem-solving, if it is to be successful, requires more in this respect than most other methods of teaching. Following this fact, then, is a question of great pedagogical significance which will occupy our attention in subsequent chapters: Are other effective teaching methods available which, despite whatever particular demands *they* make, do not make the kinds of heavy demands that are called for in problem-solving?

If we should now try to balance our account of problem-solving as a method of teaching, the following might be a fair estimate. In the hands of a skilled teacher who understands the factors that must be taken into account, there is little reason to doubt that it effectively promotes learning. Lacking such understanding, use of the method is quite likely to end in desultory, if not chaotic, activity. But even a teacher skilled in the method of conducting problem-solving may have legitimate reservations about its exclusive use. First, he may wish his students to acquire certain items of knowledge that have no immediate and apparent connection to the students' purposes. Second, and perhaps more important, he may wish his students to become disposed in a particular way toward certain items of knowledge that are unrelated to the particular purposes of which his students are aware. And third, he may wish to cultivate particular dispositions in his students without having to resort in every instance to the often elaborate preparations and controls that are necessitated by problem-solving. In each of these cases, the method of problem-solving is an inadequate means. Thus even while employing problem-solving where it is appropriate to do so, a teacher may well ask whether another method of facilitating learning is available in those cases where problem-solving is inappropriate. And of course there is. Bearing in mind that the term learning is being used to indicate the acquisition of dispositions, instances are both frequent and familiar in which people learn, both by themselves and with the help of others, even though they encountered no problems in the course of actively pursuing their own purposes. A few examples of learning that appear to occur outside the context of problem-solving may make the point clearer.

The academic lecture does not obviously fit the model of problem-solving. Consider a lecturer holding forth on a topic apparently outside the experience of his audience (a daily occurrence on nearly every college campus). On the previous account of learning, the lecture should fail—as, indeed, it often does. But not always. Occasionally it does "make an impression" or "have an impact." Most students can remember, for a while at least, a lecture from which they are willing to say that they learned—that they experienced a change of disposition, acquired a new attitude toward something. And this occurred without the students' having apparently engaged in any problem-solving.

Similarly, learning sometimes results from reading books, or seeing movies, or talking informally with friends, or from simply exercising what is called, for lack of a better name, curiosity.[11] And in these cases, again, there need not necessarily be any obvious problems in need of solution.

It would appear from common instances like these that learning can be facilitated without recourse to the conducting of purposeful activities in which problems arise. But the pedagogical problem that is presented in the above examples is: *why* do people learn when exposed to certain lectures, books, conversations, etc.? Apparently the answer to this question has not been readily available, else there would not be so many lectures and books that fail to induce learning.[12] But an answer must be sought, for unless we understand why these devices sometimes do and sometimes don't promote learning, we will remain incapable of utilizing them deliberately and effectively in schools.

## PHILOSOPHY AND EMPIRICAL INQUIRY

We have reached a point where we must look beyond problem-solving as a model for learning experiences and inquire how it is possible that people learn in other kinds of situations. How, for example, do people learn from lectures? Now it may be charged that answers must be sought in experimental psychology—not in mere philosophic speculation. This charge is, to be sure, of considerably less moment than the actual investigations that are conducted as the questions themselves are explored. Yet at least three points might be made in defense of seeking answers by looking elsewhere than exclusively in experimental psychology.

First, some experimental psychologists who study learning quite frankly state that they are not interested in the question, why people learn.[13] Their aim has been to make correlations between certain stimulus events and certain behavioral responses, such that increasingly better predictions of behavior can be made. However valuable these efforts may be, they do not explain why certain events appear together. To be able, on the basis of past observations, to predict that B will occur whenever A occurs is not to explain *why* events happen that way; for prediction and explanation are not the same thing.[14] We might suppose, for example, on the basis of watching animals behave, that they, too, are in a sense able to make predictions (or, in terms of our discussion in Chapter IV, that their behavior is predicated on their having meanings which at the same time are expectations of directly forthcoming future events). But it would be quite fanciful to suppose that animals could explain why things happen as they do. Thus the experimental psychologist who eschews theoretical explanation will be of no help in seeking answers about why learning is facilitated by lectures or cued by curiosity.

Experimental psychologists who are more prone to essay theoretical explanations offer little more help in dealing with our problem. For it appears that what at first glance look like explanatory concepts—e.g., the "habits," "drives," "excitatory potentials," etc., of Clark Hull—are not really intended to explain at all. For, as Kenneth W. Spence points out, the meanings of these concepts are provided by the mathematical equations which relate them to the known experimental variables—that is, to the environmental and behavioral measures. Thus these concepts—called by some "hypothetical constructs," and "intervening variables" by others—function not as explanations, but rather as aids to the "search for the empirical laws relating behavior to the conditions determining it."[15] Again, empirically established correlations, and not explanation, seem to be the concern of the experimental psychologist. We must, then, consult additional sources if we wish to find out why people learn from some lectures.

Second, it could be suggested that the notion of "latent learning" (learning not related to any apparent needs, purposes, drives, or deprivation states), as advanced by E. C. Tolman, might be adduced to explain why lectures and curiosity facilitate learning. This would be misleading, however, since the notion of latent learning itself was advanced as an explanation for something *else*—i.e., rapid learning rates in animals who had, for example, an opportunity to explore mazes before being subjected to experimental and ostensibly hunger-motivated learning trials. But in serving as a proposed explanation of something else, the alleged phenomenon of latent learning itself remained unexplained. Our inquiry is not advanced, then, by attempting to explain what can be empirically established (e.g., learning from a lecture) on the basis of what has neither been empirically observed nor theoretically explained (i.e., latent learning). Again, assistance from this branch of experimental psychology is no more than suggestive.

As it will become clear later on in this chapter, some observation, interpretations, and even speculations of experimental psychologists will be enormously valuable in advancing our understanding of why people learn in the kinds of situations that are now under consideration. But the third point to be made in considering why experimental psychology cannot be the exclusive resource for our inquiry is perhaps the most important one. And that is: no science of human behavior can exist without some foundation in a set of assumptions or a theory which themselves are not wholly empirically determinable. This is the case no matter how vigorously a few empirical investigators may protest, and no matter how unaware such investigators may be of the assumptions on which their observations and generalizations are based.

The above point can be illustrated by recalling the discussion of mind in Chapter IV. It was noted there that any account of human behavior that aims at comprehensiveness must include inferences about what cannot be directly observed. It was also seen that in this process, sooner or later a theory of behavior had to come to grips with a theory of mind. It was shown that what mind is, is not wholly an empirical or "psychological" question, since any answer that goes beyond superficiality must also deal with what matter is. These considerations were brought out in the distinctions made among things, events, and perceptions. And such distinctions cannot be made simply on an empirical basis because, among other things, at stake is the very question of what constitutes an event that may properly be called "empirical." Obviously, to attempt to answer such a question on empirical grounds alone involves one in hopeless circularity.

These observations can be applied to the original point at issue. If we wish to understand why people learn in certain kinds of situations we must necessarily deal with a conception of mind. And in doing so, philosophic speculation becomes as relevant and as necessary as empirical observation and testing. The test of this claim will be found in the sense or the nonsense of what immediately follows. To begin our inquiry into learning as it occurs independent of problem-solving, we shall examine what happens in what might be taken as a paradigm case of this sort of learning, the lecture.

## THE USES OF THE LECTURE

As they occur in academic settings, lectures normally have one or both of two functions: to convey information or to create an attitude or disposition toward something (toward an area of knowledge, or toward a problem or an issue, or even toward the lecturer himself). The reasons for the success or failure of the lecture in fulfilling these two functions are different. We might first look at the informational function.

Conveying information is obviously a one-way affair. Regardless of how an audience reacts to it, information is conveyed simply by the lecturer's uttering it. But it is still quite a normal use of language to say that a lecturer *tried* to convey information, but failed— that is, he did not "get it across." What is usually meant here is that, although information was conveyed, those who received it were not in any noticeable way affected by it. Neither did they use the information practically, nor did they even retain it for a very long time.

The reason a lecture may succeed or fail in fulfilling its informational function can easily be made clear on the basis of what has already been said about problem-solving. When a lecture succeeds in conveying information, it is reasonable to suppose that the learners saw some use in it—saw, in other words, that the information was relevant to purposes that they were actively seeking to fulfill. A lecture on physics, for example, may successfully convey information to Tom because he sees how he can use it in fixing his car, to Dick because he sees that his retention of it will further his ambition to become an engineer, to Harry because he sees that his retention of it may earn him a passing mark in the course, and to Ralph because he is interested in physics. The learner's purpose may be benevolent or evil, important or trivial, but if he is aware that the information conveyed will help in furthering that purpose, the lecture will succeed in that respect.

A lecture may fail in its intention when it is cast in language unfamiliar to an audience. But it may also fail because the learner simply sees no purpose in it. Information has been made available but the learner sees no point in doing anything with it. Even though he may be quite aware that simply to retain the information may get him through the course, this may not be a strong enough reason for doing so. In any case, *this* purpose will insure success for the informational function of the lecture only for a limited time. Once the course is over, the purpose for retaining the information is lost.

And so is the information. In this case, the success of the informational function of the lecture must be called a trivial one.

The nineteenth century German educator Herbart thought that if the lecture was seen by the student as relating to what he already knew (what Herbart called the student's "apperceptive mass," and what moderns sometimes call the student's "cognitive structure"), the information would be successfully conveyed. It is quite possible that the ideas of the influential Herbart, after having traveled across the Atlantic, were responsible for a good part of the verbalism that dominated nineteenth century American schools. And history appears to be repeating itself as Herbart's modern-day disciples are once again lauding the virtues of cognitive structures (a rose by any other name would smell as sweet) and recommending increased emphasis on verbal teaching and the "engendering" of "comprehension."[16]

But there does not seem to be any good reason for believing that if a perceptible connection is made between the information conveyed in a lecture and a student's prior knowledge, that, therefore, the informative function of the lecture will be successfully fulfilled. It may be a necessary, but it could hardly be a sufficient condition of success. If the learner is able to see the connection between the lecture and what he already knows, we may be satisfied that he *understands* the lecture. But understanding a thing is not the same as retaining it or using it, nor does understanding a thing, in and of itself, motivate one to retain or use it. To proclaim that when a student understands something he then "incorporates it into his cognitive structure" is merest nonsense. Such a notion implies the actual existence of a reified ghostly apparatus ("cognitive structure") to which information is somehow "attached." A moment's consideration of everyday experience is enough to remind us that we understand perfectly well much that we hear and read. Yet we quickly lose most of it.

The connection of conveyed information with what a hearer already knows is not enough, in and of itself, to insure that the information will be put to practical use or retained for any appreciable length of time. This is the case whether information is conveyed in a formal lecture or in an informal conversation. Our friends tell us innumerable things we promptly forget, despite the polite attention we pay them. What we do not forget is what they told us that we found useful in pursuing our own purposes. In fact, one of the marks of stable and deep friendships is that the parties take the trouble to say things that are relevant to the other's interests and pursuits. On the other hand, some people regale us with vast amounts of information. Whether it be gossip, occupational shop talk, or political analysis, if it does not relate to our purposes, we generally regard our informants as bores. When we have the chance, we try to avoid such people. There is, of course a pedagogical lesson here, but we have not yet provided children with adequate means of avoiding teachers who are bores.

That the only effect of some lectures is to produce boredom has even more important implications when we consider the other function that lectures may serve, that of creating or changing dispositions.[17] For it is possible for a lecture to be boring while at the same time successfully fulfilling its informational function. This may happen, for example, when the listener has no great enthusiasm for the purpose to which the information is instrumental, yet is still bent on achieving that purpose. A paradigm of this situation occurs when people are receiving a lecture on what to do in the event of a fire drill. Or again, a lecture that is boring can successfully convey information if the purposes for which the hearers attend the lecture are important enough for them to survive the boredom and "digest" the information. A paradigm is the premedical student dutifully taking in an anatomy lecture. Yet a lecture that is boring always fails if its purpose was to have an effect on the dispositions of the audience.[18] And this fact affords insight into how it is possible that people can learn from lectures.

If we recall that learning has been taken here to mean a dispositional change, and if we recall from the discussion in Chapter IV that change in disposition always involves change in meaning, change in expectation, and change in feeling or emotional quality, then it should be apparent that no case of learning occurs without having some impact on emotions. And it should be apparent, too, that what is dull, what is uninteresting, what is boring is just that which has no impact on the emotions. It is possible to learn from what is absorbing, what is delightful, what is awesome, what is terrifying, and even from what is offensive, obnoxious, or aggravating. For all these qualities connote emotion. Of course, the fact that these kinds of situations do arouse emotion is no guarantee that learning will in fact occur, but the potential is present. On the other hand, what is dull does not even have this potential. Hence, of all of the effects that a lecture might have, the only effect which necessarily precludes the acquiring of a disposition is that of boredom.

Mr. Jones knows his subject matter thoroughly but he is a boring fellow. And he is a teacher. How shall we use him? On the above account, the answer should be plain. If Mr. Jones is to have any pedagogical value at all, put him before preprofessional students who are interested enough in their future careers not to mind the boredom and who can, consequently, put to some use the information Mr. Jones has to offer. But don't turn Mr. Jones loose in a public school or in a general education course in college! This advice should be obvious on the basis of common experience as well as from what has just been said. If it is not always heeded, the most generous thing that could be assumed is that the schools suffer from an overabundance of Mr. Joneses.

If a dull lecture fails to foster dispositional changes, what succeeds? Let us take it, as a presupposition of this discussion, that the lecturer does not know his audience well and is not, therefore, attempting to appeal to the particular purposes and interests of its members. Now, it has already been seen that a necessary condition for changing or creating a disposition in a learner is that a lecture cue some kind of emotional response. This is a necessary, but it is not a sufficient condition. It is an easy thing simply to interest, delight, or anger an audience without producing any learning at all. The audiences of comedians, politicians, and ministers may be amused, stirred, irritated, or awed; teachers, when lecturing, can and have at times assumed similar postures. But the dispositions of the audience do not always change.

Yet situations readily come to mind where simply the arousal of strong emotion has affected dispositions. If, for example, a demagogue simply by arousing strong emotions through use of the familiar ploys of orators and debaters is successfully able to create or alter dispositions in his audience, then it would be proper to say that the audience had learned. The lesson to be drawn from this, however, is not that in delivering a lecture a teacher should strive to promote learning by emulating the emotional appeal of a demagogue. The reason for this will become clear if we recall what was said earlier about the kind of learning that is appropriate for schools to promote.

In Chapter II, reasons were advanced for the proposal that the chief concern of schools ought to be with teaching pupils to learn to learn. Put another way, this means that the kinds of dispositions found desirable for schooling are those which make possible the acquisition of new knowledge, skills, and attitudes. The ministrations of the demagogue or others whose verbal presentations depend for their effect largely or only on the arousal of emotion do not meet this criterion. For when the use of fact and the use of reason are not instrumental in the creation of a disposition, there is nothing in that disposition to serve as a springboard for any subsequent activity that might produce a change in the disposition, or further inquiry.

Suppose that Mr. Ballot, an uncommitted voter, listens to an address of candidate X, a demagogue. He is moved by the impassioned charge that opposition candidate Y (who, let us say, favors a certain welfare program) is sympathetic to communism, by the tender mention of X's family, by the stirring reference to X's war record, by X's heartfelt devotion to American ideals, and so forth. And having been so moved, let us suppose that Mr. Ballot leaves the convention hall believing that X is not such a bad fellow after all, and that he is deserving of support (including, among other things, a vote). Mr. Ballot has acquired an attitude toward candidate X, and perhaps a disposition toward voting, but he has acquired nothing else that could ever lead to any change in that attitude or disposition. He has acquired no facts to check, no questions to initiate further inquiry, no reasons the validity of which might bear closer scrutiny. Indeed, Mr. Ballot *may* change his new attitude toward candidate X, especially if he goes to hear an address by candidate Y. But if he listens to what candidate Y has to say, it will not be because of the attitude or disposition just acquired. Rather it will be the exercise of a prior disposition (e.g., that one should attend speeches of both candidates or hear both sides before making a decision).

For the sake of the additional emphasis that it merits, I should like to repeat the contention already made: that the above example is not an appropriate model for conducting classes in schools. The point is worth repeating because some teachers have thought that the only alternative to boring their students is to titillate them, amuse them, or carry them to the heights of passion. On college campuses, some who teach in this manner may win the title of "popular lecturer." Their classes are often well-attended but they have really missed their calling. They should have entered the entertainment industry (not politics, where their behavior might have unfortunate consequences), where, as actors or comics, they could continue to attract large audiences without having to pretend that they were fostering learning.

In examining the capability of a lecture to produce learning, we have been riding an uncomfortable pendulum that has swung from boredom to unreasoning emotion. And at neither crest of the arc have we found the lecture able to facilitate the kind of learnings appropriate for schools. But we have found one important clue that will help us in discovering how a lecture can promote such learning. This is the arousal of emotion. To fulfill successfully its dispositional function, the lecture must be able to arouse the emotions of the audience. Yet such arousal must not be dissipated so that it ends in boredom, nor can it be allowed to bear the burden of the entire lecture. What, then, shall be done with the emotion once it is aroused?

This question would introduce the payoff if this were a manual on how to lecture. Since it is not, the answer to the question will be put in very general terms so that our discussion of the lecture will be in such a form as to permit another kind of analysis of it. Generally speaking, then, if a lecture is to facilitate change in the kinds of dispositions that have an appropriate place in schools, it must not only arouse emotion (which is to say, enlist interest), but it must also focus emotion so that it will be relevant to the topic of the lecture. That is, the emotion must be emotion about the information, the questions, and the reasoning that the lecture presents. Furthermore, it will not be the lecturer's intention to direct emotion in this manner for the purpose of convincing his audience of the truth of what he is presenting (as it would be in the case of the demagogue or the indoctrinator); rather, the emotion will be directed in this way in order to underscore the significance of what is being presented.

This is to say that a lecture which facilitates learning is one that presents its content in such a manner as to appear important to the audience. Lecturers who are to some extent aware of this sometimes try to achieve this end by simply telling their audience, at various points in the lecture, that what is being said is important. This, of course, will not do. It is like asking a bemused audience to please pay attention. But however hard the listeners try, however polite they may be, they will fall back into reverie unless the lecturer is able to arouse them emotionally.

## THE LECTURE AS ART

We have said enough about the lecture to show at least that it can be presented in such a way as to facilitate learning, and that it is an instance of such facilitation that does not have recourse to problem-solving. It could be shown that when people learn from books, from the conversation of others, from explorations initiated by their own curiosity, and from other like experiences, the same conditions are present. That is, in each of these cases, emotion is aroused under conditions similar to those that have been described with regard to the lecture. Later chapters will show how this is so.

But one key question in regard to the dispositional effect of the lecture (or indeed, of any of the other devices noted above) has not yet been dealt with. Nor will it be possible to handle it in a very satisfactory way. The question is this: Granting the need for arousing emotion in the course of the pedagogical lecture, how does the lecturer go about doing it so that the requisite conditions are satisfied? The reason why this question cannot be answered very satisfactorily will soon become clear. When we witness a lecturer carefully arouse and employ the emotions of his audience, and thereby succeed in facilitating learning, we are likely to react to the event by saying, *"That* was a performance!" And indeed it was. The excellent lecturer is both a craftsman and an artist; a craftsman in the sense that his performance serves a utilitarian end (the facilitation of learning), and an artist in the sense that his organization of means must have form—that is, must satisfy aesthetic criteria. It is common to say of a lecture that promoted learning that it "had an impact," that it "made an impression." But what kind of impact or impression? Not simply a pedagogical impact, because the terms impact and impression connote direct and immediate events. Learning, on the other hand, takes time; it does not happen instantly, on the spot. One could refer to an emotional impact or impression, but not in the case of the pedagogically successful lecture, for obviously there was more going on than simply the arousal of emotions. It would appear, then, that the sort of impact that such a lecture has, given its immediacy, involves both the arousal of emotion *and* the direct perception of the organization of the lecture by means of which the emotion was related to the substantive content of the lecture. When a perception involves both the arousal of clearly felt emotion and an awareness of formal organization, it is normally termed "aesthetic." And in the case of the kind of lecture under consideration, it would seem appropriate to say that its impact, its impression, is aesthetic in nature.

This is to say that the effective lecturer who is capable of promoting learning in his students has rendered his performance into a work of art. It is not the same sort of art that is found in galleries or in theaters, but the performance nonetheless has the same features that entitle us to label paintings and dramas as art. It arouses emotion; it is carefully and formally organized with a view to the emotion's enhancing the content (and thus it will be found to have parts that closely parallel the effective development—buildup, tension, climax, etc.—of a well-wrought essay or short story), and its direct and immediate effect on an audience is aesthetic in quality. Effective lecturers, who in their performance exhibit many of the skills of a well-schooled actor, are well aware of the care that must be taken in preparing a lecture apart from the simple assembling of information. They may not be so pretentious as to refer to themselves as artists, nor do they normally refer to their performances as works of art. But the point being made here is that what they do has the *effect* of a work of art; hence their lectures *function* as art functions, regardless of whether they are called art.[19]

It should thus be easy to see why it is difficult to answer the question "How does an effective lecturer go about organizing his performance?" For the question is analogous to asking how an artist creates a work of art. We can appreciate art after it is made, or a lecture after it has been delivered, and we can analyze both of them more clearly to perceive the organization of their parts. But we cannot very easily construct a set of directions for organizing and delivering an effective lecture any more than we can make up a set of directions for creating a work of art. We can, of course, both show and tell someone how to paint a picture, and in the same sense we can tell him how to plan and deliver a lecture. But we can provide no guarantee that the picture will qualify as a work of art or that the lecture will succeed in facilitating learning. Yet while we must forego the attempt to find exhaustive rules for planning a lecture, we can still ask after the conditions that afford aesthetic quality to any experience. Thus in our quest for pedagogical effectiveness we shall in the next chapter consider aesthetic experience and art.

# NOTES

1. John Dewey, *Democracy and Education* (New York: Macmillan, 1916), p. 192.
2. John L. Childs, *American Pragmatism and Education* (New York: Holt, 1956), p. 144.
3. See Dewey, *op. cit.,* Chapter XII.
4. For a discussion of the great complexity of what are termed "molar" problems, see Harry S. Broudy, B. Othanel Smith, and Joe R. Burnett, *Democracy and Excellence in American Secondary Education* (Chicago: Rand McNally, 1964), p. 235.
5. The elaboration of problem-solving that follows owes much to

the discussion of John Dewey (especially, in *Democracy and Education,* Chapter XII). William H. Hay has gathered together, summarized, and interpreted Dewey's various statements on this topic in "John Dewey on Freedom and Choice," *The Monist, 48:3* (July, 1964), pp. 346–355. An excellent example of problem-solving behavior is to be found in Max Black, *Critical Thinking* (Englewood Cliffs, N.J.: Prentice-Hall, 1946), pp. 273–275.

6. It has been claimed by at least one critic that what is learned by means of problem-solving is either a tendency to make unwarranted generalizations (for a single successful test of an hypothesis provides little warrant for assuming that it, or others like it, is true), or systematic scepticism (bred of the realization that a single confirmation is no basis for inductive generalization). Foster McMurray has elaborated on these topics in an unpublished paper, "Pragmatic Concepts of Problem-Solving and Their Utility in Educational Theory."

7. Problem-solving as an educational method is associated with one form of progressive education. For an historical account of the demise of both, see Lawrence A. Cremin, *The Transformation of the Schools* (New York: Alfred A. Knopf, 1961) especially pp. 347–353.

8. See, for example, Jacob Getzels and Philip Jackson, *Creativity and Intelligence,* (New York: Wiley, 1962), pp. 30–33.

9. There have been many criticisms leveled at the alleged utility of problem-solving as a method of education, but most of them appear to deal with some process other than what has been presented here as problem-solving (e.g., David Ausubel, "In Defense of Verbal Learning," *Educational Theory,* 9 [January, 1961], 21–23). For a more carefully considered criticism of problem-solving, see H. S. Broudy, "A Critique of Problem-Solving," unpublished manuscript, and Foster McMurray, *op. cit.*

10. Cf. John Dewey, *Democracy and Education* (New York: Macmillan, 1916), pp. 273–274.

11. There has been much debate on the question of whether, as Aristotle seemed to think, all men desire to know. If this is what is meant by curiosity, there are plenty of cases of people who are not curious about much. But it is important to ask about the conditions that promote and hinder curiosity. This will be done in Chapter VIII.

12. The following defense of habitually ineffective lectures and books

is sometimes offered: the students are dull, lazy, uninterested, etc. Likewise, an owner may offer as an explanation of why his horse habitually runs last, that the other horses are faster. As in the above case, this explains nothing. Just as the owner had better get himself another horse, so a teacher who defends his ineffectiveness by placing the responsibility on his students should really seek another vocation. Instead, teachers often ask for another group of students (in secondary schools, there is often strong competition among teachers to be assigned to classes having brighter students).

13. See B. F. Skinner, "Are Theories of Learning Necessary?" *Psychological Review*, 57 (1950), 193–216.

14. See P. C. Dodwell, "Causes of Behavior and Explanation in Psychology," *Mind*, 69 (January, 1960), 1–13.

15. Kenneth W. Spence, "The Postulates and Methods of Behaviorism," *Psychological Review*, LV:2 (March, 1948), 75.

16. See, for example, Ausubel, *op. cit.*, and N. L. Gage, "Toward a Cognitive Theory of Teaching," *Teachers College Record*, 65 (February, 1964), 408–412.

17. Hereafter, we shall refer to this function of lectures as the "dispositional function," a convenient (if elliptical) phrase that is intended to parallel the earlier use of the phrase, "informational function."

18. A boring lecture may, of course, help create in the listeners a disposition to regard lectures as boring, but the lecturer could hardly have intended such a dispositional change.

19. The presence of artistic impact in a wide variety of events that are not normally labelled as art directs attention to the felt qualities of all experience. For a discussion of these qualities as they bear upon education, see Francis T. Villemain and Nathaniel L. Champlin, "Frontiers for an Experimentalist Philosophy of Education," *Antioch Review*, 19 (1959), 345–359.

# V I

# LEARNING AND
# AESTHETIC QUALITY
# IN EXPERIENCE

THE FORM OF A LECTURE MAY APPROACH THAT OF A DRAMATIC performance. Such a lecture promotes learning, and in doing so it functions as does a work of art. We have noted that it is not possible to provide a comprehensive set of directions which would result in the delivering of such a lecture. Yet we can gain greater understanding of what happens to people when they are exposed to such lectures (or books, etc.), and such an understanding should, in turn, provide more clarity about the conditions necessary for a lecture to be effective in promoting learning. If the lecture does function as a work of art does, then an understanding of how it is that any work of art affords aesthetic quality to experience, and an understanding of what such quality is like, will provide us with a better understanding both of what makes a lecture effective, and of how people learn.

## ART AND LANGUAGE ABOUT ART

When we consider aesthetic quality in experience, we usually think of works of art. Thus we may begin our inquiry by first considering a painting. As our account proceeds, we shall find aesthetic quality turning up in some unexpected places, but if we cannot find it on beholding a painting, we surely will not find it anywhere.

Let it first be admitted that we cannot adequately put into words what we feel and think when confronted by a painting that has withstood the test of connoisseurs over a long period of time. Precisely what a painting means is quite ineffable. If words could express what a work of art presents, we should have no need for the work itself.[1] There is, of course, nothing peculiar about art in this respect. Any experience, whether that of hearing a Bach Cantata, digging a ditch, or waiting for a bus is simply what it *is*. It can be described in words, but words strung out into discursive sentences can describe only the general features of experience—never the particulars.[2] (Thus we felt impatience in waiting for the bus, but *what sort* of impatience? For no two experiences of impatience are alike. However we try, our statement remains general, and the particular experience forever eludes us.) It would be correct to say that the artist, instead of fruitlessly trying to make a statement *about* experience, presents what functions for us *as* an experience.

Yet the fact that the uniqueness of all particular experiences forever escapes our conceptual nets has not deterred us from talking about those experiences. For we never aim to capture precisely any experience in words; rather, our purpose in talking about it is usually practical. We wish to modify it, reinstitute it, maintain it, or avoid it, etc. Or we may wish simply to understand it or to live it over again. And for these purposes, ordinary language, with all the generality of its terms, is usually sufficient. It is sufficient in talking about art, and the kind of experience to which art gives rise. If one wishes to find out *just* what it feels like to hear the Ninth Symphony, one had best put aside books about art and aesthetics, and go to a concert hall. But that is not the purpose here. We are seeking to understand how it is that works of art achieve their peculiar effect, and what conditions are involved in the experiencing of aesthetic qualities. Given this aim, we can use the same language that is used to talk about any other sorts of qualities in experience.

There is, of course, an assumption lying behind this commitment to language. And that is that paintings, poems, symphonies, and the like are no less natural events than bricks, postage stamps, and travel receipts. There are theories of art and aesthetic experience that elevate them to a realm apart from the mundane events of everyday living. Art is spoken of as the expression of a desireless will,[3] or as an intuition,[4] or as a symbolic form.[5] In each of these theories are to be found insights that make the appreciation of art richer and more satisfying,[6] but each one of them offers terms applicable to art or to aesthetic experience that have no application to any other sort of event or experience.[7] But what can one make of such concepts? If aesthetic experience is *sui generis*, how shall it be recognized and understood? If one's experience on beholding works of art is totally unlike all other experience, then it cannot be explained at all—for we should be lacking even the words. Art becomes divine, then, and the artist is likened to his own Creator.

In Chapter IV, an account of mind was presented in naturalistic terms; the discussion of art that follows will be presented in a parallel manner. It will be assumed, for the moment at least, that like mind itself, aesthetic qualities in experience are natural occurrences resulting from the interaction of events in which men play a part. That some men deliberately employ means to create objects (works of art) that facilitate such experience indicates no supernatural event imposed on humdrum nature, but rather, only betokens an achieved capacity to institute and control certain qualities in experience that men have found to be valuable.

The test of these assumptions will lie in part in the adequacy of the following discussion of art and aesthetic quality.

## FORM IN WORKS OF ART

Let us begin by considering the painting "Black Houses," a watercolor executed by Charles Burchfield. In its simplicity and economy, the picture lends itself easily to analysis. It appears to be a representation of two houses set between some dirty snow in the foreground and a large expanse of pale sky in the background. But there is both more and less than this in the picture.

There are, of course, no houses in the picture at all. Only paint. While apparently obvious, it is a distinction of great significance. The picture can be described in two ways. We can talk about the colors and the various tones of gray, the pattern of light against dark, the scattering of circular shapes against the broad, angular lines. Or we can talk about two houses

> rearing themselves up against the cold afterglow in the western sky, like gaunt black spectres which seem to be resisting the light with all the bulky power they can muster.[8]

Through particular visual means, then, the painting brings to mind a particular representation. The visual means—colors, lines, shapes, etc.—are often called the design or *form* of the painting. The representation is often referred to as the subject matter of the painting. For reasons which will be made clear later, the houses and their "bulky power" will be called the painting's *sign-content*.

A very awkward and artificial operation must now be performed: responses to each of these aspects of the painting must be examined in turn. It is awkward because, if I were asked to respond *only* to the shapes and colors, I should find it very difficult to forget that those elements were arranged to represent particular houses. And if I were asked to respond only to the houses, I should find it quite impossible to say anything intelligible about the painting at all without making reference to the particular shapes and

*Black Houses* (1918) by CHARLES BURCHFIELD, Collection of Dr. Theodor Braasch, New York

colors. This awkwardness results from the artificiality that characterizes any analysis. For we perceive the painting *as* houses *of* certain shapes and colors arranged in a certain way (or, the other way 'round, *as* the shapes and colors *of* houses). That is to say, the experience of the painting includes *both* its aspects of form and sign-content, all at once. Only under analysis may the two aspects be separated.

We shall first look at the formal aspect of the painting, and later, at its aspect as a sign. But an objection must first be met, for some theorists believe that the defining characteristic of art is form alone, and that the sort of analysis just begun is useful only insofar as it dispenses once and for all with sign-content. Clive Bell has written:

> The representative element in a work of art may or may not be harmful; always it is irrelevant.[9]

But such notions of art appear strained from the very beginning, for they start by seeking *one* defining characteristic of what is aesthetic (in this case, it turns out to be "significant form").[10] This procedure is akin to seeking the one ingredient in a stew which gives it its flavor: an enterprise destined for frustration. The error of this particular view of art is apparent from what has just been said. The experience of viewing "Black Houses," which is properly called aesthetic in quality, involves a reaction to both the form and the sign-content of the painting. So inseparably are the two united in our immediate perception that we cannot even imagine what the experience of one or the other, taken alone, would *feel* like. Thus it seems quite arbitrary to hold that aesthetic quality in experience can dispense with one of those aspects, unless one wishes to speak simply of a *different kind* of aesthetic experience.

Another way of putting the matter is to recall that experience comes as a whole, and not in analyzed parts. Experience may be *both* aesthetic *and* practical at one and the same time (the concert pianist is, after all, earning a living as he plays Mozart), but it is the *whole* experience that can be characterized either way. Neither is it partly aesthetic and partly something else in successive moments. That these latter notions are absurd is obvious in the mere stating of them. Yet they seem to be implied by a theory of art as pure form. Sign-content is not present in all works of art, but when it is, our response to it is integral with our response to the whole work. Hence that response is as relevant to what is aesthetic about the experience as is the response to the form of the work.

We shall examine the form of the painting first because, grossly speaking, it is more tangible. After all, the colors and the shapes appear unquestionably to be in the picture. But the houses, much less their "bulky power" are not actually *in* the picture; they are only suggested. Furthermore, we have seen a great many pictures in this century (not to mention rugs, wallpaper designs, etc.) that have suggested nothing recognizable at all beyond whatever feelings were aroused by the form alone: Thus the presence of form in a work of art takes on a peculiar significance for, unlike sign-content, it can elicit an aesthetic response all on its own.

We may begin with a standard definition of form: it refers to what are perceived to be the ordered relations of the nonrepresentative elements or sensuous materials out of which a given stimulus or cue for experience is made. Two things about form immediately follow from this definition. First, form is not limited to what are defined as art objects; and second, form is not really *in* the object any more than the houses are *in* the painting. Rather, form is *attributed* to an object by a viewer. Both these observations need some clarification.

Form has been defined with respect to what has been called "a cue for experience." Works of art serve as such cues, of course, and in a painting form is carried by shapes, lines, and colors. In music, form refers to the pitch, timbre, and temporal relationship of sounds. In a more complex art like literature, the form is carried not only by the sounds and phrasings of words and sentences, but by the broader organizational elements of plot structure and character type as well. But *any* cue for experience—not just art—may be perceived as having form. For example, the manner and the settings in which art works are presented to us may be characterized as having form. We are usually aware of such formal elements only when they become jarring. Too many paintings on a gallery wall spoil

the exhibition, no matter what the quality of the individual paintings. A concert stage sometimes inhibits the performance of jazz
just as a saloon would be a frustrating setting for the playing
of a sonata.

The fine arts, then, have no monopoly on form. Anything we
encounter may be organized or disorganized, and thus make us
aware of form. The man who always wears a tie is not necessarily
well-dressed, for clothing, too, is a matter of the relationships of
colors, shapes, and textures. And just as the motions of ballet
dancers *are* the dance, so the motions of hockey players *are* the
game. A choreographer pays deliberate attention to organizing
form for the dance; this makes the beholder's task easier. But if
the hockey fan attends to more than who is winning the game
(or who is about to bash whom with his stick), he can perceive form
in the changing patterns made by the skaters: in the contrasting
relationships of those patterns as they alternate from the slower,
more relaxed movements at the center of the rink to the faster and
more violent movements around the goal.

The second point to be made about form follows not so much
from its definition as it does from common sense. Events simply occur. If no one is around to participate in them, no one attributes
form to them. But do they still have form? The question is ambiguous, like the proverbial question about whether a tree falling
in the middle of a forest, far from anyone who could hear it,
makes a noise. Sound waves are emitted, to be sure, but that is not
what we ordinarily mean by noise. Now, events occur, too, and
in a particular order, although the order will be described quite
differently by different observers (no matter *how* carefully they
look) in different positions and observing at different times. The
events are not deliberately organized; *they* only *happen*. Whether
they are organized or not is a function of how particular people take
them. A forest is simply there—an unplanned, chaotic tangle of
trunks and branches, leaves and shrubbery. It may be perceived
as simply this, but often it is not. *This* part of the forest, we say,
is lovely. And we mean these particular trees, as we see them in
these particular relationships, set against that particular shrubbery.

It can hardly be argued that anyone planned that very arrangement. Our reaction to it, an aesthetic one, is a function of our having *perceived form in it.* We move a few steps and find the place not so impressive anymore. Form, then, is a function of our perception of objects and events, not of the objects or events themselves. People do not, of course, create form out of their heads. For perception itself (see Chapter IV) is a function of a total event in which a person and some part of his environment participate.

There may be an objection to this way of conceiving form. The forest may be unplanned, but the painting is not. Mr. Burchfield very deliberately painted his "Black Houses." Didn't he formally organize what he was doing? And if so, wouldn't it be proper to say that the form is *in* the painting, because he put it there? The answer must be in the negative. For if form were some genuinely and independently existing relation, it would be possible to detect it objectively and unequivocally. But such a relation is not just a relation among parts, it is a relation among parts *to an observer.* And even the most expert of observers disagree about whether, and to what extent, form is perceptible in any given work of art. Mr. Burchfield did not put form in his painting; he put paint on a plane surface. But before he did so, and while he was doing it, he thought about how he might arrange the colors, lines, and shapes (and he also thought about those matters in relation to *what* he was painting—i.e., houses, and to what particular ideas and feelings he had about them). Thus he arranged these elements in his painting in such a manner that it would be easier for him and for other viewers of the painting to perceive form in it.

To say that the painter, in organizing his materials, makes it easier for the perception of form is not to say that he always succeeds. Inexperienced viewers, for example, may be unaware of what others perceive as form in even so carefully and economically painted a picture as "Black Houses." And other viewers may take offense at representation in paintings, and may claim that the recognizability of the houses interferes with the form of the picture, adulterating the aesthetic quality of the experience they have. Finally, among those who find form in the painting, there will be disagreement as to its quality: how good it is, how effectively it is related to the sign-content, etc.

## EMOTION IN THE
## PERCEPTION OF FORM

We have seen that form might be found in virtually any cue for experience. It can, of course, be found in a lecture just as it can be found in a work of fine art. Form is found not inherently within the cue, but only as a function of the way in which an individual interacts with it—that is, as a function of one's perception. We shall want to know what the conditions of this interaction are that make possible the perception of form, but we must first carry out the present discussion to its consequences. From what has already been said, it follows that perception of form is affective in quality— that is, it has a particular feel to it. The nature of this affect must now be examined more closely.

To say that the perception of form has a particular feel to it is only to recall what was said in Chapter IV about perception: it is not simply a cold registration of perceptible phenomena after the manner of a camera but rather, insofar as what is perceived has any meaning for us, the perception is charged with an emotional tone. It is only because most of what we perceive has a minimal meaning for us that we tend to forget this fact, and attach equally little significance to the felt quality of the perception. Fire hydrants, sidewalks, mailboxes do not arouse much feeling because we behave habitually toward them. We know precisely what to do and what not to do about them, and have little occasion to be aware of their meanings. On the other hand, when one is eagerly awaiting a letter from a loved one, his perception of the mailbox when he returns home from work in the evening is loaded with special meaning and becomes charged with emotion.

But there is an interesting and important difference between the emotional perception of a mailbox which may contain an eagerly awaited letter, and the emotional perception of form in a painting. The difference is fundamental to what is meant by the term aesthetic. The meaning of the mailbox is not self-contained, but *refers* to something else: the letter (which, in turn, has meaning in terms of its writer). Most meanings function referentially, leading their percipient from one experience (i.e., that of the immediate cue—the mailbox in the illustration) to another one (the idea of the letter's possible presence). The meanings found in scientific and practical discourse and in practical affairs function in this way. And the emotion involved in the meaningful perception, like the meaning itself, is also focused on something other than the immediate experiential cue. Mailboxes do not normally make our hearts beat faster; they do so only when we think that there might be a special letter inside. Referential meanings, then, are understood and felt in terms of other things to which they might lead.

But this cannot conceivably be the case when we perceive form in some paintings. In the case of "Black Houses," it is true that at least one meaning (and one emotional focus) of the form is the houses that it represents. But in a nonobjective painting (one without any recognizable content), or in music, *there is nothing to which the form could refer.* Hence the question of the inexperienced gallery-goer, "But what's it supposed to mean?" is as irrelevant to the nonobjective painting as the same question would be if it were asked about a harpsichord sonata, a checkered tablecloth, or the medallion tip on a man's shoe. These objects *do not refer* to anything else at all; they have no referential meaning. Thus the emotional perception of form (apart from what the form may represent) does not get its felt quality because of that to which the form refers. It feels the way it does because it looks the way it does.

When the perception of form includes nothing recognizably familiar, it can have no referential meaning; thus, it can lead to no other experience of a different sort (barring, of course, the gratuitous fancies of a whimsical, or perhaps frustrated, beholder). The emotional impact of perceiving form, then, has an immediate quality not necessarily found in the referential meanings of everyday affairs. What will be meant hereafter by the term "aesthetic quality" is just this immediately and directly felt perception of form. Why such perception should feel the way it does will be considered later on, but for the moment, the linguistic context of the term aesthetic will be examined, in order to better explain how it is being used.

We can assume that works of art, at least, serve as cues for aesthetic quality in experience. Many works of art, like the painting "Black Houses," embody sign-content; that is, something recognizable that evokes ideas of specific things that are not in the work itself. Other works of art lack this and present only forms divested of all referential meaning. Most music, some painting, and architecture are all of this sort. Yet both kinds of art are said to evoke aesthetic quality in experience. If this is so, then, the presence of recognizable sign-content is not necessary for the evocation of aesthetic quality—although it will obviously transform the quality of any experience.

From this, it would appear reasonable to conclude that the necessary and sufficient condition for the arousal of aesthetic quality in experience is the perception of form. This would mean, then, that when one is having an experience that is aesthetic in quality, he is *at least* perceiving form in some cue for experience, although he may be perceiving more than that. The perception of form, as we have seen, necessarily involves the arousal of emotion, or affect.[11] Hence experience having aesthetic quality is always emotionally charged. Perceiving a mailbox as possibly containing a special letter involves emotion, too, but the experience does not have aesthetic quality. This is because we are not at all interested, at that moment, in the form of the mailbox; its only value for us lies in what it might contain. Its meaning, like its value, is referential. Thus lacking the non-referential immediacy of emotionally charged perception, our perception of the mailbox is not aesthetic. Immediacy and directness of feeling is thus but the other side of perceiving form. Experience cannot be called aesthetic in quality if it lacks immediate emotional impact or if form is not perceived.

What sort of emotion is peculiar to experience that is aesthetic in quality? Theorists present us with a formidable list of candidates for what is often called "the" aesthetic emotion. Yet under closer examination, there does not seem to be any one peculiar aesthetic emotion at all. On the contrary, there are probably an unlimited number of different ways one might feel in the course of experience having aesthetic quality. One has only to call to mind the vast differences in emotions evoked by a Wagnerian opera, a Bach fugue, a march, and "The Original Jelly Roll Blues."

Even granting the vast range of emotions that may become aesthetic in quality, there are those who claim that common to all of them is a feeling of pleasure.[12] For if we did not feel pleasure, why should we go to the trouble of seeking and cultivating such experience? If this view makes any sense, it must depend on an unusual definition of pleasure. For we normally mean by that term the feeling we have when we eat a delicious meal, receive a gift, etc. But we do not feel *this* way when we see the enactment of tragedy or look at Goya's series of etchings "The Horrors of War." Used in this way, the term pleasure, far from indicating a feeling, is probably an attempted explanation of behavior. Thus it functions much like the behaviorists' term "reinforcement." To say that one repeatedly seeks aesthetic experience because he gets pleasure from doing so is like saying he repeatedly seeks such experience because he finds it reinforcing to do so. Neither way of putting things, of course, explains anything at all, nor does either term refer to the way people feel. As we saw in Chapter III, neither "explanation" adds any more information to the simple observational report that some people repeatedly seek aesthetic quality in experience.

It is now time to consider why people seek aesthetic quality. (Of course, all people do not seek works of art, since aesthetic quality can be afforded by virtually any sort of cue for experience). The reason hinges on the conditions under which the perception of form arouses emotion, or affect. We are now ready to consider a set of related questions: under what kinds of conditions does one perceive form? How is it that such perception arouses affect?

And why is it that the affect is of a sort that people deliberately seek it? All these questions can be dealt with by considering the nature of the affective response to what is perceived as form.

## THE NATURE OF AFFECT

Our procedure will be to examine first the nature of affective responses as they occur in *any* experience, and then, to see how these responses occur in experience which is aesthetic in quality. Since we must deal now with affect at some length it will be well to have a definition of it. By affect we do not necessarily mean any particular physiological and observable events such as change in pulse rate, rate of heartbeat, or galvanic skin response. We have reference to emotional tone that is felt, and one can have feelings (especially in the course of experience which has aesthetic quality) without necessarily exhibiting any overt manifestations. What is meant by feelings is clear enough, since everybody has them. Yet it is true that to talk in such a way gives no clue as to when it would be appropriate to say, "Here is an instance of affect," since we can find no positive identifying sign of it.

Instead of trying to find some identifiable essence by which affect can with certainty be recognized, it will suffice to speak of it in terms of a relationship. Thus we may say that affect is the personally felt aspect of interactions involving persons and particular environing conditions or cues. In the discussion that follows, we shall talk in some detail about those conditions. Whether it is reasonable to say that affective responses, or feelings, are germane to those conditions will depend on the extent to which the description of them accords with common experience. Thus while we are not in a position of being able to say with certainty precisely when someone else is undergoing an affective change, we are able to say that, given a certain kind of relation to his environment, it is likely that a person will undergo such changes.

Furthermore, we shall use the term "affect" to indicate feeling that is undifferentiated with respect to the nature of the particular situation in which it occurs. Of course, most feelings are had with reference to a situation. Love, for example, or fear, or anger are particular feelings directed toward particular people or things. We will henceforth refer to these kinds of feelings as "emotions." When we speak of affect, however, we mean to *exclude* any reference to any object or situation; we mean only to refer to an excitation which may be thought of as varying quantitatively but not in quality. Hence it may be said that we experience more or less affect, but not that it varies from love to hate, or fear to security. For these latter, we reserve the term emotion.

This distinction is being made for purposes of analysis, and not as an attempt to truly characterize the world. Hence an example may make the unfamiliarity of the distinction between affect and emotion a bit less mysterious. Expecting to eat a raisin cookie, I open the cookie jar and find it empty. I am disappointed, let down. This *emotion* is, of course, about the cookies. The affect, on the other hand, is the particular excitation that is focused on (as well as aroused by) the sudden awareness of the absence of raisin cookies. The term affect, then, refers simply to an excitation; the term emotion refers to its direction, or qualitative content.

Normally, we have this or that emotion, and not a mere series of affective changes. Yet it seems to make some sense to say that one is slightly, considerably, or extremely aroused or excited and, once the point or focus of that arousal is identified, that one is having an emotional experience of slight, considerable, or extreme disappointment-at-finding-the-cookie-jar-empty. (The latter phrase is hyphenated to indicate that it is a particular emotional experience having its own induplicable quality, and not simply an instance of the general emotion, disappointment. Whatever the similarity, for purposes of classification, between disappointment at missing out on the cookies and, for example, disappointment in love, the two emotions are felt quite differently.)

In Chapter IV it was noted that all perception is accompanied by affect. It was also noted earlier in the present chapter that when the perception is of something quite familiar, the meaning of the perception is minimal, and the affect so slight as to be negligible.

Another way of putting this would be to say that our response to what is very familiar is habitual, and that habitual behavior is seldom attended by much conscious awareness, let alone feeling.

However, when what we perceive is not so familiar, and is yet perceived to be in some way relevant to our purposes or interests, the perception of it is meaningful in the full sense of the term. As we noted earlier, the meaning involved in such perception has reference to what is not yet perceived, but which may be perceived on the basis of what has already been perceived. In other words, the meaning in a perception involves an expectation about what might be perceived next, either as a function of a temporal change in events or of a clearer or fuller perception of what has already been perceived. The meaning with its expectation is an occurrence which inhibits habitual tendencies to respond. And at the same time, affect (minimally, a feeling of tension) is felt as a function of the expectation. I am speaking, now, of the general features of *any* experience. In the course of particular experiences which focus on particular things and events, affect is felt as one or another specific emotion.

Two matters need special emphasis at this point. First, what brings about the occurrence of meaning with its attendant expectation and affective quality is the perception of something unfamiliar enough to inhibit, arrest, or delay a tendency to make a habitual (or what is commonly called "unconscious") response. And second, the perception itself is *both* meaningful *and* affective at once. Perceptual experience is not turned this way and that to see whether it has any meaning, the way an entomologist examines a dead insect. Nor does the appearance of affect wait upon a deliberate determination of the relation of meaning to purpose. Neither perception, meaning, nor affect can occur in isolation; they are but different aspects of the same event, of a single psychological process.

It may help in clarifying the relationship between familiarity and unfamiliarity in perceptual experience to the arousal of affect if we consider a set of events common to the experience of most adults. Let us begin with what may be a bizarre example. Suppose that we handed the keys to our automobile to a friend who did not know how to drive, and said, "I feel an attack coming on —will you drive me to the hospital in a hurry?" We should expect his reaction to be one of utter confusion, helplessness, and frustration. This normally can be expected to result when one is called upon to respond to a situation with which he has no familiarity at all. This particular example will not occur frequently, however, because most male adults in the United States have acquired the skill of driving. But let us look at how this skill is acquired, for it is a typical (and often memorable) occasion for the arousal of strong affect.

The purpose of the driver-trainee is quite clear, and for this reason he experiences an enormous degree of affect when he first takes over the wheel. Despite what he has been told, and despite his careful observation of the instructor, he has been put into an extremely unfamiliar position. From behind the wheel he sees the street, sidewalks, buildings, pedestrians, and other cars—all of which he has seen before.[13] But now he is related to all these things in a new way. When for the first time he controls several thousand pounds of steel at 20 or 30 miles per hour, nearly everything in his perceptual field takes on the aspect (i.e., acquires the meaning) of a potential danger, a potential obstruction, a potential victim. New meanings virtually rain in on the driver-trainee from all directions, and affect is keenly felt (in this particular situation, tension may be paramount but other emotions—such as fear, anxiety and grim determination—are also involved). The first time one takes control of an automobile, then, is not a confrontation with the totally unfamiliar, but is at least an experience in which all familiar things take on an unfamiliar aspect. One is unusually conscious, for example, of where his feet are, and what they are doing. The affect typically aroused in such a situation is generally both diffuse and intense, often, so much so that it seriously interferes with what one hopes to accomplish.

But let us have a look at our driver-trainee a few lessons later (assuming he survived the first one). He is driving rather skillfully now, and he has acquired considerable confidence. But he is not yet what could be called an experienced driver. The world from the driver's seat is not yet an altogether familiar one. Consequently, although his driving *behavior* appears, from a neighboring car, to be quite like that of an experienced driver, there is an important, although covert, difference. For the trainee is still very deliberately thinking about the moves he is making and the moves he expects to make in the act of driving. He converses little with his passenger, and concentrates on the center line, on the car in front of him, on his rear-view mirror, etc. And there is another difference. He exhibits a trace of uncertainty from time to time, although for the most part the car responds as he expects it to. Given this slight, lingering uncertainty, each time he executes a successful maneuver, he experiences a marked satisfaction that is usually denied experienced drivers. Here, then, is a case typical of the arousal of affect in situations that are for the most part familiar, yet which contain enough of the unfamiliar and the unexpected to hold an individual's conscious attention and keep him from responding habitually. Perception is still marked by some tension—not enough to interfere with activity but enough to make possible a feeling of satisfaction (and sometimes exhilaration, in the present instance) in the expectation that events will be forthcoming as they have been foreseen.

Finally, let us take a ride with our former trainee several years later. As he drives, he reminisces about the past, occasionally glancing at us. We note that he adjusts his speed to other cars, slows down for signals, and continually adjusts his steering without consciously thinking about it. His driving has become so habitual that he can think and speak about other things. He is so used to driving that nearly every situation he confronts appears familiar. And in a situation of nearly total familiarity, no noticeable affect is aroused because meanings are not attended to; instead, perception is translated immediately into action.

We might summarize what has been said thus far about the conditions for the arousal of affect, so that we can see how the affective response to perceived form compares with other typical affective experiences. The four illustrations just examined extend along a continuum; at one end a situation is found to be extremely unfamiliar, and at the other end a situation is found so familiar that a habitual response is appropriate.

We tend to ignore or quickly pass over experiential cues that are almost wholly unfamiliar (as, for example, fellow passengers on a bus speaking to one another in a foreign language), although affect is rather intense and quite unpleasant if we are expected to respond appropriately to such cues. In situations where our interests and purposes are involved so that we both intend and expect to make at least relevant responses, a *great* degree of unfamiliarity arouses considerable affect. Most of it is felt to be unpleasant, since our expectations are so often unfulfilled. In situations that are *for the most part* familiar, affect is aroused but with considerably less intensity. And the fact that one is aware that most of his expectations will be fulfilled—although not, perhaps, precisely how or when they were expected to be—affords a certain confidence that renders the affect pleasant. When what is expected is delayed, affect increases; if it is delayed for very long, the affect will be felt as unpleasant. Finally, affect is not noticed at all in situations that are wholly familiar, that offer no surprises. For in such situations, nothing interferes with our tendency to make habitual responses. And in so doing, we need not attend to the immediate situation at all. Habitual actions allow us to consider other things that are not present to perception.

## AFFECTIVE RESPONSES
## TO FORM IN ART

Now let us return to situations in which form is perceived in a cue for experience. To simplify the discussion, let us take a situation in which form alone is presented—the beholding of a nonobjective painting, or a work of music.[14] How does the perception of such a cue arouse affect?

It is possible, at least in theory, to preceive the music as merely a random series of noises, and the painting as but an indiscriminate collection of haphazardly shaped colors. But the very peculiarity of talking this way is evidence enough that we do not so perceive such cues. In fact, whether or not any particular affect is aroused, we tend to perceive not individual, isolated noises and colors, but rather *relationships among* the noises and colors. That is, we perceive them as patterns.

Earlier it was said that the arousal of affect was a function of meaningful perception. Some people, obviously, experience affect on perceiving music and nonobjective paintings. But how is it possible for them to perceive such cues *meaningfully?* Where is the meaning? It cannot be in the isolated elements themselves; c-sharp and b-flat, yellow ochre and magenta obviously cannot have any referential meaning.[15] The meaning is not in each of the elements. Thus if it is perceptible anywhere, it must be in the pattern made up by the elements. For it has already been seen that cues of the sort under consideration do not refer to anything beyond themselves. Thus meaning must be found in the pattern.

When a pattern and nothing else is presented as a cue to experience, we are free either to ignore it or to attend to it. If we attend to it, what happens? It has already been noted that perception is not a matter merely of registering aspects of the environment camera fashion. To attend to some cue is to perceive meaning, to have expectations. What is expected of a pattern? At the very least, we expect it to continue. Once we perceive that a series of elements is related in a particular way (i.e., makes a pattern of some sort), we have expectations as to how it will proceed. This is not a matter of deliberate thought, of careful construction of inferences. It is direct and immediate, a part of the very perception of pattern. When we hear the first several notes of a familiar piece of music, say the ubiquitous "White Christmas," we expect the notes that will follow. But we make no inferences.

With respect to nonobjective paintings, matters are a bit more difficult to deal with, but the principle is the same since the perception of painting is as much a temporal affair as is the perception of music. There is, of course, a sense in which a painting is "seen" all at once, but this hardly does justice to the painter, let alone the viewer, if he should then wander off to "look" at the next painting. For what is seen instantaneously is but a vague impression of all that the painter has included in his picture. As one continues to look, and to look with discrimination, an increasingly greater number of nuances of color, shape, and line begin to appear (depending, of course, on the success of the painter's efforts). What was said about expectation in music will now be seen to have relevance to the perception of painting. For the "first impression" of a nonobjective picture is meaningful in that it arouses expectations of what will be seen if one continues to look, and to look more closely. If the initial perception establishes a pattern, and one continues to perceive, he expects the pattern to continue in the supporting or secondary patterns, which are discernible only through more careful attention.[16]

We have just now been speaking of patterns, but by this term, form is meant. In cues like the ones under consideration— music and nonobjective paintings—they must either appear to be meaningless or they must be perceived as meaningful in the sense of exhibiting patterns, and cuing particular expectations, either about what will be presented next (as in music), or about what will be found next (in painting). To ask how it is possible for perceptions like these to be affective in quality, it is only necessary to recall what has already been said about the arousal of affect in the course of any normal everyday experience.

We will return to the four stages of familiarity noted earlier, and to simplify matters further, speak only of music. To many Western ears, Chinese music is wholly unfamiliar. Since it lacks the melodic and rhythmic patterns and harmonic elements to which he is accustomed, a Western listener finds no meaning in Chinese music. That is, listening to any part of it, he could not conceivably have any expectations about what might come next in the music. Under such circumstances, perception would very likely go unattended; ignoring the music, the listener would not be subject to any affect. But suppose he is attending a concert of Chinese music at the invitation of friends. He is not in a position to ignore it now. And it is quite likely that affect will be aroused, in the form of feelings of unresolved tensions, confusion, and mild frustration. Had our listener been so foolish as to tell his friends how much he enjoyed Chinese music, so that they might ask his opinion of it at the intermission, it is quite likely that a feeling of frustration bordering on despair might dominate his perception of the music.

Let us examine the affective responses to music at our second stage of familiarity, and imagine a listener to whom the term "classical" music means the romantic symphonies of the nineteenth century: Beethoven, Brahms, Tchaikovsky. How will he respond to the baroque music of the seventeenth and eighteenth centuries? Here is a case where there is some familiarity with the melodic patterns and harmonic elements. But our listener is unfamiliar with the steady rhythm, the instrumental texture, the predominating contrapuntal sounds, and what appear to him to be rather monotonous dynamics in comparison with the swelling crescendos reached by the full orchestral compositions of the nineteenth century. Given what our listener *is* familiar with—melodic and harmonic patterns fundamental to nearly all European music—he *does* have expectations of what will come next: the music is meaningful to him. But what *actually* comes next hardly ever seems to come as he expected. The full orchestra never comes booming through for emphasis; there seems to be no relieving change of pace; no quiet pauses for the orchestra to gather up its energy, so to speak, and expend it in a crashing finale. And for all his familiarity with the melodic patterns, the music continually disturbs him by presenting several different melodies at once. Given his accustomed habits of perceiving melody in nineteenth century symphonic music (or indeed, in contemporary popular music), he makes an effort to block out the counterpoint and to hear only what he takes to be "the" melody. From what has been said, there would seem to be little question that our listener is experiencing the arousal of affect. And because what is familiar occurs in so unfamiliar a setting, because the listener's expectations are so frequently unfulfilled, and so often not even aroused, it would seem reasonable to expect that the affect would for the most part be felt as unpleasant.

At the next level of familiarity, consider a listener who enjoys the music of Bach, and is exposed for the first time to a concerto by Vivaldi, whose music was composed in a style similar to that of Bach's. Not only will Vivaldi's harmonic and melodic patterns appear familiar, but so will his use of rhythm, counterpoint, dynamics, and instrumentation. Yet Vivaldi is decidedly not Bach. There is expectation but not precise prediction. Vivaldi varies his melodic themes differently; his use of strings has a different texture. Thus the music is quite meaningful to our listener, and most of his expectations as to what will come next are fulfilled. Not fulfilled *exactly* as he expects, but nonetheless fulfilled. Hence his familiarity (with what is called the *style* of the music) gives him confidence in perceiving the formal pattern that is presented, and his confidence allows him to await the forthcoming formal elements with a tension felt as pleasant anticipation, and to feel them, as they arrive, as satisfying resolutions of those tensions. Affect is aroused, then, and it is felt as agreeable or enjoyable.

Our final case is that of what might be called nearly total familiarity. Consider a symphonic musician exposed to the semiclassical arrangements of a popular orchestra—say, that of Andre Kostelanetz. The melodies employed are wholly familiar, the harmonies standardized, and the rhythm and dynamics are paced according to a much used formula. For this listener, everything about the total musical pattern comes *just* as expected. There are no surprises, unexpected nuances, or developments that might delay or inhibit response tendencies. Hence the listener responds habitually to the music, which means that he no longer attends to what he is perceiving. Literally speaking, he no longer hears the music. This kind of listener, exposed to this kind of music, is not subject to arousal of affect at all. He will, in fact, be disposed to talk or to do something else when confronted by such music, which then recedes unobtrusively into the background. The unobtrusiveness of music piped into restaurants depends for its effect on this phenomenon.

## THE POTENTIAL WITHIN FORM
## FOR AFFECTIVE AROUSAL:
## CRITICS AND CRITICISM

On the basis of the foregoing, it should be clear that a *sine qua non* for the perception of form is the degree of familiarity the perceiver has with the cue that is presented to him. The cue must be fairly familiar. If it is too novel or if it is too familiar, he will not perceive form at all. In the former case, affect—if it is even aroused—will be felt as uncomfortable; in the latter case, affect will probably not be aroused at all. But familiarity is not the only condition for perception of form. The other condition is, for all practical purposes, a function of the cue itself. Commonly, we would say that *it* must have form. More accurately, we should say that the arrangement of its elements should be such as to make the perception of their pattern (or form) relatively easy. In what follows, we will, for simplicity's sake, refer to the form *of* the cue, although this is not intended to indicate any inherent property independent of a perceiver.

We have already seen that any cue for experience may be perceived as having form. If the perception of a forest or a city street is aesthetic in quality, it is clearly a matter of the viewer's having been able to attend to the formal aspects of what is before him. Surely no attempt was made to put formal qualities *into* those cues. But works of art are deliberately planned with formal qualities in mind. How, then, shall we tell whether form is "in" the work of art—that is, whether the pattern formed by the elements of the work make it relatively easy for a beholder to perceive form?

The voluminous literature on this topic goes by the name of criticism—literary, musical, artistic, etc. Whether and to what extent form is present in a work of art is a matter normally referred to an expert—a critic. The judgments of the critic are founded on his experience with artistic styles to which a particular work under consideration is related, and on his ability to discriminate how, and how successfully, elements are related to one another.[17] Thus the critic looks for harmonies, contrasts, repetitions, unity and variety, rhythm, balance, etc., within the perceived relations, and he may explicitly relate these identifiable features both to the arousal of affect and to his judgment of the value of the work in question.[18]

It is beyond the scope of the present discussion to ask how critics arrive at the discriminations and judgments they make. They disagree with one another on this matter as well as on their assessments of particular works of art. Yet agreement among critics is striking in comparison to the generally diffuse judgments made by the public. It is not by any means clear, of course, whether a critic has any greater sensitivity to elements of form than does the public in general. Many a layman has been aware of aesthetic qualities in his natural environment of which critics are quite unaware. However, what a critic does have that is lacking to most laymen is vast experience in discriminating the features of works of art, and a willingness to take them for what they are, rather than expecting them to contain referential meaning. Given these credentials, it would seem reasonable to rely on the consensus of critics or connoisseurs if one wished to find out the degree to which a particular work of art had form. But it may not be beside the point to find out whether any given critic is, in fact, a connoisseur, and is competent to make the sorts of judgments we are seeking.

While the attempt to assess a critic's sensitivity to form has been the object of much effort, it is doomed to a certain circularity. For, since form is not literally *in* the object, we cannot simply ask whether he is able to "discover" it. Instead, we should have to ask how a critic's assessment of formal qualities compares to that of some other critic's, and we should then find ourselves having to ask by what criteria the other critic was judged to be competent. In other words, testing one's ability to discriminate formal elements is always a relative affair (more defensible, perhaps, in asssessing the abilities of laymen or children in comparison to critics). It ends, finally, at the point where a critic being tested is likely to claim that the critic against whose judgments his own discriminations are being compared is not, in fact, as competent a judge as he. On the matter of sensitivity to form, then, it may be safest to assume in the absence of contrary evidence, that the critics are on a par with one another.[19]

But it is possible to test the competence of critics with respect to the extent of their relevant experience with works of art, and with respect to the extent to which they attend to formal dimensions of such works. For if one attends to form and is able to draw on a rich background of familiarity in a given style (of music, for example), his predictions as to what will come next, after a given passage within that style has been presented, should be quite accurate. To test for such accuracy should not be especially difficult. A competent critic should be able to select, of several alternative passages, the one which is most consistent with the music which has just been played prior to presentation of the alternatives.[20]

# SUMMARY: THE CONDITIONS
# FOR AFFECTIVE RESPONSES TO FORM

At the moment, we might seem to be a long way from school situations and attempts to promote learning, but it will be seen that all that has been said about aesthetic quality in experience is extremely pertinent to teaching in the schools. By way of reminder, it will be recalled that the sort of lecture that makes learning possible has much in common with art. The present inquiry into the aesthetic, in illuminating how art has an impact on people, will also show how a successful lecture gains its impact. This and other methods of schooling will receive more direct consideration in subsequent chapters. For the moment, and before going on to consider why people take the trouble to seek the sort of affective arousal that has been described, I shall summarize the foregoing discussion.

Two related topics have been under examination: the conditions under which form is perceived, and how such perception arouses affect. The perception of form and the arousal of affect are not two separate events, but one. Affect can, of course, be aroused independent of one's perceiving form, but one cannot perceive form at all without experiencing affect. The conditions under which form is perceived are, first, familiarity on the part of the beholder with the range or class of experiential cues of which a given cue is a member; and second, a posture on the part of the beholder to suspend, at least partially, his tendency to look for referential meanings or practical or cognitive outcomes. Also relevant to the readiness or ease with which form is perceived is the extent to which the perceived cue is formally organized or patterned.

The affect that is part of such perception is a function of the meaning of that perception. The meaning is apprehended in terms of what is expected to be perceived next on the basis of the patterns already perceived. And since the meaning is, in fact, an expectation, the expectation is felt as affect when it is not immediately fulfilled *just as* expected— when it is arrested, inhibited, or delayed in any way. To fill out this summary, a brief comment may be appended to each of the factors that are conditions for the perception of form.

If an individual is unfamiliar with a given range of cues, or wholly familiar with it, he cannot perceive form and to that extent he cannot apprehend the cue aesthetically. It matters little whether we speak of works of art or everyday experience. In art, the crucial factor is style; if one is wholly unfamiliar with it, he cannot apprehend aesthetic quality in even the greatest masterpiece within that style. When one is familiar with a given style, the degree of aesthetic impact or affective arousal will be a function of the extent to which the work in question is perceived to differ from what is typical of that style. It might be noted in passing that the history of stylistic change in Western art forms bears out this contention. In general, new styles have evolved from what began as merely variations within the framework of the old style. It could be hypothesized that these stylistic changes were undertaken to keep the conventions of any particular style from becoming too familiar, hence incapable of arousing affect.

Form cannot, of course, be perceived if one's attention is directed wholly to the referential meaning or practical import of the cue under consideration. To attend only to what an experience means in terms of its practical or cognitive consequences is to ignore its perceptual and aesthetic impact. There are times, obviously, when one has no choice but to apprehend experience practically. An avalanche may be lovely, but one had better get out of its way. Yet we have a tendency to treat all experience as if its consequences were as momentous and as equally portentous as a crashing avalanche. It would probably be beneficial if people attended to the fact that most forthcoming consequences of any present experience are no more important than the present experience itself. For continually to look to the future is to denigrate the present. And when that future comes, it, too, will be but a "mere" present—valueless, presumably, except for what *it* portends. The relevance of this for schooling cannot be overemphasized. Teachers and parents have their eyes on the future, to which the present is but a mere stepping stone. Yet youngsters live rather fully in the here and now. The teacher may organize what he thinks will be a learning experience wholly around what he hopes will be its future value. Yet most of the learners will be directly affected only by its felt quality here and now. So long as the two are so far apart, the teacher's efforts will be no more than a tilting at windmills.

Finally, the nature of the cue itself greatly inhibits or facilitates the perception of form. With respect to natural objects and events, whether form is perceived is largely a matter of the beholder's attitudes and experience. Yet of all the cues that are presented to one's experience, perhaps what is regularly uniform is the most inhibitory to perceiving form. Because of the uniformity of rows of identical homes in a housing development, the ticking of a clock, certain types of popular music, or the experience of working at an assembly line, they become quickly and thoroughly familiar. We then ignore them (or call them monotonous, if we have reason to expect something more) and attend to other matters. By way of contrast, works of art present occasions for deliberate attention to form. And this brings us to our last question about form: why are works of art produced and sought after at all? What is it about the arousal of affect in perceiving form that is found satisfying?

## THE ROLE IN EMOTIONAL LIFE OF AFFECTIVE RESPONSES TO FORM

The question of the worth or utility of affective responses to aesthetic form has raised much speculation, since pleasure gained in perceptual experience, unlike eating or procreation, does not appear to be a necessity for life. Some thinkers have taken pains to point this out, assigning such experience to the leisure one has after he has attended to life's necessities;[21] others have assumed that aesthetic satisfactions must function as a sort of substitute for the necessities that one cannot obtain.[22] Yet the very ubiquity of aesthetic qualities in experience seems to belie what appears to be their gratuitous nature, and other thinkers have expended much effort to show that these qualities, too, are necessities of life. Herbert Read, for example, has suggested that the perception of form satisfies a quest for order and security that cannot easily be found in the disorderly, unpredictable, and threatening world of events. He quotes Wilhelm Worringer to the effect that in art, which organizes perceptual experience, men are able to embody fixed conceptual images that for a time replace the casual and undependable images of everyday perception. His conclusion is that men would find life too harrowing without art, and without being able to preceive form.[23]

Such a view of the perception of form puts it on a par, almost, with the water that is sought by the thirsty nomad. It may not be necessary to view such experience as being quite so crucial, yet we need not lean the other way and conceive it merely as an entertainment. Aristotle, for example, was content to note how men gain pleasure from beholding, and perhaps in a sense identifying with, the graceful and competent actions of others. And he suggested that rhythms and tones (which we have been calling form) are also movement, as are human actions. Hence such rhythms, such formal elements, should be intrinsically satisfying.[24]

John Dewey's views on the role of the perception of form are an expansion on Aristotle's speculations, adding details without opposing them. Dewey speaks of the rhythms not only of graceful action, but of all of nature:

> . . . sooner or later, the participation of man in nature's rhythms, a partnership much more intimate than is any observation of them for purposes of knowledge, induced him to impose rhythm on changes where they did not appear. The apportioned reed, the stretched string and taut skin rendered the measures of action conscious through song and dance. . . . Because rhythm is a universal scheme of existence, underlying all realization of order in change, it pervades all the arts. . . .[25]

The linking of man's inner life with the rhythms of nature acts as a bridge between Western thought and many Eastern conceptions of art and life. A view common to Hindu metaphysics, that "the unity of Being becomes the rhythm and harmony (Beauty) in the process of Becoming,"[26] may sound mysterious to Western ears, but the same thought has produced ideas quite akin to those of the American instrumentalist noted above:

> In man's inner life, characterized by the interplay of his impulses and his emotions marking the rhythm of his harmony or disharmony with the environment, man unconsciously or deliberately seeks order in a harmonious and integral existence. Out of the need of this perennial inner adjustment art is born, with rhythm as its heart and core, the ultimate condition of its forms and patterns.[27]

The language of discussions like the foregoing is suggestive, and has great immediate appeal. It *sounds* eminently sensible to point out that man is a natural animal, participating in the rhythms of nature, and that he therefore naturally seeks perceptual experience consonant with those rhythms. Yet it may be of help if we attempt an explanation, in language consonant with our earlier discussion of affective arousal, explaining why it is that men seek the perception of form.

To say that people seek to perceive form is to say that they seek the concomitantly experienced affect. While the problem of what motivates behavior is far too involved for a full scale examination here, it is worth noting that evidence seems to support the conclusion that behavior is not simply a consequence of a physiological need to reduce drives. Rather, organisms at a wide range of phylogentic levels do appear to act in order to achieve positive affect—that is, pleasure, in more familiar terms. Even the lowly rat has been induced to learn with a reward of non-nutritive, but sweet-tasting saccharine. Since the saccharine could not possibly have reduced any tissue need, experimenters concluded that rats performed as they did in order to experience sweet taste.[28]

In the light of a great deal of evidence of the sort noted above, and especially in view of so much otherwise inexplicable human behavior, P. T. Young concluded that the

> elicitation of the consummatory response is more critical as a *primary* reinforcing factor in instrumental learning than the drive-reduction that is subsequently achieved.[29]

Young's term, "consummatory response," corresponds roughly to what has been called here the "arousal of positive affect." Young goes on to conclude that "neurobehavioral patterns are organized to relieve distress and to enhance (heighten, prolong) enjoyment."[30]

Under what conditions is affect felt to be pleasant, such that one would actively seek to find or institute those conditions? We have already related affective arousal, and its felt quality, to the degree to which a cue, or stimulus situation, is both familiar and formally organized. But we can now generalize still further, not altering the conclusions of the earlier discussion, but bringing them into more unified focus.

In the previously discussed examples of the driver-trainee and of the music listener, the arousal of affect was seen to be related to the difference or discrepancy between what one expected and what he actually perceived. David McClelland and his collabora-tors, using the term adaption level to mean "that to which one is accustomed," have concisely summarized the generalizations drawn from those examples:

> Positive affect is the result of smaller discrepancies of a sen-sory or perceptual event from the adaptation level of the organ-ism; negative affect is the result of larger discrepancies.[31]

According to these authors, a pleasantness-unpleasantness curve could be plotted—not against the increasing intensity of a stimu-lus, but against the size of the discrepancy between what was expected (the adaptation level—i.e., what the organism was ac-customed to) and what was perceived. Size of discrepancy, of course, is analogous to what has been called here "degree of famil-iarity." We have noted that with increasing familiarity with a given perceptual cue, what was once affect changes to boredom. This phenomenon, too, is included in what McClelland calls an "affective arousal model" of motivation:

> affective reactions to discrepancies . . . appear maximally the first time the discrepancy occurs and with less intensity thereafter because the new experience automatically interacts with the adaptation level, changes it, and thereby reduces the discrepancy. Hence there is ultimate boredom or adaptation to pain or pleasure. . . .[32]

Just as, in becoming wholly familiar with the act of driving, we pay no more attention, and just as we cease to find emotional satisfaction in works of art with which we have become overfamiliar, so

> exactly confirming certain expectations produces boredom and a tendency to discontinue the act. . . .[33]

In discussing the fact that mild arousal (i.e., small discrepancy) may be attractive, but that strong arousal cued by the same stimulus situation may be felt as repellent, D. O. Hebb finds an explanation of why risk-taking, mild threat or fear, and puzzle- and problem-solving have positive motivating value up to a certain point, but tend to discourage effort beyond that point. Even more germane to the point presently under discussion, Hebb finds that this way of conceiving human behavior affords an explanation for what we have been calling the pleasurable affect aroused through the perception of form. For he appears willing to grant this as a type of (nonverbal) intellectual activity—activity which may be undertaken just for its affective value:

> we systematically underestimate the human need of intellectual activity . . . when we overlook the intellectual component in art and in games.[34]

The affective arousal consequent upon (or more accurately, integral with) small discrepancies of perceptual experience from expectations are the conditions that D. E. Berlyne cites as explanation of *any* activities pursued "for their own sake." Among such activities, Berlyne includes recreation, entertainment, idle curiosity, art, philosophy, and pure science.[35]

If we can accept as reasonable the opinions of the above investigators, it should not be difficult to see why art, as a deliberate effort to facilitate the perception of form, is so often associated with positive affect, and is consequently so often sought after. Everyday life is not merely a series of habitual acts and nothing more. The day is full of surprises, if for the most part little ones. Each surprise is occasioned by the appearance of the unexpected—a discrepancy in perceptual experience, so to speak, from what was anticipated. Each of these discrepancies has its affective aspect, but the affect is only occasionally felt as satisfying; and at that, the satisfaction usually lies in the import of experience for the future —that is, in its referential, instrumental, consequential dimensions.

The reason why the arousal of affect in daily experience so seldom follows a pattern that might be felt as satisfying (apart from the instrumental value of any given experience) is the very adventitiousness of its occurrence. Affect may be aroused, but the press of other events and concerns may wholly prevent its resolution, or it may simply be dissipated. As a complex but nonetheless typical example of the first instance, many of us can recall going to a social event with expectations of meeting a number of unfamiliar and potentially interesting people. As the affair begins, we mix with a variety of groups, begin to find out a little about those in attendance, and become interested in how different members of different groups are related to one another. Just as our interest is mounting, we are nailed in a corner by someone who insists on relating the history of his life and his future plans. Our expectations of further social intercourse are left hanging. We experience a palpable sinking feeling as affect once aroused, bumping head-on into an irrelevant event, goes unresolved.

Instances of the dissipation of affect typically occur when we watch sporting events. In a football game, the effectiveness of the quarterback in avoiding tacklers as he circles back and forth trying to find an unguarded receiver to whom he can throw the ball is a cue that invariably arouses affect in spectators. We expect the quarterback to throw the ball, but his evasive tactics delay fulfillment of our expectations. The affect—and the expectations—are intensified when the quarterback executes a long, spiraling, perfectly aimed forward pass. But the affect is quickly dissipated, and experienced as disappointing, when the potential receiver drops the ball. Needless to say, affect experienced in such a situation is strongly colored by the extent to which we hope the team will win. Perhaps a clearer case of this sort of affective arousal occurs when we watch short films of sporting events in a motion picture newsreel.

Finally, affect aroused in everyday affairs is often resolved by events quite unrelated to those that originally occasioned the affect. Consider a department store clerk who works on a commission basis, anticipating selling an expensive suit of clothes. Arousal is high as the customer hesitates, but when he finally decides to look elsewhere and walks out of the store, the clerk may resolve his affect by heaping verbal abuse on the stockboy. When the conditions that resolve affect are different in kind from those that aroused it, the total experience is not normally felt as very satisfying.

A little later on we will examine the referential elements that can appear in works of art, but for now we can see how a work of art, taken simply as a formal organization of perceptual elements, differs from everyday affairs in its capacity to arouse, inhibit, and finally resolve affect. The difference is not, of course, one of kind, but rather one of degree.

In the sort of artistic cue that we have up to now been considering—music, for example, or nonobjective painting—affect is altogether a function of the perception of form. Hence the *same* cue (i.e., what is perceived as formal organization—a pattern) *induces* an expectation, *delays* or inhibits its resolution by presenting other elements which are discrepant—that is, which does not meet the expectation, and finally *resolves* it by presenting what was expected in a meaningful way. It is meaningful because the elements resolving the expectation as well as the affect are intrinsically related to what originally aroused it. In music, for example, the presentation of sounds related in a particular way cues expectation. The succeeding sounds may not be just what was expected, and the unexpected obstacle or discrepancy arouses affect. But eventually— and as we had anticipated—further sounds fulfill the original expectation (even if not *just* as expected) and resolve affect.

Thus the perception of form, as it is cued by a work of art, can fulfill all the criteria for the arousal of positive affect. It should not be surprising that those for whom the criteria are fulfilled will take pains to seek such perception, if it makes any sense to say that the perceived potentiality for positive affect in an experiential cue is in fact a motivating force in behavior. Those who can perceive form in works of art are thereby enabled to achieve pleasantly felt affect in a single, coherent, integrated experience. It would be accurate to say that in the perception of art one may find deliberately instituted, and in a heightened, emphasized form, a quality of experience that occurs only occasionally and by chance in the course of everyday affairs. For in the latter we are not always able to attend to formal qualities, and the cues themselves are often disorganized, chaotic, and accidental. With respect to art, we are prepared to take *to* the experience a posture of openness to immediately perceptible formal qualities, and we find the cue itself deliberately organized to make the perception of form worthwhile, interesting, or relatively easy.

Finally, experience in which aesthetic qualities are apprehended is experience valued here and now—not for what it may lead to, but for what it is. To value such experience is an antidote to the sort of practical and instrumental attitudes that denigrate the present and look only to the future. And such attitudes are common in mid-twentieth century America, where economic life is so influential in teaching us to ask, even in areas irrelevant to economic concerns, "For what can I cash it in?" Perhaps in America the lavish and grotesque entertainment industry, the unique penchant for drinking hard liquor, and the currently changing attitudes toward sexual experience, all bespeak a sort of desperate effort to salvage the present, to find something in it immediately enjoyable.

Indeed, positive affect can be found in the present through

frenzy, fantasy, distraction, and "escape." But it has been charged that these are means less calculated to make the present immediately enjoyable so much as they are intended to hide from view a future without promise. And as this latter intention is fufilled, the present, too, is lost from sight. For the normal human response to any experience is to take it both for what it immediately is, and for what it might lead to. To achieve success in subduing one aspect of experience—either its present value or its future import—is to distort it beyond recognition as human and, in so doing, severely to distort human personality. There are serious dangers in attempting to render the present valuable through excessive fantasy and frenzy, just as there are in the sort of incessant activity that continually puts off present satisfaction for the sake of a future that never materializes.

The arousal of affect, the stirring of emotion felt as pleasurable, satisfying, or absorbing, through the perception of form in experiential cues, is a natural way of apprehending experience. It is sought after because the present is not effaced but rather highlighted and fully attended to.[36] It is, in short, during the course of such experience that we feel most fully alive. And it is such experience that is best characterized as being aesthetic in quality.

## THE UNION OF AFFECTIVE RESPONSES AND REFERENTIAL MEANINGS

Although we have been attending only to the form of immediately perceived cues, we have repeatedly emphasized that seldom, if ever, is experience wholly without future import, without some freight of meaning that is not limited to the boundaries of what is immediately presented to experience. While we have spoken at length of affect simply in terms of an excitation, an arousal, affect as it occurs in human experience always seeks some reference point, always has import beyond the mere excitation, always is, in fact, experienced as some emotion, however nameless it may be. We do not experience simply excitement, simply tension, or simply resolution. Rather, we experience *something* as exciting, we feel tense *about* something, and *something* is resolved. The perception of form in human experience is never "pure," but always comes clothed in a particular emotion. The point can be illustrated by referring again to what is known (mistakenly, as we shall see) as "purely formal" art.

Arrangements of sounds, as in music, and arrangements of shapes and colors, as in nonobjective painting, arouse affect, but the affect is never simply that alone. It is neither accidental nor irrelevant to the work in question that we say the music sounds ponderous, or portentous, or joyous; or that the shapes look relaxing, or dramatic, or humorous. For the very act of perception itself is meaningful, and meaning is inconceivable without reference to something recognizable. Music need not imitate or refer to babbling brooks, and painting need not represent or refer to human figures or natural objects, in order to be meaningful. We have seen that meaning is tied to expectations, and expectations in nonobjective art works refer to formal patterns. Yet a formal pattern wholly devoid of content could not even be imagined. It is always germane to ask, "*What is it* that has a pattern?" To answer, "Just sounds," or "Just colors," is inadequate, for it begs the question, "The sounds (or colors) of what?" Hence it is the case that the sounds and colors of "formal" or nonobjective art works are meaningful only insofar as they call forth or are expressive of particular emotions (for emotions *are* recognizable members of the community of human meanings), whether those emotions are clear-cut enough to be nameable. Unless such works have an emotional impact, they are quite literally meaningless, and they have failed artistically. In *these* terms, it *does* make sense to ask of a work of music or nonobjective painting, "What's it supposed to mean?" The answer, "Nothing: it simply *is*; it simply presents certain relations of sounds or colors to one another," is genuinely absurd, if not presumptuous. *What music or nonobjective painting means, as a function of the way it is formally organized, is the emotion that it expresses.* Some examples will serve to make the point clearer.

It is not customary to ask, upon entering a room, "What does the rug mean?" It is not customary just because we expect a patterned rug to mean whatever the room itself means. If it does not, our perceptual experience is jarring: The rug *looks* out of place. We will amplify this a bit, since the triviality of the example belies the considerable human import of what is under consideration.

The very fact that it is inconceivable to characterize a rug as sad points up the fact that rugs *are* emotionally expressive. That the range of emotions is limited is probably why we class rugs (and chairs and pottery) as minor, or decorative arts. Yet a rug may *look* "homely," or "sumptuous," or "warm," or "lively" and each of these adjectives describes a way of feeling. We do not expect to find a rug that is bright and lively in a study, or one that is sumptuous in a children's playroom, or one that is homely in an expensive restaurant. For such juxtapositions produce perceptual conflict: incompatible, jarring feelings. Rooms have particular functions, and we associate particular feelings with those functions. If the furnishings of the rooms are expressive of other kinds of feelings, the result is immediately and directly felt perceptual discomfort.

All human artifacts and all natural objects are potentially meaningful in that they may be perceived as expressive of how we feel when we confront them and use them. The function of a rug, a building, a pot, or any artifact is the focus of its perceptual impact. Hence:

> function, far from being outside the aesthetic realm, is the very theme, the central subject matter of applied art.[37]

That it is possible to ignore the emotional import of function in the design of artifacts, and thus to standardize the appearance of objects, whatever their use, is only to indicate that it is possible for those who use the artifacts to learn not to attend to perceptual experience—to approach those aspects of life, in a literal sense of the term, anaesthetically. Experience so perceived is without immediate meaning, hence without immediate value. Insofar as objects of use are so perceived, our lives are focused increasingly on futures, and the value of the present is lost. In the most generous light, this is to say we become, increasingly, practical men and women. But when we have reached the zenith of practicality, when all of our meanings point away from the present, then we shall probably have ceased to be men and women at all. We will have truly become rational animals. But unfortunately, animals.[38]

Our consideration of the abstract pattern in a rug points up the claim that even works of art which purport only to exhibit "pure" form do in fact succeed or fail as art only insofar as they are perceived to be emotionally expressive. The rug was a rather humble, but nonetheless relevant, instance of a work with "pure" form—i.e., that was not made to suggest or represent anything other than itself. Yet what is true of emotional expressiveness in the rug is even more true of works of music or nonrepresentational painting, for their potential range of expressiveness is broader and deeper.

Piet Mondrian's painting "Trafalgar Square" is a case in point, for of all modern painters, Mondrian's work is said to be paradigmatic of "pure" form. "Trafalgar Square" is a grey rectangle broken by some horizontal and vertical black lines of nearly equal width. Some of the rectangles made by the intersecting of the lines, near the perimeter of the painting, are filled in with black and the primary colors, yellow, red, and blue. That is all. But one does not successively register these visual relations, evaluate them, and then appreciate them. If perception is meaningful at all, it is affective in quality, and the affect is felt as a particular sort of emotion. Of *what* emotion it is difficult to say, for feelings like these have no precise names. But it might be safe to say in this case that one feels a certain balance, and even stateliness, in the forms presented. It is even possible that this feeling is not unlike the way the painter felt about Trafalgar Square itself. If this seems like mere speculation, compare "Trafalgar Square" to the same painter's "Broadway Boogie-Woogie." In this latter painting, the lines themselves are not black, but are instead made up of juxtaposed squares and rectangles of colors, in which reds and yellows create a predominant tonality. The forms are different (within the same stylistic limits), to be sure, but what should be equally clear is the fact that the perception of the two paintings *feels* different. Of course, if these

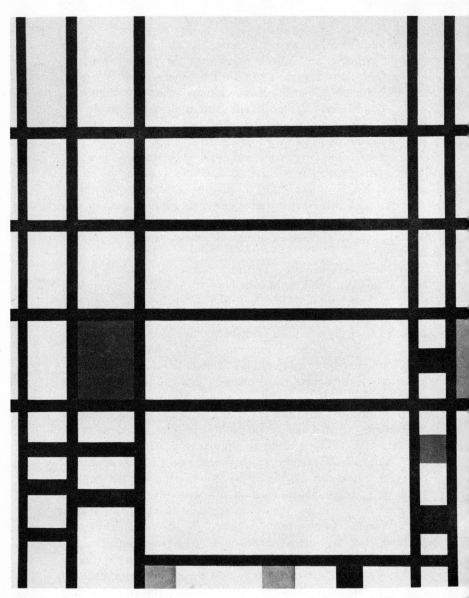

*Trafalgar Square* (1939-43) by PIET MONDRIAN, Collection of The Museum of Modern Art, New York, Gift of William A. M. Burden (the donor retaining a life interest)

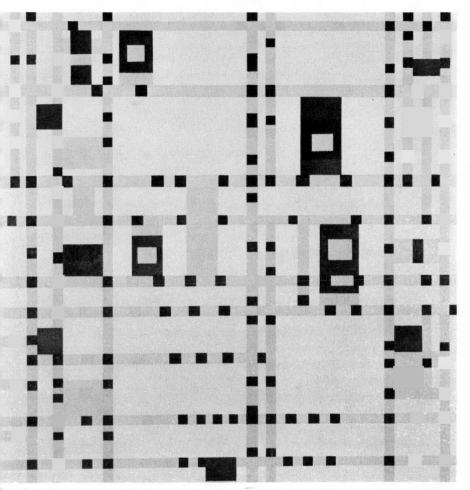

*Broadway Boogie Woogie* (1942-43) by PIET MONDRIAN, Collection of The Museum of Modern Art, New York

differences are not apparent on viewing the two paintings (as they may not be to some inexperienced viewers), no amount of argument will be convincing.

The same considerations will apply to other arts. That in Western culture certain kinds of musical passages are appropriated to certain kinds of feelings can be demonstrated by attending to the background music in a motion picture. When the heroine is on her deathbed, it would be an emotional outrage to play "Pop Goes the Weasel." Nor does Franck's D Minor Symphony appropriately accompany the antics of Laurel and Hardy.[39]

## THE ROLE OF SIGNS IN ART

The perception of form is always affective in quality, and, when we attend to the affect, it always has a particular emotional tone to it. Works of art are intended deliberately to induce and organize, arouse and resolve such feelings, and in this they may differ from the ordinary situations of life, where perceptual affect normally has a future or a distant reference, as well as an immediate one. Yet the future reference of daily experience may give greater force and depth to its emotional impact. One's work or one's children may be satisfying in an immediate sense, but they may be even more satisfying (or perhaps disturbing) because they are also perceived in terms of what they will lead to, of what they will become. If art holds the immediate moment in charmed suspension, life moves on. Yet the emotional impact of art, too, can be made more specific and more forcible when the forms perceived are at the same time suggestive of recognizable objects or events, values or beliefs, that exist in the world of daily affairs.

Consider again Charles Burchfield's "Black Houses." Thus far we have discussed the painting only in terms of the shapes and colors which constitute its painted surface. Yet obviously these elements have been so arranged as to suggest two houses in a particular setting. As noted before, this latter element is far from irrelevant to the aesthetic effect of the painting, despite the claims of formalist theories. It is no use pretending what the painting would be like or how one would react to it if it did not suggest houses, for if it did not it would simply be a different painting. More important, human perception is not normally a matter of discerning shapes and colors first, and then "cognitively" identifying them *as* the shapes and colors of these or those recognizable objects. We see shapes and colors immediately *as* particular, familiar things. Thus there is no interval of time in perceiving "Black Houses" in which one engages in some process of identification of "matching" (i.e., of the pictorial elements with some remembered visual concept of "house"). Hence the fact that the shapes and colors represent houses is neither an additional item of knowledge *added* to our original perception of the painting, nor is it some detachable part of the perception that can be dispensed with without alteration of the elements of which it is made. To perceive the painting at all is to see the shapes and colors *of* the representations of houses. Since the houses cannot be banished from the perception, and since the perception, insofar as it apprehends form, is aesthetic in quality, the perception of the formal elements *as* houses is a total experience having aesthetic quality.

The arrangement of Mr. Burchfield's colors into the shapes of houses constitutes the introduction of signs into the painting. Now a sign is "something which stands to somebody for something in some respect or capacity."[40] In that a sign stands to someone *for* something *other than itself*, a sign always has a referential function. In a manner of speaking, it points away from itself; it directs the attention of its beholder *from* consideration of itself *to* a consideration of whatever it stands for. The signs of practical discourse usually serve this and no other function. If I *point* to a ship sinking offshore, I want to direct your attention to the sinking ship, not to my pointing finger. And if I tell you, "The ship is sinking in the sea!" and you say to me, "My, but the sibilancy of your language is admirable," I shall think you are at least decadent, if not mad. For in this case "The ship is sinking in the sea" is intended to function only as a sign, and to have no intrinsic or immediate value of its own. It is neither to my pointing finger nor to the sounds of my words that I wish you to direct attention. Rather, I wish you to attend to the event to which the pointing and the words refer: the sinking of the ship.

Since signs do function in this way, we are confronted with a problem when we consider the role of signs in experience that has aesthetic quality. We have said that such experience is not referential. Yet if it incorporates signs we find ourselves attending to matters outside or beyond the immediate experience itself. Not only does aesthetic quality apprehended in daily affairs nearly always contain signs (or have sign-content), but even works of art, fashioned deliberately for the elicitation of aesthetic quality, are often full of signs, as in the iconic signs of "Black Houses," or as we nearly always find in symbolic form in poetry or literature. But when signs occur in aesthetic contexts—i.e., in contexts where perception itself has immediate, intrinsic value—they function in a peculiar way. We might take a closer look at how such signs function.

Consider a hypothetical viewer of "Black Houses." The colors arranged into the representation of houses function as signs. Suppose our viewer says or thinks to himself, "Aha, the houses look quite run down. Perhaps this is a site for urban renewal." He might then go on to consider the expense, or the social value of urban renewal. Or suppose he reacts by thinking, "So! Just like the house I was brought up in. How old was I then? Twelve—or was it thirteen?" And he might then recall how he used to play hide-and-seek under the porch.

Our viewer has not apprehended the painting aesthetically. It is he who is the object of the formalist's scorn, and not without good reason. For his reactions to "Black Houses" were no different from what anyone's reaction might be to an unplanned snapshot of a couple of houses. This viewer has simply ignored the quality of his perceptual experience, and has utilized the representative element in the painting as a *reminder* of other events, other ideas, other values. The houses in the painting have, for him, functioned *only* as *referential signs* carrying him directly from the perception of the signs to what, for him, the signs referred to. Needless to say, had it been the painter's intent for his picture to function in this way, he might as well (and with far less effort) have hung a photograph on the wall, or even the words, "two dark old houses." When any experienced event functions in this way—whether or not it bears the label, work of art, it has not been experienced aesthetically. And, it might be added, it is in virtue of the posture a beholder takes toward events that makes it possible for such humble things as trash cans to elict aesthetic quality in experience, whereas it is equally possible for a portrait by Rembrandt to fail in this respect.

If a sign functions *only* referentially, experience cannot be said to have aesthetic quality. But the function of aesthetically perceived signs is unique. They make us *aware* of things, events, ideas, beliefs, or values that are not literally *in* the art work, while at the same time *allowing our attention to remain focused on the formal elements that are the bearers of the sign.* Aesthetic quality in experience is a function of perception, and indissolubly tied to it. Hence any meaningful sign that functions within experience which has aesthetic quality must allow a beholder to incorporate those meanings *within* perception itself: in an immediate, presentational, non-discursive way. To distinguish them from the functioning of referential signs that occur in practical affairs, we shall call these *reflexive signs.* The term is adopted to indicate that such signs do not simply refer, but at the same time they *refer back* to the formal elements of which they are made.

It is possible to speak of the quality of affect involved in the perception of form, and of the quality of affect involved in the recognition of meaning in a sign. It is not, of course, a matter of *experiencing* two separate emotional conditions at once, but rather a matter of distinguishing, for purposes of analysis, two aspects of a single experience. How do these two aspects relate to each other as they occur in a single experience that has aesthetic quality?

In everyday experience, most of us are aware when form suits its content, and when it does not. We expect a big man with a deep voice to have a forceful personality. If he does not, we find it jarring. This would be a case of a denial of expectations founded on a perceptual cue. The case is the same with the perception of utilitarian objects. As noted before, the discomfort we would feel at finding bright colors and lively patterns in a room normally used for the conduct of very sober affairs (say, a funeral home) is another case of form being inappropriate to content. But perhaps matters become most frustrating when form and sign-content are incompatible in works of art, for in these cases we *expect* to find compatibility. When it does not occur, the viewer may be quite confused and believe that the problem lies in himself rather than in what confronts him. A century after it was painted, we may chuckle patronizingly at the English pre-Raphaelite painter Holman Hunt's

"Light of the World," in which a very serious sign, the figure of Christ, is shown carrying a lantern and looking for all the world like a night watchman roused from his sleep. But when such incompatibilities in form and content occur in art that is contemporary, it is less easy to tell where the trouble lies. One hundred years from now, antiquarians may chuckle at the celebrated motion picture *Cleopatra;* but the public for whom it was made must have wondered just how to react when the heroine, who has been laboriously presented as a highly intelligent, self-confident, regal lady, unaccountably behaves like the most gross sort of fishwife after a presumed rejection by her lover.[41]

It should be noted in this connection that in the hands of a skillful artist, a seeming incompatibility between the emotional impact of form and sign-content can be used to heighten the total impact of the work. An example can be found in the work of the painter James Ensor, whose figures, signs of serious religious and political themes, wear masks reminiscent of circus clowns. In these instances, the grinning masks and the gravity and importance of those who wear them can produce the single, powerful emotional effect for which the rather sardonic painter has striven. Another example of deliberate and aesthetically powerful use of incompatibility between form and content is found in the account of the death of Lieutenant Hearn in Norman Mailer's *The Naked and the Dead.* Prior to this incident, the author has spent a great deal of time elaborating the character of Hearn and enlisting interest for him. The description of Hearn's death is intended to produce feeling not just about Hearn but about war, too. Mailer writes:

> Hearn buckled his pack and hefted it to his shoulders. It was seven rations lighter now than it had been when they started, and it felt almost comfortable. The sun was beginning to give some warmth, which made him feel cheerful. As they moved along out of the hollow he felt good; it was a new morning and it was impossible not to feel hopeful. The dejection, the decisions of the previous night seemed unimportant. He was enjoying this, but if he was, so much the better.
>
> Quite naturally he assumed the point and led the platoon toward the pass.

A half hour later, Lieutenant Hearn was killed by a machine-gun bullet which passed through his chest.[42]

The foregoing examples all serve to illustrate the same point: in objects that are deliberately made by men to serve as cues for experiencing aesthetic quality, *the inclusion of sign-content serves as the focus for the affect aroused by the perception of form.* Form alone arouses certain feelings—of tension, for instance, or of balance, or lyricism, but the presence of the reflexive sign becomes a recognizable focal point around which those feelings may gather. Thus while the inclusion of sign-content is not a necessity for an aesthetic response, it can make such a response more powerful and more pointedly specific in its impact.

Art achieves as much as it can, and the aesthetic qualities of experience are richest when the possibilities of uniting the emotional impact of both form and sign-content are exploited as fully as possible. When this occurs, the effort to distinguish what is form and what is sign becomes so strained as to be almost artificial. This is sometimes most easily seen in the literary arts. One final example may illustrate how rich aesthetic quality can be when it is a function of perceiving form and content inseparably united by a skillful writer. The example is from the French novelist Colette:

> Perhaps seventy years of age, with the corpulence of a eunuch held in by stays, old Lili was usually referred to as "passing all bounds," without these bounds being defined. Her round pink painted face was enlivened by a ceaseless girlish gaiety, and her large eyes and small mouth, thin-lipped and shrunken, flirted shamelessly. Old Lili followed the fashion to an outrageous degree. A striking blue-and-white striped skirt held in the lower part of her body, and a little blue jersey gaped over her skinny bosom crinkled like the wattles of a turkey-cock; a silver fox failed to conceal the neck, which was the shape of a flower pot and the size of a belly. It had engulfed the chin.[43]

In the previous chapter, we examined the lecture, taken as typical of a variety of methods of schooling that does not apparently utilize problem-solving. We saw that the impact of the lecture, when it does in fact faciliate learning, is aesthetic in quality. Such a lecture arouses both affect and the immediate perception of the organization of its parts. By means of this perception, the affect aroused is related to the substantive content of the lecture. In the present chapter we have seen that these are the features characteristic of any experience that is aesthetic in quality, although we have given most of our attention to experience that is elicited by works of art. Yet when a work of art contains sign-content that serves as a recognizable focus for affect which has been aroused by the perception of its form, the experience of it has the *same felt quality* as the experience of hearing the sort of lecture that promotes learning. Thus while the present chapter has gone far afield from the more prosaic events of school classrooms, we find that the distance is not so great after all. A work of art and a lecture properly designed to promote learning have this in common: when they fulfill their functions, they facilitate the arousal of aesthetic quality in experience.

Later on (in Chapter IX) we will see that some of the differences between art and many other kinds of school practices are more verbal than they are real; that for practical reasons we value art for its capacity to arouse aesthetic quality, *even though we also learn from it,* and that for practical reasons we value lectures and textbooks for their capacity to promote learning, *even though* (if learning did occur) *we also have experienced them aesthetically.* When this topic is examined in detail, we will see even more clearly the close relation that exists between experience from which learning occurs, and experience which is aesthetic in quality. But before we go into these matters, we might first examine the consequences for school practices of the notion that, if they successfully promote learning, their impact is aesthetic.

# NOTES

1. See Susanne K. Langer, *Philosophy in a New Key* (New York: Mentor, 1948), p. 189.

2. "A symbol . . . cannot indicate any particular thing; it denotes a kind of thing"; C. S. Peirce, "Logic As Semiotic: The Theory of Signs," in Justus Buchler, (ed.), *Philosophical Writings of Peirce* (New York: Dover, 1955), p. 114.

3. See Irwin Edman (ed.), *The Philosophy of Schopenhauer* (New York: Modern Library, 1928), Arthur Schopenhauer, *The World as Will and Idea*, Book III, secs. 34 and 36.

4. See Benedetto Croce, *Aesthetic*, trans. by Douglas Ainslie (New York: Noonday Press, 1953), part I.

5. See Langer, *op. cit.*

6. Morris Weitz, "The Role of Theory in Aesthetics," *Journal of Aesthetics and Art Criticism*, 15 (September, 1956), 27–35.

7. For explicit criticism of these kinds of aesthetic theories, see Berryl Lake, "A Study of the Irrefutability of Two Aesthetic Theories," in William Elton (ed.), *Aesthetics and Language* (Oxford: Blackwell, 1959), and John Hospers, "The Croce-Collingwood Theory of Art," *Philosophy*, 31 (October, 1956), 291–308.

8. This is Mr. Burchfield's own description. See Whitney Museum of American Art, New York: *Charles Burchfield*, 1956.

9. Clive Bell, *Art* (New York: Capricorn Books, 1958), p. 27.

10. *Ibid.*, p. 17.

11. It will be shown later that the term "affect" is a more accurate term than "emotion." However, the more familiar term "emotion" will serve in the present context.

12. Santayana, having been labeled a hedonist in aesthetics, is said to have held this view. He may at times have done so, but at other times he surely did not; *cf.* "The Life of Reason," *Reason in Art IV*, (New York: Charles Scribner's Sons, 1946), pp. 211–212. A better example of a pleasure theory is that held by Henry Rutgers Marshall, *Pain, Pleasure, and Aesthetics* (New York: Macmillan, 1894), *passim*.

13. Of course, most people do not (fortunately) drive cars for the first time in city traffic. The example has been made extreme in order to emphasize the point under consideration; in any case, it requires little effort to imagine what it would be like to drive a car for the first time under such conditions.

14. The following discussion of affective responses to form in art is

heavily indebted to the work of Leonard B. Meyer, *Emotion and Meaning in Music* (Chicago: University of Chicago Press, 1956).

15. Some theorists have differed on this matter. The painter Wassily Kandinsky, for example, thought that certain colors and shapes invariably represented, or expressed certain feelings. See his *On the Spiritual in Art,* translated by Hilla Rebay (New York: Solomon R. Guggenheim Foundation, 1946). The simplest refutation of this view is merely to note that the "same" colors and shapes function expressively in very different ways in different works of art.

16. It would appear that these remarks would not apply to very large, monochromatic canvases that are currently fashionable in some quarters. It may be a matter of serious debate, however, whether the perception of such paintings can properly be called aesthetic in any more than an honorific sense. It may be the case that we have here an instance of sublimity (in the eighteenth century sense of transcending or defying form), or perhaps of visual nonsense (i.e., strictly speaking: lacking in "sense" or meaning). On the other hand, and apart from aesthetic considerations, a large monochromatic painting may serve to give the viewer relief from his chaotic surroundings. For a careful consideration of such painting, see Frederick M. Logan, "Education in Art for Art Educators," *School Review,* 72 (Autumn, 1964), 368–376.

17. It is also the critic's task to relate his judgments of form to whatever sign-content may be present in the work of art—a test requiring wide and sensitive experience outside as well as within the realms of artistic style. We shall for the present omit discussion of this function of criticism since our consideration of sign-content has yet to come.

18. This is normally what critics do *if* they are concerned with the presence of form in the object. However, critics may be concerned with other matters, either in addition to or instead of this one. Thus they may be more concerned with the historical setting of the work, or its social import, or with re-creating, in a reader's mind, the impression the work made on them.

19. Whether Bernard Berenson was *more sensitive* to the formal qualities of Italian sculpture cannot be proven; that he was more *familiar* than others with those qualities cannot be denied. People usually believe that degree of sensitivity is directly proportional to

familiarity. But I once knew a shopkeeper who was very familiar with a certain class of clientele; quite *in*sensitively, he would remark, "They're all alike."

20. Cf. Donald Arnstine, "Shaping the Emotions: The Sources of Standards for Aesthetic Education," *School Review, 72* (Autumn, 1964), 256; and Michael A. Wallach, "Art, Science, and Representation: Toward an Experimental Psychology of Aesthetics," *Journal of Aesthetics and Art Criticism, 18* (December, 1959), 165.

21. See, for example, Herbert Spencer, *The Principles of Psychology,* II, (London, 1855), chap. IX; and more recently, Stuart Hampshire, "Logic and Appreciation," in Elton, *op. cit.*

22. See, for example, Sigmund Freud, *A General Introduction to Psychoanalysis,* translated by Joan Riviere (New York: Liveright, 1935), pp. 327–328.

23. See Herbert Read, *Art Now* (London: Faber and Faber, 1933), p. 115.

24. Aristotle, *Problems,* 19.919$^b$ 29.

25. John Dewey, *Art as Experience* (New York: Minton, Balch, 1934), pp. 148–150.

26. Radhakamal Mukerjee, *The Social Function of Art,* 2nd ed., (Bombay: Hind Kitabs, 1951), p. 95.

27. *Ibid.,* p. 90.

28. See F. D. Sheffield and T. B. Roby, "Reward Value of a Non-Nutritive Sweet Taste," *Journal of Comparative Physiological Psychology, 43* (1950), 471–481.

29. P. T. Young, "The Role of Hedonic Processes in the Organization of Behavior," *Psychological Review, 59* (July, 1952), 250.

30. Young, *ibid.,* p. 253.

31. David C. McClelland, John W. Atkinson, Russell A. Clark, and Edgar L. Lowell, *The Achievement Motive* (New York: Appleton-Century-Crofts, Inc., 1953), p. 43.

32. *Ibid.,* p. 60.

33. *Ibid.,* pp. 61–62.

34. D. O. Hebb, "Drives and the C. N. S.," *Psychological Review, 62* (1955), 247.

35. See D. E. Berlyne, *Conflict, Arousal and Curiosity* (New York: McGraw-Hill, 1960), chap. 1.

36. A. N. Whitehead's discussion of the importance of the aesthetic in education is relevant to this point: "There is no substitute for the direct perception of the concrete achievement of a thing in its actuality." *Science and the Modern World* (New York: Mentor, 1948), p. 199.

37. Rudolf Arnheim, "From Function to Expression," *Journal of Aesthetics and Art Criticism, 23* (1964), 38.

38. ". . . the notion of the purely practical tool is as much a product of cultural decay as that of the purposeless work of art for art's sake." *Ibid.*, p. 39.

39. An excellent demonstration of the particular emotional impact of music can be found in the music Charlie Chaplin dubbed into the re-releases of his early silent films. His particular problem was to come up with a style of music that could at once express the absurdly humorous and the wistfully sad.

40. Charles S. Peirce, "Logic as Semiotic: the Theory of Signs," in Justus Buchler (ed.), *Philosophical Writings of Peirce* (New York: Dover, 1955), p. 99.

41. This scene may have been intended to convey the message that even the noblest of ladies loses control of herself when rejected in love. If so, neither the message nor its mode of conveyance was very convincing. On the other hand, comedy is often the result of the deliberate cultivation of incompatibility in form and content. A prime example is the dignified and deadpan Buster Keaton (or, more recently, Peter Sellers' portrayal of a police inspector) taking a pratfall.

42. Norman Mailer, *The Naked and the Dead* (New York: Rinehart, 1948), p. 602.

43. "Cheri," translated by Roger Senhouse, in *7 by Colette,* (New York: Farrar, Straus and Cudahy, Inc., 1955), p. 56.

# VII

## PRACTICES
## OF SCHOOLING:
## THE AESTHETIC
## AND THE ANAESTHETIC

IN THE LAST CHAPTER IT WAS INDICATED THAT ANY SCHOOL PRACTICES and materials can have a perceptual and emotional impact similar to that of a work of art. When they do, learning is facilitated. When, in hearing a lecture or reading a book, affect is aroused and resolved at least partly in response to perceived relations among sensuous elements, the experience has aesthetic quality; we may say that the lecture or book "has form." The appearance in schools of aesthetic qualities, then, need not be limited to courses in the arts. Experience in connection with any course of study may be permeated with aesthetic quality. It will be the task of this chapter to show that if such qualities do not appear throughout the studies in the school program, important avenues to learning will be blocked.

In relating aesthetic qualities to school practices, two criteria will, in turn, be applied. First, we shall ask whether a given practice is conducted in such a way that it has aesthetic impact; that is, whether it appears capable of arousing affect as a function of the relations that are immediately perceived among sensuous elements. This criterion directs our attention to the extent to which a school experience makes a direct appeal to feeling, aside from any instrumental value it may have.

Our second criterion directs attention to the relation between the form and the content of a school lesson or practice. We shall ask whether it is conducted in such a way that the affect aroused in students through their perception of form takes on a particular emotional character as a result of its being focused on the substantive content of what the practice in question purports to teach about.

After discussing school practices, we will turn our attention briefly to some of the means that would be implied for preparing teachers to conduct such practices. Throughout the discussion, I will try to show that what are essentially aesthetic criteria are also criteria for learning; that when practices do not meet such criteria, the learning that is intended cannot be expected to occur.

## AESTHETIC QUALITY AND THE ORGANIZATIONAL PRACTICES OF SCHOOLS

To what extent can school practices arouse affect through the immediate perception of relations among sensuous elements? It might be helpful to begin by citing what is paradigmatic of a complete failure to meet this criterion. Consider a roomful of students, by turns confused, bored, and threatened by the particular study or activity that the teacher has initiated. The teacher may say something like this: "All right, class, I know you're having trouble with this, and I suppose you may be wondering what the point of it all is.

Well, no matter what you think about it now, you'll appreciate it later if you'll just keep working at it."

This little speech constitutes a total denial of the potential for immediate affective value in the experience the students are presently having. What has been communicated is this: Do not look for any affective value, do not expect to have any intrinsic interest, and do not expect to gain any immediate or intrinsic satisfaction from what you are doing now. The only value of what you are doing consists in what I am promising that it will lead to. In rendering this admonition, and in assigning to the particular activity a wholly instrumental status, the teacher acknowledges (and so conducts himself) that it can have no aesthetic impact. If the students expend any effort at all, it must be based on their own clearly conceived and valued purposes (that is, in spite of what the teacher is saying), or, what is more likely, it must proceed from whatever obedience the teacher has managed to secure. Adults put into such situations label them as drudgery: evils to be suffered. Typical of such activities for most adults are washing dishes, filling out income tax forms, and undergoing dental treatment. Such things are done or undergone *only* for the results to which they lead, and because it is felt necessary to achieve those results. Hardly anyone takes pleasure in the affect aroused by such experiences, and hardly anyone would undergo them simply for the satisfaction taken in the activities themselves.

Of greatest importance for the present discussion is the fact that it is just in drudgery that our personalities alter the least—except perhaps by way of gradual deterioration when drudgery comprises the bulk of our working experience. Because they are tolerated only for their intended consequences, drudgery, "mere" routine, and purely instrumental acts are precisely the kinds of experiences during which dispositions and attitudes do not change in desirable ways. The teacher who takes the attitude that present experience can be appreciated only in terms of what it might lead to has instituted and officially recognized drudgery as the dominant theme of school work. In so doing, he may—perhaps in conjunction with certain other practices—produce acquiescence and tolerance of himself or of the topic being studied, but he is not facilitating learning.

His practices, on the contrary, make the occurence of learning highly improbable.

When an activity is tolerated only in the hope or the expectation that its eventual consequences will put an end to it, immediate perception is dullest; "mind" is elsewhere. If, in addition, the activity is mildly or very unpleasant, we are eager for the memory of it to leave us. Yet if this is the model of certain school practices, it is instructive to consider the assumption about the nature of learning that underlies it. For learning would consist in the conduct of laborious, unsatisfying activities that are imposed and directed by others. During the course of such activity, attention is least engaged; but when it is ended one has allegedly acquired a new and desirable disposition. This conception of learning is, of course, on a par with belief in magic. And stated in these rather unvarnished terms, hardly anyone would accept it. Yet actual school practices not infrequently conform to this magical conception of learning.

The reasons and causes for which people do things make a great difference in the extent to which those things have an effect on them. Two men may drive over the same country road but their experience is quite different if one is on a Sunday excursion and the other is seeking real estate to subdivide for suburban lots.

The reasons and the cause for which students pursue studies in school are classed under the heading of "motivation." It would not be inaccurate to say that the quality of the impact of whatever is done in schools is a function of the sort of motivation that operates. We may speak of two kinds of motivation. Students may pursue activities because they want to—because the affect aroused is satisfying, whether or not the ultimate goal of the activity is held to be a positive value in its own right. This is called intrinsic motivation. Students may, on the other hand, pursue activities for the sake of getting some reward or avoiding some punishment. When, in such cases, the activity is not felt to be intrinsically satisfying, when some other activity would more readily be pursued if it were found to be more efficient in producing the desired consequences, we have a case of what is commonly called "extrinsic motivation."

Because intrinsically motivated activities have immediate affective value for those who engage in them, they have the potential to be experienced aesthetically (although, when they fall short on other counts, they may not be so experienced). Activity the motivation of which is solely extrinsic does not have immediate value, and cannot have aesthetic impact. As such, it cannot be expected to promote any learning of the sort that is normally thought to be desirable.

Extrinsically motivated activity can, of course, result in the acquisition of certain isolated skills, or in the acquisition, for a time at least, of some information (see Chapter II). And it is possible for an activity that had been initiated through extrinsic motivation to *become* valued in its own right. This may happen accidently because of the background of certain students, or it may be deliberately promoted by a teacher.

We must next consider the motivational consequences of rewards and punishments, but first it would be well to note an important feature of the over-all organization of public schools. Often simply taken for granted, it conditions everything that happens in classrooms. Schooling is compulsory in the United States, and because of the increasingly limited job opportunities for those who reach the legal school-leaving age, even they are virtually compelled to remain in school. There is nothing very unfamiliar in all this, but it *would* be unfamiliar indeed if the lives of adults were so constricted. The great achievement of American democracy has been the institution of freedom of choice and opportunity. Nowhere is this freedom more significant than in the choice of one's vocation, of one's career. A person is not, at least in theory, condemned to the same status and the same livelihood as that of his father and his grandfather. He can freely choose the daily activities that will constitute the source of his support.

But for good or for ill, this freedom is not extended to American children and youth. They *must* go to school. Whether they like it or not, they are condemned to a dozen years of work that is not of their own choosing. And whether they can express it or not, nearly all young people in schools feel this very acutely. But adults, for the most part, do not. They are convinced that schools not only perform a vital function in maintaining and transmitting cultural values, but that they also offer unprecedented opportunities for the personal development and cultivation of children. Thus adults do not often consider the fact that the only other institution in American society that relates to those it serves as the school does, is the prison.[1]

Although the motives of retribution and deterrence may also operate, it is usually hoped that when a convicted criminal is compelled to go to a penitentiary, he will become a better person. The child is compelled to go to school with the hope that he, too, will become a better person. That the criminal should resent such treatment surprises no one. But when a school pupil resents the compulsion exerted on him, he is usually thought to be ungrateful. It can only be put down to blindness that adults who are otherwise sensitive and well-meaning can sympathize with the fate of the criminal while at the same time taking offense at the rese..tment many pupils have for schools.

The above observations are not intended as arguments for the abolition of public schools; after all, we are not prepared to dispense with prisons simply because prisoners are unhappy. But I am concerned to point out that some of the ideas instrumental in prison reform a century ago might well be applied to schools today. Because adults *compel* children to attend schools, *neither* for purposes of retribution, deterrence, nor reform, they are obligated to make that experience valuable to children. And yet the task is especially difficult just in virtue of that compulsion. For while compulsion is not keenly felt—if indeed it is felt at all—by children in the primary grades, it becomes increasingly apparent and increasingly onerous as children grow older. And the more strongly the compulsion is felt, the less possible will it be for students to learn what adults would like them to.

The compulsion to attend schools—with its attendant discomfort for some students—can be made more or less dominant by the ways in which teachers and administrators use rewards and punishments as motivators to activity. The primary reward, with its correlative punishments, is, of course, promotion and failure. It will be noted that, like many of the practices that will be mentioned next, promotion and failure are not *just* motivators; they are also procedures that are thought to be necessary for the smooth mechanical functioning of the school regardless of their motivational effect.

Students who are not so weak as to be in danger of failing a course are often motivated to study in the hope of achieving a high mark or avoiding a low one. More specialized motivators for achievement are scholastic honors for high marks and, for low marks, ineligibility for participation in activities like athletics and clubs. The future destinations of students are used as motivators that are relatively independent of the school's ability to reward or punish. Thus going to college and getting a desirable job are often mentioned as rewards for application in school studies, while collegiate ineligibility and unemployment are threatened as the just desserts of those who are lax. At a further remove, the more vague rewards of cultivation and culture may be promised for those who study, while it is sometimes implied that those who do not will be condemned to lives of cultural degradation. Finally, teachers sometimes deliberately and sometimes unwittingly tend to bestow a wide variety of favors on those who apply themselves assiduously and upon those whose achievement is high. Students at the nether end of this continuum are sometimes embarrassed, inconvenienced, and generally harrassed.

All of the devices just mentioned, like the paradigm example noted earlier, distract students' attention from the immediate affective value any particular school experience might have. These devices, instead, focus attention on future consequences that are not intrinsically related to those experiences, but which are procedurally bestowed on the student as rewards or punishments. To the extent that such devices predominate as motivators—that is, to the extent that they become internalized in students' value structures[2]—experience increasingly becomes mechanically and thoughtlessly instrumental, and its potential for having aesthetic quality is lost. Insofar as this is the case, learning is seriously impeded.

That learning will not normally occur under the pressures of the procedures mentioned above is implied by what has already been said about the necessity of affective arousal in order for experience to have aesthetic quality, and about the relation between that quality and learning. Yet we can analyze the impact of these school practices, when they are used as motivators, from a wholly different point of view and arrive at the same conclusion: that they are inimical to the promotion of learning. Let us, then, look at the natural history of activities that are tied to extrinsic motivators.

Suppose that a high school senior wishes to go to college, and that he is required to take a course in algebra. School authorities, and probably the instructor, think it is important for him to learn something about algebra, although he has, in this case, no particular interest in the subject. It is made clear to him that unless he gets a respectable mark—say an A or a B, he will have difficulty in entering college, or perhaps a college of his choice (thus in this case marks and college eligibility are the extrinsic motivators). He must perform well on certain examinations to get the marks, and he must attend to classroom presentations and do his homework carefully in order to do well on the examinations. Our student, for the sake of the marks and college eligibility, does what is asked of him; and although he might get some immediate satisfaction from the activities related to the course, let us suppose, as is often the case, he does not.

Now suppose the story has a happy ending for our student. He passes the course with a mark of B and is accepted at the college of his choice. Will he take anything with him to college that he acquired in the algebra course? The chances are remote. For all that he did—the textbook read, the notes taken, the skills acquired, the "problems" duly solved—was done for a particular purpose. When the purpose was achieved, those activities, not having been seen as valuable in their own right, slip easily from his mind without residue. And the student may be further encouraged by the fact that most introductory courses in college mathematics can successfully be undergone without having to remember anything from high-school algebra. Activities undertaken solely on grounds of extrinsic motivation all share this characteristic. We remember a telephone number only until we have used it, and then, it is quickly forgotten; only through frequently repeated use would we normally remember it. We remember quite well what time the plane leaves, but we forget it as soon as the trip is over.

It would, consequently, seem reasonable to say that under the dominant influence of extrinsic motivation, certain skills and items of information are acquired and remain ready for application as long as it is seen necessary to use them—that is, as long as the purpose for which they are acquired remains unfulfilled. But when that purpose is achieved and there is no other purpose for retaining the information and skills, they are quickly lost. In school situations, this means that most of what is taught is retained for a semester—roughly eighteen weeks. The loss that follows this period is quite rapid.[3]

Attention has been directed to the loss of skills and information but the acquisition of these things has not been the focus of learning in this discussion. What are the learning outcomes, then, that attach to extrinsically motivated activities? Will dispositions change?

It was noted earlier that the more dominant are extrinsic motivators, the less likely will learning result. But it would be more correct to say that the less likely will the type of learning occur that would normally be held *desirable*. In Chapter II the claim was made that desirable learning results in the acquisition of knowledge, skills, and attitudes that together build the sorts of dispositions that make it possible for a student to acquire new knowledge, skills, and attitudes. Desirable learning, in short, is that which leads to more learning. Learning may, in fact, occur as a result of predominantly extrinsically motivated activities, but it will not be of a desirable sort. We will see why this is so, continuing to use, by way of example, school marks and college eligibility as motivators.

As long as a student's fortunes are pinned on goals as crucial as school marks and college entrance, he courts disaster each time he pursues an activity that might not pay off in these terms. The senior taking physics might have been interested in building something on his own or in trying out something, but two obstacles stand in his way. If it doesn't work, will he get official credit for it? And can he afford the time, given similar extrinsic pressures that operate in all the courses he is taking? Doubt about these matters often discourages students from undertaking independent work and study. Thus what has the potential for extremely valuable kinds of learning is stymied as the student, under the pressure of external motivators, *does* acquire a disposition obediently to do what he is told and to suppress his own initiative. This may be a genuine learning outcome, but whether anyone would want it is very questionable.

School activities that are largely conducted under the dominant influence of extrinsic motivation lead to the acquisition of at least two general sorts of beliefs, each of which contributes to the formation of a characteristic disposition. In the first place, students may come to believe that the areas of adult human concern that are represented by school courses in English, science, mathematics, history, etc. are not of much real interest or value in themselves. Instead, they come to be thought of as valuable only for the consequences to which they lead. And some of these consequences—as, for example, the "democratic living" said to result from studying history, or the "cultivation" said to result from studying English—are suggested so vaguely as to cause doubt about whether certain courses of study have *any* value at all. Given the growth of such beliefs, it is little wonder that so few students ever inquire into the content of school courses after their formal schooling is over.

The second general belief generated by extrinsically motivated activity has to do with how one approaches what he is told to do. If the purpose and not the activity itself is all that matters, then, it is the part of wisdom to take whatever route is most efficient. The consequence of this is that extrinsic motivation becomes a cause for cheating in school. For if a student can get away with it, and it is less troublesome than studying, why shouldn't he cheat? Teachers may, and usually do admonish him that honesty is the best policy, but the student may be more practical. If the mark is what counts, and cheating is the best way to get the mark, then cheating is for him the best policy. The student may hope that someday, when he is working at a task of his own choosing, he can afford to be honest. In the meantime, he feels he may never get the chance to do such work *unless* he gets the mark, and gets into college. So if it works, he cheats. What is especially unfortunate is that too much success at this mode of behavior over too long a time may create a generalized disposition to cheat in *any* situation that is difficult. Dishonesty, then, is another potential (and, of course, undesirable) learning outcome when motivation is extrinsic, and activity is not valuable in terms of its immediately felt qualities.

Cheating is not an approach to activity that is condoned by the school, but other approaches that are condoned may not be conducive to better learning outcomes. Whether or not a student cheats, efficiency is still the only criterion in selecting ways of approaching extrinsically motivated goals. For students who have difficulty in dealing at more complex levels with materials, the most efficient way to get a desired school mark is to memorize as much as possible. And many students know no other way to study, even though many teachers try to discourage memorization. Apart from cheating and indiscriminate memorization, both of which have little to do with the promotion of desirable learning, the best hope for a student bent on efficiently achieving certain purposes is to do just what he is told and to hope for the best. At once, this means putting a rather blind faith in the teacher and remaining passively obedient. Attitudes like these, if through frequent repetition broadened into dispositions, are precursors to the blind faith and the unquestioning obedience that some adults render to anyone in a position of authority.

A variety of other potential learnings accrue from extrinsic motivation, none of them very attractive. Just two more might be mentioned. If the purpose is to do well on an examination and get a certain mark, then, it is impractical to stray from the specified subject matter. This may be viewed as the desirable development of power of concentration, but it may also be viewed as an undesirable narrowing of thought. For whenever adults, including teachers, do any serious thinking, the only limit to thought is relevance to the problem or topic at hand. The school's approach is often this: If the course deals with physics, sociological questions are inappropriate (but were they inappropriate for Galileo or for the scientists who built the atomic bomb?); if the course deals with military science, political questions are irrelevant (but were they irrelevant for General MacArthur in Korea?).

Finally, if one has to take an examination all by himself, it is practical to work in isolation and all for oneself. This approach to activity is frequently encouraged by schools. The conduct of discussion in classes sometimes constitutes an exception, but it is little wonder that not all students are attentive, if one's mark and one's future academic career depends on what he does, alone, on an examination. Given their lack of utility in this one important respect, discussions in class pose a genuine puzzle for many students: what *could* they be for, then? Teachers hope that discussions will promote thinking, but many students attend to discussion only in the hope of finding answers that might be useful in taking examinations.

But extrinsic motivators do not simply contribute to rendering discussions ineffective which otherwise might have been useful in promoting learning. For by encouraging individual activity, they also constitute a poor preparation for life outside the school. At home and at work, most of what adults do is done in concert with others. And just as important in the doing of them as particular knowledge and skills, are the dispositions whereby people can work and play effectively, if not enjoyably, with others. In one survey of a large business concern, the most frequently cited reason for firing employees was not a lack of knowledge or skill (for example, at typing, taking dictation, etc,), but inability to work with other people. As some critics point out, it may be psychologically harmful to have to work with others *all* the time, but, given an industrialized society, most people will have to work with others at least for a fair proportion of their time. People are evaluated on the basis of individual achievement in business and industry, too, but the *product* is also evaluated, and that is the outcome of combined effort. Insofar as schools, in relying heavily on extrinsic motivators such as examinations, marks, and college eligibility, encourage *only* isolated individual effort, they are failing to promote the desirable learning that is a function of co-operative activity.

The kinds of school practices that tend to distract attention from the immediate affective value of experience that is aesthetic in quality, focusing it predominantly if not exclusively on certain consequences, have been called extrinsic motivators. Not only do they tend to render experience virtually anaesthetic, thus precluding the kind of learning that is desired, but they also render most perishable whatever knowledge and skills are acquired in the course of fulfilling those purposes. And at the same time, *other* dispositions that are *not* very desirable *may* be acquired: the tendency to avoid certain pursuits (especially the arts and sciences) because they are felt to be intrinsically valueless, and, for some, dishonesty, indiscriminate memorizing as a mode of study, passive obedience and blind faith in authority, narrowness in thinking, and a self-centeredness born of exclusive attention to one's own activities and one's own rewards.

Are all these ills to be remedied simply by sweeping away all the practices that function as extrinsic motivators? This would probably be impractical, for however important the immediately felt quality of experience may be, the experiences promoted by schools also do have important bearings for the future. Thus some mode of promotion and some kind of evaluation are necessary if teachers are to perform effectively, and if college officials and employers are to make judgements on the basis of students' work in the schools. But the practical need for these devices in no way justifies their being used as millstones to hang around the necks of students. The methods by which they are organized and administered can be altered so as to minimize their effect as motivators. We might then consider three of these practices: examinations, school marks, and promotion policies.

Following the precedent set by colleges, secondary schools are turning increasing attention to final examinations at the end of each semester. There is a peculiarity in this, for it implies that what a student can recall and perhaps, in some cases, apply at a certain hour on a certain day is an adequate measure of what he learned as a consequence of a semester's study in a given area. Yet if all the important dimensions of learning are to be assessed, this is not adequate. For the presence of a set of dispositions can seldom be inferred from a single performance, and still less is it likely that dispositions indicative of overt behavior can be accurately assessed on a written examination. The first of these difficulties inherent in final examinations is usually met by what is called "continuous testing"—a series of lesser examinations administered throughout the semester. This mitigates the problem but does not solve it, since students are still motivated to perform well on the tests, rather than to take an interest in what is being studied on its own terms. If the felt *quality* of experience is that from which learning emerges, then, it would seem that a more sensible kind of evaluation would be to observe what the student is doing and how he goes about it in the course of normal classroom activities. This means, of course, that if a class consists largely of teacher presentations or of individual student recitations, then, there is virtually nothing available on which to evaluate most students most of the time. (It is not surprising that such teaching methods have been seen to call for special tests and examinations, since the rest of the time most students were virtually doing nothing at all.)

More specifically, teachers can note what students say in class discussions: how relevant their comments are, what information they are able to bring to bear on a topic, what kinds of questions they ask, how willingly they are to participate, how able they are to give reasons for their opinions, and so forth. In similar ways, students' participation in group work, their approach to laboratory experiences, and even their modes of individual study can all be assessed. Over a period of time, the sum of evaluations like these, made without elaborate bookkeeping, will probably afford greater insight into dispositions changed and acquired (along with the knowledge, skills, and attitudes of which the dispositions are made) than will any number of paper–and–pencil examinations.

It may be objected that the method of evaluation proposed here, which would reduce the emphasis of examinations as extrinsic motivators, tends to put too much responsibility on individual teachers. This objection is, I believe, spurious. If teachers are not seen as responsible for evaluation, why should they be thought responsible to teach? It may be claimed that evaluation by those other than the teacher (e.g., an "objective" examination) is fairer to all students. But on what grounds? Clearly, the teacher who teaches with a particular examination in mind affords an unfair advantage to his classes. And examinations, which are after all authored by people, whether they are of the essay or the multiple-choice variety, are no more "objective" than are the evaluation methods that have been proposed here.

A final objection, however, states that only through widely administered examinations can students from different classes, schools, and geographic regions be adequately compared with one another. And without such comparisons, and the norms that emerge from them, how can we make wise selections from among the swelling number of college aspirants? This reasoning, however popular at the moment, is foggy at best. The American public has overwhelmingly repudiated the European precedent of centrally administered curriculums and national norms by insisting that schools operate under local autonomy. Yet the public seems willing to accept nationally administered examinations which, the more widespread and influential they become, can only result in national norms that sooner or later eventuate in a national curriculum. All that would be left of local autonomy would be the routine housekeeping involved in administering the standard curriculum and trying to meet the national norms.

If autonomous schools and school districts are held to be valuable, then, why not autonomous teachers? Yet it is quite patent that they cannot be autonomous if they must conduct classes in such a way as to meet someone else's criterion on a widely administered examination. If teachers are to be free to set goals, or even to participate in their determination, they must be free at least to participate in assessing the extent to which those goals have been achieved. If teachers are not to be entrusted with such heavy responsibilities, then I am at a loss to discover who ought to be. They at least have had the experience of interacting with groups of pupils, and they have in most cases received some preparation for doing so. And whatever their shortcomings, it is a good bet that they know their own classes better than others do. These claims cannot be made of those who are professionally employed in the writing of examinations for wide regional and national use. Thus there are some good reasons for attending less to examinations, whether of a national or a local sort, and more to what students do day by day in the course of pursuing their studies.

The report card is a standard device used by nearly all public schools. The evaluative markings it contains, whether in the form of letters, numbers, or terms, serve as one of the most powerful of all motivators for doing school work. Nearly everyone deplores the fact that so many students work only "for grades," but if an "A" means that one is allowed to go out on week nights, or that one will be considered eligible for a particular college, and a "D" means that one must stay in during the week or seriously consider employment in the local iron works, then students will continue to work for grades. And, as a result, whatever is being studied takes a back seat and becomes a mere means to achieving the mark on the report card.

The most frequent justification for marking is the alleged need of colleges to determine who shall and who shall not enter. Whether this need is genuine is at least open to question. Thousands of high school graduates whose progress was followed in the massive Eight-Year Study[4] entered college not on the basis of school marks, but rather on the basis of recommendations of teachers and principals. They did at least as well in college studies as a comparable group whose admission to college was based on high school marks. Without belaboring the point, it might be worth eliminating school marks altogether. Any utility they have is open to doubt, and their harmful effects are obvious—not merely as extrinsic motivators that work against all attempts to promote learning, but also in leading to false comparisons (what does it mean to say that two "A" students are equally good bets for college, when they came from different schools and pursued different content in courses that bore the same title?). School marks also encourage the harmful tendency to label students whose subsequent high achievement often may be discounted by those who have, on the basis of past records, already tagged them as mediocre—i.e., as "C" students.

Evaluation is important, but mostly for the purposes of teachers. For when they evaluate, teachers can find out what changes are called for in their subsequent teaching. But there is not so much reason for assigning to all pupils permanent records of school marks that follow them all the way to their eventual employer's doorstep. A few students—the exceptionally gifted and the unusually handicapped (whether emotionally, intellectually, or physically)—may be in need of treatment so special that it becomes practical to notify others with whom they might be working later. For such students, some formal evaluation procedures (although not a simple letter or number) may be necessary. For the majority of students, however, simple promotion or whatever is analogous to it should serve as an indication of satisfactory work done. Marking students is an established tradition in schooling, and traditions—by their very inertia—constitute a serious obstacle to change. It is true that schools just would not be the same without marks and report cards. But they might be better off.

Finally, we may examine ways in which promotion policies might practically be altered in order to reduce the strength of their impact as extrinsic motivators. Just what is signified when a student is promoted from grade to grade has not always been clear. Conflicting views on promotion policy which periodically supplant one another in public favor are indicative of this. One group claims that a student's promotion is a sign of his having successfully completed study of a certain body of material. On this view, lack of success is held to be grounds for withholding promotion (i.e., for failure), while outstanding success may merit some form of accelerated promotion (i.e., skipping a school grade, or being permitted to do two semesters' work in one). Another group, fearing the embarrassing social consequences of failure, favors automatic promotion each year for all. On this view, promotion, a sign of a student's having become a year older, is merely an administrative convenience.

Those who favor automatic promotion do not, of course, use it as a reward; hence, it would not function as an extrinsic motivator. This is not the case when promotion is based on achievement. Yet in the light of what most people expect the schools to do, neither view can be accounted wholly rational. The issue becomes pointed if we look first at the policies of acceleration and failure. In both these cases it would appear that a student's fate hinges upon how he handles a finite body of material. If he learns too little of it—that is, fails to acquire enough information to pass examinations—he is required to repeat the year's work. Since his inadequate performance is as likely a sign of lack of interest as it is of any other cause, the policy of failure functions as mere punishment and would appear to have no educational value. If one is not interested in an activity, having to repeat it again holds little promise of increasing interest. But if failure really is rooted in lack of intelligence, what would seem called for is special help and remedial work where activities are appropriately altered. It should be obvious that merely repeating the work one was not bright enough to handle the first time will not make him any more intelligent after a second time around. Apparently, the policy of failure is predicated on the rather shaky assumption that the material studied is so valuable, in and of itself, that all students, regardless of intelligence, background, and interests, will be the better for it if they are simply exposed long enough to remember a proportion of it adequate for the passing of certain examinations.

The policy of acceleration is founded on the same assumption. Students who skip grades or telescope two into one apparently require relatively little exposure to material in order to pass examinations on it. But such students, allegedly the bright or gifted ones, are treated no better than those who fail. For just as the failures are given no opportunity to develop interest in the material studied or the activities undertaken, neither are the unusually "fast learners." For if genuine interests were developed—if the activities were to be perceived as valuable on their own account—there would have to be less emphasis on getting through with them in as short a time (that is, as efficiently) as possible. Both failure and acceleration, unless they are accounted entirely irrational, are founded on the notion that some materials are so valuable that a student's progress through school can simply be a function of how much time he needs to assimilate them. If schools have any other task to perform beside simply exposing this material, it is not implied by the practices of failure and acceleration.

Acceleration is sometimes seen as a means of expediting early entrance into college for some youth (no parallel rationale underlies failure). Thus the whole educational process is "speeded up" for certain students: a plan that is not without appeal for those who view each student's passage through the grades as an economic enterprise of no mean proportions. In short, accelerating students, if good for nothing else, at least saves taxpayers' money.[5] The peculiar result, then, is that some of the brightest students receive as their reward the least opportunity to avail themselves of what schools can offer. The reward for good behavior is early exit. The parallel to the treatment of sentenced criminals is striking.

If the frying pan of promotion for achievement becomes uncomfortable, some seem quite willing to hurl themselves into the fire of automatic promotion. Some difficulties are indeed avoided in this way, but new questions are raised. We know, of course, that students turn a year older every year without school promotions being necessary to remind us. What is the purpose of promotion at all, then, under these conditions? If it is an administrative convenience, what is it convenient *for*?

Given the numbers of students who go to school, it is necessary to teach them in groups. When the school population was small for a given region, the groups were unselected; teachers faced young and old in an ungraded classroom, and, if they cared to and were able, they altered their methods for different individuals. The growth of graded classrooms paralleled the growth of compulsory education, for it was thought efficient to put students together who were alike. The basis chosen for grouping was age. Reasonably enough, it was felt that, all other things being equal and nothing else known about the pupils, some similarities were sure to appear if all children in the same classroom were of the same age. Many generations later, this reasoning is no longer valid. We do know considerably more about pupils, and we find that all other things are not at all equal. That children of the same age vary enormously in physical and emotional maturity is obvious to anyone who looks. It is less obvious, but probably just as important, that in a a typical sixth grade class the level of *achievement* in such pervasive studies as English composition, reading comprehension, and arithmetical reasoning and computation varies from what is average for first and second grade levels to what is average for eleventh and twelfth grade levels.[6] Thus if automatic promotion is an administrative convenience for keeping together children of the same age, it only perpetuates a practice which is but remotely related to what is significantly similar among school children for educational purposes.

Although there is little agreement about matters of timing, it is felt that children must begin schooling at some time or other, and that there ought to be a time for them to be finished.[7] It may be simple, but it is also a bit simple-minded, to set arbitrary ages of 6 for beginning and 18 for finishing, and to institute a system of either automatic promotions or promotion based on achievement (which may accelerate or retard the process) in order to expedite the process. For this administrative paraphernalia, besides attracting undue attention and effort to its own working, is only a substitute for the more thoughtful process of making judgments, on the basis of how students behave, about what they might study most profitably, and about how they might be encouraged to go about it. The alternative to promotion policies which are either mindlessly mechanical or damaging in their extrinsic motivational effects is to return to the ungraded classroom. Yet the return need not be a step backward in history, a merely arbitrary grouping of whatever children are around. Instead, such classes might be made up of children whose background and maturity could be expected to make it appropriate for them to work and learn together.[8]

If ungraded classes were kept flexible, and the kind of evaluation discussed earlier were continually carried on, children could be moved into different groups as dispositional changes in them indicated. Instead of rushing some students through the school program and holding up the progress of others as if the school were an assembly line, and instead of assessing the results of all this by marking all students as if they were eggs, ungraded classes of the type described would enable evaluation procedures to be genuinely purposeful in allowing teachers to institute appropriate remedial methods and materials for those who needed them, and to initiate appropriately challenging intellectual activity for those who were ready for them.

Brighter children, incidentally, might still enter college earlier, but not on the basis of having simply sped through the same standard fare on which others spent more time. And duller students might be prepared for vocations and what is called (by way of gratuitous and invidious comparison) "life" with neither a mind-narrowing vocational program nor by simply repeating over and over certain academic courses until they are permanently emptied of all initiative, originality, and zest for learning. Experiments with ungraded classrooms, with and without instructional teams of several teachers and teaching interns, have been tried, and not without success.[9] The reasons already adduced, experiments like these, and the implications of earlier efforts like that of the Eight-Year Study, all point to the possible value of trying the experiment of ungraded schools. It may play hob with bookkeeping, but bookkeeping need not be the first consideration of schoolkeeping.

In the foregoing discussion, we have applied an essentially aesthetic criterion to a variety of school practices. We have asked whether those practices have enabled students to experience any satisfying arousal of affect in the pursuit of school activities. The practices discussed, such as examinations, marks, and promotion and failure, have been seen to operate as extrinsic motivators to doing school work. As such, they distract attention from the intrinsic or immediate worth of the experiences that schools promote, and focus it on the rewards and punishments to which those experiences lead. In thus tending to destroy the immediate affective value or the aesthetic quality or experience, they render it anaesthetic. For this reason, such practices constitute obstructions to learning that would be accounted desirable.

It has also been seen that these same practices can be assessed as interfering with learning wholly apart from aesthetic criteria. The remedy has been seen to consist in reducing the effect of these practices in their capacity as extrinsic motivators. This has not meant simply the abandonment of such practices altogether (although teachers might well desist from telling students that currently unpalatable activity will be "good for them someday"), but rather their alteration in such a manner that the educative purposes for which they were devised might continue to be fulfilled. Yet at the same time their potential for distracting students from the value of what they are doing can be reduced.

## AESTHETIC QUALITY IN THE METHODS AND MATERIALS OF SCHOOLING

We can now apply the other criterion, developed from the earlier analysis of aesthetic quality, to school practices. We shall ask, what is the extent to which teaching methods arouse affect in such a way as to allow for aesthetic quality in experience? It is necessary to ask this question, too, for experience in which affect is aroused, while necessary for learning to occur, is not sufficient. A child who has made hundreds of mud pies may continue making them and experience a great deal of satisfying affect; but he is probably not learning anything. For learning to occur as a result of using the methods that are presently under investigation (especially lectures, presentations and discussions, books and films), and which does not proceed from the initial institution of a problem-solving context, the experience elicited by them must have aesthetic quality. And this involves both the presence of affect and its arousal through the perception of the relations among sensuous elements (that is, of form) that remains relevant to the content of what is being presented.

When a student is reading a textbook or hearing a presentation made by a teacher, he may be feeling any number of things. For the present purpose, however, we shall attend to feelings that, because they render experience anaesthetic, markedly interfere with learning. For the purposes of convenience, we can group these feelings into three broad types, all of which are felt as uncomfortable to a greater or lesser extent. There is the discomfort that is felt as a direct response to the threat of punishment implied by the extrinsic motivators discussed above; there is confusion that is felt as a response to the presentation of certain kinds of content; and there is boredom that is felt in response to the manner in which content is presented, either in a book or in a lecture. Affect of these kinds is held undesirable on two counts. From the student's point of view, they are simply unpleasant. Until he becomes inured to feeling this way, he wonders why he is compelled to go to school and then treated in such a fashion. Teachers would like to say that students should tolerate their discomfort, because, after all, they are learning. But teachers do not always feel free to say this because, from their point of view, students who feel threatened, confused, and bored, are not really learning very much at all; at least they are pretty clearly not learning what teachers would like them to learn. In what follows, we will see that each of these kinds of uncomfortable feelings interferes with the process of learning just because they make impossible any aesthetic apprehension of experience.

Like all feelings, discomfort is not arrived at after one has assessed the import of a situation; rather, it is an inseparable part of the perception of a situation. Low marks and failure constitute a potential threat to all students, but not all students feel particularly uncomfortable about it. Students who perceive themselves as threatened, and consequently feel uncomfortable about it, are those who find a particular goal (e.g., reading a text with the intention of remembering certain materials, or following the complex instructions of a teacher) either too difficult to achieve, or not worth the trouble to achieve, or both. Since failing to achieve such goals is perceived as bringing with it certain punishments, any obstacle to such achievement produces discomfort. And since what is perceived as a threat always has some future reference (threats always refer to what *may* happen), the immediate affect that is aroused has future import. Under these circumstances, experience cannot have aesthetic quality, nor can any desirable learning occur. We can, of course, force students to do certain things by threatening them, but the only relatively permanent changes we could expect to take place will be the acquisition of an increasingly marked disposition of resentment toward both the teacher and the material he is teaching.

As it was noted earlier, the surest way of avoiding discomfort produced in students this way is to reduce the threat. This remedy can be produced relatively simply through administrative reorganization. A more difficult, and probably less certain way of reducing discomfort in students would be to modify instructional objectives in such a way that they are perceived by students both as worth attaining and not unreasonably hard. While such modifications would be desirable in any case, they are far from foolproof in reducing discomfort as long as examinations, marks, and failure to be promoted remain as threats.

Of all places, it is in schools that one expects to find clearly understood and significant meanings. For this reason, students arrive at school expecting to find meanings and assuming that those who teach in schools are there just because they have been specially prepared to make those meanings clear. Unfortunately, once class begins, meaning does not always come with the clarity that had been expected. This is not only perceived as confusing, but, insofar as the teacher is trusted, it is felt as threatening as well. For if the source of confusion is seen as in oneself rather than in a situation, one begins to doubt himself, lose confidence, and feel threatened. The meaning of what a teacher or a textbook says is analogous to the sign-content in a work of art. In both cases, meaning is a function of the way in which expectations are set up and fulfilled. Students are led to believe that they should expect *something* in schools, but if in a classroom situation matters are such that they do not know *what* to expect, meanings will not be forthcoming, and the situation will be perceived as confusing if not quite incomprehensible. The confusion clearly is not a learning situation. And at the same time, since expectations are either unfulfilled or not present at all, aesthetic quality in experience is not possible, either.

In school situations, meanings are absent and confusion is generated whenever a teacher's presentation, an activity, or a text presents anything too far removed from a student's familiarity with it. In the previous chapter we saw that unfamiliarity with an artistic style resulted in a viewer's having no expectations when presented with a particular work in that style. Because he had no expectations, he was not able to apprehend meaning in the work and as a result, the experience of it was not aesthetic. The same sort of situation holds when students are unfamilar with certain cognitive materials that may be presented in a text or in class. Without expectations, no meaning can result, hence no learning. It is probably wasted energy to consider whether a student *ought* to be familiar with what is presented in a class. The fact of the matter is that unless teachers ascertain what their students *are* familiar with, lectures and presentations are as likely to promote confusion as they are to promote learning.

Adults experience boredom when they have no choice but to attend to situations that are already too familiar to merit such attention. These situations sometimes occur at work—the more frequently when work is of a repetitive nature—and sometimes in social intercourse. Adults seek to escape boring situations, and often they can. With schoolchildren, the case is different. There is no escape from the classroom. Thus situations that might be mildly troublesome to adults who can seek ways of escaping must simply be suffered by students in schools. Boredom, for them, then, becomes understandably irritating, and illegitimate distractions, such as whispering to neighbors, passing notes, doing homework for other courses, doodling, and daydreaming, are sought. It would be otiose to observe that in such cases, learning of the sort desired by the teacher is not occurring.

Boredom in classrooms is sometimes the result of uninspired review lessons, but that is not the chief cause. Since the substantive content of most lectures, presentations, and textbooks is not so familiar to students that their attention to them should produce boredom, we must seek elsewhere for the conditions from which it arises. In fact, the conditions for the emergence of boredom have already been elaborated in Chapters V and VI.

It is not the content, but rather the *form* of many lectures and books that produces boredom and thereby inhibits learning. In the previous discussion of the lecture, it was noted that failure to elicit expectations and appropriately delay or inhibit their fulfillment—failure, that is, to afford elements of resistance and surprise in the way in which the content of a lecture is organized—results in failure to arouse affect in an audience. Absence of affect, which is tantamount to boredom,[10] not only renders experience anaesthetic, but also renders it powerless to influence dispositions. Hence learning does not occur.

The lecture, of course, is not the only potential vehicle for the elicitation of boredom. Films shown to students can be boring, too (they have, of course, strong commercial competitors), and so can a presentation intended to initiate activity, or an answer to a student's question. But a teacher is at least alive, and can elicit interest in himself, even if what he says lacks form or style. Textbooks have not this virtue, and thus become strong candidates for the most boring of all school-connected devices. It is not necessarily the case that the authors of texts are poor writers. Rather, in their attention to embracing the whole of a content area and setting it down in a clear and logical order, they simply do not attend to matters of style. Thus it may be that the problem is a case of oversight rather than inability. Attending to accuracy and logical adequacy, authors compose admirable reference works, but often forget that their books may be used for pedagogical purposes. Worse suggestions have been made that that of having subject field experts and teachers collaborate with professional essayists or novelists in the writing of textbooks.

It may be objected that if style becomes a criterion in judging the pedagogical adequacy of lectures and books, then the content will suffer. If attention is directed to style, will there not be a danger that what is said or written will lose accuracy through distortion or oversimplification? However easy it might be to improve the writing in areas that involve narrative, like history, is it not true that the school must also deal with types of complex and involved subject matter that will necessarily suffer in accuracy of exposition if cast into artistic form? Rather than try to deny this, it might be just as well to seek a reason for living with the fact. For try as they might, educators cannot always have it both ways. We may adjust the gear ratio to increase power, but we lose speed; an increase in speed sacrifices power. Yet mechanics are not distressed over this fact: what is all-important is *when* to sacrifice one for the sake of the other (on a hill, for example). Thus if the situation calls for it, educators should be as realistic in sacrificing one virtue (accuracy) for the sake of the other (style). We might, then, consider when it is appropriate to emphasize either one or the other of these aspects of teaching materials. Nonetheless, it is worth noting that lectures and books are not just like mechanical gears, and that many good available texts stand as evidence that it is possible to combine scientifically accurate and logically organized materials with artistic style in the same book.

When we examine the twelve grades of public schools, we find only a minority of studies that qualify as specifically vocational or preprofessional in content. On the contrary, nearly all courses through the junior high school level, and most of those offered in the following 3 years, are introductory in nature. They usually offer a general survey of an area of study to students who have little or no experience in it. While the student in an advanced or professional course becomes increasingly concerned with acquiring information and skill relevant to the course and to his future career, this is not so for the student in an introductory course. Our chief concern with him is to enable him to *learn about* the subject; that is, we hope that he will acquire a new or changed disposition about it through study—that he will acquire an interest in it, a concern for it, a sense of its importance, and familiarity with the modes of thinking relevant to it. In short, an introductory course has as its primary purpose the providing of an orientation.[11] For such a purpose it is vitally important that the style of the materials presented to the student does not put him off, does not bore or repel him. In cases where dispositions become the educational focus, it seems judicious to sacrifice accuracy of content when considerations of style demand it (that is, if they ever demand it).

This case is reversed when a student is taking an advanced or preprofessional course. In this event one should be able to assume (although unfortunately it is not always true) that the student *already has* an appropriate disposition toward the subject and toward becoming more proficient in it. Already interested in the subject, he is ready to come to grips with problems that arise within it, and ready to acquire whatever information and skill is relevant. When these dispositions are present, the student will continue to learn, but it is less necessary to arrange conditions carefully and deliberately to facilitate learning. Instead, more care can be spent elaborating problems, presenting detailed information, and refining skills. When a student is working at a relatively advanced level in a subject area, then, it becomes increasingly practical to attend to the accuracy of content of instructional materials, and to hope style will take care if itself.

Let us see what happens when aesthetic criteria are applied to narrative writing for the purpose of assessing pedagogical potential. For this purpose, we might compare two narratives, one taken from a psychology textbook, the other from a novel. Each passage discusses the vividness and seeming reality of dreams. We must allow that the style and aesthetic impact of each may suffer from being torn from its context, and we shall put aside, for the moment, questions of scientific adequacy. We shall ask, from which of these two passages is one more likely to experience arousal of affect, so that, were the passage read in a context of similar style, dispositions might be altered?

> Implicit and mental activities are sometimes sufficiently vivid to be recalled or rearoused by the individual after he awakens. In this event they are referred to as *dreams*. . . . As an interesting characteristic of dream processes we may notice, first of all, their seeming reality. No matter how bizarre and incongruous the content of the dream, we are disposed at the time to accept it as real. We may ascribe this to the limited range of cerebral activity. The restricted nature of this activity enables the dreamer to accept, in a manner wholly uncritical, the combinations which at any other time seem absurd and ridiculous. Only with the more complete functioning of his waking hours does he realize the incongruities of his dream.[12]

> In a morbid condition of the brain dreams often have a singular actuality, vividness, and extraordinary semblance of reality. At times monstrous images are created, but the setting and the whole picture are so truthlike and filled with details so delicate, so unexpected, but so artistically consistent, that the dreamer, were he an artist like Pushkin or Turgenev even, could never have invented them in the waking state. Such sick dreams always remain long in the memory and make a powerful impression on the overwrought and deranged nervous system.[13]

The first of the two passages was intended, presumably, to convey information, and has probably been used to promote learning. The second passage was intended to afford aesthetic quality to a reader's experience (although the author may have hoped that some learning would result as well). But we can assess the probable consequences of reading the two passages on the basis of their style, or what we have more frequently referred to as form.

The symbolic signs of language that appear in the psychology text function in a wholly instrumental way. They are utterly practical. Directing our attention away from themselves, they arouse no immediately felt affect, and permit no aesthetic quality in the experiencing of them. Unless it is crucial that we retain the information presented (for a short time at least), it is not easy to avoid boredom—especially when the cited passage is continued for many pages. In short, because the passage presents no perceptible form, its experience cannot be aesthetic and, given the effect that it does have, one of the purposes for which it is often used—the fostering of a new disposition—is not achieved.

But assuming that the passage taken from the novel is read by someone who has a little experience reading books, the possibilities of his having aesthetic quality in experience are great. For the immediate perception of the formal qualities of the words and sentences, as well as the perception of their function as reflexive signs, arouses affect. Thus the passage, especially as it is found in its context, does promote learning, even though not deliberately read for such a purpose. That is, as one reads a novel like the one from which this passage is taken, his dispositions toward people and events may be altered.

This is not to urge that textbooks should be abandoned and replaced by novels. The use of information is important in schooling, and what most texts lack in style is balanced by what most literary works lack in organized and accurate information. What is being urged, though, is the adoption of an aesthetic criterion—not simply on grounds of mercy to the student, but for the reason that without it, the kind of learning under consideration cannot be expected to take place.

*If written* (or visual or oral) *material is to be useful in promoting learning in situations that are not intimately joined with the processes of problem-solving, then the judgment of its adequacy must be based not only on logical and substantive criteria, but on aesthetic criteria as well.* In addition to asking about the importance, relevance, and accuracy of lectures and books, it is also necessary to ask whether their style has its own affective value, and whether that value enhances their substantive content. At the considerable risk of obscuring this point, I will try to illustrate it by offering a translation of the textbook passage previously cited. The translation is slightly shorter than the original and is intended to convey as nearly as possible the same information. And it is also intended more adequately to meet the aesthetic criteria that have been mentioned. The translation may not be very successful in this latter respect, but at least it may indicate the direction in which, without resorting to purple prose, textbook writing might move:

> When goblins brandishing pitchforks have cornered us on the edge of a cliff, it is a relief to wake up. Yet we remember the implicit and mental activities called dreams because they seem so real at the time. However bizarre they may be, we can accept dreams quite uncritically because sleep so limits the range of cerebral activity. In our waking hours we function more completely and the intense pleasure of the night, or what awakened us in terror, is dissolved in the clear light of knowing that, after all, it was only a dream.

# AESTHETIC QUALITY
# AND THE EDUCATION OF TEACHERS

What has been said about teaching practices in the grade schools applies equally in most respects to the preparation of teachers. This may sound contradictory at first, for it has just been noted that aesthetic considerations, while of great importance for students at introductory levels of study, are less so at more advanced and pre-professional levels. Those who are preparing to teach are commonly thought to be working at a professional level. Then why the need for aesthetic criteria in judging the adequacy of *their* educational experiences?

The reason is simply that college students who are beginning a program in teacher education are not yet functioning at an advanced or professional level, nor have they yet acquired the dispositions that would permit such functioning. Thus they will not be able to acquire the information and skills that characterize a professional worker unless they acquire the sorts of dispositions that are necessary for the relevant information and skills to have point and meaning. Of course, like most everyone else, these students have spent 12 years in the grade schools. And like some other adults, many have come to feel that if there is anything they do know about from first-hand experience, it is how schools are run and how they ought to be run. Yet nothing could be farther from the truth. Such thinking is only a little less absurd than the claim that, after a rat has been run through a number of maze experiments, it ought to be able to design new experiments itself.

For 12 years and more, college underclassmen have been students, and thus have been on the receiving end. They remember what has been done to and with them, and they usually have little idea why. Having fully acquired dispositions that may be appropriate for students, their behavior might best be described as respondent: they generally know what to expect from teachers, and they have developed relevant modes of response. But knowing how to respond to situations initiated by others is not at all the same as knowing how to initiate those situations, and having good reasons for initiating one situation rather than another. As a result, those who are beginning a teacher preparation program have neither considered the myriad problems teachers have, nor the choices they must make, nor has the very existence of those problems and choices occurred to them. And lacking these dispositions, what little information as exists that is relevant to teaching can have little meaning for them.

Even more important than acquiring the bare techniques of teaching and a body of knowledge relevant to it, then, is the necessity for prospective teachers to acquire the attitudes and dispositions that make such techniques and knowledge meaningful, and by means of which they can be enabled to make judgments about them. Thus the college student who is beginning preparation to become a teacher is as much in an introductory phase of a new field of study as a fifth grader studying American history for the first time. Because of this, the first stage of his preprofessional training must aim at cultivating an orientation, at promoting the acquisition of certain dispositions. And the procedures used for these ends must measure up to aesthetic criteria. For such dispositional learnings to result, the experience of the beginning prospective teacher must be marked by the arousal of affect as a consequence of his having perceived form in his instructional materials and procedures.[14]

What has already been said about style in lectures, presentations, and textbooks, then, applies to teacher education in its introductory phase just as it does to education in the public schools. Since those observations can readily be applied to teacher education by anyone familiar with it,[15] only one thing further will be said here about the preparation of teachers. For if it is recommended that teachers attend to the artistic quality of their preparations for classes, it would be practical if their own education enabled them to do so.

Teacher education has, of late, been the subject of close scrutiny, some of it coming from within its own ranks,[16] and some from without.[17] Attention has been directed to the critical issues of an optimum balance between required courses in general education, a subject matter teaching field, and professional education; the scope and organization of practice teaching or internship programs; the roles of state boards of education, colleges and universities, and professional accrediting bodies in teacher certification; etc. Without minimizing the importance of these matters, I should like to focus on an area of study that has seldom been thought to be of particular moment in the education of teachers. This area is education in the arts, usually considered peripheral in the controversies over which courses are most critical to the production of effective teachers.

Yet if this and earlier chapters dealing with the relation of aesthetic quality in experience to learning have made any sense, then certain kinds of experiences in the arts become quite crucial in the preparation of teachers. Any cue in the environment has the potential for eliciting aesthetic quality in experience, but the arts stand as paradigms of such cues, for they are created expressly for that purpose. If in the particular kinds of school situations we have been considering, the acquiring of dispositions is a concomitant of experience which has aesthetic quality, then, teachers will be effective in promoting such learning only insofar as they are able to make of these teaching practices an art. What could be potentially more important in teacher education, then, than the kinds of studies in the arts that can make prospective teachers more consciously aware of the features of things (such as lectures and books) that are potential cues for aesthetic experience?

College courses in the arts are not oriented to such purposes. Their emphasis is on the production and appreciation of works of art *per se*. This is usually true whether we consider studio courses or courses in appreciation, criticism, or history, and it holds equally for the visual arts, the dramatic arts, the literary arts, and music. This emphasis is such that little connection is made for any students, let alone for those who are planning to teach, between the consideration of the arts and of other, everyday activities of living. Under these circumstances, it seldom occurs to prospective teachers to utilize aesthetic cues in order to make their teaching more effective. Before considering what might be done to improve this aspect of teacher education, we might note some of the ways in which the use of the arts can directly contribute to teaching.

A college course in the visual arts can and should try to make all students more sensitive to the appearance of the world around them, and to the ways in which that appearance makes all things and events more meaningful, or less so. For those who will teach, sensitivity to aesthetic quality based on visual impact affords a variety of ways of deliberately heightening that impact—and thus better facilitating learning—in the conduct of school activities. Perhaps the most obvious focus for this is in the first thing that attracts students' attention: the teacher's own appearance. A teacher's grooming and dress may be appropriate or inappropriate, attractive, distracting, or even just silly, in terms of his own personality, of what he is teaching, of fashion, or even of the weather. Likewise, the appearance of the classroom and other rooms in the school can provide increased meaning to the activities that go on within them. And such teaching devices as educational films and book illustrations must also be judged and selected on the basis of aesthetic as well as content criteria. Failure to meet the former criteria is often the reason why the content of such visual presentations fails to promote the learning that is hoped for.

As he performs before his class, the teacher is, in fact, an actor. Just because the audience cannot escape is no good reason for his putting on a dull performance. College courses in the dramatic arts call attention, among other things, to the methods whereby means other than dialogue can attract, hold, and direct the attention of an audience. Just as the movement, gesture, and facial expression of the stage actor is deliberately calculated to heighten the impact of the thought and action of the play, so an effective teacher uses these means in a classroom. Simply to pace back and forth or to fidget before a class is distracting; to stand or sit motionless and without expression is even worse. When students are given nothing worth looking at, it can hardly be surprising that their attention wanders—and that their eyes, being useless, tend to close. The student who daydreams or dozes in classrooms may not be so much the victim of difficult subject matter or his own apathy, as of unimaginative presentation by the teacher. Doodling (or taking the sort of notes little more useful) may simply be an unwitting habit developed as a defense against the onslaught of visual and aesthetic poverty.

College courses in the dramatic arts could well make prospective teachers aware of their role as dramatic agents; of the sound of their own voices; of the impact of their speech habits on others; of the way their gestures and facial expressions look; and of how— within the limits of their particular personalities— speech, expression, gesture, movement, and timing can be controlled and modified to enhance the content of their subject matter.

Sensitivity to one's own impact as a dramatic agent is the same as being sensitive to one's total impact on other people. For some, this sensitivity is acquired "naturally." That is, having been raised in a fortuitous environment, they have been developing this sensitivity all of their lives. This has led many people to the dangerously mistaken conclusion that "teachers are born, not made." But just because some have learned such things informally is no reason to suppose that those who have not are unable to learn from deliberate instruction. There is no existing theory of dramatic presentation wholly adequate for all situations, but there is no lack of codification of rules,[18] nor is there any dearth of competent teachers or exemplars of drama. Prospective teachers, as much as and perhaps even more so than other students, could profit enormously from practicing the art of dramatic presentation, under conditions where they can observe and analyze the effects of what they have done, and where they can get competent criticism and guidance.

While nearly all students in college are exposed to courses in creative writing and the appreciation of the literary arts, all too few genuinely learn anything, if their subsequent reading and writing habits are any indication. No less than anyone else, teachers could personally profit from such courses, but the professional use they might make of them gives them added significance. In light of what they will do as teachers, few of them need to be polished writers of fiction or nonfiction, but all could make their teaching more effective by practicing greater discrimination in the evaluation of choice of textbooks and by giving attention to the literary aspects of lectures and presentations.

The point of these observations is that the study of the fine arts within the context of general education in college is emasculated when confined to looking at works of art apart from their roles in the life of society, and apart from considerations of ways in which style in the arts is related to style in conduct of all activities of living. If such college courses appear relevant only to what people can do in museums or theaters, their utility—even in advancing culture—will be slight. The remedy is not, however, the construction of special courses called "fine arts for teachers." Education departments are not normally staffed to deal with such things, and no matter who might teach such courses, the temptation is too great to turn them into cookbook courses where recipes for style in teaching are duly transmitted and reproduced. Thus, granted that attention to style in teaching might eliminate the need for much that is done under the heading of "general methods," it would probably be of little avail to extend teacher education by introducing specially oriented arts courses. What is needed, instead, is the introduction of greater practical scope in the arts courses in general education—not just for the benefit of prospective teachers, but for the sake of all the students who take such courses.

College courses in English, speech, rhetoric, drama, and the visual arts could have greater effect in the later lives of students if an attempt were made to join their content with the interests, values, and commitments of students. Indeed, if such a connection cannot be made, there would be little reason for arguing that such courses should be required of students in college. It might be objected that such a proposal merely constitutes a thinly disguised attempt to adulterate the fine arts for crass practical and vocational purposes. Indeed, many proponents of the humanities and the fine arts claim that only by exclusive attention to the content of these areas can students become truly "liberated"; that only the arts studied for their own sake can make men and women truly cultivated. I will try to show, briefly, that this claim and the objections against making the fine arts more practical, are founded on a mistaken conception of what constitutes "culture."

Rightly concerned with the preservation and transmission of culture, there are those who believe that it can be successfully passed on to the next generation simply by presenting it to students in a neat, carefully constructed package. If they were correct in their belief, we should find paradoxical the existence of magazines and newspapers, so-called "design" in furniture, automobile, and construction industries, and what is referred to in general as the "entertainment industry." Putting aside the myth that those who manage these industries only "give the public what it wants," we must realize that the people who control these media and industries are the people who attended the classes and took the examinations of the college teachers of English, speech, rhetoric, and art. Culture wrapped in academic packages was duly dispensed and duly noted by its recipients. But it was not thought to be very important, or perhaps other matters were thought more important. In either case, it is safe to suppose that the message was lost once school was out.

An hypothesis might be advanced to explain the slight impression made by packaged culture: it is not the culture, but the package, which gets in the way of culture's being genuinely acquired. For the package—that is, the courses devoted to literature and poetry, creative writing, drama, and the visual arts—keeps "culture" hermetically sealed off from the rest of the activities of living. To present the arts in such a manner, disconnected from science, history, the study of man and society, and an understanding and concern with vocations, is to communicate effectively the following message: The arts consist of objects and activities which are *sui generis* and independent of men's other concerns. If this is the case, culture will receive attention when one is *not* busied with more pressing concerns—that is, his job or his social and family life.

Thus to present culture in a package is to court the probability that the package will be resealed as soon as the formal course of study is finished. In a complex world of manifold practical concerns, few people will spend their leisure pursuing something taxing and difficult of access. These observations will need to be modified, of course, when "Under Milk Wood" competes successfully with "South Pacific," and the painting of Klee and Miro, and the animated films of the Canadian Norman Maclaren replace the creatures of Walt Disney in public favor.

More than dessert is part of a meal, culture is part of living. It is not something added to the business of living; it is a *way* one may live. If, like dessert, it is served as a separate course in college, it is likely to be skipped by those who are stuffed with the meat and potatoes of making a living, raising a family, and being responsible citizens. Thus if culture is to be acquired at all, it might be best to unseal the package, and let it permeate the rest of the things with which people are concerned.

All this simply suggests that exposure to the arts must make it possible for students to see their connection to the activities that are and will be important in their own lives. Such an approach to general education would enable prospective teachers not only to become more competent professionally, but, like students with other vocational plans, to have a better chance of finding meaning and value in the arts themselves. Study of the arts bearing on one's interests and commitments affords the possibility of their becoming genuinely functional in organizing the activities that constitute those interests and commitments. This, I submit, constitutes genuine culture, and it is the best, if not the only way, to greater breadth and refinement of culture.

In the last five chapters, I have tried to establish a base from which to speak in concrete terms about the kinds of conditions promoting the sort of learning involved in the acquisition of dispositions. The discussion of mind and thinking in Chapter IV enabled us to examine, in Chapter V, the utility and the limitations of problem-solving as a means of promoting learning. We then saw, in Chapters V and VI, how people can be helped to learn by pedagogical processes neither initiated by obstacles to ongoing activity, nor resembling, at their outset, the process of problem-solving. The present chapter has tried to exhibit some of the practical consequences for school teaching of a concept of aesthetic quality in experience that both purports to explain how lectures and books may facilitate learning, and that is itself grounded in the conception of mind elaborated in Chapter IV. In Chapter IX we shall return to the conception of mind and the notions of problem-solving and aesthetic quality that have been developed, and see how they are related to one another. But first, we must consider one more means by which people can learn: curiosity. Curiosity itself is a rather curious phenomenon, and we shall see that attempts to facilitate it are more curious, still.

# NOTES

1. In calling attention to this fact, Edgar Z. Friedenberg notes that in schools even 18-year-olds must secure special permission to go to the bathroom, and they must be prepared to answer the challenge of the hall guard on the way. How many American adults would willingly work under such conditions? See Friedenberg, "Intimations of Mortality in the Literature of Public Education," *Social Problems, 11* (1964), 306–311.

2. See David R. Krathwohl, Benjamin S. Bloom, and Bertram Masia, *Taxonomy of Educational Objectives, Handbook II: Affective Domain* (New York: David McKay Company, Inc., 1964), chap. 3.

3. See M. E. Sterrett and R. A. Davis, "The Permanence of School Learning: A Review of Studies," *Educational Administration and Supervision, 40* (December, 1954), 449–460. This review suggests that research in this area is not very conclusive.

4. Wilford M. Aiken, *The Story of the Eight-Year Study* (New York: Harper & Row, 1942).

5. See Raymond E. Callahan, *Education and the Cult of Efficiency* (Chicago: University of Chicago Press, 1962).

6. Walter M. Cook, "The Gifted and the Retarded in Historical Perspective," *Phi Delta Kappa, 39* (1958), 249–256.

7. It is not clear why it is so important to finish school. Surely no

one would admit that his education is over when school is over. If this is the case, then why abandon schools at the age of 18, 22, or any other age? An effective system of schools might well add depth to what is learned from experience at any age. This, at least is the not unreasonable argument of those who favor what is called "continuing education." James R. Kidd, *Financing Continuing Education* (New York: Scarecrow Press, 1962), p. 60, quotes Sir Richard Livingstone: "Youth studies but cannot act; the adult must act, and has not opportunity of study; we accept the divorce complacently. But action and thought, living and learning, naturally belong together and should go hand in hand. Instruct children in civics at school if you will. But when the children are adults and have votes, let such instruction be available so that their votes can be used with intelligence." Also see Renee and William Petersen, *University Adult Education* (New York: Harper & Row, 1960), pp. 9–10.

8. It is appropriate to put students together not simply when their backgrounds are *similar,* but just as important, when they are *different.* Current tendencies to try to group students on the basis of their similarities would seem to ensure their being rendered incapable of becoming familiar (in a context of cooperative, purposeful activity) with people who are different from themselves. Such lack of familiarity may result in lack of understanding, sympathy, and skills and dispositions of conjoint deliberation. The eventual result, then, may be failure to take others into account in the course of making personal, social, and political decisions.

9. See John I. Goodlad and Robert H. Anderson, *The Nongraded Elementary School* (New York: Harcourt, Brace, 1959), and B. Frank Brown, *The Nongraded High School* (Englewood Cliffs, N.J.: Prentice-Hall, 1963).

10. D. E. Berlyne argues that boredom is a function of an *increase* in affective arousal, signs of which are restlessness and agitation. He is probably correct, although the occurrence of *this* sort of arousal is a function of *lack* of arousal with respect to stimuli to which attention must be given. See Berlyne, *Conflict, Arousal, and Curiosity* (New York: McGraw-Hill Inc., 1960), pp. 189–191.

11. I take it that this is what John Dewey had in mind when he wrote, ". . . the principle [of altering dispositions through direct appreciation and keeping 'alert and effective the interest in in-

tellectual progress'] applies to the primary or elementary phase of every subject"—whether the subject appears at the first grade level or in college. See Dewey, *Democracy and Education* (New York: Macmillan, 1916), p. 273. The point made here has been put in another way by Israel Scheffler, when he wrote of introducing students to the "live and evolving traditions" of various areas of inquiry. See Scheffler, "Philosophical Models of Teaching," *Harvard Educational Review*, 35 (1965), 142.

12. F. H. Lund, *Psychology: An Empirical Study of Behavior* (New York: Ronald Press, 1933), pp. 403–406.

13. Fyodor Dostoevsky, *Crime and Punishment,* trans. by Constance Garnett (New York: Macmillan, 1956), p. 49.

14. It is to be hoped that what is being proposed here will not be confused with what often turn out to be indoctrination courses for prospective teachers.

15. To take but one instance: Great sums of money are currently being spent on the improvement of teacher education; yet, if a small fraction of it were spent on collaborative efforts to prepare textbooks that were at least interesting to read, the expense would be more than justified.

16. See T. M. Stinnett and G. K. Hodenfeld, *The Education of Teachers* (Englewood Cliffs, N.J.: Prentice-Hall, 1961).

17. See James B. Conant, *The Education of American Teachers* (New York: McGraw-Hill, 1963), and James D. Koerner, *The Miseducation of American Teachers* (Boston: Houghton Mifflin Co., 1963).

18. See, for example, Harry S. Broudy and John R. Palmer, *Exemplars of Teaching Method* (Chicago: Rand McNally, 1965), and William M. Smail, trans. *Quintilian on Education* (Oxford: Clarendon Press, 1938).

# VIII

## CURIOSITY

A PERSON WHO IS CURIOUS MAY FIND SOMETHING OUT. A PROBLEM need not arise in the course of some purposeful, ongoing activity in order for learning to be initiated. (But a curious person is one who *makes* a situation problematic for himself.) Nor are cues needed that are dominantly aesthetic in character in order for learning to be initiated. A person who is curious can acquire information, skills, and dispositions if he is simply left to himself.

It is commonly (although not very perceptively) said that children are "naturally" curious. Were there any truth in this, it would be wise to utilize that curiosity in schools. Surely any behavior normally engaged in by children that could facilitate learning ought to be capitalized on by educators.

But *how* is curiosity to be cultivated? Since children are not always curious, must teachers wait patiently for curiosity to appear, and perhaps institute other activities in the meantime? Or can they do something to promote curiosity in pupils? About what sorts of things can children be expected to be curious, and under what conditions will such curiosity thrive, so that learning can result?

## THE MEANING OF CURIOSITY

The above questions can be dealt with only insofar as we have some notion of what curiosity means. We shall have to be explicit about this, for—as will be pointed out in more detail later—we often apply the term curiosity to cases of human action that have little in common. One may be exploring the inside of a seashell, or solving some pressing problem, or engaging in social intercourse; in each case he might be described as being curious. But these actions are quite dissimilar, and we will not get closer to dealing intelligently with curiosity by using it as a blanket term to cover such disparate events. Our meaning must be narrower, then, so we can clearly and consistently distinguish among actions whose origins and outcomes are clearly different.

We often hear people say they are "curious." But if they do not tell us about it, we must infer their curiosity from observing the way they act. To say this is to imply that the noun curiosity refers to no substantive thing at all, but functions much like the noun, mind. That is, curiosity is a term applied to people when they act in certain ways. Inferred from such acts, it often purports to explain those acts. Why did he do it? Because he was curious. As we will shortly see, the explanation itself stands in need of considerable explaining. After all, why was he curious?

When curiosity is thought of in terms of overt behavior, we have in mind the explorations people make or the questions they ask. We will examine exploratory behavior in some detail, but first we need to look at how people ask questions. The term curiosity applies when people want to find things out, but people who ask questions do not always want to find things out.

Take as an example the small child who asks, "Why is the sky blue?" Such a child might be called curious, but does he really want to find something out? It is reasonable to ask this question because we are uncertain about how to answer the child. As an answer to why the sky is blue, we might mention the diffraction of light by the atmosphere, or we might say that God kicked over a bucket of blue paint, or we might even answer, "Because your eyes are blue." Any of these answers might satisfy the child, for he has no way of discriminating a satisfactory answer from an unsatisfactory one. But normally, when one wants to find out something, he is able to apply some criteria for judging what would or would not satisfy his inquiry. If this is so, we might suspect that the child's question did not proceed from a desire to find out something.

Let us approach the question, "Why is the sky blue?" from another tack. Suppose we answered the child by asking him, "Did you expect some other color?" The child probably did not, and this is one reason it is difficult to answer him. For if a person asks about something which is contrary to his expectations, we have a clue as to what a satisfactory answer might include—just as the asker of the question also has a frame of reference in which to put the answer. But when a question presupposes no particular expectations about the event in question, it becomes so difficult to provide an answer that we may reasonably doubt whether the question was, in fact, a request for information. What is being suggested, then, is that the child who asks, "Why is the sky blue?" does not usually wish to find anything out at all. Therefore, it would not be proper to call him curious.

It is more probable that this particular child is simply expressing a desire for social intercourse or a need for attention, and that he has found success in the past by putting things in the form of a question. It would not be useful to apply the term curiosity to cases like this, for if we did we should find that the attempt to utilize curiosity in school settings only lead to frustration.[1] Since such questions are not genuine requests for information, they do not easily lend themselves to cognitive development in schools.

Whether or not it is accompanied by the asking of questions, the kind of behavior that is more dependably related to curiosity is manipulatory, or more generally speaking, exploratory behavior. When people (or animals) handle things, turn them around, pull at them and shake them, or simply inspect things, we say they are curious.

But not always. When someone shakes a box he has been packing in order to find out whether he should stuff it with more tissue, or when he asks where the evening paper is, we would not say he was curious. For his overt behavior has, in these instances, been goal-directed; normally we do not describe it as curiosity behavior. When someone acts in an exploratory way to achieve a particular purpose—when his behavior is instrumental—we do not explain those acts in terms of curiosity; the "why" of the act is answered in terms of the purpose of the act.

For this reason, curiosity is normally ascribed to people when their exploratory behavior is not engaged for any known purpose. If it is not intended to produce any particular and later result, exploratory behavior, we might suppose, is engaged in for its immediately felt value. It may be worth searching for food if one is hungry, for shelter if one is cold, or for a hiding place if one is being pursued by an enemy. But if one has no such purposes and continues to explore his environment, it must be assumed that he finds the activity intrinsically satisfying. Thus a psychologist states that such exploratory behavior, insofar as it indicates curiosity, is:

> Unrelated to any goal and independent of any special internal state. . . . It is carried out for its own sake and not merely in relation to satisfying one of the conventionally accepted homeostatic needs.[2]

When someone is striving to achieve a particular practical goal or purpose—whether it be to pack a box, to read the paper, or to satisfy hunger—we normally describe his behavior in terms of trial and error or in terms of problem-solving. We do not ascribe his exploration or his question to curiosity. The more one's behavior is dominated by a strong practical goal or physiological drive, the less likely are we to call him curious. Thus while curiosity may to an extent be involved in problem-solving, it is not curiosity, but rather the chosen end-in-view which dominates and characterizes problem-solving. Of course, the curious person may indeed *set* himself a problem, and thus it would be appropriate to say that curiosity may in some instances be problem-*setting* behavior.

On the basis of this understanding of the concept of curiosity, the experience of one who is being curious shares a feature in common with experience that has aesthetic quality. In both cases, the experience is undergone for reasons other than the value of its possible consequences. Whatever those consequences might be, experience is undergone or undertaken for its immediate, directly felt value.

It is not necessary for a man to scurry about examining things in order for the term curious to be properly applied to him. A rat's explorations are limited to overt acts, but since a man can try things out *covertly* (see Chapter IV), he may in fact *be* curious without exhibiting any curiosity behavior at all. Because men can make plans and test meanings covertly, and because the meanings with which they deal (unlike the stimulus-bound meanings of most lower animals) are not tied to events perceived in the immediate environment, it is possible for men to pursue their curiosity in ways unavailable to most lower animals. If Professor Harlow's monkeys were curious about locks, they could only tinker with them[3]; a man curious about locks can speculate about them before he tinkers and, formulating questions and rejecting some answers, begin his tinkering in a more systematic and productive way.

That human curiosity may be covert suggests at least two additional features of its appearance in people. Both these features have important implications for the utilization of curiosity in school settings. First, curiosity or covert exploratory activity may set its own goals (e.g., "I wonder how that lock can be opened. . . ."), and may be pursued according to procedures similar to those found in other kinds of problem-solving situations.[4] Since the examination, overt or covert, is still without intention of practical consequence, it may still be called curiosity. That is, even though one's query about the lock may be followed by very systematic investigative techniques, the total set of acts is still a case of curiosity as long as one has no extrinsic purpose (e.g., to escape from the room) in opening the lock. In a systematized and more sophisticated form, this total set of acts may be called "scientific inquiry." The import of this for schooling is that the potentiality of curiosity for further speculative development does make it a possible springboard for school learning situations. Yet it is worth repeating that these exploratory, investigative activities—even as they are engaged in by scientists—are pursued for the immediate satisfaction derived from the conduct of the activities themselves.[5]

The other feature of men's curiosity is that overt activity may at times *interfere* with its initiation. For it is often during the times that we are not called upon to do something about which we become curious. Thus, unlike the busy laboratory animal, the curious human may not *look* very active at all. Yet it is at these very times that teachers feel impelled to apply pressures to students, for to be inactive-looking is to give the impression of idleness. Idleness not only is held to be a moral evil, but also obstructs the hopes of some educators that students be constantly and actively problem-solving, or absorbing, or reciting information. But curiosity (as it will be pointed out in greater detail later), is not always compatible with these latter activities. Curiosity often grows from inactivity and leisure.

Thus if curiosity is to be respected and cultivated in schools, a certain amount of leisure must be tolerated. Indeed, it would be surprising if students and teachers alike did not appreciate an occasional respite from the vigorous and sometimes even frantic pursuit of knowledge that marks so many classrooms. To recommend that students be given some leisure in order to learn is but to recall what the ancients believed to be a necessary condition of learning. But for the time being, we can put the matter in a negative way: so long as students are continually under pressure to complete assignments, all talk of cultivating curiosity is idle. It will be shown that *merely* to provide leisure is not necessarily to insure the arousal of curiosity.

## CONDITIONS FOR THE
## AROUSAL OF CURIOSITY

Perhaps enough has been said about what is meant by the term curiosity to consider the question, *why* are organisms curious? What makes them that way? The vitalistic and mechanistic theories of human behavior and learning considered in Chapter III both fall short of a satisfactory answer. To say, on the one hand, that curiosity emanates from some inner need or urge only begs the question, for we should want to know how it is that such inner states come into being. And we should be quite in the dark as to how to get at such a spectral emanation in order to stimulate or guide it. If, on the other hand, it is said that the behavior of organisms is but a conditioned response to specific environmental stimuli or to organic drive states, we should be at a loss to account for the appearance of curiosity, which seems to be free of both these types of influence or motivation. Yet here is a paradox: We seem to be seeking motivation of behavior which, of all activities, appears to be unmotivated. For if the term motivation refers to whatever may be taken to account for the direction, vigor, and persistence of behavior[6] (and curiosity exhibits all three characteristics), the very definition of curiosity precludes mention of the mechanisms of strict behaviorism, and seems to throw us back into the mysteries of hidden urges and instincts.

Like most paradoxes, however, this one may have been created for us by our misconceiving the nature of the activities of organisms. The dominant trend in psychology has tended to emphasize the notion that organisms are essentially passive, lying inert until the onset of some stimulus which galvanizes them into action. It has been held that action undertaken is meant only to deal with the stimulus (e.g., hunger, food, threat, etc.) in some way, and that presumably, success on the part of the organism in effect "turns it off" until the next stimulus appears. Laboratory experiments have tended to support this conception, for the investigator usually puts his animal into a deliberately simplified environment and controls the stimulus situation so that it breaks into a period of relative quiescence. Indeed, the laboratory animal may wait until it receives a stimulus. There is, after all, little else for it to do.

These highly restricted laboratory procedures have been criticized on the grounds that if an animal is subject to highly artificial and idiosyncratic conditions, its behavior will resultantly be highly artificial and idiosyncratic.[7] The conclusion for assessing such research if this: If the behavior of an animal is observed under carefully controlled and limited conditions, then, we shall understand increasingly more about *that* animal's behavior *under those conditions*. The error (and it is not necessarily the fault of the researcher) has been to overgeneralize—to assume that what a rat does under contain conditions will be done by other organisms (including men) under similar conditions, and what is worse, to assume that organisms will behave in their natural environment in ways quite similar, if not identical, to the ways in which they behave in laboratory cages and mazes.

The outcome of such thinking has been to assume that all organisms, including men, are naturally inactive, waiting for something to happen to which they can react. What is being characterized here is not necessarily a logically organized set of propositions which someone might care to defend. Rather, it is a pervasive tendency in thinking that has been encouraged by the specific directions of experimental research that has selected discrete, responsive acts on which to focus its attention. But since the notion of organisms as merely reactive is only an assumption lacking substantial support, we are at least free to entertain a different assumption.

Let us, then, attempt to deal with the question of why people are curious by assuming that all organisms, including men, are naturally active. We shall see that this assumption allows us far more easily to account for the nature of curiosity. But first it might be noted that the notion of an active organism in part controlling the very stimuli to which it is sensitive and upon which it acts is not simply the pious wish of a philosophic tradition exemplified in Liebniz's *Monadology*. For this concept of organismic life has, in fact, received serious consideration by empirically oriented psychologists ever since the publication of John Dewey's criticism of the reflex arc conception of behavior in 1896.[8] That organisms are constantly active has more recently received support from physiological studies of brain functioning.[9] Finally, current theorizing in the field of motivation has increasingly utilized the conception of an organism as inherently active and not merely waiting for something to happen to stimulate it into activity.[10]

Additional support for conceiving organisms as naturally active is found by considering what happens when they are forcibly held inactive. In one notable study, college students were paid twenty dollars a day simply to lie on a bed for 24 hours under conditions of nearly total auditory, visual, and tactile sensory deprivation. That one student quit to take a job at hard labor for less than half the pay is only one indication of the negative affect produced by the boredom enforced by the experimental conditions. After activity and sensory stimulation had been curtailed for a time, the subjects became increasingly restless, unable to sleep, and saw hallucinatory images. Consistent with what is being advanced here, the investigator concluded that variety is not the spice of life; it is the very stuff of it.[11]

According to Robert S. Woodworth, environment-directed motor- and receptor-activity is the:

> fundamental tendency of animal and human behavior and . . . the all-pervasive primary motivation of behavior.[12]

Robert White has speculated as to why this should be so. He suggests that an inherent motive to achieve competence in dealing with one's world lies behind the constant activity of organisms, and is especially significant in the play of infants and children. Their curiosity, manifested in the exploratory and manipulative behavior of examining, pulling, shaking, dropping, and tearing, is probably their only means of learning to discriminate visual patterns, of learning to handle things with facility, and of learning to build up concepts of the enormous variety of things with which they come into contact. These activities may be intrinsically satisfying for infants and children, but their long-range utility is even more important. For by what other means could people acquire the complex cognitive and motor skills that are needed to deal with the problems and needs of their later years? Considering how slow the rate of learning is in human infancy, and how much there is to be learned, White concludes that:

> children would simply not learn enough unless they worked pretty steadily at the task between episodes of homeostatic crisis.

> The association of interest with this "work," making it play and
> fun, is thus somewhat comparable to the association of sexual
> pleasure with the biological goal of reproduction.[13]

There would appear to be no lack of theoretical and empirical
support for the claim that organisms are naturally active and, consequently, naturally tend to explore and be curious. Yet even so,
the most cursory observation of our fellow men often seems to contra-
dict this. On every side we are familiar with withdrawal from environmental interaction, with the institution of inflexible routine,
with fear of experiment and risk-taking, and with lack of curiosity.
If the claim of a constantly active organism and of a natural
tendency to deal with the environment is to stand, we must account for the many instances where such behavior fails to appear.
Such an accounting will also provide a clue to the sorts of conditions that would permit and even encourage such behavior, and
would also allow for the cultivation of curiosity.

We are looking, then, for the conditions that inhibit exploratory activity and curiosity, and we may take our cue from
White's phrase, "between episodes of homeostatic crisis." For it
stands to reason that under the pressure of strong physiological
needs, any activity not directly related to their satisfaction will be
inhibited. After a hard tennis game in the hot sun, the thirsty
players do not become curious about the environing plant life.
Nor, indeed, do they become merely curious about the location of
drinking fountains. They will very likely take pains in searching
for one. Just as they inhibit learning, strong drives also inhibit
curiosity:

> the hungry child is a most incurious child, but after he has
> eaten and become thoroughly sated, his curiosity and all the
> learned responses associated with his curiosity take place.[14]

Needs that are felt especially strongly and the pursuit of goals
to which they give rise may inhibit curiosity, but inhibiting conditions can just as effectively be imposed from without. As the
anxiety produced by threat can result in a loss of flexibility in
intellectual functioning and a resultant rigidity of behavior (which

itself would preclude being curious),[15] so one of the concomitants of anxiety is a drastic reduction in exploratory play.[16] Finally, it is a matter of common observation that the more one's activities have become routinized and relatively automatic, the less curious does one tend to be. For the regulation of behavior by routine, in narrowing the meaning of that behavior, limits thinking (see Chapter IV). Yet it might be noted that once any behavioral sequence can be performed virtually without thinking, one can then afford to become curious about other things. It is because the experienced driver need not consciously consider the operation of driving his car that he can become curious about the effect of billboards on popular conceptions of truth, goodness, and beauty. Whether such curiosity is to remain merely idle and be quickly dissipated, or whether it will be pursued and transformed into a problem, is largely a matter of the kinds of dispositions one has toward the objects of his curiosity and speculation, as a residue from past experience and learning.

The conditions that inhibit curiosity—strong needs, determined goal-seeking, threat and anxiety, habit—are common enough occurrences in everyday living and are reflected, unfortunately in some cases, in school settings. Hence the observation that many people do not show much curiosity, while quite true, does not weaken the claim that organisms, including people, are normally active and (except for the aforementioned inhibiting conditions) curious. And so curious and active are people when not directly inhibited that under the conditions of sensory deprivation noted earlier, their activity will take the only path left open: deprived of the opportunity to examine or deal with the world outside, Heron's bedridden subjects became convinced they saw columns of quite purposefully marching squirrels and eyeglasses.[17]

If schools were to capitalize on curiosity, it would be necessary to do more than simply avoid inhibiting it. For we must assume that when students arrive in the classroom, they already have a range of interests, purposes, and uncompleted activities of their own. Thus if we were only to relieve them of certain threats and routines, we could expect them at once to commence pursuing their own interests and purposes. (This normally happens, incidentally, when teachers step out of the classroom for a moment. The non-academic nature of the student behavior that often ensues is some indication of the extent to which school studies have become identified with *their* interests and purposes.) If the removal of inhibitive influences is a negative condition for the appearance of curiosity, are any positive conditions available?

Whether anything can deliberately be done to promote curiosity will depend on the nature of the things and events about which people normally become curious. We have already seen (in Chapter VI) that one way of conceiving the behavior of organisms is to suppose that apart from activities directly connected to physiological needs, they strive to maintain positive affect. We have seen, too, that such affect is a function of the way in which cues in the environment arouse and satisfy expectations. If the events following the arousal of an expectation are perceived *just* as they were expected to be, interest wanes in seeking to maintain or reinstate the original cue. In human contexts this state of affairs is called boredom, and can occur whether the cue for an expectation is a school lesson, a work of art, or a personal acquaintance. If our chess partner pursues the same strategy every time we capture each other's queen, we get used to that move as a cue for the ensuing strategy. And unless that strategy continues to baffle us, we become bored with him as a partner after that point in the game. The series of events has become too familiar to remain attractive and maintain interest or curiosity.

On the other hand, attention is not likely to be maintained when we do not know *what* to expect. Suppose we have never played chess before and our friend, perhaps missing his regular chess partner, extols the virtues of the game, and insists upon our learning it at once. He sits down at the chessboard, sets up the pieces, runs quickly over the rules, and then says, "All right, you move first"! Under these conditions, when the cues are remote from our experience and we, consequently, have only the vaguest of expectations, we are likely to experience discomfort. Thus when a situation is either too familiar or too remote, curiosity is inhibited and attention wanes. We may feel boredom, restlessness, or aversion,

**and** the situation is made worse if we cannot escape it—as so often happens to adults at work and in social situations, and to children in schoolrooms.

Psychologists say that organisms will

> normally strive to maintain an intermediate amount of arousal potential,[18]

or that

> positive affect is the result of smaller discrepancies of a sensory or perceptual event from the adaptation level of the organism.[19]

What they mean in more familiar terms is that people are attracted to things in their environment familiar to them and yet still having an element of novelty or surprise. And because they are attracted to them, people will seek out such things and events and strive to maintain them once they are found—unless, of course, they are distracted by other and more pressing concerns.

Imagine a situation, then, in which a person is neither engaged in a routine activity, nor pursuing some clear-cut purpose, nor subject to any pressing needs or threats. We assume that, far from being merely quiescent, he will be alert and active. Toward what, then, will he direct his attention? On the basis of what has been said, he will seek something that, for him, has an intermediate degree of novelty—something neither too familiar nor too remote. Such things will command attention, and be explored, and may even be manipulated, or otherwise dealt with. In short, such things will arouse interest and curiosity. And they will do so because the particular sort of environmental interaction in which a slight discrepancy is present or in which there is some degree of lack of correspondence between what is expected and what is subsequently perceived, is felt to be immediately satisfying—that is, valuable for its own sake.

A discrepancy or lack of correspondence between a perceived

event and one's expectation may result either from a delay, an inhibition, or an unexpected alteration in an expected perception. We can illustrate the arousal of curiosity under these conditions by examining some typical instances.

Suppose that Mr. Kalakian is in the outer office of his doctor, awaiting his regular medical checkup. There are some old magazines on a table near him, but he is not interested in reading them. Instead, he elects to explore his surroundings. Anything he sees or hears might arouse his curiosity. Soon, Mrs. Goldberg enters the room and seats herself opposite him. After about 5 minutes she stands up and removes her winter coat. "Now, why did she sit for so long in this hot room with her coat on?" wonders Mr. Kalakian. For when she entered the room, he expected her to remove her coat. But this event was delayed, and the delay aroused his curiosity.

Mrs. Goldberg then puts her pocketbook on the table where Mr. Kalakian can inspect it. On the top of the pocketbook is a thin strip of shiny metal, bent into rectangular shape. "Will the purse open when you press that thing, or is it just a decoration?" he wonders. Mr. Kalakian has *some* expectations about what the device is for, because he recognizes it as an artifact—a man-made object—and he believes that all artifacts have a purpose. In this case, his expectation is not about the occurrence of a particular event. Mr. Kalakian is not expecting Mrs. Goldberg to *do* anything with the device on her pocketbook. His expectation, instead, is a direct function of his assumption that all artifacts have a purpose and of his failure to immediately perceive a purpose in the object before him. Nothing happens for Mr. Kalakian. Mrs. Goldberg scans through an old medical journal and her pocketbook stays on the table. In this case, since no event occurred that might have fulfilled Mr. Kalakian's expectation, his curiosity was aroused and sustained.

A short while later, Mrs. Goldberg puts on her coat and leaves. Mr. Kalakian is nonplused. "Now, what in the world did she come in for in the first place?" he wonders. Had he given it conscious attention, he would have expected Mrs. Goldberg to remain in the outer office until she had at least spoken to the doctor. But her sudden departure was an event quite different from what he expected, and again his curiosity was aroused.

## CURIOSITY AND AESTHETIC
## QUALITY IN EXPERIENCE

It has already been noted that curiosity, like experience that is aesthetic in quality, is engaged in for the sake of its immediately felt qualities. Both are held valuable because of the direct pleasure or interest they afford, apart from whatever consequences (no matter how important *they* may be) might follow. Now we see that situations facilitating the appearance of curiosity are also marked by another feature we have previously found in aesthetic experience: the arousal of affect as a function of a discrepancy between the expectation aroused by a cue for experience and what is ultimately perceived to follow that cue. Yet within this similarity is an important difference; it is to be found in the nature of what is perceived to be discrepant in the two sorts of experiences.

The perception of a discrepancy must always involve the perception of two or more related things or events. But insofar as a discrepancy is *conceived* (that is, in thought) as well as perceived, those things or events need not be directly seen or heard. In an experience marked by aesthetic quality, the discrepancy is always between at least two[20] sets of perceived (i.e., seen or heard) sensuous elements. But the case is different with curiosity. We may recall our example of Mr. Kalakian in the doctor's waiting room. His curiosity is first aroused when Mrs. Goldberg fails to hang up her coat on entering the room; her behavior constitutes a delay of what he expected. But *how* she removes her coat, and *how* she hangs it up, are of no consequence here. Thus the discrepancy of which Mr. Kalakian was aware was between the practical meaning of a directly perceived event and an event that was *not* perceived. Yet when the latter finally occurred, it was not the sensuously perceived elements of that event that satisfied expectation, but rather the *practical meaning* of that event. The case is the same in both of the other examples. When Mr. Kalakian becomes curious about the metal gadget on the purse, and when he becomes curious about Mrs. Goldberg's leaving, the discrepancy arose between the *practical meaning* of a perceived thing or event and another meaning which remained ambiguous, vague, or confused because of a *lack* of relevant (that is, explanatory) perceptible events.

Thus curiosity and an experience having aesthetic quality both involve the perception (recalling, however, that perception always involves a degree of conception) of a discrepancy; in both cases that discrepancy involves a relation between things or events (in the next chapter, it will be shown in greater detail that these conditions also appear in problem-solving). When experience is aesthetic, the relation is between the patterns found in directly perceived sensuous elements—as, for example, in words, colors, or tones. In curiosity, the relation is between sensuous elements that are directly perceived (e.g., words, colors, tones) and the import or practical meaning of such perceptions that is for some reason unclear or ambiguous. When curiosity is pursued, an inquiry is instituted which may be called problem-solving behavior, and this, in turn, may pass imperceptibly into problem-solving, either of a speculative or a scientific sort. Yet the conditions that initiate curiosity are structurally similar to those that afford aesthetic quality to experience. These conditions are also similar to those found in the initiation and conduct of problem-solving behavior, except that an initial ongoing, purposeful activity is lacking.

We called attention, in Chapter VI, to the fact that the sort of discrepancy involved in experience having aesthetic quality was a function of the perceived relations of the sensuous elements (or form) of which the cue for that experience was composed. Yet in any such experience, the discrepancy that arouses affect may also be a function of the cue's sign-content. This happens, for example, in the paintings of Goya, where the magnificent external trappings of Spanish royalty clash unexpectedly with the degenerate and haggard faces of the royal personages themselves. And it occurs when an unexpected development in a drama indistinguishably combines discrepancy of both form and sign-content. Depending on what one is familiar with, anything in his environment may be a fit subject for curiosity. Yet we have also seen that anything in one's environment may also serve as a cue for aesthetic qualities in experience.

Although conditions are quite similar for the occurrence of curiosity and the experiencing of aesthetic qualities, they subjectively feel very different. The difference in feeling may be attributed to the fact that we ordinarily *call* curiosity an experience that begins in interest and as we try to clarify practical meanings, moves forward with a dominantly cognitive intent. On the other hand, we label as "aesthetic" an experience that, while also initiated by interest, tends to follow a course in which the expansion and refinement of feeling dominates. Yet insofar as the speculation and thought initiated by curiosity is pursued for its own sake, it is positively affective in quality. And insofar as feeling is refined when experience has aesthetic quality, meanings are being altered and refined —which is to say that thought (usually of a nonverbal, nondiscursive sort) is taking place. Curiosity and aesthetic quality, then, are labels used to identify, for practical purposes of communication, different aspects of events that share quite similar characteristics.

## CURIOSITY AS A VEHICLE
## FOR LEARNING IN SCHOOLS

Having said this much about the nature of curiosity and the conditions of its appearance, we may now return to the questions with which this chapter began: Can curiosity be cultivated in school settings, and can it be utilized to promote the kinds of learnings that educators deem valuable? We shall approach these questions by confronting three more specific ones. Just how curious are children when they come to school? Is it possible or practical to alter the school practices which tend to inhibit curiosity? To what extent can schools promote learning by deliberately facilitating and exploiting curiosity?

It is said that children, of all people, are naturally curious.

This claim is consistent with the assumption of a constantly active organism. But it does not deny the fact that for every child who explores his world at every opportunity and who interminably badgers with questions every available adult, there is also a child who prefers to do what he is accustomed to doing, who does not like to explore, and who only asks questions when the answers might further his own practical purposes.

We have seen that the curiosity and active exploration of even very young children can be truncated by instituting appropriate inhibitions, but this is not the only way such behavior is reduced. If curiosity is pursued for its own immediate value, then the future, with its goals and purposes, must be put off. It is easier for younger children to do this for at least two reasons. In the first place, only very gradually does a child acquire a conception of the relation between past, present, and future.[21] The young child may *behave* in terms of past experience and expectations, but without being able to *conceptualize* a future, his behavior and his meanings are tied to present experience. Without such conceptualization, the young child has no notion of the *meaning* of a goal or a purpose not an immediate and functioning part of his present activity. Thus having no conception of a future and what it may hold in store for him, a young child focuses his attention on immediate experience and its value. He can be curious about what is around him because, in a literal sense, nothing else exists for him.

Not only do children gradually acquire conceptions of past, present, and future as they get older; they are also increasingly basing their behavior on an understood past and deliberately orienting themselves toward a foreseen future. Growing children become increasingly planful, purposeful, practical. As they become so, they have less opportunity to be curious about what is not intimately related to their plans and purposes.

On the basis of these observations, it would seen reasonable to conclude that older students can be expected to be less "naturally" curious than younger ones. Hence curiosity should be both easier to find and easier to cultivate in younger children. It bears repeating that these conclusions are based not on any assumed dullness in older children, or on any particular school practices that gradually take the edge off curiosity, but rather on the normal patterns of maturation in Western culture.

In the last chapter, we discussed several school practices that tend to distract the attention of pupils from the immediate value of their present experience. The routinization of assignments, lectures, and recitations, and the pressures of grades, failure, and future vocational and academic utility, insofar as they distract attention from the present and even constitute threats, will interfere with the arousal and cultivation of curiosity. If tasks are very extensive or very difficult, must be completed in a limited time, or have become a matter of mere routine, then, they are unlikely to arouse much curiosity. Daily translations of Caesar's Gallic Wars do not seem well-calculated to arouse a student's curiosity in Latin literature. And having to understand and remember, for examination purposes, the reasons for America's entrance into the First World War, does not, in and of itself, seem likely to arouse curiosity about the conditions under which America might enter another world war.

That it is possible to mitigate the influence of these practices has also been suggested in the previous chapter. Still, the fact that much of what is done in schools must obviously have a future reference, combined with the fact of the increasing purposefulness of maturing children, suggests that it is neither possible nor very practical to eliminate entirely the practices that inhibit curiosity. On the other hand, curiosity might be both aroused and cultivated within certain disciplinary or subject matter areas. This brings us to the last of our three questions: How can curiosity be utilized by schools in the promotion of certain learnings?

In the case of younger children especially, whose symbolic skills have not reached a high level of sophistication, it should be possible to arouse curiosity by furnishing a classroom with a changing variety of artifacts and natural objects not wholly familiar to them. So long as children do not *have* to complete assignments about these materials they can be expected to become curious about them. The teacher's role would be to encourage the development of this curiosity into problem-setting behavior, and to provide further encouragement and guidance in the ensuing inquiry.

When we consider specific areas of subject matter content, we find that curiosity can be aroused in much the same way that those areas are made aesthetically interesting. Just as interest and enjoyment in paintings, for example, can be cultivated through the judicious use of materials exhibiting what Hebb calls "difference–in–sameness"—that is, a combination of the novel with the familiar —so curiosity and interest can be promoted by the same means in other fields of study.[22] Evidence of the efficacy of such means is already available. It was Jerome Bruner's claim that any subject of study could be pursued in an intellectually honest way by pupils at any stage of development,[23] and the recent development of programs in school mathematics[24] illustrates both Bruner's claim and what has been said here about curiosity. Teaching complex mathematical concepts and processes by way of games is a case of appeal to curiosity through the presentation of difference–in–sameness. Most children are already accustomed to playing games, and a game wherein the player must discover the rules—providing they are not too complex—presents a strong appeal to curiosity. In such a case, the student's expectation is delayed until the rule is found.

The work of Richard Suchman in teaching science to elementary school children is another example of the arousal and utilization of curiosity for the purposes of promoting school learnings.[25] The development of strategies for conducting inquiry into natural phenomena not only has gamelike qualities, but also confronts children with the paradoxes that appear when an apparently simple and familiar event defies a simple and familiar explanation. A paradox—the juxtaposition of seeming contraries or, as in these cases, of the familiar with the unfamiliar—is a natural way of arousing curiosity and interest.

The presentation of paradox is equally helpful in arousing curiosity when teaching social studies.[26] Much of what we might want to teach, for example, about wages and prices, production and distribution, may appear formal, distant, and rather forbidding to students. But to present the paradox of a nation whose productivity is so high that surplus foods must be destroyed or buried, while at the same time some of its citizens go hungry, is to make a strong appeal to curiosity and interest. The presentation of a paradox arouses curiosity by altering the nature of what was expected.

When one hears that food is overproduced, he does not expect to hear that people are hungry.

The presentation of such a paradox as a springboard for further study may sound like a "problems approach" to instruction, but the resemblance is in appearance only. As it was noted in Chapter V, the notion of a problem-centered course of study originally directed attention to the intelligent examination of the student's *own* problems. What is being considered here is, however, quite different. The paradox of poverty amid plenty just mentioned, while constituting a genuine problem when it serves as a guide to inquiry and study, is initially *not* the child's problem. Even if we think students *ought* to be concerned with such a state of affairs, most of them have not confronted it in their own experience, and most of them can conduct their daily affairs without ever thinking about it. Of course, one of the tasks of schooling is, presumably, to make students aware of, and to become personally involved in problems that are of great concern to all of society, whether or not students have ever faced them personally.

The purpose of this sort of instruction, then, would be to foster awareness of important problems, to cultivate dispositions to deal with those problems and particular methods of dealing with them, and to afford relevant information bearing on those problems. The problems may not be "felt" by students at the beginning of inquiry, but it is to be hoped (just as in the teaching of science) that they will be later. The impetus for conducting inquiry and internalizing problems that are essentially social or intellectual in nature is gained through an aroused interest; this can be achieved initially by arousing curiosity. The use of paradox as one way of presenting difference–in–sameness is as effective in teaching college students and adults as it is in the public schools.[27]

A note of caution about the utilizing of curiosity in school settings might be in order. Just as a lecture can be aesthetically attractive and yet promote only entertainment rather than learning, curiosity can be aroused about a topic and soon become dissipated or trivial. To promote the kinds of learnings sought by schools, curiosity, like the appearance of aesthetic qualities in experience, must be developed into particular interests and developed along cognitive lines. It is, of course, as easy to arouse curiosity about what is trivial as it is about what is important. Yet if curiosity aroused even about socially important matters remains simply curiosity, the importance of these matters sinks to the level of relatively trivial events that often provoke momentary curiosity in the course of daily affairs.

We may, for example, evoke curiosity and some interest in a school study by making it into a game. But if that study is pursued only as a game, we may have purchased the student's interest and developing facility at the price of his adopting a relatively stable posture of game-playing toward that study or topic. A game-playing approach to mathematics may be desirable, but it may not be desirable to approach the arts or the social studies in the same manner. For the content of these areas of study is closely tied to what is of deep concern to individual and social living. These concerns are not like games at all, and to approach them thus runs the risk of trivializing and dehumanizing them. Learning to multiply by utilizing concepts in set theory may *be* a game; learning about the consequences of foreign trade for international relations is not simply a game, for it may make a difference in how students ultimately choose to live.

## SUMMARY

We have seen that the arousal of curiosity is a function of the extent to which what is presented to someone involves the occurrence of novelty within something otherwise perceived as familiar. The arousal of curiosity *can* lead to learning, but not necessarily so. For learning to occur, curiosity must be guided. If it is not, it will very likely be dissipated not far from where it began.

If the curiosity of children is inhibited or frustrated it will rapidly extinguish as a disposition. In such cases, they will welcome the routines of schooling with its consequent dulling of thought as an alternative preferable to the anxieties created by pressures and threats.[28] If, on the other hand, curiosity is cultivated and utilized, so that the results of pursuing it are satisfying, a disposition to remain curious about things may be preserved, the disposition to follow curiosity into cognitive channels may be developed, and some of the skills and knowledge that schools deem to be important may be acquired.

As people grow older and become more mature, they become more oriented toward particular goals and purposes, and curiosity resultantly becomes less frequent. As indicated in Chapter VII, much of what schools do to take the edge off curiosity can at least be mitigated. But the tendencies of normal growth and the interest that schools necessarily have in the future make it increasingly difficult for schools to utilize curiosity in older students. In these cases, curiosity will remain dormant unless special attention is given to the manner in which subjects and topics are presented.

Apart from the particular ways in which curiosity may be aroused and dealt with in classrooms, however, we have discovered something about it which may be of great theoretical (and therefore, ultimately, practical) importance. And that is its relationship to the conception of the aesthetic quality of experience previously developed. He who indulges his curiosity does not do so under the pressure of practical needs, drives, or purposes, but independent of them. His curiosity needs no justification beyond itself. In this respect curiosity and its associated activities are similar to experience that is aesthetic, which is also sought and sustained independent of any instrumental value it may have.

Furthermore, we have found a similarity in the conditions which facilitate both the arousal of curiosity and the evocation of aesthetic quality in experience. The elements in a perceptual field may cue expectations somewhat discrepant with what is subsequently perceived, either through a delay in the subsequent perception, its inhibition, or its perceived difference from what was expected (these same elements appear in the early phases of problem-solving). When awareness of this discrepancy remains focused on what is directly perceived, it arouses affect which gives an aesthetic character to experience. But curiosity, too, appears when affect is aroused as a result of having had expectations that were discrepant with what followed upon them. In curiosity, however, expectations involve meanings that are referred to in perceptions, rather than embodied in them.

Curiosity and aesthetic quality may be found in experience that is not purposeful, practical, or specifically goal-directed. Such experience is characterized by the arousal of affect upon the perception of a discrepancy between what is expected and what is subsequently found. And in both cases the extent to which one will seek to sustain or pursue the experience will depend on the degree of discrepancy. If it is very slight, then curiosity or aesthetic impact—if either is aroused at all—will be quickly dissipated. If one is forced to continue attending to the cue, he becomes bored or restless. If, on the other hand, the discrepancy is great, one is likely to respond with confusion, offense, or ridicule, rather than aesthetically or with curiosity. In any event, what constitutes the degree of discrepancy is a function of both the environmental cue and the particular background of whoever perceives it. Finally, both curiosity and aesthetic quality in experience can facilitate the acquisition of dispositions. Thus when we shift our attention back to learning, we find that whether we speak of curiosity or of aesthetic impact as its potential initiators, we are speaking of quite similar kinds of conditions.

Throughout the last several chapters, we have inquired into the conditions under which dispositions may be acquired. We have also traced their consequences for methods of conducting schooling. We have found the particular methods that might facilitate learning in schools to be highly varied—from the instituting of problematic situations, to lectures, books, and many ways of organizing and presenting them. We have also seen that all of these teaching practices appear to depend, for their intended effect, on the extent to which they promote problem-solving, aesthetic quality in experience, or curiosity. The present chapter has suggested: what arouses curiosity is quite similar to what institutes aesthetic quality in experience. The next chapter will attempt to show these same conditions must also be present if problem-solving is to occur. By thus exhibiting the intimate relations among problem-solving, aesthetic quality in experience, and curiosity, and by indicating the relation of all three to learning, a single concept of learning will be suggested that is broad enough to serve as a criterion for the assessment of any particular method of teaching.

# NOTES

1. In a recent paper, Bernard Z. Friedlander fails to make a distinction between curiosity, the desire for social intercourse, and the pressure of felt problems. He concludes that curiosity (which, as he uses the term, might mean *any* of the above events) is of questionable value for purposes of schooling. See "A Psychologist's Second Thoughts on Concepts, Curiosity, and Discovery," *Harvard Education Review,* 35 (1965), 24–27.

2. S. A. Barnett, "Exploratory Behavior," *British Journal of Psychology,* 49 (1958), 301–306.

3. See Harry F. Harlow, "Mice, Monkeys, Men, and Motives," *Psychological Review,* 60 (1953), 23–32.

4. A detailed example of the pursuit of such curiosity that could *not* be said to have originated in an existentially problematic situation can be found in John Dewey, *How We Think* (Boston: D. C. Heath, 1933), pp. 92–93.

5. To say that the conduct of systematic exploratory activities (consequent upon the arousal of curiosity) is immediately satisfying, is to observe that the process of problem-solving itself may be permeated with aesthetic quality. And to say that a scientific investigator may pursue inquiry for this reason, *initially,* is *not* to say that after the inquiry is under way, he may not adopt new (and sometimes quite practical) ends and purposes.

6. See John W. Atkinson, *An Introduction to Motivation* (Princeton, N.J.: D. Van Nostrand, 1964), p. 274.

7. See, for example, William S. Verplanck, "Since Learned Behavior Is Innate, and Vice Versa, What Now?" *Psychological Review,* 62 (1955), 139–144.

8. "The Reflex Arc Concept in Psychology," *Psychological Review,* 3 (1896), 357–370.

9. See D. O. Hebb, *The Organization of Behavior* (New York: Wiley, 1949), *passim;* and K. H. Pribram, "A Review of Theory

in Physiological Psychology," in P. R. Farnsworth and Q. McNemar (eds.), *Annual Review of Psychology, 11* (Palo Alto, Calif.: Annual Reviews, Inc., 1960), 32.

10. See Robert W. White, "Motivation Reconsidered," *Psychological Review, 65* (1959), 297–333, and John W. Atkinson, *op. cit.,* 295–314.

11. Woodburn Heron, "The Pathology of Boredom," *Scientific American, 196* (1957), 56.

12. Robert S. Woodworth, *Dynamics of Behavior* (New York: Holt, 1958), pp. 124, 125.

13. White, *op. cit.,* p. 329.

14. Harlow, *op. cit.,* p. 25.

15. See Ernst G. Beier, "The Effect of Induced Anxiety on Flexibility of Intellectual Functioning," *Psychological Monographs, 65* (1951).

16. See E. G. Schachtel, "The Development of Focal Attention and the Emergence of Reality," *Psychiatry, 17* (1954), 309–324. With reference to a different, but closely related topic (creativity), John Dewey wrote: ". . . the demands of a particular problem and particular purpose inhibit all except the elements directly relevant. Images and ideas come to us not by set purpose but in flashes, and flashes are intense and illuminating, they set us on fire, only when we are free from special preoccupations." [*Art As Experience* (New York: Minton, Balch; 1934), p. 276].

17. Heron, *op. cit.,* p. 53.

18. D. E. Berlyne, *Conflict, Arousal, and Curiosity* (New York: McGraw-Hill Inc., 1960), p. 200.

19. D. C. McCelland, J. W. Atkinson, R. A. Clark, and E. L. Lowell, *The Achievement Motive* (New York: Appleton-Century-Crofts, 1963), p. 43.

20. Other discrepancies, for example those cued by sign-content in works of art, may also be involved in experience that is aesthetic in quality.

21. See K. C. Friedman, "Time Concepts of Elementary School Children," *Elementary School Journal, 44* (1944), 337–342, and J. Piaget, *The Psychology of Intelligence* (London: Routledge and Kegan Paul Ltd., 1947), pp. 136–137.

22. "Too much that is easy gives no ground for inquiry; too much that is hard renders inquiry hopeless. . . . unless the familiar is

presented under conditions that are in some respect unusual, there is no jog to thinking . . ." John Dewey, *How We Think* (Boston: D. C. Heath, 1933), p. 290.

23. Jerome S. Bruner, *The Process of Education* (Cambridge, Mass.: Harvard University Press, 1960), p. 33.

24. See Max Beberman, *An Emerging Program of Secondary School Mathematics* (Cambridge, Mass.: Harvard University Press, 1958).

25. J. Richard Suchman, "Inquiry Training: Building Skills for Autonomous Discovery," *Merrill-Palmer Quarterly*, 7 (1961), 147–169.

26. Insofar as the paradox is of little pedagogical help when students are wholly unconcerned about what is paradoxical, the concerns of the students cannot be ignored. See Richard E. Sullivan, "Clio in the Classroom," *The Centennial Review*, 7 (1963), p. 369.

27. For example, in pursuing with prospective teachers the relations that hold between the school and its supporting society, the writer found it useful to present the following paradox: It is often believed both that schools are maintained for the benefit of individual children and their families, and that everyone should be taxed to support schools. Confronted with the paradox of holding both these beliefs, students are encouraged to consider the relation between schooling and societal aims, as well as issues of private and public support of schools.

28. Remarking on the "interest" children sometimes show in the duller routines of schooling, John Dewey remarked: ". . . through custom we finally embrace what at first wore a hideous mien. . . . I frequently hear dulling devices and empty exercises defended and extolled because "the children take such an 'interest' in them." Yes, that is the worst of it; the mind, shut out from worthy employ and missing the taste of adequate performance, comes down to the level of that which is left to it to know and do, and perforce takes an interest in a cabined and cramped experience. To find satisfaction in its own exercise is the normal law of mind, and if large and meaningful business for the mind be denied, it tries to content itself with the formal movements that remain to it. . . ." in "The Child and the Curriculum," in Martin S. Dworkin (ed.), *Dewey on Education* (New York: Bureau of Publications, Teachers College, Columbia University, 1959), pp. 108–109.

# I X

## DISCREPANCY:
## THE BASIS OF
## GENERAL METHOD
## IN SCHOOLING

THE WORLD IS NOT SIMPLY OUR STIMULUS. IT IS ALSO OUR OYSTER. At times we must cope with it, but at other times we play with it. And sometimes we just contemplate it. At any of these times, we can learn from it. In the foregoing chapters we examined three general kinds of situations from which learning might result. These situations briefly can be characterized in terms of what initiates them, and how our responses to them are typically described.

294

1. Within the course of any activity we may be struck by the patterned relation of sensuous elements in something that is perceived. The quality of such experience is called aesthetic and its pursuit and refinement, whether or not it is focused on a work of art, is called appreciation.

2. In the relatively quiet periods between goal-directed activities we may encounter something novel within a familiar context. We react with curiosity about it. If the curiosity is followed up, we create a problem for ourselves and then engage in speculation or what may be called "scientific inquiry."

3. Bent on the pursuit of some goal or purpose, we encounter an obstacle. The obstacle may be some thing or event that interferes with activity from without, or it may be some shortcoming in ourselves; in any case, it is perceived as blocking activity that may be either overt or covert. The attempt to deal with the obstacle is called problem-solving.

What initiates each of these situations is the perception of a discrepancy. To that extent the situations are alike, but they differ insofar as the discrepancy involves different elements in each case. Experience itself, of course, does not come neatly encased in one or another of the paradigm cases described here. Any discrepant situation may, at one and the same time, involve a personal problem, a matter of curiosity, *and* perceived patterns of formal elements. For the purpose of the following analysis, however, three distinct kinds of discrepant situations will be discussed. Before examining the kinds of discrepancies involved, it will be well to recall what happens in the perception of any discrepancy.

## DISCREPANCY AS A PRECONDITION
## OF BOTH THINKING AND LEARNING

A discrepancy is a particular sort of relation, and the relation is usually one of slight difference. Because it is a relation, it is not possible, strictly speaking, to say it is directly perceived even in the way we speak (loosely) of directly perceiving, for example, a color, like red. Any perception of a discrepancy also involves some conception of relevant similarities and differences, whether or not the conception can be verbalized. But because the conception is so seldom brought to consciousness, we may speak of an immediate perception of a relation. When we are presented with two slightly different shades of red, we are directly aware of the discrepancy between them. Hence it is reasonable to say the discrepancy is immediately perceived, even though conception is also involved (the perception is not, of course, to be confused with knowledge, which must undergo some test). Similarly, should we run across the word "elephunt," the discrepancy between it and its proper spelling, while obviously involving conception, is still perceived directly. What distinguishes the three discrepancy situations discussed above lies in the character of what is directly perceived to be related to what. We will first examine the discrepancy relation involved in experience marked by aesthetic quality.

When one attends to the pattern found in the relations of sensuous elements as in tones, colors, or shapes, one must necessarily hold in suspension goal-directed or purposeful activities. Insofar as a pattern *is* found in directly perceived sensuous elements, we say it is meaningful, or it has artistic or aesthetic form. The meaning thus found cues certain expectations about how the pattern of perceived elements will continue or be filled out. When what we subsequently perceive is not in accord with those expectations, we become aware of a discrepancy. Thus the sort of discrepancy in experience that is aesthetic in quality involves the relation between the pattern found in a set of directly perceived sensuous elements and some other set of sensuous elements that is subsequently directly perceived.

When one is not actively pursuing a particular purpose, he may, instead of attending to the pattern of sensuous elements that is presented to perception, attend to the practical meanings of what he perceives. (Some people dispositionally attend to patterns, others to practical meanings. Most people, without strong dispositions in either direction, will let their attention be guided by the nature of the perceptual cue. Thus if a pattern does not strikingly emerge in the perception of an unfamiliar cue, one is likely to seek its practical import or associative meanings. The neophyte confronted by unfamiliar contemporary art forms, unable to find a pattern, is likely to ask, "What's it supposed to be?") Insofar as a perceived event has a practical or cognitive meaning, it functions as a sign, and its meaning is, therefore, indicated by, but not contained within, the perceived event. Thus the referential import or meaning of something perceived is a function of the way we connect it in thought to what is not directly perceived. As we apprehend such a meaning, we also have a relatively clear expectation about what it is that the perceived thing or event indicates.

When we run across something unfamiliar and attend to its practical or cognitive import, we find that we do not quite know what to expect. Because expectation is blocked, the meaning of the thing is unclear or ambiguous. Under these conditions we may, if not under the pressure of other concerns, become curious. This blockage, this confrontation with the novel, may be characterized as a discrepancy. The kind of discrepancy that marks curiosity involves relations of different sorts of elements from those in the discrepancies that characterize aesthetic quality. In curiosity, the discrepancy involves the relation between what is directly perceived and practical or instrumental meanings that are unclear because of what is not directly perceived.

When things and events are being dealt with in the course of pursuing particular goals or purposes, their meanings are perceived in relation to those goals and purposes. Thus the expectations we have are functions of the hypothesized connections we make between what is directly perceived, what is not perceived, and what we are aiming for. The expectation of achieving a purpose may be thwarted either by something that is directly perceived or by what is suggested by some perception. In either case we become aware of a block, an obstacle to purposeful (overt or covert) activity which, when subject to thought, may be conceived as a problem and pursued in the manner called problem-solving. One's initial perception of the obstacle, one's thwarted expectation, may also be characterized as a discrepancy. But this kind of discrepancy constitutes a relation between kinds of events different from those in the perceived relations that signaled curiosity or aesthetic quality in experience. When an obstacle to purposeful activity is met, the discrepancy involves a relation between meanings found in what is directly perceived and the purposes that we entertain.

Given the fact of a perceived discrepancy, what we want to know is how it eventually figures in the sort of experience in which learning occurs. What is of greatest importance, then, is what one *does* in face of such discrepancies. But what one does will first of all be a function of how he feels. When a perception does not arrive when expected, when it does not come as expected, or when it wholly fails to fulfill an expectation, affect is aroused. The affect which accompanies the awareness of any discrepancy first of all arouses and focuses our attention on our immediate situation. Routine, habit, or the automaticity of our responses is, for the moment at least, destroyed. In this moment, the attraction of attention and the arousal of affect is pregnant with the possibility of new meaning. It contains the germ of aesthetic appreciation, of speculation and science, and of practical intelligence. Whether the arousal of affect through the perception of discrepancy will yield such fruits depends on our manner of response to the discrepancy, to the means adopted to resolve or settle it. But this, in turn, depends on the size of the discrepancy. Thus, before examining ways of dealing with discrepancies, we shall first note how their size or extent affects subsequent operations, even to the point of preventing them from taking place.

In previous chapters we have seen how too small a discrepancy goes unnoticed or leads to boredom, and how a discrepancy that is too large arouses negative affect. It only remains to bring together those several discussions and show how the size of a discrepancy produces similar effects in any of the situations that are now under consideration. It should be remembered that however large or small a discrepancy actually "is" depends not simply on the nature of an environmental cue, but even more on what a given person is already familiar with.

When the pattern of sensuous elements in a work of art is so familiar that our expectations about continuations of that pattern are fulfilled just as expected, our attention lags. If we cannot escape the situation, we become bored and restless. Such is the effect of minute or imperceptible discrepancies; when affect is aroused, it is negative. Precisely the same effect obtains when, relieved of the pressure of goal-directed activity, we allow our curiosity free rein. If our surroundings are so customary that nothing novel presents itself our attention is not held, and we seek other surroundings (or, in woolgathering, we ignore our surroundings altogether). In both these situations no opportunity is presented for intelligent, minded behavior; there is nothing for mind to do. Yet the same holds in cases where activity is purposeful and goal-directed. If the expectations concerning what we are about are continually and fully confirmed by each succeeding event, just as we expected, there is literally no need to think about what we are doing. Discrepancies are minimal or nonexistent, and we act by habit. In such cases we may not even attend to our acts, although, if for some reason we must (as, for example, school children must when they are mechanically learning their multiplication tables), the affect that is aroused is negative.

We may summarize the above by saying that in any human situation, if one's expectations are fulfilled just as expected, or if the discrepancies from one's expectations are very slight, then thought cannot occur—whether that thought might have taken the form of appreciating aesthetic quality, pursuing curiosity through speculation or scientific inquiry, or intelligently conducting practical affairs. Thought and intelligence need something to chew on, something to be directed toward, some resistance. They do not operate in a vacuum or feed on themselves. And when thought is absent, the kind of learning on which this study has focused cannot occur. Conditioning, of course, *can* occur in the absence of discrepancies, as is admirably set forth in the theory of programmed instruction which recommends that pupils learn by proceeding by very minute degrees ("small steps") through a program of instruction designed in such a way that errors are unlikely to occur. When obstacles (and discrepancies) are removed, conditioning proceeds unhindered. But conditioning precludes the operation of thought, and should, therefore, not be confused with the acquisition of dispositions that could be accounted desirable.

If very slight discrepancies in experience cannot be expected to eventuate in learning, the same conclusions must be drawn for cases in which discrepancies are quite large. We said earlier that a viewer is likely to turn away from a work of art done in a style that is wholly unfamiliar to him. If he experiences any affect at all, it will be negative. Similar consequences for the arousal of affect follow when we freely explore our surroundings, although in the realm of perceptual events that are practically meaningful, it is seldom that we confront the totally unfamiliar. Perhaps an instance can be found, however, if we recall how it felt to wake up in the morning in a hotel room in a strange city. Until mind begins to function normally, the affect aroused by the totally unfamiliar surroundings is usually mildly negative. Or take the case of a visitor to an international fair, beholding a full-scale cutaway model of an airplane engine. In the face of such overwhelming complexity and unfamiliarity, he is unlikely to be curious about it and speculate on how it works (although he may react to it as an *aesthetic* cue); as likely as not, he moves on to the next exhibit.

The same consequences for affective arousal result when very large discrepancies from our expectations occur within the course of purposeful, goal-directed activity. The affect that accompanies such large discrepancies is sometimes called shock. The discrepancy may be so great that it indicates failure to achieve the goal if the present line of action is sustained; in some cases, it may then be deliberately ignored in an effort to resolve the affect. On the other hand, its very size may turn shock by degrees into discouragement, whereupon the activity, instead of being blindly sustained, is simply discontinued, and the goal is abandoned.

In each of the above illustrations of a large discrepancy from expectation, experience either sought a new focus of attention or was exhausted of any minded component. As in the case of a very small discrepancy, then, a large discrepancy is not conducive to thought. And as such, it is not conducive to learning, either. If one's attention is to remain focused on the conditions that gave rise to the discrepancy, then, some intermediate degree of discrepancy must be found, wherein what is novel or obstructive appears in a context of what is familiar. Earlier, this was referred to a "difference-in-sameness." As often happens in genuinely problematic situations, affect need not be felt as positive in order for one to deal with the discrepancy in some way; yet it must not be so intensely un-comfortable that one is impelled to escape the situation entirely. Strongly held goals, of course, may enable one to deal with some very unpleasant problems, but only slightly negative affect may be enough to thwart curiosity and destroy aesthetic quality in experi-ence. The implications of these observations are significant for the control of the affective climate in school settings.

If a situation is to preserve its potentiality for promoting learn-ing, the discrepancy perceived in it must be of such a degree that an individual is impelled to deal with it in some way. What, then, could he be expected to do about the perceived discrepancy? His perception is accompanied by affect. When it occurs in a situa-tion most of whose components are recognizeable (as in any pur-poseful activity, in exploration, and when confronted by art con-taining sign-content), affect is normally felt as a more or less specifiable emotion. Thus in such situations one's feelings may be characterized by terms like surprised, concerned, mystified, confused, thwarted, amused, stirred, moved, and so on. But common to each one of these feelings is some degree of tension, doubt, and uncertainty. For whatever the situation may be, an unfulfilled, delayed, or surprised expectation will always be accompanied by affect that is suffused with tension and uncertainty. And, if the affect is neither too weak nor too strong, one will seek to resolve it. The way in which such affect can be resolved is to reinstitute meaning in the perceived situation. This will involve either overtly or covertly dealing with the situation in such a way that one's expectations can be altered to become consistent with what will be subsequently perceived. This can be done either by re-assessing the situation, by making overt changes in it, or by doing both. In any case, the discrepancy will be made to disappear, or to be greatly reduced. And when expectations are made secure, meanings become clear and stable.

Just what one does by way of reinstituting meaning in a situa-tion depends on the kinds of things involved in the relations that are perceived as discrepant. We have already seen in earlier chapters how aesthetic quality in experience may be pursued, how curiosity may be developed, and how practical difficulties may be dealt with intelligently. Now we can examine these several kinds of development together, relate them to the kinds of discrepant relations discussed earlier, and see how each of the modes of development is related to the conception of thinking presented in Chapter IV.

## THINKING: THE PURSUIT OF DISCREPANCIES INTO THE AESTHETIC, THE SPECULATIVE, AND THE PROBLEMATICAL

The moment when one's attention is attracted by a perceived discrepancy in a pattern of sensuous elements contains the germ of the aesthetic. But whether aesthetic quality does subsequently come to permeate experience depends on what follows from that moment. If the discrepancy is neither too great nor too small, and if one is disposed to suspend pursuit of practical meanings and one's own personal goals (apart, that is, from the goal of perceiving form), he may achieve aesthetic quality in experience by continuing to attend to the sensuous forms which first presented the discrepancy. This continued attention is precisely what was spoken of (in Chapter IV) as "covert trials" within the process of problem-solving. The differences between this covert activity and that which occurs in the process of solving problems are essentially two: (1) the problem in this case is not an obstacle in the way of purposeful activity, but rather is a problem one *makes for himself* in the very commitment to attend further to the perceptual cue; and (2) there is not normally any overt test of one's "hypothesis" or solution in this kind of covert trial. For these reasons, it is not always possible to tell by observation whether a person confronted by a landscape, a poem, a painting, or a symphony is achieving any aesthetic quality in his experience. However, because observation is unreliable, it is no indication that the concept of the aesthetic, therefore, has but a ghostly reference. That to which the concept refers is easily enough explained and understood; when we have done this, we can always ask a person when his experience could be so characterized.

What sort of covert trials does one make that lead to experiencing aesthetic quality? To ask this question is to ask, "How does one come to appreciate art?" or, more generally, how does one come to appreciate the patterned sensuous elements in any perceptual cue? There are, obviously, no exhaustive rules for answering this question, but some indication of an answer can be given. Most important, one must continue to attend to the sensuous elements that initiated the discrepancy. This means that for a time one must keep in the background other particular goals and whatever other meanings may be associated with the sensuous elements under consideration. What one tries to find in the course of this attention is a relation of sensuous elements or a pattern that affords a new meaning. Such a new meaning will alter one's expectations in such a manner as to become consistent with the sensuous elements subsequently perceived. This process, while not limited to responses to works of art alone, is often called "appreciation of the formal qualities of art." It is not undertaken overtly, nor is it often carried on with the help of language symbols. Thus the process is both covert and nondiscursive. Familiarity with styles and formal types in the arts, such as "mannerist painting" or the "Italian sonnet," serves as an aid in identifying patterns, although they are often taught in schools for other more obscure and less defensible reasons.

When a pattern is found, then, meaning is reinstituted and expectation becomes more trustworthy; discrepancy is thereby reduced and its attendant affect is resolved. It might be noted in passing that complete success in making such covert trials would result in our becoming bored with the set of perceptual cues in question. Thus works of art that have achieved continued fame over the centuries are usually those that contain enough internal formal complexity, and enough elements of surprise (that is, liberties taken within their stylistic genre), that one's efforts to find regularities and clarity in pattern seem never to be quite wholly satisfied.

The curiosity aroused when one's attention is attracted by some perceptual cue, the practical import or meaning of which is ambiguous or unclear, contains the germ of speculative thought and scientific inquiry. But again, whether these latter events will, in fact, issue from curiosity depends not only on the size of the perceived discrepancy, but on one's willingness to suspend other activities connected with previously entertained goals and purposes as well. Since the discrepancies involved in cases of curiosity have to do with the associative meanings of what is perceived (rather than only with a perceived pattern of sensuous elements), the development of experience that begins in curiosity will involve, among possible other things, covert trials at generating and establishing new meanings.

The less one is able to use language, the less one can think discursively. Hence an infant confronted, for example, with an unfamiliar package is likely to pick it up and rattle it by way of manifesting curiosity. But an adult's curiosity is more likely to be exercised covertly. He may simply regard the package, and after wondering what is in it or what it is for (discrepancy between what is perceived and what its import is), begin to project hypotheses about it. That is to say, he *makes a problem for himself.* For example, the way it is marked suggests that it came in the mail; its size indicates that it may contain a small appliance his wife is known to have ordered; etc. This process is normally called speculation; it is usually discursive—except for those moments called "insight" when a connection is suddenly made between previously disparate and half-hidden recollections—and it is always covert. As indicated in Chapter IV, testing is possible in the process of speculation, although it, too, is covert. For example, the hypothesis that the package just arrived is rejected when a postmark dated a week ago is noted. We see here that even the process of speculation may involve empirical observation; as it does, speculation more closely conforms to what is usually called "scientific inquiry." One may finally pick up the package and, finding it to be quite light, reject the hypothesis that it contains an appliance. Here one's covert trials have eventuated in an empirical test—that is, in the institution and observation of a change in conditions rather than simply an observation of what is there. This behavior, common as it may be, is quite analogous to the more elaborate and controlled procedures of experimental science.

Curiosity, then, if it is pursued, results minimally in a kind of speculation which is covert and usually discursive (involving either inductive or deductive reasoning, or both). It may also involve more careful observation of the perceptual cue and even include an overt test of an hypothesis, thus approaching in form scientific inquiry. If one's hypotheses receive more than a merely tentative confirmation, either in a covert or an overt test, then, a more stable meaning is achieved for the original perceptual cue; the discrepancy is overcome and the affect is resolved. Curiosity would seem to be the sole motivation for inquiry into problems that do not otherwise affect one's personal affairs. Yet it can quite reasonably be asked, why should young people in schools be curious about what is presented to them? And what guidance is given that might facilitate the processes of speculation and inquiry that have been described here?[1]

We have already spoken in detail about the process of solving practical problems, so it will be necessary here only to summarize that earlier discussion and relate it to the role that is played in it by the arousal of affect. The perception of an obstacle to ongoing, purposeful activity is an affective situation; perception and affect occur together and are indissoluble. The discrepancy lies between that of which we are immediately aware (including both what is directly perceived and its meanings) and our expectation that present activity will achieve our purpose. It makes little difference whether subsequent activity is described as an attempt to solve a problem, settle a discrepancy, reinstitute a meaning, or resolve affect; what happens is the same. As in the cases of speculation and scientific inquiry, covert trials involving hypotheses and tests, discursive thought, and data-gathering, are made. But unlike speculative inquiry, this process of dealing with an obstacle to purposeful activity must sooner or later eventuate in an overt test. For its function, after all, is to reinstitute not just meanings, but activities that will lead to the achievement of a goal. Since the affect aroused in connection with the initially perceived discrepancy is intimately connected with the conception of one's purpose, only resumption of activity that can be expected to achieve that purpose (or another purpose we are willing to substitute for it) can satisfactorily resolve the affect. But it might be noted that the discovery that one's purpose is, in fact, unattainable is another way of resolving affect, although the processes by which one reaches such a discovery are the same as those that lead to resumption of the original purposeful activity.

In discussing the ways in which discrepancies and affect are resolved in the development of experiences involving aesthetic quality, curiosity, and problem-solving, we have for purposes of exposition simplified matters. For in point of fact, very few of the experiences one actually has are "pure" cases of any one of these three types of activity. The events of daily life usually involve combinations of two or all three of these kinds of activities occurring at once in experience. A few examples may help in showing this. At the same time they will show how particular events of living come by the special qualities for which we prize them.

Most works of art present to a beholder what we have called sign-content as well as form. Thus the relations that arouse affect need not simply be those of perceived patterns of sensuous elements. Sign-content evokes ideas, beliefs, and values that, insofar as they are meaningful, relate to our purposes. Discrepancy in expectation may thus also be a function of sign-content, and the arousal of affect is, then, a function of both perceived form and discrepant expectations about meanings related to practical, social, religious, or intellectual purposes. In this last regard, affect aroused by art has a quality not unlike the affect aroused in meeting obstacles to ongoing, practical activity. And the resolution of this dimension of affect aroused by art is not unlike what has been called "speculation." Yet as long as the attention of the beholder remains focused on the sensuous elements in the work of art, his experience is properly said to have aesthetic quality, no matter what other kinds of covert activities are occurring simultaneously.

The work of contemporary potters illustrates this point. In regarding a pot, we normally are aware not only of its formal design, but at the same time, of how we would expect to *use* it (which is to say, our perception of the *function* of any utilitarian object consists of our relating what we see to what we could or would *do* with it—that is, to a real or hypothesized *purpose*).[2] Thus the affect aroused by a pot, a pitcher, or a basin involves our relating its shape to how it might contain or pour its contents, how we might hold it, and how its shape would affect its feel or balance. These latter considerations are seldom made discursively, but are simply and immediately a part of our perception of the pot. Some contemporary pottery, however, has been made with such sculptural qualities that it could not conceivably contain or pour anything. Thus a beholder could not imagine how to pick it up so that it would be balanced. This brings more discrepancy in expectation than normally can be experienced pleasantly, for perception becomes confused. In a sense we cannot, because of its unusual shape, perceive such pottery *as* pottery. But because the potter felt constrained to include in his work some rudimentary spout(s), we cannot perceive it as simply free-standing sculpture, either. The resultant confusion is often great enough to destroy aesthetic quality in experience, and the case is clearly illustrative of the interaction of responses (with their affective qualities) to perceived patterns and to practical purposes.

Most of us at one time or another have seen the type of mantel clock whose finely machined brass works are enclosed in a glass dome.[3] We are immediately struck by the perceived pattern of sensuous elements in it (its form) and are at the same time fascinated by how the clock might work. This would be a case, then, of affective arousal at once the product of both aesthetic quality in experience and curiosity. Depending on dispositions formed by past experience, observers may continue to attend to the form of the clock (the development of aesthetic quality) or may perform covert trials in an attempt to find out how it works (the speculative development of curiosity).

The pursuit of scientific inquiry has earlier been identified with certain types of speculative development of curiosity. Yet except in the cases of some children and a very few adults, curiosity is not the sole source of affective arousal in the pursuit of science. Scientists, like anyone else, are also working at a job, and the conduct and success of their inquiries is related not simply to their scientific concerns (i.e., what initially aroused curiosity) but also to the security, prestige, and status they hold as employed workers. Thus affective arousal in scientific inquiry is not wholly free of felt qualities associated with personal security and advancement, just as the solution of an intellectual problem for the scientist may, at the same time, be a solution of a personally practical problem (of, for example, whether and where to seek another post), or of a social problem (e.g., a cure for a disease). So prevalent is this multidimensional aspect of affective arousal in scientific inquiry that the danger is always present of its affecting the *outcomes* of inquiry. That is, one's concerns about personal status and prestige (or social amelioration) affect not only subjects selected for inquiry, but may also affect and even distort the results one reaches.[4] Thus one of the established criteria for judging the professional worth of a scientist (or worker in any intellectual discipline) is the extent to which his activities remain uninfluenced by, although not necessarily free from, personal and nonscientific concerns. This, I take it, is what is meant by "objectivity" (rather than the "truth" of the results of one's investigations), and in this sense historians, literary critics, philosophers, and indeed workers in *any* field can be just as objective as experimental chemists.

This conclusion leads us to consider the affective components of the activities of workers in other, so-called nonintellectual vocations. The work that adults do comprises a significant proportion of their waking hours; insofar as people learn from their work— that is, insofar as the *way* they work forms certain dispositions about dealing with a variety of tasks, their work influences the way they approach activities off the job.[5] To the extent that one's vocational tasks are dictated by authorities, and to the extent one's job is routinized into repetitive, unthinking habits, one can be expected to carry the dispositions thus formed into his personal and social affairs. Thus such workers are often found seeking authority away from the job, routinizing their leisure activities, or seeking escape from routine through entertainments that similarly exclude thought, but in different ways (e.g., drinking, television watching, gambling, etc.). Yet the number of jobs which by their nature *must* be dictated and routinized are, through automation, becoming fewer, and increasingly more vocations allow, to a greater or lesser extent, for the exercise of thought. We might consider a problem that might confront a shoe salesman, by way of showing not only the multidimensionality in affective arousal and in modes of resolving affect, but also the identity of response patterns of workers in any field, be they shoe salesmen or chemists.

Styles in shoes change and the changes cannot always be accurately predicted in advance. Thus some shoe stores find themselves with a fairly large inventory of perfectly good, but currently unfashionable shoes on their shelves. Since it is not good business to keep a large stock of nonmovable items on hand, one problem that shoe salesmen face is how to sell a shoe to a woman which may fit comfortably, and look attractive on her, but is not consonant with the latest fashion. The point at which the problem becomes most acute (and, for some salesmen, the first time they become aware of the problem) is after the customer has tried the shoe on, stands up in it, and says, "It feels good, and I like the color, but it looks sort of out–of–date." The salesman now has a very practical problem to solve, the outlines of which are perceived at the moment the obstacle (". . . but it looks out–of–date") arouses affect. He is not merely curious about how this woman can be sold the shoes, but, since his own personal goals are involved in the selling—especially if he works on a commission basis—he must arrive at some overt test of whatever speculations he makes about the successful reinstitution of his own purposeful activity.

In a situation that calls for immediate action, the speculations of our shoe salesman must necessarily be nondiscursive, although he may risk "thinking out loud." The important point, however, is that his trials, both overt and covert, may involve the same procedures as those of any laboratory scientist. He must imaginatively consider what might work and reject at once those acts whose failure can be forecast without overt testing. As the same time, he must gather or recall as much data as is relevant to the problem. For example, he might be inclined to tell his customer that the fit and comfort of the shoes are more important than fashion, but a glance at her dress and grooming (i.e., data-gathering) leads him to believe that such an approach will not work (on the basis of the memory of previous experience which has yielded data of a psychological sort). Like the experimental scientist, he must make an overt trial—for example, "But the color of the suede is a good match for your handbag"—and like the former, he must be prepared to try something else if it does not confirm the hypothesis (which in this case was the unverbalized, "she will be disposed to buy the shoes if she can be convinced that they match her accessories"). The woman's next comment, "Oh, but I'm not planning to keep this handbag," sends him, in effect, back to the drawing board.

We tend at times to think the salesman's activity differs from the scientist's, whereas the differences are only ones of degree and emphasis. The arousal of affect initiates and initially guides activity and in both cases activity is terminated when the original affective situation is resolved by some overt or covert test. It makes no difference whether one's aim is to sell a pair of shoes or find some generalization that is true about cosmic rays. But the context is different in the two cases: the salesman is under the pressure of having to act overtly; normally he cannot, although he sometimes does, step to the back of the store to consider what to do next. The scientist normally is not under this sort of pressure (although he might be as, for example, in being limited in what he can do by the length of time during which an eclipse is total). The salesman's acts are perceived as being directly involved with his own purposes —e.g., to make his commission—so that curiosity is limited. The scientist's activity is not always perceived as having this direct personal connection (although he may be well aware that a promotion or the control of plague depends on the truth and originality of his generalizations). Yet, just as affect was seen to be multidimensional for the scientist, so it may also be for the salesman. For when he first encountered his customer, he may have thought, "This woman, given her age and appearance, can easily be sold a pair of shoes from the shipment that arrived yesterday, but I wonder if she can be persuaded to buy a pair of last year's shoes that are on the top shelf at the back of the store?" Thus, as in the case of the scientist, curiosity and practical goals may both be involved in the salesman's experience.

One further thing might be said about the vocational activities of both salesman and scientist. Insofar as they are not routinized or dictated by someone else (or by the absolute necessity of prior events), they may (as indicated in Chapter VI) be perceived aesthetically. When the sequence and connection of events in which one participates can be perceived at the same time as if one were at a distance from them[6]—when, that is, one is aware of one's self doing interrelated things instead of merely being aware of the separate things one is doing, one's experience of those events can become permeated with an aesthetic quality of the sort one achieves when reading a novel or attending a play. Yet the emotions one has are not like those felt when reading or at the theater, because they are indissolubly combined with the emotions that attach to one's curiosity, one's speculations, and one's personal and sometimes crucial goals and purposes. When the arousal of affect proceeds from experience in which aesthetic factors, curiosity, and personal goals all have a role to play, experience is felt as being most intense, rich, and personally satisfying. Such experience, involving the multidimensional arousal of affect, is probably akin to what Abraham Maslow has called "peak experience."[7]

We have previously spoken of the aesthetic quality in the experience of witnessing athletic events. We can now better understand the great emotional impact of some of those events since more than aesthetic factors are usually involved. There are obviously elements of curiosity involved in watching any game or athletic event, and they may relate to our practical goals as well (e.g., defending the honor of school or city, or winning a bet). But some of our most deeply held values also come into play before certain kinds of games. Thus the drama in a bull ring or on a football field, symbolic of the struggle between life and death, man and nature, or man in competition with his fellows, often arouses affect in connection with personal values and goals held at so deep and fundamental a level that we seldom deliberately think about them.

As the above experiences and situations have been described, it may seem that one is sequentially subject to three different sorts of affect: that involved in aesthetic quality, curiosity, and practical problems. And it might seem that one could be quite confused in trying to determine which sort of feeling or type of environmental

cue to deal with first. This, however, would misconstrue what has
been said, for the analysis of experience produces conclusions that do
not themselves look at all the way experience feels before analysis.
It is worth reminding ourselves that experience comes just as it
is, unanalyzed, and we feel all at once and together. Affect does not
make its appearance in a series of neatly labeled packages, each
package corresponding to some relevant psychological dimension
of the cue. What gives some experience its felt unity, however, is
just the way affect is aroused and resolved. For it is the basic event
of a perceived discrepancy in expectation—*no matter what* was expected—that it arouses affect. And it is the reinstitution of meaning
—*no matter what* kinds of relations are involved—that resolves the
situation in which affect was initially aroused. Thus as a person
reacts in a situation—as his feelings are aroused and he searches
for new meanings—there is no need for him to sort out the
different sources of affect and deal with them serially. His deliberate
response need deal only with what he perceives as being important
to him. But if we are to understand the nature of his responses and
how they are involved in learning, with a view to understanding
better how we might teach him, we must divide his experience into
categories that meet logical criteria even while doing violence to the
felt character of experience itself. It might also be added that the
units into which we have divided experience must serve to recon-
stitute the original experience when they are put back together, else
the analysis is invalid.

Before we examine the kinds of learning that result from the situations that were described above—assuming for the moment that
learning does occur—we might attend to a feature of all of them that
is significant for the way we think about any kind of learning. We
have seen that learning conceived as the acquisition or alteration of
dispositions involves those covert and not necessarily discursive activities that characterize minded behavior. In the present chapter we
have brought together and compared the various components of a
wide variety of human situations, and have seen that in each case the
occurrence of minded behavior has been a function of the way affect
is aroused, and the way affect and the conditions that aroused it are
dealt with. At the moment many theories of learning compete for the

attention of those who teach, all the way from personality and Gestalt theories to behavioristic theories and their subclasses of contiguity, drive-reduction, and reinforcement theories. But if the foregoing discussion has been correct, and if learning does in fact result from the sorts of conditions described, we can understand and deal with any kind of learning in terms of a single set of categories. On the basis of what has been said, learning (that is, the acquisition of dispositions, along with related knowledge, skills, habits, and attitudes) is a function of the arousal and minded resolution of perceived discrepancies from expectations. For lack of a better name, we might call the notion of learning that is being presented here (with due respect and apologies to others who have also discussed learning in these terms) an "expectancy-discrepancy" conception of learning.

## THE IMPACT ON LEARNING OF TIME AND THE OUT-OF-SCHOOL ENVIRONMENT

We must assume that the way one usually acts has a greater influence than anything else on how he will act in the future. In a certain sense, there is much truth in contiguity theories of learning.[8] The theory holds, however, that one's previous bit of overt behavior is most relevant in predicting his next bit of overt behavior when the conditions eliciting that previous behavior are repeated. What I am claiming here, however, has less specificity. For it would appear safer to say that the *disposition* according to which one acted previously is most relevant to his behavior in a subsequent situation, when the conditions are repeated that previously brought that disposition into play. In other words, the sort of contiguity with which we need to be concerned is that which holds between molar, but not molecular bits of behavior; that which holds between dispositions and behavior rather than between separate overt acts.

An example may help to illustrate this point. Suppose little Willie is sloppy—he leaves his toys where he last used them, he tosses his coat on the floor when he enters the house, etc. Now let us suppose we wish him to acquire a disposition to be neat or to put things where they belong. We can, of course, arrange conditions (e.g., a reward or a punishment) so that Willie will enter the house and hang up his coat. But simply in virtue of this, it does not appear to be a very safe bet that Willie will head upstairs and pick up his toys. Indeed, it would be hazardous to predict that he will hang up his coat the *next* time he comes home. One act does not a disposition make. But if, by working *with* Willie, we arrange it so that he hangs up his coat—*and* picks up his toys, etc.—on a great many successive occasions, and under a variety of conditions (e.g., when Willie is home on time and when he is late, when he is happy and when he is out of sorts, when he is hungry and when his bladder is full, etc.), we may come to believe (or at least to hope) that he has acquired a disposition to pick up after himself—and that he will tend to do particular things relevant to that disposition. When there is evidence for such a disposition—that is, frequently observed acts of putting things where they belong—we may then, but *only* then, predict his overt behavior respecting what he will do with his coat the next time he comes home, or what he will do with his toys when next he finds them on the floor. Needless to say, the identification of a disposition, like its acquisition, does not come at a particular moment in time.

By considering these relations between dispositions and behavior, we can also corroborate what we have already known for a long time. Pervasive learnings do not occur instantaneously, as if by magic. Except on very rare occasions—as, for example, in what is reported as being religious conversion[9]—learning, the acquisition or alteration of dispositions, occurs slowly and by imperceptible degreees, over a never fully definable period of time. One's future behavior is a function of the dispositions he brings to certain situations, and the only way that such dispositions are formed is by repeating, with forethought, certain modes of action over and over again. For only through frequent yet thoughtfully discriminated repetitions of certain ways of behaving, under a wide variety of conditions, can stable dispositions be formed. These observations, pedestrian though they may be, are sometimes forgotten by teachers and parents who are impatient for children to "learn" ("I *told* William to hang up his coat when he came in. Now, why won't he?"). Yet nothing could be more relevant in understanding how it is that people learn from the kinds of situations in which an initial arousal of affect is developed into experience having aesthetic quality, into speculation and scientific inquiry, and into problem-solving.

We can conclude from the above that only in exceptional (or what we call "memorable") cases is a great deal learned in terms of changed dispositions from any one textbook, from any one teacher, or from any one source of study in schools. Again, this accords with familiar experience. If we were asked how our school experience had influenced our ways of behaving later on, we should hesitate to make very many direct connections, but probably say that over the long haul, a great deal of what happened to us in school "sunk in." This observation is correct as far as it goes, but for affording us guidance in making schooling more effective, it does not go very far. But when we examine the ways in which affect is aroused and thoughtfully resolved, and connect those ways to our observations about what is necessary in terms of time and frequency to change dispositions, we begin to see the mechanics of what is implied in the phrase "to sink in."

When we consider the kind of future behavior it is hoped schooling will influence, we have in mind especially (although not exclusively) those future situations which are in some sense problematic or insecure: those future situations, in which expectancies—whatever their context—are not fully met. If these are situations that schools are designed to help us meet, then the only means by which they can perform their task is to offer guidance in meeting and handling such situations in schools. The patterns of overt and covert action that we develop to meet novelty in schools, then, might be expected to carry over into out-of-school situations. Yet school children and youth are also developing patterns of thought and action after school, at home and in the neighborhood.

These out-of-school patterns often conflict with those the school hopes to teach. But the school has one enormous advantage over these informal influences which it has hardly begun to exploit. Behavior patterns are formed fortuitously in home and neighborhood, and because they are unplanned and accidental, they conflict with one another. The school, on the other hand, can call its shots. It offers people who are specially prepared to control deliberately the influences that bear on the behavior of young people. Thus whether it is currently operating or not, the potential is present in schools to offer consistent guidance for the formation of stable dispositions toward acting in the presence of the novel, the unexpected, and the problematic. And insofar as its impact *can* be consistent, the school is potentially more influential than the strong but scattered and contradictory influences that are met out of school.[10]

Before we consider the formation of dispositions more specifically, two qualifications must be made about the potential impact of the school. First, dispositions are already formed and sometimes quite strongly, by the time children first enter school. For this reason the school's task, if it is to succeed in whatever it attempts, will often be one of changing dispositions already formed (and in some cases of strengthening them) rather than simply cultivating new ones. We might consider a child who enters the first grade with a disposition to fly into a fit of rage when he confronts obstacles to his purposeful activities. The school cannot then directly begin teaching him to meet those obstacles intelligently. The temper tantrums cannot be ignored: they must be altered themselves gradually into more effective behavior. The same cues and same motive forces that lead to problem-solving also lead to temper tantrums. Those cues— that is, obstacles to purposeful activity—realistically can never wholly be eliminated (hence the futility of trying to set up a "warm, accepting, nonevaluative, and free environment"), nor can the energy that underlies a fit of rage on the one hand, or thought on the other, be ignored. Whatever the psychosocial dynamics of cases like these, they do point up the great impact of what a child has already learned before he comes to school.

The other qualification has to do with consistency and inconsistency of influence in the home and neighborhood. It was claimed above that such influences were scattered and inconsistent, hence not so potentially powerful as the consistent influence exerted by schools. But this is not true in all cases. It is probably true when a child is reared in a heterogeneous environment: when he interacts with a relatively large family and a variety of other people representing a wide range of religious, social, and economic backgrounds.

But it is much less true when a child grows up in a fairly homogeneous community, as increasingly seems to be the case in the United States. It stands to reason that the more similar the educational background, the religion, the income, and the social status of the people with whom a youngster interacts, the more consistent will the influences be that go into forming his dispositions. The more consistent those influences are, the more impact on dispositions will they have.

If the impact of this informal education is a bit unsettling when we consider the plight of children raised in the deteriorating cores of our larger cities, it is no less cause for concern with respect to children raised in the suburbs. The dispositions sought by schools may come into conflict with dispositions formed in both kinds of neighborhood. For example, however docile they may be in school, it is probable that some suburban children acquire dispositions incompatible with those sought by teachers. Such children sometimes learn to approach art with only impatience disguised by the appearance of politeness; to approach the world that is seen and felt and heard by ignoring the sensible and sensuous patterns within it (indeed, how else could the visual appearance of suburbs be tolerated?); to approach the novel by seeking ways to turn it to personal advantage; and to approach obstacles to purposeful activities with the assumption that all problems can be solved if only one has a neat appearance, good manners, influential friends, and enough money. These dispositions are as contrary to what schools aim for as dispositions of undisguised aggression, procrastination, and dishonesty that are allegedly acquired in slum neighborhoods. Aggression and dishonesty, even when they appear in the minority of slum children and youth, more obviously attract attention, but the "social dynamite"[11] in the suburbs only has a longer, slower-burning fuse. The impact on thought made by an afternoon on the golf course at the country club is potentially no greater and no less than that made by an afternoon in the poolroom. Nor are the dispositions acquired by the young golfer *necessarily* any less socially reprehensible than those acquired by the young pool player.

The dispositions formed in children are of great consequence for the maintenance of the sort of society that adults want. The homogeneous environments in which some children are raised can be and often have been criticized for the narrowness of attitudes they create in people toward their fellow men. But this narrowness is only one dimension of a more pervasive debility fostered by homogeneous environments: a total set of rigid dispositions and habits that is not easily subject to change.

There is now a growing tendency for communities to become socially, economically, ethnically, and racially homogeneous. Because of the consequences this may have on the growth of children, it might be worth the effort to insure that the populations of our schools remain heterogeneous. Such an effort might involve the redrawing of school districts, the construction of giant "educational parks," or the transporting of children to school by bus. Yet these are not matters for the schools to handle alone. They are public problems, and as the public deals with them, so will it define its own philosophy and formulate its own meaning for democracy. In no realm of action is the intimate relation between the aims of the school and the goals of society more clearly seen. For as the powerful educational impact of homogeneous communities begins to render ineffective the teachings of a school designed to serve equally all those communities, we must either tolerate a glaring incompatibility or face a crucial question: Shall our schools be made to "fit" each of our subcultures at the risk of freezing each growing child into the social group into which he was born? Or shall the schools educate widely different kinds of children under one roof, in the hope of enabling each to seek the sorts of groups with which his growing and increasingly many-sided personality is most compatible?

When the above questions are put in language relevant to the conditions of learning, the import for the organization of schools becomes even more clear. A child whose growth suits him for membership in only one kind of social group is a child in whom many dispositions have become so fixed as to resemble rigid habits. Such a child's capability for continued learning is severely limited. When, on the other hand, a child's education enables him to meet the varying demands of different kinds of groups, his dispositions remain open and flexible. Thus he remains prepared to deal intelligently with the new situations that different groups present to him. In short, such a child has learned to learn.

## LEARNING IN SCHOOLS THROUGH THE PURSUIT OF DISCREPANCY SITUATIONS

We have elaborated in some detail the influence on children's dispositions of their out-of-school environments. Yet the school does have an impact, and it will become greater as school practices are made more consonant with the ways in which children learn. We have considered the relation between the patterns of action we call dispositions and the behavior likely to result from them. These considerations can now be applied to the ways that dispositions are formed.

How a person frequently reacts to situations has an impact on the ways he will react in later situations. If we now re-examine the varieties of responses discussed earlier, we will be able to see what sorts of dispositions might be expected to result if schools institute the appropriate situations of expectancy-discrepancy, and provide guidance in dealing with those situations.

Aesthetic quality in experience, and the disposition to be receptive and open to such quality, is not effectively cultivated by taking children to a museum or a children's concert once or twice a year. Nor is it effectively cultivated by simply exposing them to objects of art, or by telling them of the aesthetic worth of those objects, and admonishing them to be appreciative. Appropriate dispositions will be acquired only if students have an opportunity to enjoy and be moved by such things. For that is, after all, their only value; if those values are not made to operate, no amount of knowledge about paintings, music, and books, and no degree of simple but unrewarding exposure to them will ever dispose students to seek and enjoy them, and to be receptive to aesthetic quality later on. It may be natural for some adults to be patronizing, if not, indeed, to denigrate the sorts of things young people are capable of responding to aesthetically. But teachers cannot afford to do this, for their only means of developing positive dispositions toward aesthetic qualities is to capitalize on what students *are* capable of, and begin refining students' responses from that point.

The above recommendation is not intended to apply only to this or that specific subject of study in school. It is intended to hold for all school studies, for at least two reasons. Aesthetic quality can be a part of any experience in which thought is involved, and deliberately to limit its consideration to classes in the arts is both to miss its significance and to afford a distorted approach to it. If children and young people are disposed to look for aesthetic quality only in works of art, they will seldom find it. First, most people are normally exposed to art of any kind but rarely, and such exposures cannot be expected to increase if the arts are made to appear wholly different from, and unconnected to, the other activities of living. Second, when the aesthetic dimensions of other activities (whether of a meal, a church service, or a job) remain unperceived, they are drained of much of the richness that could make them more meaningful and immediately worthwhile. And third, if the connections between works of art, aesthetic quality, and other activities are not made apparent, the meaning and emotional impact of works of art themselves are bound to be impoverished. For much of this meaning and impact is directly a function of the way art is perceived to relate ideas, beliefs, and values that are only suggested or evoked by the work itself.

The other reason why continuous sensitivity to aesthetic dimensions of experience should be cultivated in all school activities relates more directly to the conditions under which any disposition is formed. Those conditions suggest that success in promoting learning will take place only if certain kinds of behavior are fostered repeatedly and in a wide variety of contexts. If this is so, then a disposition to be open and receptive to aesthetic quality can be cultivated only when teachers of all school subjects and in all school grades are sensitive to those qualities, and can help develop a similar sensitivity in their students. Put in these terms, it might seem as though the task is hopeless, but it is not nearly so hopeless as it is when aesthetic quality is thought to be the sole province of the arts teachers and when they, in turn, focus attention on time-honored objects far beyond the capacities of young people to enjoy. The geometry teacher who takes pleasure in working through a complicated proof is experiencing, among other things, aesthetic quality. Dispositions toward such quality, as well as toward geometry and logical thought in general, would be more effectively cultivated if that geometry teacher better understood the reasons he liked geometry, and was able to communicate his own satisfaction and enthusiasm to his students. Little can be said for those who teach without genuine interest in what they are teaching. It is probably far too late for *them* to learn.

The disposition to inquire, both speculatively and scientifically, is one with the disposition to be curious. Because current schooling seldom enables children and young people to pursue problems related to their own affairs, and because it seldom focuses on aesthetic quality in experience, about all that is left for it to cultivate in the light of what it *does* present, is a disposition to be curious. To put this the other way 'round, if schooling as it is typically found operating is *not* at least cultivating curiosity in its students, it is hard to imagine *what* desirable dispositions it is developing.[12]

To try to promote learning by limiting school methods to the exploitation of curiosity does not seem very wise, but matters are made worse, if not ludicrous, when schools do not even present subjects to students that they can be curious about. Yet this is quite typically found in many classrooms. Students are assigned things to read and remember, and "problems" to solve, and are expected to pursue inquiry just *as if they were curious*. But when the materials of study and the teacher's presentations do not elicit curiosity, it is little wonder that some students begin to think that schooling is some monstrous, mindless game invented to torment them. It may well be that those students who openly resent such practices are far more realistic about schooling than many of their teachers who may never ask themselves whether the activities they initiate make any sense to their students. There is a time-honored, familiar way of conducting classes: "Today we will study participles. . . ." or "Now we will turn to the Revolutionary War. . . ." or "What, class, makes it more difficult for some elements to enter into chemical combination with others?" But this approach only produces the wooden carrying out of assignments. It arouses curiosity and initiates genuine inquiry for no one, except perhaps for those who have the least need for teachers and schools: youngsters who have already acquired scholarly dispositions.

In view of the fact that we live in a world that must be dealt with practically, and because it can be found meaningful and enjoyable aesthetically, it does not make good sense to expend all the school's efforts on cultivating the kinds of dispositions that depend on curiosity alone. Yet if the latter is to be done at all, it might as well be done effectively. In Chapter VIII we discussed at length the kinds of teaching practices, like the presentation of paradox and anomaly, that could be expected to arouse curiosity. If a genuine disposition to be curious and to inquire is to be developed, then such practices must pervade all school classes and all grade levels. That it is more difficult to do this, and at times less wise, in the upper grades of school than in the lower grades cannot be denied. Yet one must seriously wonder at the sanity of those who claim it is appropriate for small children to pursue curiosity, but that adolescents in the secondary schools really have not time to be curious. What *have* they time for? If they are neither dealing with genuinely felt problems, nor experiencing aesthetic quality, nor pursuing curiosity, there is but one thing left for them *to* do: follow directions and do what they are told, while thinking about it as little as possible. It is both the great triumph and the unhappy tragedy of American public schooling that so many students have, through repeated exposure, become disposed to do just this[13] ever afterward.

The reluctance shown by many people who have an interest in schools to institute the methods of problem-solving may be understandable from a psychological point of view. It is often enormously difficult to deal with problems, let alone to identify them. And the solutions, not always predictable in advance, can be most upsetting. But adults can hardly afford to act as if problems did not exist, or to let others deal with them. This alternative is not conducive to health or longevity, either for individuals or for nations. Thus it would appear advisable for schools to institute problem-solving activities—even if it is difficult, and even if some solutions arrived at by students are not particularly palatable in the short run.

Of all worthy dispositions the disposition to recognize an obstacle to activity as a genuine problem and to deal with it as such is the hardest to develop. For each time a problem is met, a purpose or a goal and a value is called into question:

> Let us admit the case of the conservative; if we once start thinking, no one can guarantee where we shall come out, except that many objects, ends, and institutions are surely doomed. Every thinker puts some portion of an apparently stable world in peril and no one can wholly predict what will emerge in its place.[14]

Thus it is emotionally far less taxing to hold one's goals and values lightly, so that obstructions to achieving them can be met simply by adopting new goals and values. This adaptability to change suits chameleons, but does not lend much dignity to men. Perhaps one instance of recent efforts by schoolmen systematically to avoid cultivating the disposition to deal with problems will make the point clearer.

In the discussion that follows, I intend only to illustrate the way problems can be avoided, rather than dealt with, by the simple expedient of giving up values and goals not seriously held in the first place. I also hope to show how the disposition to abandon goals and values can come to be proposed as a school aim. At the same time some light will be cast on the enormous complexity of some problems, and on the way they have of ramifying, of spreading out into other areas of concern. Thus one may have the very best of intentions and approach matters with the utmost gravity—as those in the following example do who propose "education for vocational adaptability"—and still avoid solving a problem by focusing on its more immediate dimensions and missing its long-range significance.

It has been correctly observed that in the mid-sixties, and for a long time to come, the jobs of many workers will be threatened by technological unemployment. The increasing automation of industries and offices (not to mention the varying needs of national defense), in putting people out of work, raises the problem of what they will do to support themselves and their families. This has been viewed by some as essentially an educational problem, one affecting both secondary schools and adult education. As a remedy, it has been proposed to educate workers for change and adaptability, so that, not being too committed to their present job, they will smoothly learn a new one when new industrial and business methods demand it.

The problem is a poignantly real one, but the solution is not a solution at all: It is an avoidance of the problem. However rapidly times change, the point and meaning in the lives of most adults has been and will continue to be very importantly shaped by the work that they do (if the lives of some adults are consequently felt as largely pointless and meaningless, it would make more sense to re-examine and re-structure the nature of vocations rather than to pin one's hopes on the efficacy of sermons about meaningful living —whether they be delivered by ministers, teachers, or therapists). Given this fact, the recommendation to take one's job so lightly that one would be willing to switch to another one without undue strain is a recommendation to avoid commitment to the values around which many, if not most people, focus their lives. Thus the appearance of a problem (the threat to the existence of one's job) does not cue intelligent thought and action leading to a solution at all. Instead, it merely cues the disposal of one set of values and the adoption of another. Under these conditions, one could not risk thinking that his job was important, or identifying himself with and finding self-respect in his work. Under the conditions of "playing it cool" towards one's work, we should have to ask what *will* afford self-respect? And what will result in work done with care and pride? Simply the ability to adapt to changing conditions, while valuable in itself as a means of self-preservation, is not enough to make one *feel* valuable to himself or anyone else.

Without adaptability the disintegration of personality inevitably follows, but few people can maintain stability and self-respect *simply* by adapting to change. They need also to believe that what they are doing is somehow worth doing. Yet this belief cannot be had when one is prepared to give up quickly what he is doing at the behest of extrinsic conditions. To recommend this attitude as a goal of schooling is to make a joke of personal and social responsibility—for one will change jobs simply in reaction to what others have done, not by participating in the decisions that involve major industrial and economic changes—and deliberately to cultivate the attitude of the drifter. This latter attitude and those in whom it functions, have doubtless made some genuine contributions to society (for example, some American folk music and, indirectly, influences on social legislation), and in a few cases such people have even led personally satisfying lives. But deliberately to foster a nation of drifters does not seem well calculated to maintaining a healthy society, let alone a democratic one.

The above discussion scarcely suggests a solution to the problems of technological change and unemployment. It was only intended to show the difference between short-circuiting a problem and dealing with it, to show what sorts of considerations must be taken into account when dealing with a problem, and to show what is involved when one seriously recommends that schools attempt to cultivate in students a disposition to be sensitive to problems and to deal with them. If one should ask how the disposition to recognize and deal with problems is to be developed, the answer must be the same as that respecting the cultivation of the dispositions to be curious, to inquire, and to be open and receptive to aesthetic qualities. It is, simply, that real problems for students must be raised and attacked at all levels of schooling, and in as many kinds of courses as the subject of study permits.

Without continuous and repeated attention to problems—which necessarily involves taking students' purposes into account—a disposition to recognize and meet problems cannot be developed. Yet at the same time it is worth noting that it would be a mistake to assume from this that *all* school activities must be problem-solving activities: This would be neither possible nor desirable if it were. Life is a great deal more than a series of problems demanding resolution, and so, too, should be the schools. A school or a life given over wholly to the solving of practical problems would be as distorted as either one's being wholly concerned with the cultivation of aesthetic delights.

## THE ROLE OF THE TEACHER

If we can assume that, over an extended period of time, dispositions can be acquired by the means indicated; if, in other words, the expectancy-discrepancy concept of learning that has been advanced adequately accounts for the sort of learning we are considering, then, the role of teachers can clearly be seen. Their primary tasks would be to initiate situations in which expectations of students were in some way unfulfilled, and to offer some help and guidance to students in dealing with those perceived discrepancies. Thus the teacher's tasks are conceived primarily as two in number: initiation and development of discrepancy situations. Within such a context, the knowledge and values communicated by teachers will take on point and meaning.

We have already spoken at length about ways of setting up situations that, in presenting students with affect-arousing discrepancies from their expectations, attract their attention and interest and thereby create the possibility of developing experience in ways that will promote learning. In Chapter V we considered ways of instituting problematic situations; in Chapters VI and VII we saw how it was possible to create conditions that would allow for the experiencing of aesthetic qualities; and in Chapter VIII we considered ways of setting up situations that might provoke curiosity. But the mere initiation of these kinds of situations is no guarantee that they will subsequently develop into experiences of genuine aesthetic quality, into speculation or inquiry, or into problem-solving.

Earlier in this chapter we saw how discrepancy situations are ideally developed through thinking, so that certain dispositions are acquired. Yet what could happen ideally is not always what in fact does happen. Before appropriate dispositions are stably formed one is easily distracted from aesthetic qualities, one's curiosity may quickly dissipate, and obstacles seen as problems are often short-circuited rather than tackled. We shall examine ways in which teachers might help students stay with a discrepancy situation and follow it to wherever it might lead. There are, of course, no precise rules to follow, but we shall see how it might be appropriate for teachers themselves to cultivate certain dispositions—even though they can never, of themselves, serve to dictate precise "teaching behaviors." We may also get additional light on our problem by noting what teachers often do, quite deliberately and as a matter of accepted procedure, that inhibits thought on the part of students and stands in the way of their developing the dispositions we are seeking.

We might begin with a precautionary note. Students are often mystified before certain works of art, halted in inquiry, and stumped by problems. Teachers sometimes "help" these students by simply supplying the answers, or by telling them just where to look, so that the difficulty will be immediately overcome. This often seems like the benevolent course of action to take, and students so helped are often grateful. And it is less strain for a teacher simply to supply an answer than it is for him to offer substantial help that still leaves the student to his own resources. But insofar as the teacher has done the thinking *for* the student, the quick and easy settlement of the discrepancy at hand is bought at the price of eliminating thought in the student, and curtailing the development of the dispositions in him that are sought. Learning under these conditions does of course occur, in the sense that dispositions are being acquired. But they are not dispositions that teachers would very likely cultivate deliberately, if they knew what they were doing. By short-circuiting the student's thought, the teacher develops a disposition to seek an answer quickly, without the effort of thought; a disposition to seek help elsewhere instead of relying on one's self; a disposition to put implicit trust and faith in authority, since the inhibition of thought unfits the student to make judgments on his own or to check on what the teacher says.

The only way for the student to learn is to do the work himself, to do his own thinking, to get his own ideas, to check his own hypotheses. This is not intended to be an unusually heroic view of learning. To emphasize the individual's own activity and responsibility in no way minimizes the fact that his own thinking and learning may be broadened, deepened, and made more fruitful when it is joined with that of others—both the teacher and his peers. Not only do some problems demand cooperative effort, but thinking itself, conceived as a deliberate and conscious effort, could not be developed at all independent of the participation by others. Yet this is not to suggest that others can do one's thinking and learning *for* him. A disposition to act cannot be *given* to a student the way information can; it is acquired only as a function of how he himself behaves. This means that the teacher's chief task, once affect has been initially aroused in a discrepancy situation, is to provide guidance and encouragement to the student as he begins dealing with the discrepancy.[15] Teachers must, of course, do other things, such as planning and organizing activities, evaluating both students and himself, attending meetings, etc. But we are speaking here of behavior toward students in the classroom. And it could be added that all other teaching tasks are ancillary to, and optimally supportive of, what is done in the classroom.

In guiding and encouraging students to deal with discrepant situations, the teacher must try to understand and assess the ways students are thinking and the directions in which they are heading. Without this, little guidance can be given, and students whose thoughts are derailed will be left to get back on the track wholly on their own. In the course of the students' activity, the teacher will attempt to encourage thinking while discouraging easy answers, superficial ones, blind trial-and-error, and avoidance of whatever has presented a discrepancy and aroused affect.

But just as there is no exhaustive set of rules to follow that guarantees the solution of problems, the satisfaction of curiosity, or the appearance of aesthetic quality in experience, so there is no exhaustive set of rules for a teacher to follow in encouraging and guiding a student's thought.[16] We are speaking here of dispositions in teachers, not behavioral acts or responses to specific stimuli received from students. Thus to help a student avoid a blind alley in thought may call for criticism at one time or in one case, praise in another situation, or the asking of a key question in still another case. And to encourage a student may mean a smile or a kind word in one case, or again, the right sort of question in another; and encouragement can even be given in the form of admonishment. It may be worth recalling that teaching is not a science, and certainly not a rule-bound activity like installing television sets; rather, it is an art.[17]

In trying to get a good look at something in the dark, as any effort to view effective teaching must be, it is often helpful to look off to the side of what has attracted our interests. Thus, in order to get a better view of the teacher's role in guiding and encouraging thought, we might look instead at the pattern of a great deal of what is called (by courtesy only, as I will try to point out) "teaching." The pattern is typically this: First, the teacher presents an assignment as clearly as he can. He may also utilize class time to demonstrate how the assignment could be completed, or to provide an exemplar of what part of the completed assignment would look like. Second, he allows time—sometimes in class, sometimes at home—for completion of the assignment. And third, he asks for evidence that the assignment was successfully completed. This may come in the form of written homework or oral recitations in class. Or it may be provided for on a test or examination. In showing how this pattern of teaching does not promote learning, we can find some further indications of what would constitute effective teaching.

To begin with, no fault could be found in giving assignments clearly; too often they are presented otherwise. But clarity is not enough. Just because I am told what to do *clearly* does not constitute a sufficient reason or motive for doing it. Enough time has already been spent considering the nature of the teacher's presentation to belabor this point any further.

It is at the second phase in the pattern cited that the possibility of learning begins to disappear, if it has not already departed at the first phase. The student who must complete the assignment by himself, either in class or at home, gets no help in the actual performance of the task which is supposed to be a learning experience. A demonstration or exemplar provided by the teacher when the task was first assigned may be of some help, or it may work to the detriment of learning. For the student, grasping at straws, may only attempt to imitate what the teacher did rather than to think through the assignment in his own terms. When the student is assigned the task of completing work by himself, he is being told in effect to learn by himself. One does not need a specially trained teacher to make such assignments. They can be presented just as well by a sales clerk, a newspaperman, or an admiral. But why teachers should not be expected deliberately to assist students in thinking, and thereby deliberately to promote learning, eludes explanation.

The third phase of the teaching pattern is perhaps the most peculiar of the three when considered in relation to learning. Given the present usage of learning as the acquisition of dispositions, the providing of evidence, oral or written, of successful completion of the assigned task is not evidence of learning at all. Rather, it constitutes evidence in most cases of the short-term acquisition of information or skills, isolated from any meaningful use of them. It might, however, be evidence only that the student successfully produced answers by imitating the teacher's acts, copying another student's work, or enlisting the assistance of his parents.[18] It is rather hard under such circumstances to be sure of just what constitutes cheating.

We see, then, that at least one typical pattern of what is called teaching yields, on analysis, some suggestions about what teaching is *not*. The pattern that has been examined turns out to be an appropriate set of procedures only for administering certain kinds of tests. Unless teaching is taken to *mean* testing, such a pattern is *called* teaching by mistake.

If the pattern of "teaching" described above is to be avoided, no equally clear pattern has been suggested to replace it. At this point then, one might reasonably ask, how can an expectancy-discrepancy conception of learning (or indeed, any theory of learning) be of any utility to teachers in a classroom? People are not going to teach with a ruler in one hand and a rule book in the other; neither shall doctors meet patients with a stethoscope in one hand and a codification of medical ethics, supplemented by rules for diagnosis, in the other. Yet an understanding of how people learn may become a part of a teacher's disposition toward teaching, just as medical ethics and diagnostic procedures (i.e., understanding how certain symptoms relate to underlying physiological conditions) became a part of a physician's disposition toward the practice of medicine. Let us abandon the analogy and examine the matter more closely.

People acquire all sorts of dispositions—to set an attractive table, to be considerate of one's children, to drive a hard bargain—without ever learning precise rules of their exercise. Yet in every case of an acquired disposition there is also an understanding of certain relevant knowledge, a holding of certain attitudes or values, and an ability to exercise certain skills. It is not, of course, simply the acquisition of knowledge, skills, and attitudes that automatically produces the disposition, but it is their acquisition combined with their use over a considerable period of time. What is being suggested here is that if those who teach acquire knowledge, values, and skills relevant to teaching within a context of being able to exercise what they have acquired, they will come to be disposed to teach more effectively than they otherwise would.

In directing attention to how people learn, we are especially concerned with the role of knowledge in the disposition of teachers. It would seem reasonable to suppose that if a teacher were aware of the conditions under which learning occurs, he would (other things being equal) be less disposed to practice the inadequate patterns of teaching that have been frequently mentioned here. It might also be expected that such awareness, gradually becoming part of a teacher's professional disposition, would incline him to behave compatibly with what he understands about the conditions of learning. Such behavior would include the short and long range planning of classroom activities, evaluation, and probably last, in view of the difficulties inherent in making decisions implicitly and quickly, the teacher's immediate responses to students in and out of classroom situations.

If one knows that the learning he hopes to promote cannot result unless situations affective in quality are initiated and appropriately developed, one can deliberately plan to create such situations, to assess what is happening in a classroom with such a criterion in mind, and to capitalize on such situations when they arise.[19] And if one has some understanding of the ways in which thought can transform such discrepancy and affect-laden situations, both overtly and—what may be more important—covertly, one can become sensitive to the points at which he can be of genuine assistance to students when they are in the process of dealing with situations. These are the points, then, where a conception of how people learn comes into contact with how one teaches.

Still, a major obstacle remains that can never be wholly overcome. Because a student's efforts are largely covert, the teacher often finds himself in the position of having only the *results* (either in written form or orally) of the student's covert trials to work with but not the trials themselves. It is true that the teacher can make reasonable inferences about the nature of those covert trials on the basis of the observable results in which they eventuate, but this is not always enough to go on if the teacher hopes to be of help in the student's conduct of those trials. The teacher's inferences are not always correct, and frequently what the student does overtly provides no adequate basis for making an inference about how he arrived at what he did. One of the greatest difficulties in responding helpfully to papers that students write is in trying to understand what impelled them to write the often unexpected and strangely irrelevant things that they do. This is simply to say that teachers cannot always infer just *how* students were thinking, and that they are, consequently, shackled in their efforts to be of any help.

But to be aware of the key position of covert activity in thinking and learning stresses the necessity of making those activities overt whenever it is possible. This is, at least, one of the most important pedagogical justifications for carrying on discussions in classrooms. For in the course of talking about situations that are discrepant, in the exchange of questions, answers, and speculations that constitutes dialetic (or what in more exalted language has been called "the great conversation"), one prompts students literally to "think out loud." They make their covert trials overtly, so that they can be examined, questioned, criticized, and guided as they occur. Given this use of discussion (or what in less exalted terms has been called "verbal behavior") in the classroom, its employment simply to elicit from students how much they remembered of what they read or were told is recognized as only the appearance of teaching, and constitutes, in fact, only testing of a rather superficial sort. Thus to remove the blindness that causes well-meaning persons to confuse testing with teaching[20] is to be able to utilize discussion in classrooms as one of the chief means of providing guidance and direction to the actual processes of students' thinking. (Good intention can, of course, be misguided, and even collection plates can be used as weapons. The danger is always present that the means by which thought can be assisted and guided can also be misused to dictate it.)

We have spoken at great length about how people learn; it remains for us in the final chapter to consider more directly *what* it would be worthwhile learning. We have dealt in this and in the foregoing chapters chiefly with the problem of how dispositions are acquired. In that discussion we have seen how crucial is the role of affective arousal as it occurs in situations where expectations are balked by discrepant events. We have also seen how this analysis of the initial phase of a potential learning situation covers equally well cases where aesthetic qualities are focal in experience, where curiosity, speculation, and scientific inquiry are focal, and where obstacles to purposeful activity predominate. In the case of aesthetic quality, attention is directed to discrepancies in the perceived relations of sensuous elements. In cases of curiosity and speculation, attention is directed to incomplete meanings found in perceived things and events. And in cases where purposeful activity is blocked, attention is directed to discrepancies found between perceived events and our expectations of achieving our purposes. We have also seen how crucial to all of these situations is the role of those covert efforts called "thinking," and how teachers might usefully direct their efforts toward both the initiation and the guidance of such thinking.

Yet in all this there has been little mention of what might constitute a public school curriculum, little mention of the goals of American society, and little mention of the goals of schooling and their relation to social goals. Nor has there been much discussion of what particular knowledge and skills it might be important for students to acquire. Important as these matters are, they have been put off until the concluding chapter quite deliberately. For a discussion of how the content of schooling is related to social values and aims can make sense only when one is clear about the conditions under which learning occurs. Otherwise, we arrive at a set of aims and a curriculum so divorced from the actualities of practical implementation that they stand as unattainable ideals. Theory then justly deserves the charge of being unrelated to practice.

Certain assumptions have, of course, already been made about school aims. I have assumed that it is intended that schools promote learning when it is conceived as the acquisition of dispositions to behave in certain ways under certain types of conditions. But more than this has been assumed about the aims of both school and society. For learning that is desirable has been under discussion, distinct from just any kind of learning, and I have proposed, in a very general way, to call desirable any kind of learning which holds open the possibility of continued learning.

Unlike the previous assumption, this value commitment respecting the kind of learning that is desirable may require some defense, for such a school aim presupposes the desirability of freedom of thought. This would not be compatible with the aims of a society in which it was held desirable to limit deliberately the thought of its citizens. For example, criticism of dominant political, social, and economic institutions might be thought dangerous and, therefore, undesirable. If so, then the school aim of promoting the sort of learning that leads to more learning, and which considers no men, ideas, or institutions as eternally correct and thus exempt from examination and criticism, would sharply conflict with such a social norm. Since this is not an essay in political or social theory, I do not propose explicitly to defend this commitment about educational and social goals. Instead, I shall assume (or perhaps hope) that very few Americans would publicly object to freedom of thought, inquiry, and speech, or to any school aims which supply the means of carrying out, and thus giving meaning, to this freedom. When communities seek to censor the reading materials of high school seniors, and when states pass legislation to insure the teaching of the "evils" of communism, they are, of course, abrogating this freedom. Yet it is a tribute both to the strength of the ideal of freedom of thought, and to the difficulty of actually maintaining it, that such violations of it are made *in its very name.* Thus some people are heard to say, "We must teach that certain ideas, like communism, are wrong in order to preserve our freedom." It might even be surmised that the Presidential election of 1964 indicated, among other things, that those who fail to condemn groups that openly act to limit freedom of thought and action are themselves doomed to political extinction.

If choices about classroom activities demand a hierarchy of values, then a commitment to the desirability of learning to learn must take precedence over any values thought to be inherent within any bodies of organized knowledge. This has been implied in all the foregoing discussion, for more lasting in its pedagogical effect than the substantive content of *what* has been taught are the particular attitudes and modes of thinking involved in *how* one is taught. Yet without having in mind some content to teach, one might be at a loss as to how to initiate activities in a classroom. There may not be anything that is both so important that everyone ought to know it, and so difficult to find out that the schools must teach it. Yet it might still be claimed that, in light of how people learn, and in light of the value commitments that have been made explicit here, our efforts to live well in the sort of world we have created suggest that some things are more worth knowing than other things. What those things might be, and how they might find a place in the curriculum, will be the concern of the next chapter.

## NOTES

1. Once again, research like that of Suchman's not only suggests hope for the future, but at the same time reflects unfavorably on more traditional school practices. See J. Richard Suchman, "Inquiry Training: Building Skills for Autonomous Discovery," *Merrill-Palmer Quarterly,* 7 (1961), 147–169.

2. Cf. Rudolf Arnheim, "From Function to Expression," *Journal of Aesthetics and Art Criticism,* 23 (1964), pp. 29–41.

3. I am grateful for many discussions with Mr. Charles Juister and Mr. Peter F. Stone for any truth that may be found in the following point.

4. Experimental evidence of the influence of the opinions of others on one's observations may be found, for example, in Solomon Asch, "Effects of Group Pressure upon the Modification of and Distribution of Judgments," in H. Guetzkow (ed.), *Groups, Leadership, and Men* (Pittsburgh: Carnegie Press, 1951).

5. See John Dewey, *Democracy and Education* (New York: Macmillan, 1916), chap. 23.

6. See the discussion of "psychical distance" in Edward Bullough, "Psychical Distance As a Factor in Art and an Aesthetic Principle," *British Journal of Psychology,* 5 (1912–1913), 87–118.

7. See Abraham Maslow, *Motivation and Personality* (New York: Harper, 1954), chap. 13.

8. See, for example E. R. Guthrie, "Conditioning: A Theory of Learning in Terms of Stimulus, Response, and Association," in N. B. Henry (ed.), *The Psychology of Learning,* Forty-first Yearbook of the National Society for the Study of Education, Part II (Chicago: University of Chicago Press, 1942).

9. It is likely that even in such notable cases, the moment of conversion was preceded by a long period of germination, both conscious and unconscious. What went on in this earlier period, then, was part of the process of learning.

10. Respecting the impact of schooling on values and attitudes, Hilda Taba urges a role for the school as a "countervailing force to the impact of culture outside the school." See Taba, *Curriculum Development: Theory and Practice* (New York: Harcourt, Brace & World, 1962), p. 66.

11. See James B. Conant, *Slums and Suburbs* (New York: McGraw-Hill, Inc., 1961).

12. It may be objected that schools may at least cultivate attitudes of honesty, obedience, promptness, etc., independently of developing curiosity and/or problem-solving. But the objection is unfounded, for these attitudes are *ways* of dealing with problems

or of pursuing curiosity. The attempt to develop them independent of the latter is doomed to failure, for it can result only in the appearance of honesty, obedience, etc. These appearances, mechanically performed, may quickly disappear when students are called on to deal with genuine problems.

13. An implied invidious comparison with schools of other nations is not intended here. Rather, attention might be called to what American schools *do* accomplish in comparison to what they *aim* at, in the light of typically Amedican ideals (e.g., independence and freedom of speech and thought).

14. John Dewey, *Experience and Nature* (LaSalle, Ill.: Open Court, 1925), p. 182.

15. This point is forcibly put by John Dewey in *Democracy and Education* (New York: Macmillan, 1916), p. 188.

16. See Israel Scheffler, *The Language of Education* (Springfield Ill.: Charles C. Thomas, 1960), pp. 69–71.

17. If true, this calls into question the utility of the rapidly growing collections of materials descriptive of "teaching behaviors." Lists of such behaviors may acquaint one with the kinds of things teachers have done, but no act or behavior on the list carries with it a signal for when to use it. This is a matter of judgment. And since such judgments in the classroom must be made at once, they are matters of exercising a disposition.

18. In helping their children with homework, some parents do what the teacher is ostensibly hired to do. Children who are not so fortunate, whose parents have had little schooling themselves, or whose parents are not interested in the academic problems their children bring home, are sooner or later labeled "slow" students. They will then be routed into vocational courses and, eventually, shops and offices and factories. Those who were helped at home to think and learn—usually from "better" homes, are sooner or later labeled "bright" or "gifted," and sent on to college. There is much irony in the fact that schools sometimes even take the credit for "developing" the "bright" youngsters—just as teachers perceive themselves as being instrumental in the academic successes of their students, but attribute failure to causes "within" the student rather than in connection with their own teaching. See Thomas J. Johnson, Rhoda Feigenbaum, and Marcia Weiby,

"Some Determinants and Consequences of the Teacher's Perception of Causation," *Journal of Educational Psychology,* 55 (1964), 237–246.

19. It is only too familiar a situation when students arrive in a classroom buzzing with interest over, for example, some recent political event, only to have a teacher squelch what might have been turned into a genuine learning situation by saying, "Settle down, now, class, and let's see what you can recall about the Mexican War."

20. That testing is one of the things that teachers legitimately do is not a justification for the substitution of testing for teaching.

# X

# THE CURRICULUM

THE TERM CURRICULUM USUALLY REFERS TO THE PARTICULAR knowledge and skills taught in a school. Sometimes, however, it may be defined as "the sum of the educational experiences that children have in school."[1] If the latter definition were adopted, to find out about a school's curriculum would be an enormous undertaking. We should have to ask not only about the knowledge and skills that are taught, but also about habits and attitudes, values and dispositions, and indeed about nearly every school-sponsored activity that might be thought to be educational. Those who use the term curriculum in this broad sense have their own reasons for doing so,[2] but such a usage tends to make redundant the term schooling. Since we have already used schooling in a very broad sense, and since we have considered at some length the cultivation of dispositions, we shall for the sake of convenience adopt the more ordinary meaning for the term curriculum: namely, the knowledge and skills included in a school program.

When schooling is under discussion, the curriculum is usually one of the first topics to be considered. After all, it is thought very important to know what the school teaches. In this discussion, however, the knowledge and skills that comprise what the school teaches come last for consideration, and deliberately so. It is not that the curriculum is unimportant. Rather it is only that, without satisfying the prerequisite learning conditions that have been discussed, it will not matter very much what appears in the curriculum.

The knowledge and skills presented by schools are to be acquired by students. But they cannot be acquired other than mechanically and on a short-term basis unless they are found meaningful by them. The kinds of meanings with which schools are concerned are, for students, new meanings. But new meanings are not acquired (as we saw in Chapter IV) independent of change in disposition, which is to say, of one's tendency to act. Thus it follows that, *unless knowledge and skills are presented in a context in which appropriate dispositions have been formed, or are in the process of formation, they will not be acquired by students in any meaningful sense.* If knowledge is unrelated to relevant dispositions, it matters little what a student is exposed to. For he will not acquire it in any lasting sense.

A doctor readily acquires new knowledge about anatomy because he is so disposed. To want to acquire what will make him a more effective doctor is a part of his professional obligation, which, in turn, has become a part of his character. With a little more difficulty, a medical student will acquire new knowledge about anatomy. That knowledge will be meaningful to him, too, for his dispositions are undergoing change. He is learning to become a doctor. But one who is neither a doctor, nor has any intention of becoming one (nor of becoming a worker in some other field to which anatomy is relevant), nor whose curiosity has been sufficiently aroused, will not acquire new knowledge about anatomy in any meaningful sense. This is what is meant by the claim that the question of what to teach is beside the point unless an appropriate context of learning has been created. And this is why learning has been the focus of this book, and why discussion of the curriculum has been delayed until now.

Once conditions for acquiring dispositions have been established, it makes sense to consider the knowledge and skills that are taught. But disagreement is as strong about this as it is about how people learn. Nearly everyone has his own candidates for what ought to be taught, but later in this chapter I will propose that, whatever may be included in the curriculum, it be selected by someone who has an understanding of the relevant knowledge involved and is ·in a position to be responsible for teaching it. This means, in most cases, teachers. Furthermore, we will examine the learning process itself and find that, far from being a series of neutral events, it embodies and implies very particular personal and social values. These values do not in themselves indicate what knowledge and skills should be included in the curriculum. But I will propose that choices of what to teach be made in light of these values, so as not to be incompatible with them.

The main tasks of this chapter, then, are to show how the selection of content for the curriculum is related to a conception of how people learn, and to relate this process of selection to the role of the teacher. These concerns, however, are not always found in more conventional efforts to formulate a curriculum for public schools. Thus we must first take into account some important considerations about learning and schooling that these efforts have overlooked. We shall begin by examining what is usually taken to be a crucial question about the curriculum, asked a century ago by Herbert Spencer. What knowledge is of most worth?

## THE KNOWLEDGE
## "OF MOST WORTH"
## FOR A CURRICULUM

Finding the knowledge that is "of most worth" is sometimes thought to be a matter of selecting for the curriculum a fair sampling of available knowledge as it has been organized and preserved in the various disciplines or subject matter areas. There is a *prima facie* plausibility to this procedure. After all, civilization's best minds have labored for thousands of years to discover, create, organize, and store knowledge. Without it, we should probably be living in caves and trees again. So why not expose students to a fair sampling of it?

However plausible sounding this procedure may be, it is a rather formidable problem to decide just what *is* a fair sampling of all the knowledge we possess. And the more we accumulate, the more difficult it is to decide. Those who attempt to arrive at a curriculum by sorting out this knowledge and choosing samples from it often arrive at very different conceptions of what a curriculum should be like.[3]

One difficulty in formulating a curriculum from the organized knowledge that is available is that the more an expert knows about his own field, the less likely he is to be well-informed in other areas of knowledge. Of course, highly knowledgeable experts have a dismaying tendency to make pronouncements about areas in which they are not experts, by drawing ingenious but often ingenuous analogies from their own field to others. Thus when educators look for worthy samplings in the knowledge that is available, they are faced with a babble of specialized experts, in which none is an "expert" in all knowledge.

The curriculum-maker is thus situated much like the child in a candy store with a nickel in his hand. But educators, being less adventurous than some children (and with considerably more at stake), usually choose varieties of curriculum content they have tried before. Thus the American public school curriculum, in spite of the rapid growth of knowledge, has been very long-lived. But for the gradual disappearance of Latin and Greek and the division of broader areas of knowledge into narrower and more specialized ones, the curriculum (although not curriculum *theory*) has changed little over the past several generations. It may well be, as some have suggested,[4] that in light of so much knowledge being available, the traditional school curriculum is about as good a sampling as any other. But the traditional curriculum usually omits studies like psychology, anthropology, and economics—to mention but three areas of knowledge without which any sampling might justly be thought incomplete.

There are endless schemes for organizing and classifying the knowledge that is available, and each one is justified in terms of the purpose for which the knowledge is intended to be used. To say this, however, casts suspicion on the notion that a defensible curriculum can be formulated simply by sampling available knowledge. For while it is obvious that knowledge taught in school must be drawn from what is available, we have now suggested a criterion for selecting it that is not intrinsic to the nature of the knowledge itself. Our mode of selecting curriculum content has shifted from simply sampling the knowledge available, toward some conception of the purposes to be served by that knowledge.

The question, what knowledge is of most worth? can then be countered with another question: *For what* is the knowledge supposed to be worth? In asking about the purposes for which knowledge is to be selected for the curriculum, we uncover another nest of experts, each claiming, this time, to have found the true purpose (or purposes) that education is to serve. The purpose, like a bucket, is sent down into the well of knowledge, and the curriculum drawn up is found fitting for the bucket that holds it. We will briefly review some of the leading candidates for the purpose of education and their corresponding curriculums.[5]

For the purpose of what is sometimes dramatically epitomized as "national survival," some educators have been concerned about discovering who is most talented among our school children, and to develop and train them for highly specialized tasks. The curriculum thought appropriate for this purpose emphasizes mathematics, scientific and technological studies, and foreign languages. Schooling designed for this purpose may also include a guidance program which strongly encourages all academically promising students, whatever their particular abilities and interests, to study in these areas. It is hoped that such curriculum content will provide the knowledge and skills most likely to produce military and political strength for the nation. Critics point out that the nation has other needs besides political and military ones, and also argue that students may have needs and interests of their own which are not easily translatable into a program of national needs.[6]

Rather than strengthen society and its institutions as they now exist, some educators view the purpose of education as building a new and more humane society. The curriculum chosen to suit this end emphasizes social science areas such as anthropology, sociology, economics, and political science. It might also be helpful to bring these studies to bear upon topics and problems that point up the need for a reconstructed national and world society: the conservation of natural resources, the exploding world population, the United Nations, etc. The arts may be utilized to dramatize world problems and their solutions. Few would object to the importance of the topics and problems to which this kind of curriculum is addressed. But it falls short of universal appeal because there are other concerns calling for knowledge and skills that receive but little attention in this curriculum.

Many current curricula are not pointed toward the fulfillment of any particular national or international needs. The purpose of education, for them, is simply to make individuals fit to live adequate personal lives. The curricula differ with respect to differences in what is thought to be an adequate personal life. Thus one kind of curriculum contains knowledge and skills to acquaint students with the various arts and sciences, for the purpose of making them knowledgeable and cultivated. Another is proposed to help students adjust to a complex, changing environment; knowledge and skills are presented that are relevant to such matters as working effectively with others, exercising wise consumership, achieving emotional stability, etc. And still another kind of curriculum is designed to help students prepare for careers; the knowledge and skills taught are related to preprofessional (or "college preparatory") courses, business and secretarial courses, shop courses, and work-study programs related to clerical and sales training.

There is nothing wrong with any of the purposes mentioned above except that each one of them tends to ignore the reasonable claims of the others. If we send only one bucket down into the well of knowledge, we leave much that is important still in the well. If we try to bring it up, too, the bucket overflows. But if we send down all the buckets, we end by flooding the schools.

Aside from fomenting endless arguments over what "the" purpose of education might be, there is inherent in this manner of selecting curriculum content a very serious threat to learning. All the purposes mentioned above are quite independent of the learning process itself. Yet we have seen that if what a student learns is to enable him to go on learning, his own purposes must become involved in the process. A student who is learning to learn is, among other things, developing his own aims and purposes. Teachers may arrange the conditions of schooling in the hope that those purposes will become significant and worthy ones. But there are many worthy purposes. If the purposes chosen by others do not coincide with those of students, then, any means selected to achieve those extrinsic purposes will interfere with learning.

The selection by schools of a purpose extrinsic to the ways in which people learn may then subvert learning to the achievement of that purpose. While it is fortunate that no single purpose for schooling is likely to win public approval, it is true that many, if not most, of the purposes proclaimed by individuals and groups are in themselves quite valuable. For this reason, and because it is the business of the school to attend to the nation's needs and to its students' futures, the school cannot afford to conduct its affairs as if those purposes did not exist, or were unimportant.

It is valuable to prepare for a career, and it is important to strengthen society. It is worthwhile to be knowledgeable and cultivated, it is important to be able to adjust to one's environment, and to make that environment a better place to live is worth everyone's attention. But it is unlikely that all students in schools will do all of these things effectively. In a society that values freedom of choice and self-determination, there are good reasons for enabling the students themselves to make their own selections about how much effort they will expend in which of these roles. Yet children, it may be claimed, are too young to make such important choices. If the children are too young, and if the choices are important ones, then the school might well equip them to make those choices thoughtfully. They can be made by people who are disposed to be sensitive to and interested in the world around them, and who are disposed to recognize and deal with problems that face them. And students will acquire these kinds of dispositions if the school helps them learn to learn.

We are concerned, of course, that the knowledge and skills

contained in the curriculum be of such a nature that students can meaningfully acquire them. To succeed in this effort, they must be presented in the kind of learning context in which dispositions are being formed. But when it comes to selecting the content of the curriculum, we can go further than this and see that the process of learning itself provides an indication of what to teach. The main topic of the preceding chapters of this book has been how people learn, and we have seen the difference it makes in how one might teach. But any conception of learning necessarily involves a commitment to certain kinds of values. It remains for us to see how the expectancy-discrepancy conception of learning discussed earlier, and the values that it implies, also serve as a guide to the selection of content for the curriculum.

## INDIVIDUAL AND SOCIAL VALUES IMPLIED IN THE PROCESS OF LEARNING

The discussion of learning throughout this book has not been intended to be "purely" descriptive in nature. Whether or not value choices are recognized for what they are, they are assumed at the start of any inquiry into the learning process, and they are implied by the results of any such inquiry. Thus it is possible for an understanding of *how* people learn to serve as a guide in selecting *what* people shall learn. The discussion that follows will attempt to make clear the following generalization: Any reasonable selection of content for the curriculum must include knowledge and skills that are relevant to the promotion of the values implied by an understanding of the ways in which people learn.

Before we could say very much about how people learn, we first had to be clear about what we were going to call "a case of learning" (see Chapter II). The term is always used, of course, to refer to some sort of change in a person. But as it is ordinarily used, learning refers both to many *ways* in which people change, and to many different *results* of change. To call all these changes learning emphasizes many important similiarities among them, but more careful study leads us to many different and sometimes conflicting conceptions or theories of learning.

What confounds those who would employ the various extant theories of learning is the fact that each has a measure of plausibility and applicability in certain kinds of situations. Some of the confusion could be assuaged if we considered them not so much theories of learning as theories of human change. There is no trouble in accepting the fact that people change, and are changed, in many different ways. To accept and use the various learning theories simply as theories of change would be the kind of pluralism that leads to greater understanding and more intelligent practice. But to conceive them all as theories of learning (without taking special care to be clear about the sort of learning that is meant) invites ambiguity and contradiction.

The discussion of learning in these chapters has directed attention to the sorts of changes in which intelligent action is involved, and in which dispositions are acquired. When it is proposed to foster such changes in schools, then, very particular value choices have already been built into the proposed school program. The nature of those values may be made clearer when we consider how a disposition to continue learning is expected to function in an individual's life.

No one can be quite sure about the kinds of situations a school pupil will face after he leaves school. But an important reason for sending him to school—if not the most important reason —is to enable him to deal more capably with those situations later on, whatever they might be.

Because the future is always more or less indeterminate, there is no way of telling just what particular items of knowledge, or what bits of behavior, or even what specific habits and attitudes which, if acquired in school, will be brought to bear in some future situation. On the other hand, the person who is prepared to deal with an indeterminate future is acutely aware of his natural and human surroundings. He is able to accept and enjoy them as they are while at the same time remaining sensitive to what is problematic about them. He has the confidence to meet problems and deals with them in terms of their widest consequences, for others as well as himself and those close to him. Moreover, he is disposed to deal with those problems on the grounds of objectively found factors in the situations themselves and his own carefully considered values and purposes, rather than merely on the basis of personal bias and desire.

To speak of human action in this way is to speak in terms of character and dispositions. One's tendencies to act are under consideration, rather than one's knowledge, particular response patterns, or habits. Of course, dispositions do not function independently of these more particular responses, but one who is appropriately disposed can acquire those responses when they are needed. A man who is sensitive to problems and aware of the importance of dealing with them may lack relevant information or skills. But he will be disposed to get the information and skills he needs. He may, of course, fail in the attempt, but no preparation and no disposition, once acquired, can guarantee success.

When people learn, they change, but any description or account of learning necessitates choosing from among the many ways in which people change the kind of change on which attention is to be focused. This choice, as long as it suggests school practices, has moral implications. To illustrate, we may note that punishment, in many instances, has the effect of negative reinforcement (that is, particular behaviors are conditioned by the withdrawal of the punishment). While punishment may be counted as a way of facilitating learning, negative reinforcement is not currently popular as a general method of schooling. It is not merely that the use of the rod, for example, is now held to be inhumane. For it is also thought that only passive obedience resulted from using it: that is, a kind of conditioned behavior that gave little reason to hope that the child would remain obedient without further use of the rod or some psychological substitute for it.

Current conditioning theorists and educators who favor the schools' fostering discrete behaviors are not inhumane. They recommend the use of positive reinforcement (approval, or immediate knowledge of the results of one's efforts) rather than negative (the rod). But positive reinforcement is still conditioning, and conditioning is different from the kinds of events that have been under consideration in this study. The conditioned student is changed, but is not *he* who is the agent of change; he remains passive.

The rod of negative reinforcement is undesirable on two counts. It is inhumane, and the victim is simply changed—he remains passive, not responsible for the change. Conditioning conceived as positive reinforcement avoids the first charge, but does not escape the second. Those concerned with schooling must choose, then, between changing students by conditioning them or by some other means. This choice of process is a moral choice, and the particular values that underlie this study are indicated by the kinds of dispositional changes in people that throughout have been the focus of attention.

The moral implications of the kinds of learning for which the school is responsible have important social consequences. If, as I have claimed, the acquisition of certain kinds of dispositions prepares one to deal adequately with an indeterminate future, then the acquisition of discrete behaviors and particular attitudes and preferences is least likely to constitute such a preparation. For unless those particular behaviors and preferences are just the ones that are relevant to new situations when they come (and the odds are against this), the individual must either succumb to them or let someone else meet them for him. Thus commitment to a process by which students acquire specific behaviors and preferences has significant implications for social and political organization. For when many people are effectively schooled in this way, they must all let someone else meet their futures for them. The complexities of modern civilization may demand that we often consult experts, and the size of nations may demand representative government. But the abdication of all individual initiative, participation, and decision-making soon leads to tyranny.

The values implied in what I have called an expectancy-discrepancy conception of learning suggest a different kind of social organization. To be disposed to continue learning, and to be committed to the earlier noted values that are implied in aesthetic sensitivity, alertness and intellectual curiosity, and sensitivity to problems and skill in dealing with them, is to have a certain kind of character. But it would be difficult, if not impossible, to maintain such qualities of character if one had continually to interact in a type of society which arbitrarily limited freedom of thought and criticism, which put arbitrary limits on the scope of human inter-action, and which exercised an authority over individuals that did not afford them the means of participating in it. We can see more clearly the relation between the conception of learning and the im-plied qualities of character that have been advanced here, and some more general features of social organization by considering a few examples.

The dispositions discussed above could neither be developed nor exercised in a society so bent on utilitarian ends that its members found no time for privacy and leisure. For the enjoyment of many kinds of artistic qualities and the pursuit of curiosity cannot proceed in an environment where a practical purpose constantly dominates thought and action. Privacy and leisure are not just the blessings of childhood. They are conditions without which an adult must remain something less than fully human.

Similarly, arbitrary restrictions on social intercourse put blinders on curiosity and breadth of interest and concern, and by that much both vitiate men's intellectual and scientific pursuits, and dilute the satisfactions that can be found in a wide variety of human relation-ships. More important, such restrictions, in separating people from one another, narrow the scope of human purpose and render opaque the full consequences for others of what men do. Thus problems that affect everyone grow unheeded because they are hidden behind tra-ditional barriers that are largely irrelevant to personal qualities of character.

The qualities of character implied in the conception of learning advanced here include orderly ways of thinking: having respect for evidence and a sense of its relevance, being disposed to make careful inferences, and feeling an obligation to test one's conclusions. But none of these dispositions can be developed or exercised in a society which limits freedom of thought or excludes some of its members from participation in the decisions which affect them. For when one's thoughts and one's destiny are controlled by others, there is neither motivation nor practical need for thinking carefully on one's own. Aristotle was correct when he observed that slaves were not quite like men. But they were not born that way. They were made that way by the institution of slavery, just as other men are made thoughtful and independent by virtue of living in a free society. It is no criticism of this conception to point out that not all Americans think critically, develop broad interests, or live fully aware of their own purposes. Rather, this merely indicates that freedom for all is not created simply by the signing of a declaration. The biases and the gaps in men's thinking each indicate not some congenital inadequacy, but a sector within some social institution, an area of human interaction whether intimate or remote, that for them has not been free.

The norms of social organization under consideration are probably not very different from the ones usually mentioned when the curriculum of the public schools is under discussion. Insofar as these norms are not fully realized throughout the wider society, they suggest what is often termed "social needs." Some curriculum makers are then disposed to draw up a program of studies designed to satisfy these needs. But the attempt to draw out a curriculum from beliefs about an ideal society and the inferred needs of the present one suffers from at least two serious difficulties. The first is that ideal conceptions of society are either too vague to imply curriculum content or so specific that attention is distracted from schooling and toward political controversy. With some notable exceptions,[7] the references to an ideal society found in most discussions of the curriculum often begin and end with homage paid to democracy, the worth of the individual, and the dignity of mankind. Until those generalizations are made more explicit in terms of concrete institutional contexts, they imply little about a curriculum. But when they are made explicit, attention is turned away from the curriculum and toward controversy over political and social beliefs. A conception of a curriculum always implies a particular social philosophy, but the detailed working out of political and economic problems should not be mistaken for proposals about the school curriculum. *Those* proposals, on this conception of curriculum design, would be kept waiting (perhaps forever) until partisan political disputes were settled. In a pluralistic society, the attempt to fit a curriculum to a conception of an ideal social order is at best impractical. As already indicated, *general* forms of social organization are surely suggested by the qualities of character that result when young people learn to learn. But the attempt to draw implications for schooling from one's conclusions about specific political, economic, and social institutional forms only ends in a plan for indoctrination—not education.

The danger of indoctrination suggests the second difficulty involved in trying to fit a curriculum to one's beliefs about an ideal society. For the attempt to do so distorts the process of learning. The imposition of beliefs about a social ideal bends the futures of children to a particular set of social norms, instead of fitting them to examine and adjust their own society as they become older. This, as we saw, is indoctrination, no matter how benevolently conceived. Such a role for schooling limits human choices instead of making them more free and more thoughtful.

Schooling and society are related, but there is a more defensible way of making the relation between the two explicit and functional than by picking the social order one likes and then organizing what the school teaches to prepare students for it. That way is to begin with the conditions of learning and schooling rather than with one's conception of an ideal society. For when one is clear about the kind of learning process that he is willing to have the schools promote, then generalized principles of social organization are already implicit. Those norms will, of course, be those that are required to maintain the qualities of character developed in the process of learning itself. A disposition to learn can neither be acquired nor exercised independently of the kinds of freedoms outlined earlier.

## A CRITERION OF SOCIAL RELEVANCE FOR THE SELECTION OF CURRICULUM CONTENT

The kinds of social norms implied in the process of learning provide one criterion for the selection of content for the curriculum. If the qualities of character developed by the schools require for their maintenance certain kinds of social organization, then students should be made thoughtfully aware of it. The criterion for curriculum content can then be put this way: Knowledge and skills should be selected that will help students in understanding, maintaining, and criticizing a society in light of the criteria of freedom of thought, decision, and social interaction. We will see that this criterion of social relevance is neither a strong nor a rigid one. It will give some guidance in selecting content for certain courses of study, but it may be more useful in its negative application—that is, in suggesting what should be excluded from the curriculum. And there are some kinds of school studies to which the criterion has no direct application at all.

A fact is, of course, just a fact and no more. Children who acquire knowledge about the distance from here to the moon, or the knowledge that Washington spent a winter at Valley Forge, are not any better prepared to understand or criticize one sort of society than they are another. Being able to multiply seven by six does not prepare one any better for democracy than it does for fascism, or for capitalism than it does for communism. Thus the application of the criterion of social relevance cannot be taken to imply that a curriculum maker can find facts and skills that carry their socially beneficial qualifications with them. The criterion is, then, only intended to suggest that bodies of knowledge and skills be organized and used in schools in such a way that their relation to the organization, maintenance, and improvement of social institutions is made apparent.

The way in which the criterion is to be applied obviously suggests methods of teaching, but it is relevant to the selection of content as well. To see the difference it might make, consider the teaching of biology. What is taught may be strictly limited to knowledge about certain processes, like photosynthesis and the structure and function of cells, and the parts of selected forms of organic life—perhaps amoebae and paramecia, ferns and flowers, flies and frogs. But the teaching of biology can include some of this knowledge in a context of pursuing questions about the human and social uses of biological knowledge—especially at those problematical points where society is undergoing reconstruction. Is the fluoridation of water harmful? Are the causes of illness natural? Are some people naturally superior to others? Does biological knowledge help in understanding what is meant by the term "natural"? Does the concept of evolution have any relation to an understanding of social organization?

Such questions may be inappropriate for immature learners, but when properly raised are not for adolescents. Their inclusion and pursuit in a biology course radically alter its content. Yet this way of studying biology is of far greater relevance to the general education of all students than is the detailed study of ferns, flowers, flies, and frogs. To consider questions of social relevance is appropriate for all students whatever their special interests, for they may become disposed to attend to the relevant biological considerations of human and social problems. But the detailed study of certain forms of organic life is especially appropriate for students already disposed to incorporate biological understanding into their thinking. Many of these students will be interested in biology as a career, but what is appropriate study for those interests is not necessarily appropriate for all students.

To be concerned with the social relevance of biological studies is not to deny students the chance for detailed study of organic life. If curiosity and interest have been aroused, many students will want to do so, and they should be encouraged and assisted in this. A criterion of social relevance is not opposed to specialized scholarship, but it does recognize the fact that the obligation to be scholarly is not so universal as the obligation to understand and deal intelligently with the institutions within which one lives.

Because of the nature of teaching and learning, the criterion of social relevance must be qualified. It would be pointless to try to present *all* of what the school teaches as it bears on social aims and organization. It is not because there is any particular virtue in teaching what is socially irrelevant, but only that the concept of social relevance is itself too loose to become a rigid and inflexible criterion of content selection. Consider a class pursuing inquiry into why plants grow up in spite of gravity, or involved in a mathematical game. Both kinds of study are eminently worth including in a curriculum yet neither would be called socially relevant in the ordinary sense of the term.

It is worth noting that the school classroom itself is a miniature social institution, having a set of functions, formally and informally organized functional groups, and a power structure. In his career as a student, the learner lives in many such miniature societies, and it would be reasonable to suppose that their accumulated impact has an influence on the dispositions with which he will function as an adult in the wider society. If, then, the studies that are presented should create an undesirable social climate in the classroom, they might best be left out of the curriculum. This is, of course, as much a matter of how the content is presented as it is of the nature of the content itself. In any case, we may remember that students are often bored, confused, or threatened by what is presented to them. Order and control in a classroom of such students is not maintained by the nature of the inquiry itself, but is, instead, achieved only by force, the promise of extrinsic rewards, or more subtle substitutes for them. Not only is this a poor climate for desirable kinds of learning to occur, but it is also likely, if frequently encountered, to engender in students the kinds of dispositions appropriate to living in an authoritarian society. If the choice of content is responsible for such conditions, these are reasons enough for making another choice.

Given our understanding of the learning process, a child simply could not learn to learn in a classroom in which arbitrary restraints were placed on his freedom of thought, of decision, or of social interaction. Restraints there must be, of course, and more of them for younger and less civilized children. But if they are exercised in the interests of the children's learning, then the restraints are not arbitrary. Thus, if a child in school is acquiring a disposition to acquire new knowledge, skills, and attitudes, his social climate cannot be incompatible with the broader social norms discussed earlier. If this is so, then the knowledge and skills involved in what is being learned *are*—by virtue of the nature of the process itself—related to the understanding and maintenance of a society that prizes freedom of thought, decision, and social interaction. For the child as he learns is *living* in just such a society.[8] In areas and at levels of maturity where it is appropriate, content can be made more directly socially relevant if developing dispositions are brought to focus on topics and issues related to contemporary industrialized and interdependent society.

When we understand the importance of the relation of curriculum content to the societies within and outside of the school, we also gain some insight into the kinds of curricula that are inappropriate for schooling. Such a curriculum would be one that deliberately organized knowledge and skills in such a way that their relation to broader social concerns *could not* practically be pursued. Studies designed as a specific preparation for a specific subsequent activity are limited in this way. They may qualify as vocational or pre-professional education, but not as general education. For the content of such courses, however appropriate to this job or that career, is not of sufficient generality or importance for all students to be exposed to it. It might be objected that the schools ought to prepare students for careers, and that since they have different abilities and interests, different curricula or "tracks" are called for. Elsewhere I tried to show how job preparation (or any other single function) considered as an exclusive school aim was opposed to the interests of students in a free society. This can be made more explicit in light of the foregoing discussion.

The particular track into which a student is placed bears a marked relation to his home background. Most students in college-preparatory tracks are representative of more favored social and economic groups; students in the business and shop courses are generally drawn from lower socioeconomic classes. Native ability is probably less responsible for these groupings than is the influence of home, neighborhood, and the opinions and the prejudices of others upon one's growing abilities and aspirations. But once students are separated in schools in this way, restrictions are placed not only on their future academic and career choices, but also on their social intercourse. Thus students are unable to learn from, work with, or understand students in other tracks. Yet it is probably these skills and understandings, more than any other specific curriculum content, that are most relevant to understanding, maintaining, and criticizing a free society.[9]

How a single-purpose conception of schooling tends to determine a student's future for him has already been mentioned. We can see how particularly this applies in the case of vocational and other specific preparatory curricula. Not just a person's job, but his modes of thought and feeling as well are largely a function of the kind of career he chooses. Some vocational programs are begun as early as age 14; this would seem rather early for the making of so important a choice. But without having a clear public mandate to do so, the school may make this choice for the student. Having assessed the student's abilities and attitudes (and not allowing for or even providing for any important changes in these later on), the school usurps the socially important and personally crucial task of specifically deciding his future. The school may claim that putting the student onto a track is only "fitting education to the needs and abilities of the child." But this would seem a mockery of the idea of teaching personal responsibility by thus withdrawing it from students. Rather than exert pressures on young adolescents to choose careers, or choose for them, schools might be better advised to afford the resources and foster the learnings with which students might be enabled later on to make better choices.[10] Nearly 3 generations ago, Charles W. Eliot argued that too early a selection of one's career was incompatible with the notion of a free society:

> It is common in Europe to classify children very early into future peasants, mechanics, tradespeople, merchants, and professional people, and to adapt deliberately the education of children from a very early age to this decreed destination. In a democratic society like ours, these early determinations of the career should be avoided as long as possible, particularly in public schools. . . . who are to make these prophecies [about future careers]? Can parents? Can teachers? Can university presidents, or even professional students of childhood and adolescence? . . . the individual child in a democratic society has a right to do his own prophesying about his own career, guided by his own ambitions and his own capacities, and abating his aspirations only under the irresistible pressure of adverse circumstances.[11]

We may hope that advances in science and industry since Eliot's era have not rendered obsolete this conception of freedom and responsibility.

## THE ORGANIZATION OF KNOWLEDGE AND SKILLS FOR TEACHING

A criterion of social relevance suggests how some knowledge and skills may be treated in schools, and suggests that some modes of organizing the curriculum are inappropriate for general education. But it does not suggest what particular knowledge and skills to which our criterion can be applied should be chosen initially. Thus one may ask, "Where do the candidates for curriculum content come from in the first place?"

We will see shortly that this question is not worthy of an answer. There are plenty of lists of knowledge and skills to be found. They are all different, but if one of them actually did win universal approval it would be far out-of-date by the time it was translated into a set of curriculum materials. This does not suggest that school studies might as well be selected at random. Rather, one may infer from it that the important question to ask about curriculum is not, "which one is the right one for the schools?" but rather, "who should select it, and for whom?" This latter question raises the important considerations, for content selection, of competence and responsibility.

When we ask who is competent to select knowledge for a curriculum, and what it would mean to be responsible for the selection, we are no longer considering simply the knowledge itself that might be selected. But before directly pursuing the questions of competence and responsibility, we must very briefly consider the place of the organization of subject matter in the curriculum.

Various organizations of content have had their champions from time to time. Content should be presented as it naturally enters into children's ongoing activities; or it should be presented in the form of the logically organized disciplines. A wide sampling of content should appear in the context of dealing with social problems; or it should appear in the form of two or three disciplines hitched together and pulling the same freight of topics or issues. Content should be called "subjects," so students will respect the internal logic of each; or it should be called "core," so students will respect the interrelations of the disciplines with each other and with life patterns.[12]

I have not mentioned these organizations of content until now because it does not matter very much which one is chosen. If the discussion of learning in the previous chapters has any merit, then children *can* learn, however the content of the curriculum is packaged. On the other hand, no organization of knowledge and skills in itself can guarantee that children will learn. Of course, some extremes of content organization can make it unlikely that students will learn. If *all* the knowledge and skills presented to students must wait until they become relevant to the students' own particular interests, then most children will learn very little. If, on the other hand, the *only* knowledge and skills presented to children must follow undeviatingly from somebody's notion of the immutable inner logic of the disciplines, then learning will probably suffer in the students' efforts just to remember what they heard and read. In both organizations of curriculum content, the conditions under which learning might occur are absent. When children's activities follow *only* their own interests, they are often put off by discrepancies and problems that might have borne educational potential. In the face of such discrepancies, they may simply abandon those activities. On the other hand, when presented only with content that, in its rigidly logical organization, is isolated from other concerns, there is little opportunity either for the experiencing of aesthetic quality or for the encountering of problems relevant to personal concerns. And the danger is present that even curiosity may not be aroused.

But aside from these extremes, most modes of content organization can be utilized, as long as the teacher attends to the conditions under which people learn. Thus there is nothing that has been said here about learning that does not apply, for example, to the organization of content by subjects. Since the subject curriculum is conventional, the easiest to organize, and still the most popular one, we might take a moment to consider the relation between the growth in students of dispositions to learn, and the development of subject matter from the more general to the more particular and precise.

If schooling does promote the sort of learning that enables and encourages more learning, then the ways in which children focus their interests should change over a period of time. New dispositions gradually become a significant part of their character. Eventually they will become able to direct their attention to increasingly more specific and more logically organized areas of study. For as one learns to learn, he acquires knowledge, skills, and attitudes whereby he both wishes to pursue and is capable of pursuing more detailed and specific problems and topics. Thus knowledge pursued in the elementary grades under the more general headings of "science" and "social studies" will increasingly be studied, as students become more mature, under the narrower headings of physics and biology, or history and economics.[13] What remains important, however, is that students who reach a level of sophistication that enables them to pursue more specialized studies do so in light of an understanding of the relation of these studies to other topics and concerns. And it also bears repeating that different students will be ready to pursue more specialized studies in different areas and at different times. Arbitrary requirements for content acquisition, then, only delay the more sophisticated student and confuse the others.

The same considerations for the growth of subject matter conceived as knowledge apply in general to subject matter conceived as skills. Younger students lack the sophistication (i.e., the appropriate dispositions) to study language, or mathematics, or critical thinking *per se*. But because little else can be learned at all without some skills in these areas, they must be practiced from the beginning of schooling and ever afterward. How they can effectively be practiced has already been indicated. Mathematical reasoning and the skills of computation are natural concomitants to the study of science, and the study of all subjects is fruitless without increasing facility in the use of language and logic. Thus teaching in all knowledge areas must be teaching in skills as well. But while some skills, like reading, cannot even be imagined without some connection to relevant curriculum content,[14] others can be effectively practiced in isolation from any other relevant concerns. We have already spoken of the presentation of mathematics in the form of puzzles and games. The same may apply, for example, to the teaching of critical thinking.[15] The finding of reasons and the drawing of valid conclusions must, of course, be taught and practiced in connection with the study of every subject to which verbal discourse is relevant. But if such skills can be sharpened through deliberate practice, students might be presented with both relevant and irrelevant data and be asked to solve a "crime," or sit on a "jury."

A game worth playing involving the practice of a skill may ultimately have important social consequences. Not many people in our culture, for example, need very much in the way of mathematical skills, but a few people are sorely needed who know a great deal about mathematics. The fact that society needs such people, however, does not in itself motivate children to acquire those skills. Good mathematicians are invariably people who *like* the subject. Thus if children are taught mathematics through games and in ways that are enjoyable—rather than through interminable drill in getting the right answer—it could reasonably be hoped that enough people will acquire favorable attitudes toward mathematics for society to get the mathematicians it needs.

Yet a word must be said for the repetitive and isolated practice of skills that is called drill. Drill appears in the practice of schooling just about as often as it is maligned in theory. What makes it problematical is the fact that it is too often practiced at the wrong time. It is useful to practice a skill in isolation from other activities when a disposition to use the skill has already been formed, or is in the process of being formed. An aspiring secretary readily practices her typing, even though the material typed is of little interest to her. And people seriously concerned with musical expression are willing to spend hours practicing the techniques of their instruments. What makes drill ineffective and offensive is the often unwarranted assumption that an appropriate disposition has already been formed. The classic example is the otherwise bright little boy who is so inept at practicing the piano, no matter how much instruction and drill he receives. He fails because he is more disposed to do something else than to become a pianist. There are some who say that drill is warranted, whether or not a child sees the point of it, because he "needs" it. But good reasons are seldom offered for *why* students need it. Much mischief is done when the very complicated concept of need is taken as if it were obvious.[16]

## RESPONSIBILITY FOR CONTENT SELECTION: THE ROLE OF THE TEACHER

A little earlier it was suggested that the important question to ask about the curriculum was not, "what knowledge and skills should be included in it?" but rather, "who should select the knowledge and skills that are to be included in it?" The conclusion seems inescapable that such people should be familiar with the area of knowledge from which the content of the curriculum is to be drawn, and they should be responsible for their selection. The first of these two qualifications is clear enough. A person unfamiliar, for example, with science is hardly competent to select knowledge and skills for the curriculum in that area. The second qualification may be less clear: what would it mean to be responsible for the selection of content?

Responsibility in this sense means simply that whoever selects content for the curriculum be prepared and in a position to take the consequences of his selection. But what *are* the consequences of selecting content? They are hard to measure in terms of long-run effects on students. Consequences can directly be seen in terms of what happens when content is presented in a classroom. Of course, the student takes the consequences of selecting this rather than that content, but since he lacks the background to make competent choices himself, he cannot be held fully responsible for curriculum selection.

The only other person in the classroom who suffers the immediate consequences of what is taught, and can alter activities accordingly, is the teacher. In light of this, and in light of his knowledge of the area from which content is drawn, the teacher becomes chiefly responsible for selecting the content that appears in the curriculum. To see the meaning of this more fully, consider an extreme case of irresponsibility in content selection.

Some legislatures have enacted laws making it mandatory to teach about the evil consequences of drinking in all the elementary schools of the state. The good intentions of legislators and their constituents cannot be doubted. Habitual drinking is a bad thing, and the sooner one realizes it, the better. But it is safe to assume that very few legislators have ever presented a unit on the evils of drinking to a classroom of elementary school children. The results of the attempt are, of course, as ineffective as they are ludicrous. Thus it would also be fairly safe to assume that if the legislators who enacted the law  had to teach what they made mandatory, they would soon see its pointlessness. This is a case of irresponsibility in curriculum content selection because those who made the choice left it entirely to others to suffer the consequences. Such a mode of decision-making suits the military, where decisions must be made and carried out quickly, and where the consequences of those decisions are close at hand, measurable, and painstakingly assessed. But the military serves as a poor model for organizing an institution bent on preparing young people to live in a nonauthoritarian society. The distance from the Pentagon to the battlefield is not nearly so great as it is from the legislature to the classroom. When selections for curriculum content travel that distance, there are no controls against irrationality and caprice.

The teacher is knowledgeable and skillful within certain subject areas, and the teacher takes some of the consequences of what he teaches. Thus the knowledge and skills worth serious consideration for inclusion in the curriculum are what teachers are competent to select and teach. The most important determinant, then, of the overall curriculum of a school is the nature of the areas of competence of its teachers.

No examination of knowledge in the abstract, and no examination of society, or of children, can produce a precise, fully rational, and universally acceptable selection of content for the curriculum. Selecting content before one knows who will teach it (and who is to acquire it) is thus putting the cart before the horse. If teachers are unprepared to teach the content that is given to them (because it is part of some ideal curriculum), what follows cannot be very good education. If teachers are not given the opportunity to teach what they *do* know (because it is not part of the ideal curriculum), then their own knowledge and skills are wasted. To find a curriculum, one must start with the teachers he has, or better, try to staff a school with teachers whose competence ranges over a broad variety of fields of study.

To focus on what a teacher can teach rather than on an abstract list of studies is to recognize the importance of teachers in the process of schooling. Yet public school systems have traditionally been organized in such a way as to deny that importance. Teachers are often expected to transmit knowledge and skills that appear in curriculum materials prepared by others. More recently, they have been expected to prepare students for high achievement on examinations constructed by others. Under these circumstances, teachers are not responsible for content selection, and others are irresponsible. The teacher is cast in a subservient role respecting the selection of what he is to teach, despite the fact that his own education has presumably prepared him to make the selection himself. For in most cases he has spent at least 4 years acquiring knowledge and skills in his area of teaching, and acquiring knowledge, skills, and dispositions relevant to the process of teaching.

The consequence of organizing a school system in such a way so that teachers are not always responsible for selecting what they teach is to discourage the kinds of people who prefer to make their own choices from becoming teachers. The conditions of employment, in this as in any other field, are powerful determinants of the kinds of people who will enter the field. Strongly independent people seldom seek employment in a field where, as in teaching, the dictated plans of others entail long hours, hard work, and emotional strain—but little responsibility.

Given his conditions of employment, it is not surprising that the image of the American teacher is not a particularly exciting one. But it does reflect a person willing to work very hard at carrying out the decisions other people make. His own abilities and purposes, not to mention those of his class, are often quite irrelevant to those decisions. But so willing is he to execute them that he is even prepared to try whatever "new methods" of teaching may be fashionable, in the hope of transforming the sow's ear into a silk purse.

At present, 2 million people teach in the public schools. Many of them make what choices they can about curriculum content, and for some, the breadth of choice is considerable. But there may be nearly as many people who left teaching for other work, because they could not adjust themselves to meeting professional standards of teaching in circumstances where professional decisions about what to teach were withheld.

The subservient role of many teachers is not unremarked by students. If the teacher is to initiate them into an area of study, it is he who must serve as a model of intellectual curiosity, critical thought, and the profound concern that is the mark of total absorption in the immediate quality of a situation. But one who carries out the decisions of others, who has not chosen the content he teaches, can be no such model. It is hoped that schools will dispose students to be independent, to exhibit initiative, and to become responsible. But if these dispositions are not exercised by the teacher, it is to be wondered from whom they will be acquired. The teacher to be sure does function as a sort of model. But what the student often learns from him is to go through certain motions obediently and without undue complaint, or to resent any authority because it so often seems arbitrary, or to become cynical and avoid personal involvement in activities where the purposes of others must be taken into account.

To argue that teachers be responsible for their own selections of curriculum content is to deny neither the importance of cooperatively made curriculum decisions, nor the importance of available curriculum materials. Insofar as the scope and sequence of curriculum content has importance, it is necessary for teachers to adjust their decisions about content to those of other teachers. Thus the more general decisions about curriculum must be made by teachers acting in concert.

Moreover, the quality of teachers' choices of content is directly related to the availability of curriculum materials. Curriculum guides, textbooks, films, tapes, and the teacher's own lesson plans are resources, each suggestive of possible content. The teacher is hamstrung only when one of these is used to define what to teach, rather than to be a resource for teaching. Insofar as content selection is concerned, the same principle holds for the effective operation of the instructional team, wherein two or more teachers share responsibility for teaching the same group of students. Team teaching works when the strengths of each member are utilized, when through consultation those strengths are shared and deepened, and when the person designated as leader suggests and advises about content rather than dictates it. The individual teacher can profit from the use of curriculum materials in the same way. His selection of content is the richer for being able to draw from many materials at hand. But if he is limited to presenting the content contained in a single one, either he subordinates his judgement to that of someone else or he spends much of his time in class supplying to students what he judges that the text or the curriculum guide lacks. There are far better ways to utilize time in the classroom than for the teacher to become a supplementary talking text.

To sum up, there are at least four compelling reasons for teachers' making their own choices of the content that shall constitute the curriculum. First, there is no ideal curriculum available on which all experts would agree. And if there were, it would be as unlikely that many teachers would be prepared to teach it as it would be likely that the special competence of many other teachers would lie unused. Second, by dint of their preparation, teachers are at least as qualified as anyone else to select curriculum content. If they are not, the fault lies with those who certified them to teach. Third, of those with the knowledge requisite for making content selections, only the teacher is in a position to be responsible for what is taught. If the content, once introduced in the classroom, turns out to be inappropriate, it is the teacher who must deal with the resulting situation. It is he who must amplify it, alter it, or withdraw it. And finally, the student suffers even more than the teacher when someone else assumes responsibility for content selection. For not only is the student burdened with having to acquire knowledge and skills that often seem arbitrary, but his own habits, attitudes, and dispositions are disastrously shaped when he continually witnesses and interacts with a model of subservience to the decisions of others.

It is not surprising, then, that the organizational and administrative practices which interfere with responsible teaching also minimize the possibility of students' acquiring dispositions to acquire new knowledge, skills, and attitudes. Since the restraints and controls exercised on teachers are of the same sort that teachers sometimes (but not necessarily by choice) exercise on students, the criticism of those latter restraints (Chapter VII) applies with equal validity to their exercise by others upon teachers. In other words, learning itself can be enhanced only when those responsible for promoting it are free to teach. The consequences of this for the administration and control of schools are beyond the scope of this book. But it follows that if what is taught in schools, as well as the way it is taught, are means or conditions for the promotion of learning, and if teachers are responsible for those means, then responsibility for many kinds of educational decisions must shift from school boards and administrators to teachers. It would also follow that only strongly organized teachers can bring about such a shift.[17]

## QUALIFICATIONS FOR TEACHING

In bringing to a close this discussion of learning and schooling, we have found reasons for believing that the interests of public education are best served if the means of schooling are left in the hands of those who teach. When our concern shifts from curriculum content to teachers, it becomes pertinent to ask about their qualifications. Thus we will conclude by noting the kinds of competence needed by teachers to select content that functions effectively in the promotion of learning.

To begin with, it is clear that a teacher must have a fairly thorough understanding of the subject or subjects that he teaches. He must also have some understanding of the relation of these to other areas of knowledge. For without this, his classroom teaching must either turn into the sort of specialized training that for most students is premature, or simply sink to the level of pedantry. What the teacher knows is not to be presented in all its detail to students, but rather is to be drawn upon in deciding what part of it is appropriate to teach. When a teacher understands what his students presently know, familiarity with his subject helps him to select what is appropriate for them to come to know, or to be exposed to. No amount of sympathy for children or skill at interpersonal relations will substitute for knowing his own field when a teacher seeks content to include in his curriculum.

Secondly, the content a teacher selects must also be based on his knowledge of whom he is teaching. Not that he must visit his pupils' homes, looking for competence in the parents or rivalry among the siblings. In cases of more enigmatic or problematical children, a teacher may wish to consult with an informed guidance counselor, but the information needed about most students can be acquired in the classroom. For the effort to teach is helped by knowing how students respond to what is taught, and how it is taught, and how, in learning situations, they respond to each other. Of course, the less free students are to respond in class, the harder it is to find out anything helpful about these matters.

Students come to class with very different kinds and qualities of prior experiences, and of course, they differ greatly in the extent to which they can deal with certain kinds of content. This is sometimes thought to be a good reason for selecting different "levels" of content—for example, one for the quick, one for the average, and one for the slow students. But the reasoning behind such a procedure is faulty. First, it assumes that, since there are differences among children, the differences will disappear (or at least be reduced to manageable proportions) within each of, say, three different groups. This is incorrect. Even if we rashly ignore all the differences among children except those relating to their ability to acquire a certain kind of content, the variation among children within a group will be as striking as the variation between groups.

Second, grouping according to ability to acquire content assumes that a particular selection of knowledge is so universally beneficial that it ought to be parceled out in different dosages to different students. But we have already seen how difficult it is to defend any single selection of curriculum content. Under the guise of ministering to individual differences, such grouping only seeks to pigeon-hole and thereby transcend those differences through the imposition of an omniscient choice of content. The point of trying to understand students is not so they can all be set to acquiring different amounts (or levels of complexity) of the same thing. Rather, it is to be able to find content that is appropriate for each.

In planning a lesson, a teacher selects a certain range of content for presentation to all the students in his class. But if he has some relevant understanding of his students, what he will expect or hope each one to acquire will progressively differ for each. When teaching is effective, and when students use a variety of materials in pursuing their studies, we should expect them to become increasingly different from one another respecting what they know. But it is unfortunate that the benign wish for students to come to know more be translated into the practice of getting them to know more of the same.

One final qualification must be mentioned in considering the competence of teachers to make their own selections of knowledge and skills for inclusion in the curriculum. In choosing content, a teacher must be concerned about its role in the promotion of learning. Stated so baldly, this may appear obvious. But in light of the way learning has been discussed in this book, it may not be so obvious at all.

Some teachers are concerned that their students acquire certain kinds of knowledge and skills. Some are concerned that their students acquire certain kinds of habits and attitudes. And only some teachers are concerned that their students acquire dispositions that enable them to go on learning—that, in short, they learn to learn. It is good for teachers to have varied concerns, but variety in this respect may not lead to happy consequences. To select content to teach simply because it is thought that students ought to acquire it is a curriculum rationale that is, as we noted earlier, hard to defend. Other curriculum makers each have their own favored selection of content, and in any case most students tend in the classroom to reject this approach to teaching. Selecting knowledge and skills in the hope that they will contribute to the formation of certain habits and attitudes is little short of indoctrination. The choice of content will be based on the particular habits and attitudes desired, but in any case the student never quite knows what is happening to him. His attitudes result not from his own judgment, but from exposure to a biased selection of content. Attitudes so formed are not easily subject to expansion or change.

If schooling is to promote dispositions to acquire new knowledge, skills, and attitudes, then content must be selected for the curriculum with this aim in mind. But the learning that has been discussed here is a process dependent on many conditions, not all predictable in advance. Study may be initiated and pursued in a context in which experience has aesthetic quality; it may follow on the presentation of something that appeals to curiosity; or it may result from inquiry into what is personally problematical. In each case the student has an expectation that is thwarted in some way. But what he expects, and what will be discrepant with his expectations, is sometimes a surprise to the teacher as well as it is to the student himself. While planning in advance is necessary, it does not relieve the teacher of making decisions about content in the midst of the give-and-take of the classroom.

For these reasons, a teacher cannot simply be told what decisions to make about selecting content. He must instead be prepared to make decisions in certain ways. A teacher competent to select curriculum content has not, then, simply acquired certain kinds of knowledge or skills. Instead, he has acquired a disposition: one to employ the curriculum in the service of the kind of learning he hopes to promote.

Because of the infinite variety of situations in which learning may occur, a teacher's successful choice of curriculum content is not simply a matter of his knowing this or that, and not simply a matter of his having acquired a particular skill or pedagogical technique. It is a matter of his own disposition. He must have a tendency to see content in its role as an aesthetic cue, as a prod to curiosity, or as a cue to awareness of a problem, and to see it as supplying the material for the pursuit of these initiating situations. To select appropriate content, the teacher must view it as the natural passenger for the vehicle of his students' thoughts—not simply as a burden to be acquired and retained until examination time. To be disposed to treat curriculum candidates in this way is no mechanical skill, no behavioral response to some specific set of stimuli. It is the way a competent teacher lives: the way he plans his semester's work and his daily lesson plan, and the way he makes judgments about how and where to direct the discussion and the activities of his class.

We are speaking now of a disposition to teach—that is, to provide the conditions under which children can learn. To cultivate such a disposition is the special task of institutions that prepare teachers. This preparation may be made more specific in terms of the special problems of teaching and learning that are relevant to the procedures exemplified in different fields of inquiry. Yet many people who never had any special preparation for it have dispositions that are suited for teaching. This should neither be surprising nor should it lead to the nonsensical conclusion that teachers are born, not made. If teaching is conceived as the fostering of the kind of learning with which we have been dealing, then it is the process by which one human being makes it possible for another to become alert, grow sensitive to his world, and think independently. Without making over his pupil into an image of himself, such a person enables a learner eventually to do without him. This, of course, is how we should want all adults to act; it represents the best that could be hoped for of anyone's education.

Some do learn to act this way: to acquire the dispositions that make for an effective teacher. They may learn it by deliberate intent of their parents, through contact with a few influential teachers, or through the accident of a congenial social environment. But institutions that prepare people to teach are not rendered unnecessary simply because some people teach effectively without them. The dispositions of such people did not appear miraculously at birth; they were acquired, whether by accident or design, over a period of time. And if they can be acquired at all, they can be acquired more effectively and more widely when they are deliberately and thoughtfully taught.

## NOTES

1. See Robert H. Beck, Walter W. Cook, and Nolan C. Kearney, *Curriculum in the Modern Elementary School* (Englewood Cliffs, N.J.: Prentice-Hall, 1960), p. 181.
2. See Israel Scheffler, *The Language of Education* (Springfield, Ill.: Charles C. Thomas, 1960), p. 23.

3. Evidence for this conclusion may be found by comparing the very different proposals for curriculum content that tap what is essentially the same source: the organized knowledge that is available. See, for example, Harry S. Broudy, B. Othanel Smith, and Joe R. Burnett, *Democracy and Excellence in American Secondary Education* (Chicago: Rand McNally, 1964); Edward A. Krug, *The Secondary School Curriculum* (New York: Harper, 1960); and Philip H. Phenix, *Realms of Meaning* (New York: McGraw-Hill, 1964).

4. See Krug, *op. cit.*, p. 544.

5. Most of the examples mentioned below are included in Philip H. Phenix (ed.), *Philosophies of Education* (New York: John Wiley & Sons, 1961).

6. A satiric criticism of the view of curriculum under discussion can be found in John Hersey, *The Child Buyer* (New York: Knopf, 1960).

7. See, for example, B. Othanel Smith, William O. Stanley, and J. Harlan Shores, *Fundamentals of Curriculum Development* rev. ed. (Yonkers, N.Y.: World Book Co., 1957).

8. The relation between the social climate of the classroom and the learning of norms that are appropriate for the wider society outside of school is put in another way by Hilda Taba: "Capacity to behave democratically does not develop from learning facts about the beneficial effects of democracy. Conditions need to be provided which approximate the conditions under which values and feelings were acquired in the first place: in social interaction, under conditions that evoke feeling and entail reality of purposes. . . ." See *Curriculum Development: Theory and Practice* (New York: Harcourt, Brace, & World, 1962), p. 70. For a further elaboration of this point, see Richard S. Peters, *Authority, Responsibility, and Education* (New York: Paul S. Eriksson, 1960), p. 106.

9. For a discussion of the importance of his classmates in what a student learns, see Christopher Jencks, "Slums and Schools," *The New Republic, 147* (September 10 and 17, 1962).

10. Some have argued that business and industry would like well-trained applicants for jobs. One might answer that such training is their own responsibility, and not that of the public schools. In any case, business and industry are finding it increasingly

more practical to train their own employees after they are hired.

11. Charles W. Eliot, "The Fundamental Assumptions in the Report of the Committee of Ten," *Educational Review*, XXX (1905), in Edward A. Krug (ed.), *Charles W. Eliot and Popular Education* (New York: Bureau of Publications, Teachers College, Columbia University, 1961), pp. 152–153.

12. A comprehensive review of these various modes of organization may be found in Harold Alberty, *Reorganizing the High School Curriculum* rev. ed. (New York: Macmillan, 1953).

13. The development of curriculum content suggested here follows the proposals of John Dewey, in his discussion of the development of subject matter from starting points of history and geography. See *Democracy and Education* (New York: Macmillan, 1916), chap. XVI.

14. This suggests that while the study of literature itself may be worthwhile, such studies as "reading" and "English," considered as disconnected from both children's interests and other areas of study, have little place in the school curriculum. For further discussion of this point, see Broudy, Smith, and Burnett, *op. cit.*, pp. 169–172.

15. For a discussion of critical thinking as a particular kind of language skill and as a subject of school study, see Robert H. Ennis, 'A Concept of Critical Thinking," *Harvard Educational Review*, 32 (Winter, 1962), 81–111.

16. An analysis of the concept of needs can be found in B. Paul Komisar, " 'Need' and the Needs-Curriculum," in B. Othanel Smith and Robert H. Ennis (eds.), *Language and Concepts in Education* (Chicago: Rand McNally, 1961).

17. For an extended discussion of those issues, see Myron Lieberman, *The Future of Public Education* (Chicago: University of Chicago Press, 1960), especially chap. XI, *passim*.

# INDEX

Abstract art, *see* Nonobjective art
Acceleration and acquisition of knowledge, 243–244
Acculturation, *see* Informal learning
Achievement words: and learning and knowing, 20–21
Acquisition of knowledge: and cognitive structure, 165; for its own sake, 48 n.; in introductory and professional courses, 252–253; and lectures, 163–166; and problem-solving, 153–154; as a school aim, 158; and school promotion, 243–245
    *See also* Knowing; Knowledge
Activity: as characteristic of organic behavior, 274–276; in introductory phases of schooling, 154–155; overt and covert, 130–131; and problem-solving, 149–150; and school methods, 140–141; of students, in learning, 327–328
Adaptability and technological change, 323–325
Adaptation level: and affective arousal in curiosity, 279; and familiarity, 205–206
Adult education, *see* Continuing education
Aesthetic quality: and affective arousal, 193–197; and boredom and uniformity, 202; and curiosity, 271, 281–283, 289–290; in emotional life, 202–210; and emotions, 187; as human, 212–213; and intrinsic value, 209–210; involving form and meaning, 180–181, 221; and learning, 222; and lectures, 170–172, 221–222; and motivation, 230–231; as a natural event, 177; obstacles to, in schools, 248–252; and perception, 185–186, 193–197, 296–298; pervasive, in curiosity and thinking, illustrated, 306–311; and problem-solving, 291 n., 302–303; and reflexive signs, 219–221; and rewards and punishments, 233; and rhythm, 203–204; and school practices, 228, 247, 251–256, 319–321; in teacher education, 256–263; in vocational activities, 310–311
Affect: in curiosity, 278–281; defined, 188; distinguished from emotion, 189, 210–

211; and expectation, 190; and habit, 189–190; negative, in boredom and inactivity, 275; negative, and size of discrepancies in perception, 298–301; positive, and motivation, 204–205
Affective arousal: and adaptation levels, 279; in aesthetic experience, 283, 290; in curiosity, 278–281, 283, 290; and discrepancies between expectation and perception, 205–206, 298–301; to form in art: and discrepancies between expectation and perception, 206–209; and immediate experience, 201–202; and impact of meaningful content, 215–217, 219–221; instances of occurrence, analyzed, 194–197; and novelty, 195–197; and perception of pattern, 193–195; and specific emotions, 195–197 and habit and familiarity, 190, 193, 205–206; in lectures, 166–170; and meanings, 210–211; and novelty, 190, 193, 205–206; occurrence, analyzed, 190–192; in perception, 190; in practical affairs, 207–208; in problem-solving and risk-taking, 206; sought by organisms, 204–205
Age grouping, *see* Graded classrooms
Aiken, W. M., 264 n.
Aims in education: and curriculum choices, 342–345; and school methods, 6–9, 333–334; of students, and acquiring knowledge, 84–85
    *See also* Purposes; School policy
Alberty, H., 373 n.
Allport, G., 88 n.
American ethos, emphasis on instrumental values, 209
Analysis, conceptual, and school methods, 9–10, 11
Anderson, R. H., 265 n.
Anxiety: and curiosity and intellectual activity, 276–277; and extreme novelty, 191
Apperceptive mass and cognitive structure in acquiring knowledge, 165
Appreciation of art, 303; and discrepancies between expectation and perception, 298

Change: implied in learning theories, 347; intelligent, values implied in, 347–348; perceived meaning of successive events, 125–126
*See also* Novelty

Chaplin, C., 226 n.

Character: and indeterminate futures, 347–348; traits of, and dispositions, 38
*See also* Dispositions

Cheating: as illicit socialization, 150; and rewards, 236; in schools, and teaching methods, 330

"Cheri," 221

Childs, J. L., 10 n., 141, 172 n.

Chomsky, N., 79, 91 n.

Classroom, *see* Social structure of classroom

Club eligibility as motivation for study, 233

Cognitive structure and acquisition of knowledge, 165

Colette, 221, 226 n.

College education and practical and social concerns, 261–263

College preparation and social irrelevance of studies, 356–358

Collegiate eligibility as motivation for study, 233

Commitment as focused by vocation, 324–325

Community: activities of, and schooling, 154; impact of, on disposition formation, 316–319

Compartmentalized thinking and school rewards, 237

Competence as motivation of behavior, 275–276

Competition and school rewards, 237–238

Compulsory schooling: influence of on learning, 231–232; similarities to prisons, 231–232

Conant, J. B., 266 n., 336 n.

Concepts, meaning and expectation, 119–120

Conditioning: in animals, 110–111; as indoctrination, 82–83; as learning, 71–75; and learning of habits, 29; long-term effects of, 85–86; as operant, 71–75; as precluding thought, 299; as respondent, 71; and values of passivity, 348–349
*See also* Bribery; Reinforcement

Confidence as learning outcome, 347–348

Consciousness and meanings, 135

Contiguity in learning theory, 313

Continuing education and the concept of "finishing" school, 264–265 n.

Cook, W. W., 264 n., 371 n.

Cooperation, *see* Socialized attitudes

Correlation and explanation, 161–162

Counseling, *see* Guidance counseling

Covert Trials: in curiosity, 271–272, 303–305; independent of language, 115; and purposes, 117–118; and refining hypotheses, 144–149; of students as focus of teaching, 332; in trial-and-error behavior, 111, 114–116, 117–118; within experience having aesthetic quality, 302–303

Creativity and freedom from problematic situations, 292 n.
*See also* Aesthetic quality; Curiosity; Problem-setting; Problem-solving

Cremin, L. A., 88 n., 173 n.

*Crime and Punishment,* 254, 266 n.

Critical thinking: developing skill in, 361; requiring more than skill, 25–26

Criticism of art, *see* Art criticism

Croce, B., 223 n.

Crowder, N., 91 n.

Culture and the vocational and practical in education, 261–263

Curiosity: and aesthetic quality, 271, 281–283, 289–290; and affective arousal, 278–281; appearance of, in children, 283–285; and asking questions, 268–269; combined in experience with thinking and aesthetic qualities, illustrated, 306–311; and competence motivation, 275–276; confusion in use of term, 291 n.; and covert trials, 271–272; defined, 268–272; and discrepancies between expectation and perception, 279–282, 296–297; as dispositional outcome of schooling, 288–289, 321–322; and drive-reduction, 270, 276; and expectations, 269; and exploratory behavior, 269–272; inhibited by political organization, 350; inhibitors of, 276–277; and learning, summarized, 288–289; and leisure, 272; motivation for, 272–281; and novelty, 278–279; and overt behavior, 268, 272; and problem-solving and problem-setting, 269–272; and purposes, 269–270; and school methods and materials, 285–288; and scientific inquiry, 271–272; and speculation, science, and practical affairs, 303–305; and stimulus deprivation, 275,